Auguste Edouart's Silhouettes of Eminent Americans, 1839–1844

Presented to Miss Catherine Hutton previous to my departure for America.
Birmingham 23d Augt. 1838. Augn Edouart

Andrew Oliver

Auguste Edouart's

Silhouettes of Eminent Americans, 1839-1844

Published for the National Portrait Gallery, Smithsonian Institution

by the University Press of Virginia, Charlottesville

Publication of this book
was supported by
The Barra Foundation, Inc.
Philadelphia, Pennsylvania

THE UNIVERSITY PRESS OF VIRGINIA
Copyright © 1977 by the Rector and Visitors
of the University of Virginia

First published 1977

Frontispiece: Lithographed
self-portrait of Edouart.
Metropolitan Museum of Art,
Bequest of Mary Martin, 1938.

Library of Congress Cataloging in Publication Data

Édouart, Augustin Amant Constance Fidèle, 1789–
1861.
    Auguste Edouart's Silhouettes of eminent Americans,
1839–1844.

    "Catalogue of 3,800 named and dated American
silhouette portraits by August Edouart" by E. Jackson:
p. 508.
    Includes index.
    1. Édouart, Augustin Amant Constance Fidèle,
1789–1861. 2. Silhouettes—United States. 3. United
States—Biography—Portraits. I. Oliver, Andrew,
1906– II. Jackson, Emily, 1861– Catalogue of 3,800
named and dated American silhouette portraits by
August Edouart, 1789–1861. 1976. III. Title.
IV. Title: Silhouettes of eminent Americans, 1839–
1844.
NC910.5.E3044   741.9'4   76-21073
ISBN 0–8139–0632–6

Printed in the United States of America

Contents

Preface

THE HISTORY and provenance of the volume of silhouettes reproduced here are incomplete. It may be one of the sixteen albums saved from the shipwreck in 1849 in which much of Auguste Edouart's work was lost. The first notice of it that has come to light in this country is a bill dated "Feby 3, 1923," reflecting the sale by E. F. Bonaventure Inc. of 536 Madison Avenue, New York, to Miss Sarah C. Hewitt of "1 Vol. Silhouettes of eminent Americans by Edouart—net $1200." Bonaventure was said to have acquired the volume in Paris. Thirty years later, on October 15, 1955, at the Norvin H. Green sale at Parke-Bernet Galleries the volume was acquired by John D. Shapiro of Baltimore, and when Mr. Shapiro disposed of it a few years ago it came into the possession of its present owner.

Not only are the silhouettes themselves prime examples of the art, but the persons included in this extraordinary gathering were, with a handful of possible exceptions, prominent either nationally, statewide, or in their own community. Though the identity of a few has eluded discovery, most of the others merited inclusion in one or another of the well-known biographical dictionaries.

The cover of the volume measured 11½ by 9¾ inches and the pages 11 by 8 inches. In order to obtain photographs for reproduction here, the volume was disbound; but the order in which the silhouettes appear has been preserved. Although at first glance the order seems to be haphazard, there is a clue to it which cannot be detected from these reproductions alone. Edouart started out with a blank scrapbook with short stubs to which pages or other items of interest could be glued or tipped in. Between the stubs were tissue paper pages to protect or separate whatever might be tipped in. With a few exceptions, noted hereafter, the pages inserted by Edouart were lithographed scenes on what turned out to be the right-hand, or odd-numbered, page and blank on the reverse, left-hand or even-numbered, page. The silhouettes were pasted on afterward. On the blank pages a simple ink-wash ground was sketched in on which the subject could appear to stand. The exceptions are a few sheets where the background has been entirely drawn in in ink or wash; these usually have a silhouette on one side only, and the sheet has been tipped in wherever it suited Edouart's fancy. A good example is the first to appear, which was placed in the volume immediately before the first numbered page. Others are figs. 5, 12, 17, 38, 276, and 346. It then appears that as a general rule Edouart pasted in the silhouettes more or less chronologically on the right-hand, or lithographed, page and then came back to the beginning and began to fill in the blank, or left-hand, pages. Ninety-one pages display two silhouettes, sometimes taken on the same day, sometimes of persons closely related or connected, and at other times apparently placed together by fancy only. There are twenty-five different lithographed backgrounds, used from two to nine times each. The first use of each type can be seen in figs. 2, 9, 14, 22, 25, 27, 29, 31, 34, 39, 41, 44, 46, 48, 51, 55, 57, 64, 78, 84, 95, 102, 118, 120, and 125. (These figure numbers refer to the biographical sketches and their facing silhouettes in the present volume).

Edouart himself, as Mr. Mayor tells us in the Introduction, gives us a clue to how he worked in his *Treatise on Silhouette Likenesses*. There he tells us: "It has been my invariable practice, to ask the names of my sitters, and write them on the backs of the duplicate, which duplicate I place in my book." In the process of disbinding the volume it was possible to examine the reverse of one or two silhouettes which had become partly unglued. Written on the back in Edouart's hand was the name of the subject. What also appeared were pencil lines close to the edge of the silhouette, from which we can deduce that he sketched the profile on the white side of the page before cutting it out. This would have given him an opportunity to make changes as he went along, which would have been impossible with scissors. Folding the paper and cutting both silhouettes at once would result in the finished profiles appearing reversed from each other, and such turns out to be the case. Where we have found the sitter's counterpart of a silhouette included here, it has turned out to be facing the opposite way.

Edouart exhibits great skill in cutting out the most minute objects which one might expect to find sketched in later in ink. To cite but a few of many examples, eyeglasses (figs. 54 and 71), small objects (fig. 108), and canes (figs. 81, 87, and 89) are all cut out of the same sheet of paper as the figure itself. One of Edouart's telltale marks is the ubiquitous white collar—for example, in fig. 70. It is not as might be expected a triangular slip of white paper pasted on the black. The method was to cut a slit in the neck and insert a piece of white paper which would be pasted both underneath and above the slit. In many instances the black shade was also embellished with silver markings to show hair style, buttons, military braid, lapels, and the like.

Each biographical sketch is given a number corresponding to the figure number of the individual's silhouette. The full name and the year of birth and death are given where known. Under the name appear the place and date given on the silhouette itself unless otherwise indicated.

In almost every instance the silhouette bears beside or above it the autograph of the subject, sometimes with date and place of taking, and descriptive titles. In a few instances the sitter signed the lithographed background first and the silhouette, when pasted in, covered over part of the writing (figs. 105, 325). At the foot of the page in Edouart's hand (and he had two styles of writing, each of which is usually apparent) appears the name of the subject, date, place, and some item of miscellaneous interest, in one case the height of the subject, in another his weight. A few of the pages are signed by Edouart (figs. 1, 6, and 205).

Fig. 1 is a curiosity. It appears that Dr. Loomis was cut in Saratoga, but it does not appear when. On the lower right-hand side, however, appears Edouart's signature and a date: "Augt. Edouart, fecit. 1838." But in 1838 Edouart was still abroad. He arrived in America in July 1839 and did not go to Saratoga until July 1840. This is a wash drawing on which the silhouette was pasted, and the whole was tipped in ahead of the first numbered page, perhaps as a sort of frontispiece because of the signature; or perhaps the sheet was prepared in advance for such a purpose when Edouart was planning to come to America. Dr. Loomis of himself hardly seems a likely subject with which to commence such an extraordinary collection.

It is more likely that the volume served two purposes: to preserve for Edouart a personal record and the means of making duplicates of his most prominent sitters and, as Mr. Mayor suggests, to use for advertising purposes—to show a prospective sitter what prominent personages had had their profiles taken. If so, the project was a marked success, for included are profiles of four presidents of the United States, five members of the Supreme Court, six state governors, six college presidents, eighteen mayors, six commodores, thirteen generals, thirty state or federal court judges, fifteen authors, and at least twenty-nine physicians. As will be noticed throughout the volume, and as would be expected of most prominent people, many of the subjects knew and had intimate connections with each other, and cross-references in the biographical sketches will make this abundantly clear.

A complete bibliography or citation of the sources used in preparing the brief biographical sketches would be lengthy and impracticable. The principal sources have been James G. Wilson and John Fiske, eds., *Appleton's Cyclopaedia of American Biography* (1891–1900); Allen Johnson and Dumas Malone, eds., *Dictionary of American Biography* (1928–); *The National Cyclopaedia of American Biography* (1898–1968); Franklin B. Hough, *American Biographical Notes* (1875); *Webster's Biographical Dictionary* (1958); Clifford K. Shipton,

Biographical Sketches of Those Who Attended Harvard College; Franklin B. Dexter, *Biographical Sketches of the Graduates of Yale College* (1885–1911); William D. Lewis, *Great American Lawyers* (1907–9); Rossiter Johnson, ed., *The Twentieth Century Biographical Dictionary of Notable Americans* (1904); William B. Sprague, *Annals of the American Pulpit* (1857–65); Henry Simpson, *The Lives of Eminent Philadelphians* (1859); J. Thomas Scharf and Thompson Westcott, *History of Philadelphia, 1609–1884* (1884); Thomas H. S. Homersly, *Complete Regular Army Register of the United States (1779–1879)* (1880); and Nicholas B. Wainwright, ed., *A Philadelphia Perspective: The Diary of Sidney George Fisher Covering the Years 1834–1871* (1967), as well as individual biographies and memorial tributes too numerous to mention. The gathering of the source material was ably carried out for me by Bryant F. Tolles, Jr., now the director of the Essex Institute, Salem, Massachusetts, who also wrote the sketches accompanying figs. 2 through 11; the balance were written by me. I owe a debt of gratitude to Whitfield J. Bell, Jr., librarian of the American Philosophical Society, for tracking down what had been to me elusive Philadelphians. My daughter Ruth F. O. Morley reproduced in typescript as closely as was possible my crabbed hand with a watchful eye to errors. My wife heard me read aloud most of the biographical sketches with critical interest and sometimes with amusement at the anecdotes that have survived the century and a quarter since Edouart used his scissors.

Included as an appendix is a list of 3,800 silhouettes cut by Edouart during his ten years in America.

The men and women who occupy the following pages covered every facet of American life in the early nineteenth century and in the aggregate supply a skeleton history of that period. Edouart is said to have cut perhaps more than 4,000 silhouettes in America; here we see preserved the cream of the crop, a veritable portrait gallery of distinguished Americans.

ANDREW OLIVER

Boston, Massachusetts
July 14, 1975

Introduction

THE PROFILE PORTRAIT has come and gone in history for quite definite reasons. The Egyptians and Greeks insisted on being clear to the point of drawing the brow, nose, lips, and chin in side face to make up an unmistakable head. Since then, profile portraits have twice reappeared in two ages of classic revival. Pisanello medals and Pollaiuolo portraits expressed ideals for the early Italian Renaissance, while the most conscious and programmatic profile head, the silhouette, became all the rage in the epoch of David's paintings of Roman history, of Adam's "Etruscan" drawing rooms, and Greek Revival porticoes.

In 1806 Goethe connected black-figured Greek vases with the silhouettes of his contemporaries by saying, "I like to think of silhouettes as linking two irrevocably sundered ages." Yet the two kinds of black pictures were made with two entirely different intentions; for the archaic Greeks painted figures in solid black to decorate their pottery with the boldest possible patterns, while the silhouettists reproduced a shadow cast by a horizontal beam of light.

This new thing, the accurate black profile likeness, must have appeared in England about 1700, when William and Mary are supposed to have had their silhouettes taken. By the 1720s it sounded like an established novelty when Swift described a lady cutting a man's profile with her "scissars":

> One sloping cut made forehead, nose, and chin,
> A nick produced a mouth, and made him grin.

Yet thirty or forty years later a Paris newspaper noted what seemed like a new fashion in France: "Our ladies are all drawing the portraits of their friends on black paper, cutting them out, and even giving away their own portraits without this being ill thought of. This useful invention reproduces sweet faces everywhere."

Here was a novelty in search of a name. A fortnight before this Parisian newspaper notice of December 1759, Etienne de Silhouette was dismissed after nine months in office as controller general of French finances. This reformer, having lost his popularity by cutting pensions and sinecures, was hooted into disgrace, and his name was tacked onto everything skimpy, such as pocketless breeches that had no place to put money. Were the black profile portraits named after him because they are shaped by snipping away paper? Or because they suggest shadow without substance? Or because M. de Silhouette may have made them? Whatever the reason, the black profile portraits had come to stay; and they lacked a name in France, so the nickname stuck.

The word *silhouette* spread quickly over the Continent but tardily into Britain, where such portraits had long been familiar under the pretty name of *shades*. As late as 1806 an Englishman wrote: "Whenever they send me their silhouettes, or what do they call them, I chuck them out of the window." Even in the 1830s Edouart found that the word *silhouette* still meant nothing in country districts.

The silhouette might have passed away as a parlor amusement had it not happened to become associated with popular science in 1775 and 1778 when Johann Kaspar Lavater, a Zürich evangelical parson in his mid-thirties, published an international best-seller, *Essay on Physiognomy, for the Promotion of the Knowledge and the Love of Mankind*. Some years earlier Richardson and Rousseau had started people scrutinizing faces to ferret out God's noblest work, an honest man. Psychological typecasting now looked easy with Lavater on hand to classify a curving forehead as effeminate, a projecting underlip as phlegmatic, and so forth.

For laboratory specimens Lavater needed portraits of machine-made accuracy, and he found them in silhouettes traced from the shadow cast by a profile. "I have collected more physiognomical knowledge from shades alone than from every other kind of portrait," he wrote. "Whoever would study physiognomy should apply himself to the study of shades. If he has no physiognomical sensation for shades, he has none for the human countenance." This exhortation, printed beside what are thought to be the first printed black profile portraits, helped spread a craze for silhouettes throughout the north of Europe, and especially in England, where Lavater's bulky work was published in four separate translations in twenty years. The advantages claimed for silhouettes were precisely those later claimed for photography—cheapness, speed, accuracy, and the possibility of dispensing with art training. Goethe remarked: "Everyone is skillful and no traveller may stop for a visit without having his shadow traced on a wall in the evening." This procedure was used by Martha Washington's nineteen-year-old granddaughter Nelly Custis to trace George Washington's larger than life-size shadow cast by a lamp on white paper. She then cut out the inside and pasted the hole on black cloth to make what is called a hollow-cut shade, rare outside the United States.

Americans in the struggling young Republic felt important enough to want their portraits done and they found them at the modest prices that they could then pay in profiles, either cut with scissors or traced with a French machine called a physionotrace. The first copious maker of profiles was a young French army officer, Charles Balthazar Févret de Saint-Mémin, who found himself stranded in New York in 1793, the year of the Terror, with his family to support. Using the artistic skill that was then a part of any polite education, Saint-Mémin made nearly a thousand profile portraits, either drawn life-size on pink paper or reduced with a pantograph to palm-size etchings. His profitable example was soon followed by many American silhouettists who traveled about with profile machines or a mere pair of scissors. One of the busiest was Moses Williams, a dexterous black who made little hollow-cut silhouettes at Charles Willson Peale's museum in Philadelphia. The competition brought forth freaks like the armless Miss Honeywell, whose label claims that she cut likenesses "with the mouth." One must admit they look it.

The craze for silhouettes was waning in 1839 when the most prolific silhouettist ever to work in the Americas arrived in New York, originally driven from France by the hard times under Napoleon, just as Saint-Mémin had been driven by the French Revolution. This was Augustin (or Auguste) Edouart. Let us hear about his early life in his own words and spelling as he wrote it to a Miss Catherine Hutton in Leamington in September 1837, when he was forty-nine:

In compliance with your request I give you a short abstract of my life.—I was the sixteenth and last child of my family; born the 27th January 1788. at Dunkerque département du Nord, France, my christian names are *Augustin, Amand, Constant, fidel*, my parents from independance, were ruined in the course of the French revolution—My mother died when I was 7 yrs. of age.—5 of my brothers paid their life in the service of their country—When 15 yrs. of age being left with an unmarried sister to take care of our father who was paralettic, I began at that age to provide for myself:—at 19 I was director of a China manufactory at St. Iriex la Perche [where kaolin was discovered in 1765], in the south of France, having 120 workmen under my direction, where I remained about 2 yrs. when I returned to Paris and obtained a commission as *Inspecteur des Fourrages* in Holland; from thence went into Germany where I had several services to fulfill, and was attached to the suite of *La grande Armée* going to Russia; Illness prevented me and returned to Holland—I was in Bergen-op-zoom when the English who stormed it were defeated—By the requisitions I made in the country I was the means of support in Antwerp in the time of the Siege; it is in that place that my military career ended. Being brought up in the Revolution, and likewise all devoted to Napoleon, I would not give my adhesion to Louis 18th on which account I was compelled to expatriate and arrived in London the 1st of August 1814. From that time to the present I support myself by talents which I had never thought of in my time of prosperity.

I beg you Madame to receive my most sincer thanks of gratitude for the honour confer on me and here take the liberty of subjoining my silhouette likeness.

This likeness is reproduced in the frontispiece. It and the letter were bequeathed to the Metropolitan Museum by Mary Martin in 1938.

Despite his avowed aversion to Louis XVIII, Edouart had cut seventy-eight silhouettes of him and his exiled court at Holyrood in 1831. These are now in the Bibliothèque Nationale in Paris.

Edouart told a great deal about his professional practice in a book that he had printed at Cork in 1834 with a London title page dated 1835 to prepare publicity for working and exhibiting in the capital. The title is a puff for snobs: *A Treatise on Silhouette Likenesses by Monsieur Edouart, Silhouettist to the French Royal Family, and patronised by His Royal Highness the Late Duke of Gloucester, and the principal Nobility of England, Scotland, and Ireland.* The eighteen illustrations had previously been lithographed in Cork on thin paper pasted down on more substantial sheets. The silhouettes were printed in solid black on the same gray or sepia backgrounds of rooms or landscapes that he used for mounting the cuttings that he sold. Edouart did not himself draw these backgrounds, or the tiny lithographed letters, newspapers, and open books that he cut out to paste into the hands of his silhouette figures. He proudly said: "I have Artists (and I may say not inferior ones) employed to draw these backgrounds. . . . I have likewise my frame maker who works under my directions." The English frames are of flat maple with an inner edge of narrow gold molding. What with these frames for sale, his albums, and his traveling exhibition of forty framed silhouette scenes and portraits and forty-five hair-work pictures, he gradually accumulated three tons of baggage.

Edouart's book tells much about his life in the British Isles. "When I first came to England I supported myself by my industry. I invented Mosaic Hair Work," used for portraying the pet dogs of the Duchess of York and Queen Charlotte. In 1825, shortly after his wife died, he accidentally discovered his vocation during a call on an English family, when he criticized some machine-cut silhouettes of the father and mother. The daughters challenged him to do better. "I could stand it no longer, and in a fit of moderate passion, I took a pair of scissors, that one of the young ladies used for her needle work; I tore the cover of a letter that lay on the table; I took the old Father by the arm and led him to a chair, so as to see his profile, then, in an instant, I produced the Likeness; the paper being white, I took the black of the snuffers, and rubbed it on with my fingers. The ladies changed their teasing and ironical tone, to praise, and asked to have theirs also, but in revenge I declined to do so." Only nine years later he claimed to have cut "more than 50,000 likenesses," to which one must add the more than 3,500 made in the United States. After practicing with heads only for about a year, he ventured on entire bodies, which he scaled exactly to what he called his "military Standard."

He began each silhouette by studying "the line of the forehead, relative with the nose; the nose with the lips, and lastly the line of the lips with the chin; the relation of the mouth and chin; I deliberate in my mind upon the points, which come forward, and those that retire." For children, after cutting the faces, "I leave them free to run about the room, and by these means, I am better able to judge their figure." He cut from sheets of thin paper printed in solid black on one side only. He folded each sheet down the middle, white side outward for better visibility, and held the fold toward his left. He first pierced any holes there might be, then cut the features while moving the paper as much as the scissors, if not more, to curve smoothly. The best scissors were those made for embroidery, with a loose pivot. Edouart separated the two silhouettes that he had cut simultaneously and mounted the one for the client on plain paper or on a lithographed background. On the back of the mount he pasted a label with his list of prices. His English labels have survived for Oxford,

Cambridge, and Cheltenham, and he must certainly have had others printed for his busy seasons in London, Edinburgh, New York, Philadelphia, and Saratoga. He kept one of the duplicate cuttings for his records and labeled it, on the white back and in ink, with the name and profession of the sitter, the place, and the date. He said, "I keep my duplicates all defended with a patent lock" in albums that he indexed to facilitate cutting copies when asked for. He scrupulously copied ladies' portraits only for the ladies themselves, and never for eager young gentlemen. His library of cuttings became a source of income like a photographer's stock of negatives.

England must gradually have furnished less and less work, for on August 23, 1838, he inscribed his portrait for Miss Hutton with a farewell on his departure for America (frontispiece). He cut his first American silhouette on July 10, 1839, in New York, where he stayed a year, with some excursions; from early July to mid-September 1840 he was in Saratoga, where he was to spend five summers. He returned often to Saratoga Springs for the same reasons that had brought him to the English spas at Bath, Cheltenham, and Leamington. The *Daily Saratoga Sentinel* for the summer of 1842 lists dozens, sometimes over a hundred, arrivals each day. The medicinal waters and the famous races attracted political bosses and the rich, who in turn attracted a thousand hangers-on, lured by the hope of scraping profitable acquaintance. However occupied the visitors may have been at home, the springs freed them with money in their pockets and whim and leisure to spend it. What pleasanter pastime could there be than to have one's shade cut by quick little Monsieur Edouart? And quick he surely was. In 1840 a Baltimorean, George Buchanan Coale, wrote: "A little Frenchman named Edouart has the most remarkably accurate eye I have ever seen. I send you a full length which he snipped, cut in two minutes. He cut two for me after an interval of a day, both from my face, and when compared the outlines fitted as if they had been cut from a double paper from the same cutting." This accuracy did not come easily, for Edouart confessed that "to preserve a steady hand, I am obliged to be very particular in my diet; strong tea, coffee, spirits, or any other excitements, would soon destroy it." Yet varied and full of character as Edouart's faces are, the identical little slippers all dangle as if levitated.

Edouart's travels in the United States can be pieced together from the notes on his silhouettes. From early November 1840 to mid-January 1841, he was in Baltimore, then spent six months in Washington. After the usual Saratoga summer, he moved for September and October to Troy, and in November through June he was in Boston. September to early June 1843 found him in Philadelphia, where he must have done well, for he returned after Saratoga on October 1 and stayed until mid-December. He then went to New Orleans until late April 1844, with possible excursions to Natchez. During May and June he made his way north, through Louisville and Lexington, Kentucky, to his old haunts in Saratoga. By then he had to travel more in search of sitters, for he worked during November and part of December in New York, then pushed on for a few weeks in Philadelphia and Baltimore before returning to New York until July, 1845. His career as a silhouettist ended with his last and shortest stay in Saratoga, where he cut his last surviving shade on August 16, 1845.

What is astonishing is not that he ultimately failed but that he could keep going so long in the face of competition from photography. Only two months after he had cut his first silhouette in New York on July 10, 1839, the directions for making daguerreotypes arrived in the United States. Since the French government gave this relatively simple process to the world without a patent, hundreds of people in every city and small town in North America were soon making these beautifully clear likenesses. It is remarkable that Edouart cut so many of the outstanding Americans in this album in 1843 and 1844, when he must have begun to feel the full threat of the daguerreotype. Is it possible that he met his competition by offering to portray well-known people free of charge in the hope that their example would pull in the small fry? In England, after all, he had made headlines of his noble and royal patrons. Certainly he must have displayed this album of conspicuous men as a central feature of his traveling exhibition. It is thanks to his methodical habit of keeping record silhouettes that we know his name today, for almost all the silhouettes that he sold at the time have since vanished.

Edouart may have spent the end of the 1840s in New York, possibly supporting himself by giving French lessons as he had done in his early days in London. In 1848 his painter and photographer son Alexander, born in London in 1818, came to New York, where he probably helped his father pack his bulky baggage and embark on the ship *Oneida* in 1849. This flight from failure brought on his crowning disaster, for a December storm wrecked the ship off Guernsey. Edouart escaped with ten albums of British silhouettes and six of American ones out of a total of some fifty-odd, plus a certain number of frames. He gave all of this to the Lukis family, who cared for him with touching compassion, and went on his way to France. He died at Quines, near Calais, in 1861.

The sixteen albums remained in the Lukis family until about 1910 when Mrs. F. Nevill Jackson bought them. She sold parts of the British albums to public collections in London, Edinburgh, and Dublin. She photographed all the American silhouettes and made prints for various American institutions. The album reproduced here was the only one kept intact. The other five albums supplied nearly 3,000 silhouettes to descendants of the sitters; 861 unsold silhouettes from the five broken albums were bought by the Reverend Glenn Tilley Morse of Newburyport and bequeathed by him to the Metropolitan Museum of Art in 1950. The American portraits have been listed in the following publications:

Catalogue of 3,800 named and dated American Silhouette Portraits by August Edouart (1789–1861) Discovered by Mrs. F. Nevill Jackson. [London, n.d.]

A Collection of American Silhouette portraits cut by August Edouart on Exhibition at 12 East 45 Street, New York. Preface by Arthur S. Vernay. New York, 1913.

Ancestors in Silhouette cut by August Edouart, by Mrs. F. Nevill Jackson. London, 1921. This lists 8,000 English, Scottish, and Irish silhouettes beside 3,600 American ones. It has a great deal of information, often inaccurate in detail. Edouart's birth date is given as 1789 instead of 1788, as he wrote it to Miss Hutton.

A. HYATT MAYOR

LIKENESSES IN PROFILE
Executed by Mons. Edouart,

Who begs to observe, that his Likenesses are produced by the Scissors alone, and are preferable to any taken by Machines, inasmuch as by the above method, the expression of the Passions, and peculiarities of Character, are brought into action, in a style which has not hitherto been attempted by any other Artist.

Numerous Proof Specimens may be seen at the house lately occupied by Mr. Trinder, at the bottom of the High-street, Oxford.

	s.	d.
Full Length	5	0
Ditto, Children under 8 years of age	3	6
Profile Bust	1	0
Duplicates of the Cuttings to any quantity, are for each Full Length	3	0
Ditto, Children	2	6

††† Attendance abroad, double, if not more than two Full Length Likenesses are taken.
Any additional Cutting, as Instrument, Table, &c. &c. to be paid accordingly.

LIKENESSES IN PROFILE,
Executed by Mons. Edouart,

Who begs to observe, that his Likenesses are produced by the Scissors alone, and are preferable to any taken by Machines, inasmuch as by the above method the expression of the Passion, and peculiarities of Character, are brought into action, in a style which has not hitherto been attempted by any other Artist.
Proof Specimens may be seen as above.

	s.	d
Full Length	5	0
Ditto, Children under 8 Years of Age.	3	6
Profile Bust	1	0
Dupliate of the Cuttings to any quantity, are for each Full Length	3	0
Ditto, Children	2	6
4, Colonnade, Cheltenham.		

☞ Attendance abroad, Double.

LIKENESSES IN PROFILE
Executed by Mons. Edouart,

Who begs to observe, that his Likenesses are produced by the Scissors alone, and are preferable to any taken by Machines, inasmuch as by the above method, the expression of the Passions, and peculiarities of Character, are brought into action, in a style which has not hitherto been attempted by any other Artist.

Numerous Proof Specimens may be seen at Mrs. BAYS's, Trinity-Street, Cambridge.

	s.	d.
Full Length	5	0
Ditto, Children under 8 years of age..	3	6
Profile Bust	2	0
Duplicates of the Cuttings to any quantity, are for each Full Length	3	0
Ditto, Children	2	6

†.† Attendance abroad, double, if not more than two Full Length Likenesses are taken.
Any additional Cutting, as Instrument, Table, &c. &c. to be paid accordingly.

Edouart's English labels. Metropolitan Museum of Art, Bequest of Mary Martin, 1938, and Glenn Tilley Morse, 1950

Auguste Edouart's Silhouettes of Eminent Americans, 1839–1844

1

R. Loomis

Saratoga, [undated]

R. Loomis, a distinguished and proper-appearing gentleman, was a dentist and may well have been in demand at the fashionable upper New York resort of Saratoga. There is no clue to Edouart's choice of Dr. Loomis to appear first in the volume. Perhaps he considered the signature and date "Augt. Edouart, fecit. 1838." an appropriate frontispiece. Edouart did not arrive in America until July 1839, nor did he reach Saratoga until July 1840.

R. Loomis. Dentist
Saratoga.

Augt. Edouart fecit.
1838.

2

William Henry Seward   1801–1872

[New York], October 2, 1839

Statesman and diplomat extraordinary, Seward was one of the most attractive, as well as one of the most important and industrious, figures of the critical years before and during the American Civil War. An affable, generous, and equitable man, he abhorred personal controversy and exhibited great versatility in his interests and broad perceptivity in his views. His public appeal was such that one historian actually described him as "lovable." Dwarfed during his peak years by the towering personality of Lincoln, Seward has long been denied full recognition for his adroit, conciliatory accomplishments in public life. Edouart displays him as he appeared when governor of New York.

Born of Welsh-Irish ancestry in Florida, Orange County, New York, young Seward attended a local academy and in 1820, at the age of fifteen, graduated at Union College with high honors. He read law for the next two years, was admitted to the bar in 1822, and commenced practice in Auburn, New York, which remained his residence for the rest of his life. Influenced by the political philosophies of John Quincy Adams (fig. 172) and his lifelong friend Thurlow Weed, Seward entered local politics, winning election to the state senate in 1830 and soon becoming its recognized leader. Nominated unanimously for governor in 1834, the determined young man was defeated by William L. Marcy (fig. 6). In 1837–38, with the political conditions ripe, Seward again challenged for the governorship and on this occasion was victorious, as he was a second time in 1840. During his four years as governor he displayed a strong ardor for political combat, an optimistic temperament, and powerful humanitarian sympathies. At this point in his career he staked himself as an advocate of internal improvements, a believer in democratic public education, and one of the first active proponents of abolition. Historians have assessed Seward's governorship in highly favorable terms.

In 1848, with antislavery sentiment high, Seward was elected to the United States Senate, where he was to remain for two full terms until 1861. Whig partisan, nationalist, and republican, the New Yorker stood fast on moral conviction, often opposing compromise measures calculated to appease the contending factions in the North and South. Attaching his fortunes to the rising star of the new Republican party, he made a strong bid for the presidential nomination at the 1860 Chicago convention, only to lose to the irrepressible Lincoln, who after his subsequent election victory offered Seward the cabinet post of secretary of state.

It was as secretary of state in the Lincoln and Johnson administrations that Seward made his real mark. Conducting diplomacy with a keen eye to domestic public opinion, he compiled a nationalist-expansionist record of accomplishment that has won him praise ever since. During the Civil War he adroitly handled the threat of possible European intervention, initiating protests against Great Britain as a basis for the later *"Alabama* claims," and securing from the French the promise of evacuation after their impetuous adventure in Mexico. In 1867 came his greatest accomplishment—the acquisition from Russia of the vast northern territory of Alaska, the contemporary epithet for which, Seward's Folly, has been proven fallacious in modern times. In 1870–71 he made a ceremonious trip around the world, the first American of his rank to do so. Death came a year later at his Auburn home.

Yours faithfully
William H. Seward.
October 2d 1839.

3
Charles Anderson Wickliffe
1788–1869
Saratoga, July 13, 1844

Nicknamed "The Duke," Charles A. Wickliffe was not an overly popular man with those not of his own social standing, because of his often haughty, aristocratic, and disagreeable manner. At Saratoga in 1844, as postmaster general, he must have been in his element. His legal and political comrades, too, held him in generally high esteem, and he acquitted himself creditably in the various state and national positions that he held during his career. Born near Springfield, Kentucky, Wickliffe attended local schools and Wilson's Academy at Bardstown before reading law in the office of his cousin M. D. Hardin. Admitted to the bar in 1809, he joined a group of Bardstown lawyers and quickly established a reputation as a bacchanalian and a gambler for high stakes.

Wickliffe's service to Kentucky was varied and extensive. He was first a member of the state House of Representatives from Nelson County in 1812 and 1813, returning in 1820 and 1821 after duty as an aide to General Samuel Caldwell during the War of 1812. In 1823 he was sent to the United States House of Representatives, where he remained for ten years. He was an unsuccessful candidate for United States senator from Kentucky in 1831. Upon his return to his home state, he was again elected to the legislature for three years, becoming lieutenant governor on the Whig ticket in 1836. Upon the death of Governor James Clark in 1839, Wickliffe succeeded to the governorship, in which he continued for the next year.

With his appointment by President John Tyler (fig. 258) as postmaster general in 1841, Wickliffe again shifted back to national politics. In 1845 he became a Democrat over the Texas question and was therefore eligible for appointment during the same year as a diplomatic agent by the new president, James K. Polk. Back in Kentucky he worked for revision of the constitution and statutes, and was once more elected to Congress in 1861, this time as a Union Whig. At the close of his term he again changed political stripes and was the Peace Democrat candidate for governor, but was defeated. In his last term in Congress he was thrown from his carriage and was seriously crippled for the rest of his conflict-filled life.

4
William Ellison Miller, M.D.
Saratoga, August 20, 1844

A physician from New York City, William Ellison Miller may well have attended Charles A. Wickliffe when both vacationed at Saratoga. Wickliffe was known to have had a history of health problems. That they were social acquaintances is more than likely.

C. A. Wickliffe
Kentucky
Saratoga July 13th 1844

Dr. Wm. Ellison Miller
New York
Saratoga Augt 20th 1844

C. A. Wickliffe Post Master Genl. of U.S.
Kentucky   Saratoga 13th July 1844.

Dr. Wm. Ellison Miller MD
New York. Saratoga 20th Augt 1844

5
Isaac L. Varian   1793–1864
New York, November 22, 1839

A portrait of Isaac Varian adorns the wall of the
Governor's Room at New York City Hall and,
like the Edouart silhouette, gives evidence of his
personal confidence and integrity. As an "old
school Democrat" and a member of the Tammany
Society, Varian rose through the political ranks
and was twice elected mayor of New York, holding
the office from 1839 to 1841. Like several other
mayors, he was a member of the Volunteer Fire
Department and was associated with many significant personages of the city, gaining him valuable support for his election campaigns. In 1841
he served as a state senator. Even Philip Hone
(fig. 8), known to be a bitter opponent of democ-
racy, admitted that he was an excellent man. Born
on the old family homestead in the city, Varian
resided there for many years, ultimately removing
to Peekskill, New York, in 1845, where he later
died.

James Esturan
New York Nov 22th 1839

Isaac L. Varian Esq.
Mayor N. York Nov 22nd
1839

6

William Learned Marcy 1786–1857

[Location unknown], September 3, 1839

It is highly appropriate that Mount Marcy, the tallest mountain peak in New York State, is named for William L. Marcy, prominent lawyer, jurist, and statesman. Marcy was without doubt one of the most able and esteemed public figures of his time. Born in Southbridge, Massachusetts, he attended the local schools and Leicester and Woodstock (Conn.) academies, was graduated from Brown University in 1808, taught school in Newport, Rhode Island, studied law, and then removed to Troy, New York, where he was admitted to the bar in 1811. Commencing the practice of law in that city, he remained there until 1821, a period broken only by brief service on the Canadian frontier during the War of 1812. While in Troy he held the post of city recorder and edited the *Budget*, which became an influential Democratic journal allied with the forces of Martin Van Buren (fig. 230).

With the aid of the friendly interest of Van Buren, Marcy was offered the state comptrollership of New York in 1823 and moved from Troy to Albany, which was his home thereafter. Success in this capacity led to his appointment again by Van Buren as associate justice of the state supreme court, a position in which he displayed erudition, courage, and a strong sense of justice. His legal career, really his first love, soon became overshadowed, however, by service in public office. Resigning from the bench in 1831, he accepted reluctantly an election to the United States Senate, where he remained until 1833, acting as chairman of the Judiciary Committee. Upon his nom-

ination for governor he returned to New York, carried the election, and served for three terms through 1838, losing his bid for a fourth term to William L. Seward (fig. 2). He left his mark upon the state, organizing the first geological survey and settling the boundary dispute with New Jersey. Edouart shows him just after the end of his last term as governor.

From 1840 to 1842, as a member of the Mexican Claims Commission by appointment of President Van Buren, he exhibited ability at conciliation and, with his colleagues, secured settlements for American claimants. Marcy's papers show conclusively that after 1840 he set his mind on a high federal post, and in 1844 he accepted the post of secretary of war in the administration of James K. Polk. With the election of Franklin Pierce in 1852, Mr. Marcy moved to the job of secretary of state, where, in the estimation of most later diplomatic historians, he distinguished himself as one of the best men ever to serve in this capacity. Over the four years of his tenure, he was chiefly responsible for the negotiation of twenty-four treaties, of which four are most significant: the Gadsden Treaty with Mexico (1853); the Reciprocity Treaty with Great Britain (1854); the trade treaty with the Netherlands (1855); and the treaty with Denmark abolishing the Danish Sound dues (1857). With the close of the Pierce administration in March 1857, Marcy's public life abruptly ended, and a year later he died suddently at Ballston Spa, New York.

W. L. Marcy

W. L. Marcy Ex Governor State of New York 3. September 1839

7

Hamilton Smith
Louisville, Kentucky, May 15, 1844

Hamilton Smith is listed as an attorney-at-law and a notary public in the *Louisville Directory* for a ten-year period from 1839 to 1849. For a time he served as a director of the Louisville Gas Company Bank and resided outside of the city at his country home on the Bardstown Road. He is one of a large group of lawyers and physicians taken by Edouart in Kentucky in May 1844.

8

Philip Hone   1780–1851
Saratoga Springs, July 27, 1843

Prosperous merchant, philanthropist, politician, and leader of society in New York City, Philip Hone left a diary of his life and times that has served as perhaps the most significant firsthand account of New York in the period 1828–54. Hone's origins, however, were humble. He was born in New York of German-French ancestry; his father was a joiner of limited means. At an early age, Hone began his rise to prominence as a partner to his brother John in an auction business which gradually grew to be one of the most profitable in the city. At age forty, worth at least half a million dollars, Hone retired from business, toured Europe, and settled himself, his wife Catherine Dunscomb, his six children, his library, and his art collection in his Broadway residence adjacent to City Hall Park.

In taking leave of active business management, Mr. Hone was launched into the local and national limelight in political, literary, and social circles. The combination of wealth, integrity, personal charm, and public spirit was an irresistible formula for success. In 1825 he was elected mayor of New York for one year when the Democratic city council split over rival candidates. By virtue of this experience he became conspicuous in exclusive social circles. He then became a local Whig party leader and was active in civic, religious, and charitable organizations. In addition Hone was a founder of the Mercantile Library in New York and was one of the projectors of the Delaware & Hudson Canal and part owner of coal mines near its terminus, Honesdale, Pennsylvania, named in his honor.

It is through his famous diary, however, that one gets the most complete picture of Mr. Hone, his city, and his eventful life. Traveling widely, he explained his interests in politics, the letters, and the arts. He was known to have been an intimate of Henry Clay (fig. 147), William L. Seward (fig. 2), John Quincy Adams (fig. 172), and, most particularly, Daniel Webster (fig. 164), whom he visited often in Marshfield. Although he was defeated for the state senate in 1839, he was an indefatigable organizer of the Whigs. Until late in life he was a devoted theatergoer, developing friendships with many stage people of note. His contacts with the writers' community were equally broadspread. In the panic of 1837 Hone lost a part of his estate; he reentered business unsuccessfully and was appointed naval officer of the port of New York by President Taylor. A tour of the western United States left him in poor health, but he was able to continue his valuable diary until five days before his death.

Hamilton Smith.
Louisville Ky.
May 15th /44 —

Yours faithfully
Philip Hone
Feby 27th 1843.
Saratoga Springs

Hamilton Smith Counsr. at Law.
Louisville Kenty 15th May 1844.

Philip Hone of New York.
Saratoga Springs 27th July 1843.

9

Cornelius Van Wyck Lawrence
1791–1861
[New York], September 28, 1839

A native of Flushing, Long Island, the son of a prosperous merchant, Lawrence made a high reputation in both business and politics. His boyhood years were spent working on his father's farm. Upon the completion of a common school education, he removed to New York City in 1812 and successfully engaged in mercantile and financial pursuits, forming the firm of Hicks, Lawrence & Company, well-known auctioneers. Active in politics and a prominent member of the Tammany Society, he was elected to the United States Congress as a Jacksonian Democrat in 1833. A year later he resigned this office to take up the duties of mayor of New York. He was the first person chosen mayor under the new city popular suffrage law. Previously, this office had been filled by a member of the board of the Common Council.

Mr. Lawrence served as mayor for two successive terms and in 1836 was a presidential elector on the Van Buren–Johnson ticket, acting as president of the electoral college. During his second administration as mayor, the famous 1837 flour riot took place. For twenty years he held the honorable position of president of the Bank of the State of New York. At the same time he was a director of several other banks, trust companies, and fire and mutual insurance companies. During the presidency of James K. Polk he occupied the post of collector of customs of the Port of New York. In 1856 Lawrence retired from business on account of ill health; he spent the closing days of his life at his country seat in Flushing, where he ultimately died. Supposedly, he was distantly related to Walter Bowne (fig. 275), mayor of New York four years prior to his own election. Lawrence was married to his cousin Lydia A. Lawrence, the daughter of Judge Effingham Lawrence and the widow of Edward N. Lawrence.

4.

C. W. Lawrence
28 September 1839

C. W. Lawrence Esq Mayor of N.Y.
28th Septemb. 1839

10
James Logue
Lexington, Kentucky, May 29, 1844

In 1813 James Logue emigrated from Letter Kenney, Ireland, to Lexington, Kentucky, where he resided with his father for a time and opened an academy for girls and boys. As an educator, he was highly successful, and the fruits of his labor enabled him to acquire several properties in the city. In recognition of his literary interests, he was elected librarian of the Lexington Library, a position which he held for some twenty-five years. Late in his career, the directors of the library showed their appreciation of his services by presenting him with a handsome walking cane.

In 1846, two years after he stood to Edouart, Mr. Logue was elected mayor of Lexington for a one-year term. He is said to have filled this station to general satisfaction. During his active career he made trips to Ireland, England, Europe, and to other parts of the United States.

11
James Stevenson   1788–1852
Saratoga Springs, July 15, 1843

Wealthy, zealous in public affairs, and a polished gentleman, James Stevenson was an able servant of his native city of Albany, New York. After graduating from Williams College, class of 1807, he studied law under John V. Henry and was admitted to the bar. Although of proven competence as a lawyer, he paid slight attention to his profession but instead focused his interest on the city, working for local enterprises and serving repeatedly as a member of the Common Council. He was a trustee of Albany Boys' Academy and one of the first governors of Albany City Hospital.

Running as a Whig in 1826, Stevenson was elected mayor of Albany, succeeding Ambrose Spencer. Two years later he won reelection to the same office. Despite much success and popularity, in 1838 he tendered his resignation due to the pressures of personal business. Though regarded as "high-toned" and "old-school" by some, Stevenson gave his attention to useful public activities with sound judgment and unobtrusive modesty. He was known to be notably loyal to the Episcopal church. As a testament to his stature in the community, his funeral was attended by the Common Council as a body. Appropriately, Edouart pairs Stevenson with James Logue, a man holding a comparable political office and sharing his keen devotion to local civic affairs.

4½

James Logue, Mayor of
Lexington Ky.
May. 29. 1844 —

Jas. Stevenson —
Saratoga Springs July 15th 1843 — —

James Logue Mayor of Lexington Ky.
Lexington 29th May. 1844.

James Stevenson Mayor
of Albany 36
Saratoga Springs 15th July 1843.

12
James Biddle 1783–1848
Philadelphia, October 19, 1843

Bachelor son of the Philadelphia Quaker family and educated at the University of Pennsylvania, Commodore Biddle's career was in the navy, which he entered in 1800. He was captured in 1803 when the *Philadelphia* grounded near Tripoli. In 1815, as captain of the *Hornet,* he ran the blockade at New London and off Tristan da Cunha heroically captured the British brig *Penguin.* He took possession of Oregon Territory in 1817, later serving in the West Indies, South American waters, and the Mediterranean. From 1838 to 1842 he headed the Naval Asylum at Philadelphia, known as "Biddle's Nursery" and the forerunner of the Academy at Annapolis. In 1846, as commodore of the East India Squadron, he negotiated the first treaty with China. He was an older brother of Nicholas Biddle (fig. 271). Edouart displays the commodore only a few months after he left the "Nursery."

James Biddle
U. S. Navy
19 Oct. 1843

4 bis

Commodore James Biddle U. S. N.
Philadelphia 19th Octob. 1843.

13
Mary Austin Holley 1784–1846
Lexington, Kentucky, June 1, 1844

A New Haven–born Episcopalian, Mary Austin
married the Congregational minister Horace Holley, who for ten years served Boston's Hollis
Street Church. But Boston's theological liberalism
undermined his Trinitarian belief and he and his
wife embraced Unitarianism. He later accepted
the presidency of Transylvania University at Lexington, Kentucky. At his death in 1827 his widow
contributed an appendix to the biography of her
husband, *A Discourse on the Genius . . . of the
Reverend Horace Holley*, written by Dr. Charles
Caldwell (fig. 79), and after a few years she emigrated to Texas with the aid of her cousin
Stephen F. Austin, the founder of Texas. There
she wrote her great work *Texas: Observations
Historical, Geographical, and Descriptive*, published in 1833, for which she is deservedly remembered. Her long interest in Texas earned her the
title "first lady ambassador at large" for the Austin Colony and the Republic of Texas. She had
hoped that her large landholdings in Texas would
rise in value assuring her of financial security,
but she was doomed to disappointment. "It is
truly in Texas," she wrote, " 'Man never is, but
always to be—blest.' You are put off—put off-
forever."

Mary Austin Holley
Lexington Kentucky
June 1st 1844.

1 Letters on Texas -
the first work
published on the
Subject, & on which
all the rest were founded. 1832

2 Mr Holleys Texas - 1b

Widow Mary Austin Holley of Texas.
Lexington Ky 1st June 1844.

14

David Spraker   1801–1873
New York, September 14, 1839

Born at Sprakers, New York, Spraker moved to
Canajoharie after his marriage in 1826 and lived
there as one of its prominent residents until his
death. He graduated from Union College in
1822 and then became a lawyer. He served as a
member of the Supreme Court Commission, as
judge of the Court of Common Pleas of Montgomery County, and as state senator from 1836 to
1839. Six of his eleven children lived to maturity;
one of them, Ferdinand, became a founder and
vice-president of the Baseball Hall of Fame at
Cooperstown. His silhouette was made just at
the end of his term in the state senate.

D. Spraker

David Spraker New York State Senator and member of the Court for the correction of error New York 14th Sept 1839.

15
James Kent 1763–1847
New York, November 2, 1840

Kent was first dubbed "the American Blackstone" by Justice Joseph Story. The Constitutional Convention of 1821 required New York's judges to retire at age sixty, and so in 1823, at the peak of his abilities, Kent left the bench after nineteen years of service. He moved to New York City, where he was reappointed to the law professorship at Columbia. For two years he lectured, unsuccessfully he believed. Then his son William urged him to rewrite his lectures; he did and published them in four volumes as his *Commentaries on American Law*, the American counterpart of Blackstone's work and one which became a classic, six times republished during his life and many times thereafter.

In 1781 Kent graduated at Yale College, where he was a founder of its Phi Beta Kappa Society. While in college he first read Blackstone's *Commentaries* and determined to be a lawyer. He commenced practice in Poughkeepsie and then moved to New York. He sought public office and was thrice elected to the assembly; he also served as the first professor of law at Columbia College. In 1798 Governor Jay appointed him judge of the supreme court; in 1804 he became chief judge and in 1814 chancellor. He established the practice of giving opinions of the court in writing and was virtually the creator of equity jurisdiction in the United States. His place on the court in New York equaled that of Chief Justice Marshall on the Supreme Court. Kent's sparkling wit and friendship with Story shows in toasts they reportedly exchanged at a Phi Beta Kappa Society dinner at Harvard. Story gave, "The State of New York, where the law of the land has been so ably administered that it has become the land of the law," to which Kent replied, "The State of Massachusetts, the land of Story as well as of song."

It is fitting that Edouart posed Kent and Story together so carefully, the older man seated, pointing to one of his opinions, the younger with deference continuing the argument.

16
Joseph Story 1779–1845
Boston, June 9, 1842

A graduate of Harvard College in 1798, Story studied law under Samuel Sewall, later chief justice of Massachusetts, and delivered the eulogy in Marblehead on the death of Washington. Later, as a member of the committee to consider the establishment of a court of chancery, he, with Kent, helped found the chancery system in this country. He was a member of Congress, a member and speaker of the Massachusetts House of Representatives, president of the Merchants Bank of Salem, overseer of Harvard, and a fellow of the Corporation. In 1811 he became associate justice of the Supreme Court of the United States, the youngest person ever appointed to the position. He sat on the Court with credit for thirty-four years. The Law School of Harvard owes much of its beginnings to his efforts as a professor of law. The statue of him by his sculptor-son William Wetmore Story stands appropriately in the great doorway to Langdell Hall, the Law School's library.

Early writing of poetry gave way to numerous learned works on law: *Bailments* (1832), *On the Constitution* (1833), *Conflict of Laws* (1834), *Equity Jurisdiction* (1836), *Agency* (1839), to name but a few. Only a lawyer can fully appreciate the breadth of knowledge and perseverance required to produce such volumes.

It was a pleasant coincidence that in 1901 Story, Kent, and Chief Justice Marshall (fig. 196), the three great judges of the age, were elected to the Hall of Fame for Great Americans at New York University on the same day. It is also evidence of Edouart's perspicacity that in this, the surviving volume of his great collection of silhouettes, he preserved likenesses of these men.

New York November 2d 1840 *Remember* 5½

Author of "The Commentaries on American Law." & Chancellor of New York. —

June 9 1842 Boston

Joseph D Story

Author of the "Commentaries on the Conflict of Laws".

obt. 10th Sept 1845

Chancellor James Kent State of N.Y. New Y. 2d Novemb. 1840.

Judge Joseph Story of the Sup. C U. S. Boston 9th June 1842.

17
Subject Unknown
Date and place unknown

There is no clue to the identity of this tall, handsome figure. However, the duplicate of this silhouette, with statistical information about this
subject, may well still remain in private hands.

18
James Trecothick Austin
1784–1870
Boston, March 28, 1842

Educated at Andover, Boston Latin School, and Harvard College in the class of 1802, admitted to the bar in 1805, Austin married Catherine, daughter of Vice-President Elbridge Gerry, in 1806. He served as county attorney for Suffolk County, Massachusetts, from 1807 to 1832, as overseer of Harvard, as state senator, and in 1829 as commissioner to settle the boundary between Massachusetts and Connecticut east of the Connecticut River. He served as attorney general of Massachusetts from 1832 to 1843. Recognized as one of the leading lawyers of Massachusetts, he became president of the Suffolk County Bar Association and, as a staunch Republican, was an opponent of the antislavery movement. Harvard honored him with an LL.D. in 1835, and he was a distinguished member of the American Academy of Arts and Sciences and of the Massachusetts Historical Society. He contributed regularly to the *Boston Emerald* and the *Boston Patriot* and wrote his well-known *Life of Elbridge Gerry* in 1828.

19
Greene Carrier Bronson   1789–1863
[Saratoga], August 28, 1840

Able lawyer, judge, and politician, Judge Bronson was the leader of the Hard Shell wing of the Democratic party. He began his practice of the law in Utica in 1815 and became surrogate of Oneida County in 1819. Elected to the assembly in 1822, he was soon chairman of the Judiciary Committee. He served as attorney general of the state of New York until 1836 when he became a justice, and later chief justice, of the Supreme Court of New York. In 1847 he became a judge of the court of appeals. Having lost his fortune in unwise speculations, he retired from the bench and became collector of the port of New York in 1853, unsuccessful candidate of the Hard Shell Democrats for governor in 1855, and corporation counsel in 1859. During the first years of the Civil War he was a member of the New York Union Defense Committee. As a prominent member of the bench and bar he is appropriately paired by Edouart with Austin.

G. C. Bronson
Albany N.Y. Aug. 8 1844

James T. Austin
Attorney Gen'l Massachusetts

James T. Austin
Attorney Gen't of Mass. Boston 28th March 1842

Greenson
Judge of the Supreme Court Albany

20
John Marsh, D.D.   1788–1868
Saratoga, August 4, 1842

Born in Wethersfield, Connecticut, a graduate of
Yale in 1804, Marsh studied theology with his
father, served for several years in a variety of
churches, and accepted a call to the Congregational church in Haddam in 1818. But his interest lay in the Temperance Movement. As corresponding secretary of the American Temperance
Union he was editor of its *Journal* and in 1839
established the *Youth's Temperance Advocate*.
Jefferson College honored him with a degree of
Doctor of Divinity in 1852. Titles of his publications show his bent: "The Rum-Drinking Christian: A Short Sermon" (1829), "The Pool of Bethesda; or, The Unfortunate Drunkard's Call for
Help" (1841), "Frauds in Intoxicating Liquors—
The Sin of Drunkard Making" (1856). He was
engaged in raising money for the Yale Divinity
School when he suffered a fatal stroke. A worthy,
hard-working reformer, his best-known lecture,
"Putnam and His Wolf" (1829), sold over 150,000
copies. There is no clue to his being paired by
Edouart with the first mayor of Brooklyn.

21
Cyrus Porter Smith   1800–1877
Washington, April 23, 1841

Having been brought up on a farm, Smith worked
his way through Dartmouth, graduating with
honors in 1824. He read law with Chief Justice
T. S. Williams of Hartford and supplemented his
scant resources by teaching in singing schools.
After moving to Brooklyn, New York, in 1827, he
entered politics, became clerk of the Village
Board of Trustees, corporation counsel from 1835
to 1839, and enjoyed a growing law practice. He
was the first mayor of Brooklyn, elected in 1829
under the new law, and became the moving spirit
in the development of its system of public education. During his term as mayor he and General
Robert Nichols established a city hospital which
ultimately became the Brooklyn City Hospital.
As managing director of the Union Ferry Company and acting president of the Brooklyn City
Railroad Company, he merited the reputation of
being one of the most influential of Brooklyn's
early citizens and earned the affectionate title
"Uncle Cyrus."

6.½

Rev John Marsh
Cor Sec Amer.
Temp. Union
Aug.   New York
4. 1842

C P Smith
Mayor of the City
of Brooklyn
Ab. 23. 1841.

Revd. John Marsh. Corresp: Secretary
Saratoga 4th Augt. 1842.   Amern. Temperance Union
of New York.

C.P. Smith Mayor of the City of Brooklyn
taken in Washington 23d. April 1841.

22

John Neilson, M.D.   1775–1857
New York, September 26, 1839

A youthful graduate of Princeton College, 1793, Neilson studied medicine in New York under Dr. Kearny Rodgers and practiced his profession for upwards of sixty years as one of the foremost physicians of his time and with what is believed to be the largest practice among the physicians of that day. He was surgeon to the army during the War of 1812 and later was consulting physician to the Lunatic Asylum at Bloomindale. He bravely remained in the city during the yellow fever and cholera epidemics of 1822 and 1832. In 1798 he married Abigail, daughter of Anthony Lispenard Bleeker (whose names are perpetuated in two of New York's streets), and was blessed with six sons and six daughters. Edouart preserves his well-known "fine and erect physique."

Mc.Brillon

7.

John Neilson M.D.
Bener Hall 26th September 1839

23
Edward Cornelius Delavan
1793–1871
Saratoga, August 3, 1842

Having amassed a fortune as a wine merchant, Delavan built the famous temperance hotel in Albany, the Delavan House, and devoted the rest of his life to the Temperance Movement. It was at this hotel that the tea merchant Matthias Bruen (fig. 116) died in 1846. Delavan was one of the organizers of the New York State Temperance Society and engaged in the delicate discussions of the risks of the use of wine at communion. When the *Journal of the American Temperance Union* was first published, with the Reverend John Marsh (fig. 20) as its editor, Delavan financed the printing and distribution of 50,000 copies. To emphasize the risks of intemperance, he distributed in the state of New York in 1840, two years before he stood for Edouart, over 100,000 colored, engraved plates of the human stomach showing the bad effects of alcohol. He was born in Westchester County, New York, married first Abby Smith of Lyme, Connecticut, and second Harriet Schuyler, daughter of Cornelius Schuyler of Albany, and died in Schenectady.

24
Reuben Dimond Mussey, M.D.
1780–1866
Saratoga Springs, July 20, 1842

Dr. Mussey was a prominent physician and professor of surgery at the Ohio Medical College at Cincinnati when taken by Edouart, who probably paired him with Delavan because of their common interest in the Temperance Movement. Mussey, born in New Hampshire, was a graduate of Dartmouth in 1803 and received his M.D. in 1809 from the University of Pennsylvania at the time Dr. Benjamin Rush was head of the Medical Department. He practiced medicine in Salem, Massachusetts, for six years with considerable success in association with Dr. Daniel Oliver and in 1814 moved to Dartmouth to become professor of materia medica and therapeutics, and later professor of obstetrics, and anatomy and surgery. He served as president of the New Hampshire Medical Society, was an ingenious and forward-looking physician, the first person to tie, successfully, both carotid arteries. In 1852, after fourteen years at the Ohio Medical College, he began lecturing on surgery at the Miami Medical College and in six years returned to Boston. He married first Mary Sewall and second Hetty, daughter of Dr. Osgood of Salem; two of his four sons became physicians. He received the degree of A.M. from Harvard in 1806 and an LL.D. from Dartmouth in 1854 and was an honorary member of the Massachusetts Medical Soriety and of the American Academy of Arts and Sciences.

7 1/2

Edward C. Delavan.
"
Ballston Centre
Saratoga Co.
Aug 3 a 1842

R. D. Mussey M.D.
Prof. of Surgery
Cincinnati Ohio July 20.

Edw.d C. Delavan of Ballston N.Yk
Pres.t of Temperance Soc.ty Saratoga 3.d Aug.t 1842.

Dr. R. D. Mussey Professor of Surgery Me Coll.
of Ohio
Cincinnati
Saratoga Springs 20th July 1842.

25
Jacob Hayes 1772–1850
New York, October 25, 1839

Master "thief-taker," "terror to evildoers," Old
Hayes, as he was called by the criminals of his
day, never forgot a face that once attracted his
attention. Of Jewish descent, he embraced Christianity, moved from Bedford, New York, his birthplace, to New York City, where Mayor Livingston
appointed him high constable (chief of police), a
post to which he was reappointed by each succeeding mayor and which he held half a century
until his death, when the office was abolished. He
earned the fear and respect of the criminal classes.
His reputation rivaled that of Townsend, the celebrated Bow Street officer of London. Edouart
portrays him hot on a trail. A fascinating account
of Old Hayes is given in Augustine E. Costello,
Our Police Protectors (1885), with enough anecdotes to satisfy the most ardent reader of detective
stories.

Jacob Hays

Jacob Hays, High Constable, Sergeant at Arms and Crier of the Court of Sessions. New York 28th Octob. 1834.

26
Charles Cromwell Ingham
1796–1863
Saratoga, August 25, 1843

The *Death of Cleopatra*, painted by the Dublin-born portraitist Ingham when only nineteen years old and shown at the first exhibition of the American Academy of Fine Arts in New York, gave him notoriety and business. He moved to New York, became a founder of the National Academy of Design and a member of the Sketch Club, and painted many well-known sitters. His portrait of Lafayette was so well received that the head became the basis for the full-length portrait of the general painted for the State Department in Albany. Romantic portraits of young girls and pretty women, such as *The Laughing Girl* and *The Flower Girl*, became his popular pieces. Edouart presents a charming likeness of him at his easel at the height of his career, at about the time he painted his portrait of that center of controversy, the explorer Commodore Charles Wilkes.

8½.

Charles C. Ingham of New York taken in Saratoga 15th Augt 1843
Portrait Painter

27
Daniel Bryant Tallmadge
1793–1847
New York, October 1, 1839

Tallmadge earned his reputation as a lawyer by
reversing the conviction in the "conspiracy cases"
of Jacob Barker and others against the advice of
their own lawyers who thought their cases hope-
less. Though he lost the case before the state supreme court, he carried it to the Court for the
Correction of Errors, which reversed the lower
court and set his clients at liberty. It was a great
victory. His practice consequently flourished, and
he was appointed a judge of the superior court in
the city of New York to fill out the term of Judge
Hoffman, who had died. He held this post with
honor. Born in Chatham, New York, he had
no collegiate education but studied law under
Charles H. Ruggles and Elisha Williams and was
admitted to practice in 1818. His reputation was
furthered by his review of the supreme court's
opinion in the *McLeod* case, which was cited with
favor by Daniel Webster. He died at the height of
his career while in Virginia trying to recover his
health.

Dan.ᵗ B. Tallmadge . Oct. 1ˢᵗ 1839

9.

Honᵇˡᵉ Danˡ Bᵗ Tallmadge . Judge of Superior Court
New York 1ˢᵗ Octob. 1839

28
Henry Myer Phillips 1811–1884
Saratoga Springs, August 21, 1842

A Philadelphia lawyer and the son of a Philadelphia lawyer, a product of Philadelphia schools and the Franklin Institute, Phillips is caught here by Edouart as a young man at the start of his career, as if declaring, "Here am I, Lord." His career was distinguished, if stereotyped. He became a member of the Thirty-fifth Congress, 1857–59, a trustee of Jefferson Medical College, a member of the board and subsequently president of the Fairmount Park Commission, a member and later president of the Board of City Trusts, a director and president of the Academy of Music, and a director of the Pennsylvania Railroad Company.

9½

Henry M Phillips
Counsellor at Law.
Philadelphia
August 21. 1842

Henry M. Phillips Counsellor at Law
of Philadelphia.   Saratoga Springs 21st Augt 1842.

29
John McKeon 1807–1883
New York, September 28, 1839

Born in Albany, graduated from Columbia College in 1825, admitted to the bar in 1828, McKeon was elected to the state assembly in 1832 and to Congress, where he served from 1835 to 1837 and 1841 to 1843. Upon the resignation of Charles O'Conor (fig. 252) in 1853 as United States attorney for the Southern District of New York, President Pierce appointed McKeon to fill the unexpired term. He later was a delegate to the Democratic National Convention in 1864 and the Union Convention in 1866. In 1881 he was again elected district attorney of the county of New York, a post he held until his death. He was a distinguished and merciless prosecutor, one of his most sensational cases being that of the notorious Madame Restell, the proprietress of a fashionable abortion establishment on Fifth Avenue.

15.

John McKeon

Washington 1 Septr. 28. 1839

John McKeon Late Member of Congress N.Y. 28th Septr 1839

30
William Valentine 1802–1865
Saratoga Springs, August 3, 1841

Dr. Valentine, widely known as "the Humorist,"
was born in New York City, studied medicine under the celebrated Dr. Chesseman, and graduated
from the New York Medical College. His marriage
to Marian Bedell of Hempstead proved unhappy
and barren and perhaps gave rise to his career as
a humorous lecturer, a superb delineator of character and scenes, a ventriloquist, and a flutist,
which caused him to travel throughout the country. He must have been a welcome addition to the
Saratoga Springs vacationing assemblage.

10½

Dr Wm Valentine
Saratoga Aug. 3d 1841

Dr. "Wm." Valentine, Comic lecturer
taken at saratoga springs
Aug 3d 1841.

31
Matthew Livingston Davis
1773–1850
New York, October 29, 1839

At dawn on July 11, 1804, Davis, with Aaron Burr and two others, rowed across the river from New York toward Weehawken. Shortly after sunrise, upon the heights twenty feet above the water, in a spot six feet wide and eleven paces long, Burr mortally wounded Alexander Hamilton, who died the next day. The coroner's jury a few days later brought a verdict of murder against Burr. Davis was later committed to prison for refusing to testify against his friend.

Davis, a journalist, collaborator with Philip Freneau on the *Time Piece* and *Literary Companion*, became grand sachem of the Tammany Society and as an adventurer was convicted (though on appeal acquitted) of massive swindles. As a lifelong friend of Burr he came into possession of Burr's papers and his voluminous correspondence "indicating no very strict morality in some of his female correspondents." Burr died in September 1836, aged eighty-one, leaving Davis as his executor. In the preface to his *Life of Burr* (published in 1836, though surely commenced earlier—the preface being dated November 15, 1836) Davis wrote: "These letters contained matter that would have wounded the feelings of families more extremely than could be imagined . . . and created heartburnings that nothing but time could have cured." And then he added the words so many had hoped for: "With my own hands I committed to the fire all such correspondence, and not a vestige of it now remains." Though this self-serving declaration was soon after questioned, Davis must have been a figure of great interest and whispered concern as a member of the New York community in 1839 when he was cut by Edouart. In his later years he was Washington correspondent of the London *Times* under the name of "the Genevese Traveler" and of the *Morning Courier and New York Enquirer* as "the Spy in Washington." Known as "the Old Boy in Specs," justly famous for his anecdotes and reminiscences, he died in Manhattanville and was buried in Trinity Cemetery.

Matthew Livingston Davis,
New York
29" Oct. 39-

M. L. Davis
New York 29 Oct. 39

11.

Matthew Livingston Davis

32
Paul Beck Goddard, M.D.
1811–1866
Philadelphia, October 3, 1842

A native of Baltimore, graduate of Washington (now Trinity) College, Hartford, 1828, Goddard received his M.D. from the University of Pennsylvania in 1832 and acquired a wide and well-deserved reputation as editor of many medical works of a varied nature. He was a demonstrator of anatomy at the University of Pennsylvania and a skillful surgeon. But, like many able men, he had another side. Fascinated by Daguerre's photographic discovery, Goddard discovered that the use of vapor of bromide on the silvered plate used by Daguerre greatly accelerated the photograhic process. This discovery furnished the basis of future progress in photography. His discoveries were laid before the American Philosophical Society in 1839, and in 1840 he became a member of that society. As a newly elected member of that distinguished gathering, he must have been a doubly interesting character for inclusion in Edouart's repository of shades of prominent persons.

33
James Waddell Alexander, D.D.
1804–1859
Philadelphia, October 3, 1842

Grandson of James Waddell, the "blind preacher" made famous by William Wirt, Alexander, born in Virginia, graduated from Princeton College in 1820 and then spent four years at the Princeton Theological Seminary. From 1828 to 1832 he had charge of the First Presbyterian Church in Trenton and from 1833 to 1844 was professor of belles lettres and rhetoric at Princeton. Later he occupied the chair of ecclesiastical history and church government in the theological seminary. In 1851 he accepted a call to the Fifth Avenue Presbyterian Church in New York, where he served out his life. He was a prolific writer of hymns and popular theology and a contributor to many publications including the *Biblical Repertory* and the *Princeton Review*. Edouart catches him at the time he was a Princeton professor and shortly before Lafayette College awarded him an honorary D.D.

11½

Paul. B. Goddard. M.D.
Demon: of Anatomy
University of Pennsylvania
Oct: 3d 1842

James W. Alexander, Prof.
Coll. of N. Jersey.
Oct. 3. 1842.

Paul B Goddard M.D. Demon: of Anatomy
University of Pennsylvania
Philadelphia 3d Oct. 1842.

James W. Alexander, Professor
College of New Jersey.
Philadelphia Oct. 3rd 1842

34

James Barron   1769–1851
Philadelphia, April 4, 1843

Son of a Revolutionary War merchant captain, Barron took part in the last days of the war. He entered the navy in 1798, served on the *United States* under Commodore Barry, and had a command in the Mediterranean with Commodore Preble's fleet. After a few years of service he took command as commodore in 1807 of the *Chesapeake*, thirty-eight guns. The vessel had been hastily and inadequately fitted out and after sailing off Hampton Roads was attacked by the fifty-gun British *Leopard* in search of deserters. After receiving a burst of gunfire which killed several of his crew, Barron hauled down his colors. The alleged deserters were seized and the ship released. The British later paid substantial amounts in reparation for what was considered an illegal seizure.

On reaching home, however, Barron was court-martialed for not having fought longer by a court which included among its members Commodores Decatur and Bainbridge. Though acquitted of cowardice, Barron was suspended for five years for neglecting "on the probability of an engagement" to clear his ship for action. When he reentered the service, his efforts to obtain a command were blocked by his brother officers. Believing Decatur to be the ringleader of opposition, Barron challenged him to a duel in 1820, and on March 22 at Bladensburg, Maryland, Decatur was killed and Barron himself severely wounded. Decatur's popularity served thereafter to prevent Barron from getting a post. Though in 1839 he became senior officer in the navy, the rest of his life was spent waiting for orders, as he is so poignantly shown by Edouart, the coveted commands lying at anchor in the distance. It is the judgment of history that Barron had not been at fault but was a victim of circumstances.

James Barron

Philadelphia
April the
4th 1843

12.

Commodore James Bar[ron]
Born 15th Sept. 1768.

35
Mirabeau Buonaparte Lamar
1798–1859
New York, November 18, 1844

Lamar, from 1838 to 1841 the second president of the new Republic of Texas, won his post at an election the results of which were assured by the suicide of both of his opponents shortly before the vote was taken. Though during his term the independence of Texas was recognized by many European powers, its state university founded, and the capital moved from Houston to Austin, Lamar's administration was financially disastrous. Born in Georgia, he became an Alabama merchant but failed in business; then he acted as secretary to Governor George M. Troup of Georgia and later founded the *Columbus Independent*, a states' rights paper, and in 1833 was editor of the *Columbus Enquirer*. Becoming interested in the crisis developing in Texas, he joined Sam Houston's army, distinguished himself at the battle of San Jacinto, and in 1836 became vice-president under Houston and two years later president.

At the end of Lamar's term as president, Houston was reelected. Not long after, Lamar reversed his political opinions and by 1844 (at the time Edouart cut his silhouette) sided with those favoring the annexation of Texas as necessary to preserve slavery. In 1846 he saw action in the Mexican War under General Zachary Taylor, with outstanding service at Monterey, and later he commanded a company of Texas rangers. After the admission of Texas as a state Lamar served a term in the legislature and for a time served as minister to Nicaragua and Costa Rica. In 1857 he published his principal work, *Verse Memorials*. Lamar County and the town of Lamar in Aransas County both serve to perpetuate his name as one of the pioneers so active in the early political life of Texas.

Mirabeau B. Lamar
Texas
18th Novr 1844.

Genal Mirabeau Bonaparte Lamar
Late Presidt of Texas Æ Fifty 18th Novr 1844

36
Catherine R. Williams   1787–1872
Saratoga, July 18, 1844

Mrs. Catherine R. Williams, described by Edouart as "Authoress," was indeed a poet, novelist, and biographer. She was born in Providence, Rhode Island, the daughter of Captain Alfred Arnold, whose father, Oliver Arnold, was attorney general of Rhode Island. Her sea captain father, unable adequately to look after his daughter following the early death of her mother, entrusted her to the care of two maiden aunts, under whose guidance she received her education, heavily tinged with religious overtones. At the age of thirty-seven she was married in New York to Horatio N. Williams by the Right Reverend Benjamin T. Onderdonk (fig. 39). The marriage was short-lived, and in a few years she was divorced and returned to Providence with her infant daughter. She turned to writing, discovering a popularity that greatly surprised her. Commencing with a book of poems in 1828, many of which were written in her youth, she followed with *Religion at Home* in 1829, *Tales, Natural and Revolutionary* in 1830, and *Aristocracy; or, the Holby Family* in 1832. In 1833 she published *Fall River*, an account of the sensational trial of the Reverend Ephraim K. Avery for the murder of the youthful Miss Sarah M. Cornell, of whose guilt Mrs. Williams had little doubt. *The Neutral French; or, the Exiles of Nova Scotia*, which she believed her best work and which foreshadowed Longfellow's *Evangeline*, appeared in 1841, reflecting the experiences she had while journeying through the provinces the previous year. Lastly she published in 1843–45 her two-volume *Annals of the Aristocracy; Being a Series of Anecdotes of Some of the Principal Families of Rhode Island*. It was at this period, at the height of her career, that she visited Saratoga and was taken by Edouart in a significant pose, manuscript in hand, no doubt as she was often seen.

37
William Cooper Mead, D.D.
1795–1879
Philadelphia, May 4, 1843

Dr. Mead was, for over forty-three years, the saintly and beloved rector of St. Paul's Church in Norwalk, Connecticut, to which he was called in 1836, succeeding by a few months the farsighted Jackson Kemper, later missionary bishop in the Old Northwest and founder of Kenyon College. Mead was born in Greenwich in 1795, ordained deacon in 1824, and priest in 1825 by Bishop Hobart of New York. Before he was called to Norwalk he served at Grace Church, White Plains (which he founded), from 1824 to 1826, Christ Church at Reading, Pennsylvania, for a few months, and Trinity Church in Philadelphia for almost ten years until 1836.

During his memorable tenure at St. Paul's, Norwalk, he was responsible for erecting the church building and later Trinity Chapel in South Norwalk—and lastly his own tomb. In his sermon preached on the twenty-fifth anniversary of his coming to St. Paul's he remarked that during his rectorship 3,775 sermons had been preached, 2,717 by himself. It was said of him that his faith was summed up in the text of the last sermon he preached in the old church building: "We preach Christ crucified."

At his death, on the forty-third anniversary of the death of his old Philadelphia friend Bishop William White, the bells of St. Paul's tolled his age, spreading the sad tidings of the loss of a beloved member and servant of the community.

Catharine R Williams
of Providence R.I. July 18th 1844
Taken in Saratoga

Wm Cooper Mead
May 4th 1843.
Norwalk, Conn.

Wm Cooper Mead DD.
Rector Saint Paul's Church, Norwalk, Conn.
Philad. May 4th 1843

Mrs Catherine R. Williams Authoress
of Providence (R.I.)
Saratoga 18th July 1844.

12¾

38
Solomon Etting   1764–1847
Baltimore, November 8, 1840

It was not without cause that Solomon Etting in his old age was affectionately referred to as Father Etting. Born in York, Pennsylvania, in 1783 he married Rachel, a daughter of Joseph Simon, the Indian trader who was also a founder of the Pennsylvania Academy of the Fine Arts. At the age of twenty-one Etting was one of the founders of the Masonic Lodge No. 43 of Lancaster, rising from treasurer to junior warden, to worshipful master before he moved to Philadelphia in 1790 following the death of his wife. He then married another Rachel, daughter of Barnard Gratz, and removed to Baltimore, where he lived until his death. He became a leader in the movement to permit Jews to hold public office. After many years effort on his part the disability of Jews was removed by the legislature and Etting himself became the first Jewish member of the city council in Baltimore, finally becoming its president. Among his other public activities was his part in the organization of the Baltimore & Ohio Railroad, of whose first board of directors he was a member.

He was a devoted public servant, a man of presence and dignity, some of which Edouart, in his shade, has caught; but a shadow cannot adequately reveal the respect and affection felt toward him by the community.

12½ in

Solomon Etting
Baltimore 8 Novr. 1840

Solomon Etting.
Union Bank. Baltimore
8th Decr. 1840

39
Benjamin Tredwell Onderdonk, D.D.
1791–1861
New York, April 14, 1840

Upon his consecration in 1830 at St. John's Chapel in New York by Bishops White and Brownell and his own brother Henry, Bishop Onderdonk became the fourth bishop of the Episcopal Diocese of New York, succeeding the revered Bishop John Henry Hobart, who had ordained him to the diaconate and the priesthood.

He was a New Yorker by birth, a graduate of Columbia College in the class of 1809, and after taking orders became an assistant minister at Trinity Church, thereby occupying a position that was a proverbial steppingstone to the episcopacy in the Diocese of New York. From 1821 until his death he also occupied the chair of professor of ecclesiastical history at the General Theological Seminary and filled many posts in the diocesan convention. Untiring in his devotion to his calling, vigorous, uncompromising, and High Church, in the end he aroused his enemies and contributed to his own downfall. In 1845, after a long and painful trial before an ecclesiastical court acting under a canon of only three months' standing, the court found him guilty of having committed immoral acts, and he was suspended from all exercise of his spiritual and ministerial functions. It is apparently true that he was at times given to overindulgence or, as it was alleged at his trial, "improperly excited by vinous or spiritous liquors," but such indiscretions of man-

ners as may have followed from such a condition could not, in the opinion of his supporters, support a charge of "immorality with a deliberately impure intent." Opinions of churchmen were strongly divided, but the "proceedings of the ecclesiastical court were almost universally reprobated." The suspended bishop lived in seclusion in his state of ecclesiastical suspension until his death in 1861 despite an almost successful attempt to have his suspension lifted. During this long period, the Reverend Jonathan M. Wainwright (fig. 40) was elected provisional bishop of New York so that the diocese could continue to function.

The approbation which the bishop received during his last years was borne out by the extraordinary number of devoted and loyal friends who attended his funeral. There is little doubt that the harsh treatment he received was as a victim of what could fairly be termed a conspiracy. The whole sad tale is told in a series of pamphlets representing both sides of the controversy and bound and published together in a fat octavo volume that appeared late in 1845.

Edouart's silhouette shows the bishop at the summit of his episcopal career, in ecclesiastical surroundings as though in the act of preaching, and oblivious to the disaster that lay ahead.

13

Bishop T. Onderdonk,
New York, April 14. 1840.

Bishop of New York Dr. Benjamin T. Onderdonk

40

Jonathan Mayhew Wainwright, D.C.L. 1792–1854

Boston, April 2, 1842

The fact that this silhouette of the Reverend Dr. Wainwright immediately follows that of Bishop Onderdonk, whose shoes as bishop of New York he filled for a time under unusual circumstances, is of course a mere coincidence. In 1842 when this shade was cut, Dr. Wainwright was minister in charge of St. John's Chapel in New York, a branch of Trinity Church. He had been born in England and received his early education there, later coming to America and graduating from Harvard College in 1812. He was ordained deacon by Bishop Griswold and priested by Bishop Hobart. For a time he served as assistant minister of Trinity Church, then as rector of Grace Church in 1821. The reputation he earned as a preacher and pastor led to his call to the rectorship of Trinity Church in Boston in 1831. Yet after four years of useful service in Boston he welcomed his recall to New York to assume charge of St. John's Chapel.

In 1852 he was sent to England as a delegate to the fiftieth anniversary of the venerable Society for the Propagation of the Gospel in Foreign Parts, where he was received with distinction and was granted from Oxford the honorary degree of D.C.L. On his return to America he was elected provisional bishop of New York, a post devised to fill the apparent ecclesiastical gap caused by the unfortunate suspension of Bishop Onderdonk (fig. 39). His consecration was the first in America in which an English bishop (Bishop Fulford) took part. Also present was Bishop Doane of New Jersey (fig. 245). The circumstance of the Diocese of New York's having been without an active diocesan for twelve years laid a heavy burden on Bishop Wainwright, one which he did not shirk from bearing but which brought him to the grave in two years. During that short period it was recorded that he had consecrated fifteen churches, ordained thirty-seven deacons and twelve priests, and administered the sacrament of confirmation to 4,127 persons. He was indeed a good and faithful servant.

13½.

Jon.ª M. Wainwright
Boston April 2ᵈ 1842.

Revᵈ. Dᵣ. Jonᵃ. M. Wainwright of New York.
Sᵗ. John's Church. N.Y.ᵏ   taken in Boston 2ᵈ April 1842.

41
Laurens Hull, M.D.   1779–1865
[New York], October 25, 1839

Dr. Hull, a native of Bethesda, Connecticut, studied medicine under Dr. David Hull of Fairfield and received his license to practice in 1802 from the Connecticut State Medical Society. For the next thirty-four years he practiced his profession with devotion and success in Oneida County, New York, at the same time taking an active part in civic affairs. He was a delegate to the State Medical Society in 1817 and later for two more terms of four years each, becoming a life member in 1824. For two terms he served as vice-president of the society and twice as president, receiving considerable acclaim for his distinguished address to the society on quackery. He was honored with the degree of Doctor of Medicine from the College of Physicians and Surgeons of the University of New York, of which he became a fellow in 1828.

His political activity commenced in 1813 on his election as a member of the assembly from Oneida County. From 1837 to 1841 he was a member of the state senate, which was also the Court for the Correction of Errors; this accounts for the legend at which he is looking in Edouart's representation. Although the place where the silhouette was taken is not indicated, it was cut on the same day as that of Jacob Hays (fig. 25), October 25, 1839, which, as stated on its face, was cut in New York.

14.

Laurens Hull M.D.
Senator from 6th Senate
District & member of the
Court for the correction
of Errors in the State
of New York
Oct 25th 1839

42
John McVickar, S.T.D.   1787–1868
Saratoga Springs, August 24, 1843

Clergyman and professor, Dr. McVickar was born in New York, the son of a well-to-do merchant. At the age of seventeen he was graduated from Columbia College, having ranked first in his class throughout his term. He was ordained priest in the Episcopal church in 1812 by Bishop Hobart, who remained a lifelong friend and whose biography McVickar published in 1834–36. In 1809, on marrying Eliza, the daughter of Dr. Samuel Bard of Hyde Park, he became rector of St. James Church there, a parish organized by his father-in-law. In 1817 he was called to Columbia College to be professor of moral philosophy (to which he added instruction in rhetoric, the history of philosophy, and political economy). In 1857, when the great Francis Lieber (fig. 185) took the chair of political economy, McVickar took the chair of evidence of natural and revealed religion, which he held until 1864.

On two occasions for a short period he was acting president of the college but to his disappointment was never elected president. From 1844 to 1862 he served as chaplain of the army post at Fort Columbus on Governor's Island in New York harbor, where he was responsible for the building of the Chapel of St. Cornelius the Centurion, still actively maintained by Trinity Church, New York. As superintendent of the Society for Promoting Religion and Learning in the State of New York he was largely instrumental in the establishment of St. Stephen's College at Annandale-on-Hudson as a training college for Episcopal clergymen. His name and beneficence are still remembered at this institution, which is now known as Bard College.

Dr. McVickar is shown here at about the time of his second stint as acting president of Columbia, which would account for his addition of the words "Col. Coll." below his signature.

43
Benjamin Franklin Butler
1795–1858
Saratoga Springs, August 31, 1840

For a large part of his life Butler was one of the ornaments of the New York bar. Edouart portrays him during one of his terms as United States attorney for the Southern District of New York, shortly after his distinguished service as attorney general of the United States. Born in Kinderhook Landing, he took up the study of law at an early age under Martin Van Buren (fig. 230) and was his law partner in Albany for four years. In 1821, when Van Buren became United States senator, Butler was appointed district attorney of Albany, a post he filled with ability until 1825. At that time he was appointed by the legislature to a commission to review the statutes of New York, a task which earned him the approbation of Chancellor Kent (fig. 15). For six years he served in the assembly. On the election of William L. Marcy (fig. 6) to the governorship of New York, Butler was offered his seat in the Senate, but he declined out of a desire to devote himself to the practice of law. Not long afterward, on the urging of his friend Van Buren, he accepted appointment as attorney general of the United States under President Jackson and for a brief period served as secretary of war. For two terms, under Van Buren and Polk, he accepted appointment as United States attorney for the Southern District of New York. He was constantly engaged in public service, filling positions which he felt not incompatible with his devotion to the practice of law. In 1833 he was appointed to the commission to settle the boundary between New York and New Jersey; in 1838 he was instrumental in developing a department of law in the University of the City of New York; and in 1845, with Daniel S. Dickinson (fig. 45), as a member of the electoral college of the state he cast his vote for Polk. In 1858, on a trip to rest from his labors, he died in Paris of Bright's disease.

B. F. Butler, Saratoga Springs
August 31. — 1840 —

John McVickar
Cu. Coll.
24th Augt 1843

Professor John McVickar, Columbia Coll. N.Yk
Saratoga Spgs 24th Aug. 1843. Philosophy

Benjamin Franklin Butler
Late Attorney Gl. of the United States
Saratoga Springs 31st Augt 1840.

44
James R. Manley, M.D.   1782–1851
New York, August 1, 1839

Dr. Manley described himself in Edouart's likeness as "Resident Physician" of the city of New
York, a post to which he was appointed by the
governor and which he held for twelve years.
Though born in Philadelphia he received his education in New York at Columbia College, from
which he earned his bachelor's degree in 1797 and
his M.D. in 1803. He served for many years as professor at the College of Physicians and Surgeons
in New York and lectured on obstetrics and
diseases of women and children. He is said to
have attended Thomas Paine in his last illness.
Throughout his career he enjoyed a high reputation in his profession and it is not surprising to
find Edouart seeking him out. There is a record of
the artist having cut another likeness of Manley
dated August 20, 1839, and he also took a fine
silhouette of Manley's poetess daughter, Emma
C. Embury (fig. 64), in October of the same year.

15.

Dr. James R. Manley M.D.
Resident Physician
of city of New York
Aug 1st 1839 —

James R. Manley M.D. Res. Phs. of the City
New York 1st Augt 1839

45
Daniel Stevens Dickinson
1800–1866
Saratoga Springs, September 3, 1840

Senator Dickinson's silhouette was cut toward the end of his senatorial term and only a few days after that of his fellow member of the electoral college, Benjamin F. Butler (fig. 43). Born in Goshen, New York, Dickinson was apprenticed to a clothier; but having an acute and inquiring mind, he studied Latin and mathematics, taught school, and turned to the law, being admitted to practice in 1828. He commenced his legal career in Guilford but shortly moved to Binghampton. Active in politics, he became the first president of Binghampton and was elected to the state senate in 1836 and lieutenant governor in 1842, in which capacity he presided over the senate's functions as the Court for the Correction of Errors. Upon the resignation of N. P. Tallmadge (fig. 179) from the United States Senate, Governor Brouck appointed Dickinson to fill the vacancy; he was later elected to a full term, serving as chairman of the Committee on Finance. His strong position on the slavery question raised him to the leadership of the conservative Democrats in New York and gave him national prominence.

Like many an able lawyer and politician, he filled many positions. He was delegate to the Democratic National Convention in 1848 and 1852, he declined appointment as collector of the port of New York, and he was elected attorney general of the state of New York in 1861. Although nominated by President Lincoln to settle the Oregon boundary with Great Britain, he declined the office, as he did also a seat on the state court of appeals. He did, however, accept appointment as United States district attorney for the Southern District of New York in 1865, serving to the satisfaction and benefit of all until his death. His singleness of purpose and strong interest in preserving the Union made a strong and lasting impression on his colleagues. On receiving word of his death, the United States Senate unanimously adopted a resolution recording that it was filled with mournful recollections brought by the return of the day on which Lincoln was assassinated, and that it had received an additional sadness by the sudden death of the Honorable Daniel S. Dickinson "formerly President of this body as well as the worthy incumbent of many offices of honor and trust under the State and Nation," and adjourning "as a proper mark of respect for the memory of the departed."

15½

D. S. Dickinson Saratoga Springs
State Senate N.Y.   Sept 2 1840

D. S. Dickinson State Senator N.Y.
Saratoga Springs 3d Sept. 1840.

46
Samuel Griswold Goodrich
1793–1860
New York, October 26, 1839

Although the name of Samuel G. Goodrich does not appear in many dictionaries of English literature, and today scarcely anyone remembers his nom de plume, Peter Parley, he wrote, published, and sold more volumes than many of those whose names are recorded. His Connecticut father, grandfather, and brother were well-known clergymen, and two uncles were prominent lawyers, but apparently due to financial problems and lack of interest, his own education was limited. He went to work as a merchant's clerk at the age of fifteen, was unable to enter college, and fell back on self-education. His publishing career began at the age of twenty-three and was a financial failure. Following the death of his first wife in 1822, he went abroad and met Scott, Lockhart, and Hannah More, who, as he later wrote, had a strong influence on him. By 1826 he had married Mary Booth of Boston and had resumed his publishing career; for many years he edited and was principal contributor to the *Token*, a so-called gift book annual in which many of Hawthorne's tales made their first appearance. The year 1827 saw the first of the *Tales of Peter Parley*, which were followed by over a hundred volumes. In 1833 *Parley's Magazine* appeared, and then *Robert Merry's Museum*, both children's periodicals. On the side Goodrich dabbled in politics, serving a term in the Massachusetts legislature and for three years as United States consul at Paris.

Despite doubt as to the authorship of some of his books (Hawthorne was known to have helped him with one), Goodrich's *Recollections of a Lifetime*, published in two volumes in 1856, reveals that by his own count his published works numbered upwards of 170, most under the name of Peter Parley, and that some seven million copies had been sold. He even listed twenty-eight spurious "Parley" books published in England. The literary quality of his works leaves much to be desired. His popularity was undoubtedly due in part to the dearth of children's books at the time.

In 1839 when he signed his name above Edouart's silhouette likeness of him, he was at the height of his publishing career. His popularity is evidenced by the fact that at his death it is reported that his remains lay in state in St. Bartholomew's Church in New York, and that at his interment in Southbury, Connecticut, children preceded the funeral procession strewing flowers in its way.

S. G. Goodrich
author of Peter Parleys Tales. Oct 26. 1839

16

Samuel G. Goodrich
author of Peter Parleys Tales. Boston
N. York 26th October 1839.

47
Benjamin Winslow Dudley, M.D.
1785–1870
Lexington, Kentucky, May 29, 1844

At the time this silhouette was taken, Dr. Dudley held the professorship of anatomy and also of surgery in the Medical Department of Transylvania University in Lexington. He had been active in reorganizing that department of the university in 1817 to the extent that disagreements with his fellow students had terminated in a duel between him and one Richardson, in which the latter was severely wounded and his life saved only by the prompt action of Dudley in stopping the flow of blood with his thumb. Dudley was born in Spotsylvania County, Virginia, but grew up in Lexington, where he studied under Dr. Frederick Ridgely. In search of further training he traveled abroad, partly on a financial venture, and spent four years studying under such men as Sir Astley Cooper and John Abernathy in London. While there he became a member of the Royal College of Surgeons.

He was one of the experimental surgeons of the day, and his success earned him the reputation of being the ablest surgeon west of the Alleghenies. His successful removal of a cataract, thereby restoring sight to a man long blind, was a pioneer operation in the West. It is told of him that he performed 225 operations for the stone, without anesthesia, with the loss of only a half-dozen patients and the necessity of only one repetition of an operation. Dr. Dudley was ahead of his time in his insistence on the proper care and preparation of a patient before an operation. His health was impaired in his later years due to an infection received during an operation, and he died at an old age after an illness of but a few hours. This silhouette is the first in this volume of many likenesses taken by Edouart of physicians in Lexington and Louisville, Kentucky, in May 1844.

B W Dudley M D
Lexington K. 29 May 1844

B. W. Dudley ND
Lexington Kentucky 29th May 1844.

48
Washington Coster   d.1846
New York, November 11, 1839

One of the most successful commercial houses in
New York during the last decade of the eighteenth
century was that of the merchants Coster Brothers
& Co. The two brothers, Henry and John, had
each been born in Haarlem, Holland. With a
spotless reputation for ability and integrity,
everything they touched turned to gold, and they
amassed large fortunes and reared large families.
But money spoiled the sons of Henry Coster.
Harry, the elder, was a spendthrift; money was no
object, but his way of life drove him to death
before he could spend what he had. Washington
Coster, the younger brother, married Miss Depau,
daughter of Francis Depau and granddaughter of
the comte de Grasse, who had commanded the
French fleet off the coast of America during the
Revolution. Washington was for a time a partner
in the well-known firm of Christmas, Livingston,
Prime & Coster, bankers and brokers, and it was
perhaps during this period that Edouart cut his
shadow, surely that of a well-to-do merchant banker, strolling through his estate, tall, handsome,
and prosperous. But he had some of his older
brother's weaknesses. He is said to have had a
reputation for good eating and drinking. On his
last outing, following several sleepless nights, he
was given a dose of morphine to help put him to
sleep. It did, on a sofa at Blancard's Globe Hotel
on Broadway, from which he never arose.

Washington Coster
New York Nov 11th 1839

Washington Coster Esq.
New York Nov. 11. 1839.

49
Jedadiah Cobb, M.D.   1800–1860
Louisville, Kentucky, May 20, 1844

A native of Maine, graduate of Bowdoin College in 1820, Cobb moved to Boston, where he studied under Dr. George C. Shattuck; he received his M.D. from Bowdoin in 1823. He intended to practice in Portland, Maine, but was called to the Medical College of Ohio at Cincinnati as professor of the theory and practice of medicine and later as professor of anatomy. These chairs he held until 1837 when he moved to Louisville, Kentucky, as professor of anatomy at Louisville University. His reputation as a lecturer and surgeon and his ability to draw out the best from the members of his faculty all united to make the Louisville Medical School one of the outstanding medical institutions in the West.

In 1852 he returned to the Medical College of Ohio, but after two years he retired because of ill health and withdrew to Manchester, Massachusetts, where he died. His eldest son became a physician and demonstrator of anatomy at the Medical College of Ohio and it was to further his career that Dr. Cobb had returned there in 1852.

50
Thomas Leaming Caldwell, M.D. 1799–1875
Louisville, Kentucky, May 17, 1844

May 1844 was Edouart's month in Kentucky. Here we see another physician, Dr. Caldwell the younger, active in the practice of his profession with his father, Dr. Charles Caldwell (fig. 79). Not much is known of Thomas's early life except that in 1824 he was a director of the Botanical Garden of Transylvania University. Later he attended the Medical Department of Transylvania University and received his medical degree in 1836. For at least one term he was a councilman for the Fifth Ward of Louisville; during the Mexican War he served as brigade surgeon; later he was associated with various branches of the Louisville Fire Department. His contributions to his profession were his skill as a surgeon and his interest and ability in clinical training of young medical students. His family life does not appear to have been happy. His parents separated when he was young, and in his later life he is reputed to have fought a duel with his unfaithful wife's lover, maiming him for life.

W. J. Cobb. M. D. Professor of
Anatomy Louisville Med-
ical Institute. May 20th 1844.

Thos. L. Caldwell M. D.
Louisville Ky May 17th
1844.

J. Cobb. MD. Profr. of Anat. Louisville Med. Inst.
Louisville 20th May 1844.

Thoms. L. Caldwell MD.
Louisville Ky. 17th May 1844.

51
Alexander Hodgdon Stevens, M.D.
1789–1869
New York, November 13, 1839

Stevens, a son of John Stevens, who took part in the Boston Tea Party, was born in New York City. Graduating from Yale College in 1807, he studied medicine for a time under Dr. Edward Miller, professor of clinical medicine at the College of Physicians and Surgeons. He then transferred to the University of Pennsylvania, where he studied under Dr. Benjamin Rush and received his M.D. in 1811. On the way to Europe to continue his studies, he was captured and imprisoned for a short time in England. When freed he studied medicine under Sir Astley Cooper and John Abernathy, as well as under the leading physicians in Paris. He served as professor of surgery at Queen's College, now Rutgers, from 1815 to 1826 when he removed to the College of Physicians and Surgeons in New York, where he was professor of clinical surgery for over twenty years. He served as president of the college from 1843 until 1855. It was here that he introduced to New York the practice of bedside instruction, something he had learned under Dr. Rush. He also served as president of the American Medical Association in 1848, and of the Medical Society of the State of New York in 1849–51. Author of numerous articles on medical subjects, editor of two New York medical journals, he appears before us as he did in the midst of his career, holding in his hand perhaps a draft of one of his learned articles.

52
Charles Danforth   1797–1876
Saratoga, August 5, 1844

After a long, hard start in business, Danforth was at last becoming financially successful at the time he visited Saratoga in 1844, a fact suggested in his silhouette. Born in Norton, Massachusetts, he had a limited education but developed a strong bent toward the mechanical arts. After going to sea as a common seaman during the War of 1812 and a brief stint at schoolteaching, he returned to the cotton manufacturing business which he had first tried at Norton. At Sloatsburg, New York, where he acted as a machinist and carder, he invented, and in 1828 patented, the so-called cap spinner, which was widely received and, to his financial disappointment, pirated. However, he moved to Paterson, New Jersey, joining the firm of Godwin, Rogers & Clark to manufacture his spinner. Before long he took a leading part in the firm, expanded its business to embrace machine tool making, with immediate success. In a few years his firm, changed to Danforth, Cooke & Company, built a large number of locomotives for the Delaware, Lackawanna & Western Railroad. In time their locomotives were widely sold and in 1865 the Danforth Locomotive and Machine Company was formed, Danforth serving as president until 1871. He amassed a large fortune and was reputed to be a leading expert in the manufacture of spinning machinery. He was not active in civic affairs but served one term as president of the Paterson City Council. There seems to be no reason for his likeness being paired with that of Dr. Stevens.

18.

Alex^r H. Stevens.

Nov 13. 1839.

Dr Alex^r H. Stevens M.D. / Honble Th^s L. Danforth
New York 13th Novemb 1839 / Schohaire N Y^k Sarat 5th Augt 1844

53
Robert Fuller   d.1851
Saratoga, August 28, 1844

Fuller is described on his silhouette as of Boston. Not much is known of his life. He was a selectman of the town of Cambridge from 1832 to 1834 and a representative to the General Court in 1834. By 1850 he is recorded as living in Cambridge but in business in Boston as an iron merchant. In 1850 a young Cambridge man named Robert Oliver Fuller, who, presumably a relative, had been named after Robert Fuller, entered into business with the elder Fuller, whose death soon put an end to the association. He was not listed in the *Boston City Directory* after 1851. His presence in Saratoga and his confident stance and fine signature suggest confidence and prosperity.

54
John Binns   1772–1860
Philadelphia, September 24, 1842

After two years' imprisonment during the revolutionary movement in Ireland, Binns came to this country, first to Baltimore and then to Northumberland, Pennsylvania. There he founded the *Republican Argus*, a step which strengthened his influence with the Democratic party. In Philadelphia, from 1807 for twenty-two years, he published the *Democratic Press*, a leading state paper until it opposed Jackson. For twenty years Binns served as alderman of Philadelphia, a fact which did not deter Edouart from describing him as "John Binns of Ireland." His publications include an autobiography in 1854 and *Binns's Magistrate's Manual* in 1858. It is told in Scharf and Westcott's *History of Philadelphia* that in 1819 Binns published an engraved reproduction of the Declaration of Independence which *Port Folio* said "far surpasses anything that the pencil and burin have hitherto produced in this country." It is unlikely that he ever met the ironmonger with whom he is paired.

15/1

John Binns.
Ald.n Phila.d Sept.r 24 1842.

Alderman John Binns of Ireland
Philadelphia 24th Sept. 1842.

Robert Fuller of Boston
Saratoga 28th Aug.t 1844.

Alderman John Binns of Ireland
Philadelphia 24th Sept. 1842.

55
B. F. Skinner
Saratoga, July 8, 1840

Little is known of Judge Skinner, whose signature
is as bold and handsome as his silhouette, except
as appears in the inscription at his feet. He was a
judge of the Court of Common Pleas, Cambridge,
Washington County, New York. He is shown in
1840, perhaps in middle life. The proximity of
Cambridge to Saratoga would explain his being
there, and that he was a judge would seem to justify his presence in Edouart's volume.

19.

B. F. Skinner

Judge B. F. Skinner   Court of Common Pleas
Cambridge, Washington Co. N.Y. taken at Saratoga 8th July 1840.

Benjamin Bosworth Smith, S.T.D.
1794–1884
Louisville, Kentucky, May 16, 1844

It is not surprising that during his month in Kentucky in 1844 Edouart should have sought the opportunity to take the silhouette of Bishop Smith, who was the first bishop of the Episcopal Diocese of Kentucky and at the time was superintendent of public instruction in charge of the public school system there.

Smith was born in Bristol, Rhode Island, and graduated from Brown in 1816. Brought up in the Congregational church, he was ordained priest in the Episcopal church by Bishop Griswold in 1817. Thereafter, he served at St. Michael's Church, Marblehead, Massachusetts, St. George's in Accomack County, Virginia, and Zion Church, Charleston, Massachusetts. For five years he was rector of St. Stephen's in Middlebury, Vermont, and in 1828 was in charge of Grace Church mission in Philadelphia. For five years, until 1837, he was rector of Christ Church, Lexington, Kentucky. In 1832 in St. Paul's Chapel of Trinity Church, New York, he was consecrated bishop of Kentucky, where he served for many years with devotion. In 1868 he became the senior and hence presiding bishop of the Episcopal church. He held that post until 1872 when ill health caused him to retire. He edited several church journals and wrote scholarly works on ecclesiastical subjects. He died in New York City. Edouart shows him perhaps as he used to appear in the act of delivering his pastoral charge.

19½.

B. B. Smith { Bp: of the P.E. Ch:
{ in the Dio: of Ky.

May 16. 1844.

B. B. Smith

B   B.B. Smith Bishop of the Prot.t Ep.al Church
Louisville 16th May 1844 in the Dio: of Kentucky

57
Robert Hunter Morris   1802–1855
[New York], March 11, 1840

Morris in his own hand proudly notes that he was recorder of the city of New York, a post to which he was appointed in 1838 by Governor Marcy (fig. 6) and from which he was removed in 1841 by Governor Seward (fig. 2). The removal grew out of the Glentworth conspiracy that threatened to implicate many prominent Whigs for employing questionable tactics at the time of Seward's election. Following Seward's action, Morris, the Tammany candidate, was in 1841 elected to the first of his three terms as mayor, following Isaac L. Varian (fig. 5).

Morris was born in New York, a member of the Revolutionary family that had settled in Morrisania, Westchester County. After a clerkship with Elisha Williams, leader of the Columbia County bar, Morris commenced practice at Johnstown but in 1827 removed to New York. He was for a time assistant to James A. Hamilton, United States attorney for the Southern District of New York, and later was instrumental in establishing a modern police force in lieu of the old watch system. He held the position as postmaster of New York under appointment by President Polk and in 1846, with Charles O'Conor (fig. 252) and Samuel J. Tilden, was a member of the state Constitutional Convention.

20.

Robt: H. Morris
Recorder of the City of
New York
March 11th 1840

Robert H. Morris Recorder of the City of New York

58
Thomas B. Pinckard, M.D.
1797–1860
Lexington, Kentucky, May 23, 1844

Dr. Pinckard was a native of Virginia; his mother was related to President Monroe. He was a graduate of the Transylvania Medical College and well thought of for his amiable disposition and professional ability. He was thrice married: in 1826 to Catharine, daughter of Captain Vance of Lawrenceburgh, Indiana; in 1840 to Lucy Ann, daughter of John Lyle of Fayette County, and in September 1844, shortly after his silhouette was cut, to Mrs. Mary Eaton, daughter of James Harper of Lexington. He was for many years a member of the Episcopal church in Lexington.

59
John L. Price, M.D.
Lexington, Kentucky, May 23, 1844

It has not been possible to identify firmly which Dr. Price it is who described himself as surgeon and physician and is shown perhaps explaining one of his medical problems to his companion Dr. Pinckard. A Dr. J. L. Price informed the public in 1834 through the *Lexington Gazette* that he was residing with his father a few miles west of Lexington, where he would "attend to the practice of Medicine and Surgery, etc, etc, in all their various branches." Another notice in the *Lexington Observer and Reporter* in May 1844 records the concern of a dozen patients of Dr. J. L. Price lest, while he was canvassing as a candidate for a seat in the legislature, they should be neglected, and they attempted to withdraw his name from the race as it would be "better for him, as well as for us, that he shall be engaged in attending to the afflictions of his friends and neighbors than to be in the strife and struggle for office." This is the John Lewis Price who commenced the study of medicine in 1832 and graduated shortly afterward from Transylvania Medical College. This man succeeded in being twice elected to the legislature, was the author of a bill giving Negroes the right to testify, was acquainted with Lincoln, and was a staunch emancipationist.

201½. T. B. Pinck and M. L. Jno Price MD Surgeon &
Lexington Ky. Physician Lexington Ky
May 23d 1844 May 23d 1844.

Thos. B. Pinckard MD Partner with John L. Price MD Surgr. Le
Lexington Ky 23d May 1844

60
Charles Edwin West, LL.D.
1809–after 1897
New York, October 26, 1839

This young man, standing in classical surroundings, was no doubt proud to sign himself "Principal" of "Rutgers Female Institute," established
in 1838 by the regents of the state university as
the first institution to offer a college course to
women. West served as its first principal for
twelve years, until he took charge of the Buffalo
Female Academy, where he remained until 1860.
In that year he became the principal of the Brooklyn Heights Seminary following the retirement of
Alonzo Gray and held the post for twenty-nine
years.

He was born in Washington, Massachusetts,
and graduated in 1832 from Union College, Schenectady. His early career was in private teaching,
founding the Albany Classical School and for a
short time occupying the chair of chemistry and
natural history at the Oneida Institute. But his
great reputation rests on his long career as head
of the early women's institutions of learning. It
is estimated that upwards of 15,000 women had
studied under him. He was a man of wide intellectual interests and lectured on art, architecture,
literature, science, law, and medicine. The University of New York gave him an honorary M.D.,
Columbia an M.A., and Rutgers College an LL.D.
He was a member of many learned societies and
the author of several works dealing with his career
and the institutions with which he was connected.
He was for twenty-five years a member of the
Century Association, retiring in 1898. He was also
a noted collector of paintings, engravings, and a
wide variety of Japanese art.

21.

Charles E. West
Principal
Rutgers Female Institute
New York Oct. 26th 1839

Charles E. West Principal of Rutgers Institute for Females 26th Oct. 1839.

61
Lunsford Pitts Yandell, M.D.
1805–1878
Louisville, Kentucky, May 15, 1844

Here was a man of boundless energy, ability, and versatility of interest. He successfully combined three careers, medicine, paleontology, and the church. He was born in Hartsville, Tennessee, and at the age of seventeen commenced the study of medicine under his father. After a short term at the Medical Department of Transylvania University at Lexington, he went to the University of Maryland, from whose Medical Department he graduated in 1825, aged only twenty. After six years' practice in Murfreesboro and Nashville, Tennessee, he was elected to the chair of chemistry in Transylvania University, which he filled with distinction until 1837. He then removed to Louisville, which he believed offered wider opportunities, and with Dr. Charles Caldwell (fig. 79) and others organized the Medical Institute there, which later became the medical department of the University of Louisville. Here he remained for twenty-two years, teaching in the fields of chemistry, physiology, and pathological anatomy. In 1858 he joined his son in Memphis as professor of theory and practice of medicine in the Memphis Medical College. During the Civil War he was active in hospital service, and it was during these years that he was ordained a Presbyterian minister and pastor of the Dancyville Presbyterian Church. He later returned to practice medicine in Louisville. At various periods he was editor of the *Transylvania Journal of Medicine* and of the *Western Journal of Medicine and Surgery* with T. W. Colescot (fig. 298). A year before his death he was elected president of the College of Physicians and Surgeons of Louisville.

At the time he was carrying on his active medical career, he was also engaged in what was his greatest contribution to knowledge, the study of the geology and paleontology of Kentucky. He assembled one of the outstanding collections of fossils and geological curiosities, and his name was given to many first discovered and classified during his scientific years.

He wrote and published widely on medical and geological and paleontological subjects.

62
Henry Miller, M.D.   1800–1874
Louisville, Kentucky, May 15, 1844

Edouart succeeded in capturing the likenesses of most of the faculty of the Medical Institute of Louisville, and it is but natural he should have caught Dr. Miller and Dr. Yandell the same day and have placed them in familiar conversation with each other.

Dr. Miller was a physician of distinction but lacked the wide interests of his colleague Yandell. He was born in Glasgow, Kentucky, and received his M.D. from Transylvania University in Lexington in 1822. He was demonstrator of anatomy at Transylvania for several years when, as a result of personal disagreements with the faculty, he removed to the health resort Harrodsburg, where he practiced nine years. He then accepted the chair of obstetrics on the opening of the Medical Institute of Louisville; after it became the Medical Department of the University of Louisville, he remained on the faculty until 1858. He returned in 1867 as professor of medical and surgical diseases of women for one year, changing to the same chair at the newly established Louisville Medical College, where he remained until his death.

He left his mark as a distinguished obstetrician and gynecologist and was a pioneer in the use of ether in his obstetrical practice, especially during labor. Though he had a poor speaking voice and a weak delivery, he wrote forcefully and fluently, both books and articles, for learned journals, his *Principles and Practice of Obstetrics*, published in 1858, long being a standard work on the subject.

212.

L. P. Yandell, M. D. Professor
of Chemistry in the Medical
Institute of Louisville.
Louisville. May 15th 1844.

L. P. Yandell, M. D. Professor
of Chemistry in the Medical

L. P. Yandell MD Prof of Chemistry in the.   H. Miller MD Prof of Obstetrics &c
Medical Institute of Louisville 15th May 1844.   Louisville 15th May 1844.

63
Barnard R. Mathews
Saratoga Springs, July 26, 1845

Details of Mathews's life have eluded discovery. The inscription under his signature "Great Western S.S." is the clue that he was an officer of one of the first transatlantic steam vessels, the *Great Western*. James Hosken (fig. 346), in a similar setting at an earlier date, is described as an officer of the steamship *Great Western*, then being in fact its captain.

64
Emma Catherine Embury
1806–1863
New York, October 25, 1839

It was a happy coincidence that the talented daughter of a distinguished physician should have been captured by Edouart only three months after he took her father, Dr. Manley (fig. 44). It was from her father that Emma developed her love of books, and the result was an almost unending flow of verse and story. She was a constant contributor to the *New York Mirror* and was well on the way to a literary career in 1828 when she married the well-to-do, cultivated Daniel Embury, the president of the Atlantic Bank of Brooklyn. Poetry, romantic if sentimental tales, and essays poured from her pen. Her publications, too numerous to detail, had commenced, by the time of her marriage, with *Guido, a Tale; Sketches from History and Other Poems.* And so they continued, but they did not interfere with her charming talent as hostess and leader of a salon. The *Dictionary of American Biography* says of her that "book reviewers habitually confused Mrs. Embury's literary achievements with her virtues as a wife and mother and her charm as a hostess." There is quoted the perceptive criticism of Edgar Allan Poe: "She is not so vigorous as Mrs. Stephens, nor so vivacious as Miss Chubbock, nor so caustic as Miss Leslie, nor so dignified as Miss Sedgwick, nor so graceful, fanciful, and *spirituelle* as Mrs. Osgood, but is *deficient* in none of the qualities for which these ladies are noted, and in certain particulars surpasses them all." Despite her sentimentality and perhaps preciousness, she was a fine example of the golden age of the poetess in America.

22.

Emma C. Embury
New York, Oct. 25th 1839

Emma C. Embury Wife of Daniel   Authoress
Daughter of Mr. James Manley   New York 15th November 1839.

65
Charles Delucena Meigs, M.D.
1792–1869
Philadelphia, October 19, 1842

The professorship of midwifery in the Jefferson
Medical College in 1841 and the publication of
the second edition of his *The Philadelphia Practice of Midwifery* in 1842 conspired to give Dr.
Meigs the confidence and poise which he shows,
sitting in a federal chair to the French silhouettist.

Dr. Meigs was born in Saint George's, Bermuda,
and taken by his family first to New Haven, Connecticut, and then to Athens, Georgia, when his
father became president of the University of Georgia. He obtained a familiarity with the classics
and, by a happy acquaintance with the emigrant
M. Petit de Clairvière, a knowledge of the French
language. Graduating from the University of
Georgia in 1809, he pursued a course in medicine
at the University of Pennsylvania, where he graduated, after a few years absence, in 1817. An early
attempt to practice in Augusta was thwarted by
his wife's feeling toward slavery and he moved to
Philadelphia where he practiced for many years.
Obstetrics, or midwifery as it was termed, was
his specialty, and he wrote on and taught the subject for years. In 1841 he was elected professor of
obstetrics and diseases of women at Jefferson Medical College, a post he held to the benefit of the
community and his profession for twenty years.
Then, unlike so many of his contemporaries, he
retired from medicine to live home in the country, Hamanasett, Connecticut, where his declining years were spent in gentle husbandry, reading
and enjoying the association of family and friends.
His many contributions to the medical journals of
the day testify to his knowledge of his subject and
to his untiring efforts to relieve the sufferings of
his fellow mortals. He contributed a memoir of
Dr. Samuel G. Morton (fig. 177) to the *Transactions of the Academy of Natural Sciences* in
1853.

22/2

Ch. D. Meigs. M.D. Philad.
Oct. 19th 1842.

Ch. D. Meigs MD. Philadelphia 19th Octob. 1842.

66
Francis M. Johnston, M.D.
New York, November 12, 1839

Dr. Johnston, as he himself testifies after his signature, was in 1839 president of the Medical Society of New York. As he stands in the arched
doorway where Edouart placed him, the wind has
lifted the edge of his coat and at the same time
has blown beyond ready reach any notice of his
medical career. But this was the season in 1839
when the silhouettist cut many of the prominent
figures of the day, lay, clerical, and medical, and
there is little doubt that despite the dearth of
readily discoverable records, Dr. Johnston merited
Edouart's scissors.

23

Francis N. Johnston M.D. Pres. Medical Society of New York

Francis N. Johnston MD
Pres.t Medical Society New York
N. York 12th Jan.y 1844

67
John Kearsley Mitchell, M.D.
1793–1858
Philadelphia, October 13, 1842

After three voyages to China as surgeon with a medical degree received from the University of Pennsylvania in 1819, Dr. Mitchell settled in Philadelphia. In 1824 he lectured on the institutes of medicine and physiology in the Philadelphia Medical Institute and in 1826 held the chair of chemistry. The Franklin Institute called him as a lecturer on chemistry as applied to the arts in 1833. At the time this likeness was taken he occupied the chair of theory and practice of medicine in the Jefferson Medical College. He served in various city hospitals in Philadelphia and was handsomely rewarded for services performed during times of pestilence. He was a brilliant lecturer and wrote a great deal on medical subjects, as well as a few literary works. His literary and scientific genius were inherited by his somewhat more prominent and better-remembered son Dr. S. Weir Mitchell.

68
Henry Bond, M.D.   1790–1859
Philadelphia, May 5, 1843

Though he was a physician of standing and skill, Dr. Bond is probably best remembered for his great genealogical work, *Genealogies and History of Watertown*, published in 1855, a product of his later life after retiring from active practice of medicine. Family interest led him to the history of Watertown, and his historical interests resulted in his membership in the New England Historic Genealogical Society, the Massachusetts Historical Society, and the New-York Historical Society.

He was born in Watertown, Massachusetts, entered Hebron Academy in 1806, and graduated from Dartmouth College with honor in 1813. He studied medicine under Dr. Cyrus Perkins at Dartmouth and received his medical degree in 1816. He became a fellow of the New Hampshire Medical Society and in 1819 moved to Philadelphia to take advantage of the high standing of its medical institution. There he was an officer of the Philadelphia Medical Society for years and a fellow of the Philadelphia College of Physicians. For many years he served as president of the Philadelphia Board of Health. His ability and reputation subjected him to calls for assistance in every branch of Philadelphia's medical service, and he was never found wanting. It was a fortunate circumstance for him that when ill health induced him to resign his medical practice, it did not prevent his fruitful historical and genealogical activities. Edouart shows him aged fifty-three, two years before his retirement from the practice of medicine.

23½2.

J K Mitchell M.D. Prof. Pract. of Medicine
Jefferson Medical College Phil.ª —
13 Oct 1842. —— Henry Bond M.D.
Phila May 5. 1843. ——

Dr J. K. Mitchell MD. Profʳ of Medicin
Jefferson Coll. Philadelphia 13th Octob 1842.

Dr Henry Bond MD
Philadelphia 5th May 1843.

69
Joseph L. M. Stevens   b.1804
New York, September 25, 1839

What little we know of Major Stevens we find
written on his silhouette. It appears he was born
in the county of York, Maine, and in 1839, when
described by Edouart as the "American Dwarf"
was forty-two inches tall and weighed fifty pounds.
The top hat he holds so jauntily must have ac-
centuated his size. Details of his life have escaped
our notice, but it is not unlikely he was a well-
known figure in his day.

Joseph L. M. Stevens the 2.d June 1804.
American Dwarf, born in
the County of York, the State
of Maine, and is 42 inches high
34 Years old and weighs 50 pounds

Major Joseph L. M. Stevens American Dwarf. 42 Inches 34 Years old
New York 25.th Septemb. 1839.   born 2.d June 1804, in the County of York State of Maine

70
Reynell Coates, M.D.   1802–1886
Philadelphia, April 25, 1843

71
Benjamin Hornor Coates, M.D.
1797–1881
Philadelphia, March 25, 1843

Dr. Coates, shown standing in front of his older brother, had by 1843 given up the active practice of medicine and was devoting himself to writing, principally though not exclusively on medical subjects. He had contributed articles to Hays's *American Encyclopedia of Practical Medicine and Surgery* and to the *Philadelphia Medical Journal*, and his *First Lines of Physiology* appeared in its sixth edition in 1847. He was born in Philadelphia and received his medical training at the University of Pennsylvania, from which he graduated in 1823. On being appointed surgeon to an East Indiaman he voyaged to India and was in Calcutta at the time of the Burmese war. In 1824 he returned to Philadelphia and began his practice. He was professor of natural science at Allegheny College at Meadville, Pennsylvania, for a short time, practiced in Bristol for two years, and then gave up general practice. He was associated with his brother Benjamin, and with Drs. Bache (fig. 189), Bond (fig. 68), and others in the short existence of the Philadelphia Medical Academy. In the early planning of the South Sea expedition he was appointed comparative anatomist, but to his disappointment the undertaking as originally planned was broken up. He died in Camden, New Jersey, whither he had retired in 1845.

Benjamin Coates, five years older than his brother Reynell, attended the Friends' Grammar School in Philadelphia and graduated from the University of Pennsylvania as a medical student in 1818. As an apprentice at the Pennsylvania Hospital he learned "the art and mystery of medicine." He soon had a successful practice and in 1828 was elected attending physician at the hospital, where he continued as physician and clinical lecturer until 1841. His reputation led to both honor and public service. He became a fellow of the College of Physicians, president of the Philadelphia County Medical Society, a member of the Academy of Natural Sciences, senior vice-president of the American Philosophical Society, and vice-president of the Historical Society of Pennsylvania, of which he was a founder. With Dr. Bache (fig. 189), Dr. Bond (fig. 68), Dr. Wood (fig. 190), and Dr. Meigs (fig. 65) he enjoyed membership in the "Tea and Toast Club", a social club with medical improvement as its secondary purpose. He was a prolific writer on both medical and historical subjects. His works include *A Memoir of Thomas Say, Naturalist*, and one of Charles Caldwell (fig. 79). He was a man of greater stature than his younger brother, but it is a pleasant reminder of their relationship to have them standing side by side. Their father, Dr. Samuel Coates, was himself a distinguished physician, and his large life-size portrait by Thomas Sully belongs to the Pennsylvania Hospital.

24½.

B H Coates, M. D. Philadª.
Mar. 25ᵗʰ, 1843. (Benjamin Hornor)
12 years attending physician, and 5 years house
surgeon to the Pennsylvania Hospital. Vice President of the Medical Society of Philadelphia.

Dr. Reynell Coates MD
Philadª 25ᵗʰ April 1843

Dr. B. H. Coates MD Vice Presdt of the Society Medical
12 yrs Physician of the Penna Hospital
Philadelphia 25ᵗʰ March 1843.

72

John Clarke, M.D.   1773–1846

Saratoga, July 20, 1840

It was the Yorkshireman Dr. Clarke and Chancellor Walworth (fig. 119) who were largely responsible for the growth and development of Saratoga Springs. At the age of fifty Dr. Clarke, who for years had operated New York City's first soda fountain and accumulated a fortune from the popularity of carbonated beverages, retired to the country to live out his life in peace. He had been one of the leading physicians at Saratoga early in the century and after his satisfactory financial career in New York City found it easy to return.

He purchased acres of land around Saratoga, among which was the magical fountain of youth, Congress Spring. Clarke knew a good thing. Within a few years thousands of bottles of Congress Spring water were being sent over the world with claims of having the properties to cure all manner of complaints, both real and fancied. The spring itself was enclosed in a Doric pavilion, and soon people were flocking to Saratoga to bathe in the pool, to drink the waters of the spring, scooped up by little boys with tin cups fastened to long sticks at a penny a cup, to the accompaniment of Johnson's brass band. Old hotels, such as Union Hall, Congress Hall, and the Columbian, were renovated; new ones, the Pavilion and the United States Hotel, were built; and the town thrived.

Dr. Clarke was a leading figure in the community, not only to his own benefit but to that of the townspeople at large. He was for some years a vestryman of the appropriately named Bethesda Protestant Episcopal Church. Generous and farsighted, to him goes the credit for devising the plan whereby each taxpayer received a rebate of $62\frac{1}{2}$ cents for each tree planted in front of his property, thus creating the shaded avenues of which Saratoga became so proud. He died in 1846, aged seventy-three.

Edouart shows us the handsome, confident proprietor of the springs as he appeared in his sixty-seventh year, peering out over his small but happy empire founded on his ability to persuade people to drink water.

26

Dr J Clark
Saratoga Springs

Dr J Clark Proprietor of the
Saratoga 20th July 1840. Congress Springs

73
Lyman Bradstreet Walker
1785–1857
Saratoga Springs, July 28, 1843

The Honorable Lyman B. Walker, attorney general of New Hampshire, would have been a welcome guest at Saratoga, not only for his high professional standing but for his ready wit, his amusing and entertaining conversation. He was an addition to any social gathering.

Born in Brookfield, Massachusetts at an early age, he was taken by his father to Vermont, where he spent his youth. At some time between 1811 and 1815 he commenced the practice of law in Gilford and by 1819 became solicitor for Strafford County, an office he held for fifteen years. For ten years, from 1817 to 1827, he served as judge advocate of the Second Brigade. He was a representative for Gilford in the legislature from 1828 to 1829. He moved to Concord when appointed attorney general, where he served his five-year term. As an able and successful lawyer, his quick wit stood him in good stead in his trial practice. He died in Gilford.

74
Henry Walton   d.1844
Saratoga Springs, September 3, 1840

It has not proven possible to pick up Judge Walton's trail, but Edouart was aware of his death and noted it in the lower right-hand corner of the silhouette. Walton had a fine flourishing hand, as his inscription indicates, and his profile supports the conclusion that he was a man of determination.

26/2

Henry Walton

Lyman B. Walker
Attorney General of N.H.
Saratoga Spring 28th July 1843 —

Saratoga Springs 3d Sept
1840

Lyman B. Walker Attorney Gal of New Hampshire   Judge Hy Walton   Obt 16 Octo 1844.
Saratoga Springs 22th July 1843.   Saratoga Springs 3d Sept 1840.

75
Francis Wayland, D.D., LL. D.
1796–1865
New York, April 25, 1840

Seated as though on the steps of Brown University's recently completed Rhode Island Hall, Dr. Wayland, Brown's fourth president, appears in Edouart's silhouette shortly before his trip to France, England, and Scotland, caught possibly as he was about to embark.

From humble beginnings, Wayland pursued a remarkable career, his star ever in its ascendancy. His father, an immigrant from England, was first a leather merchant and then a Baptist minister in upper New York State. Young Wayland graduated from Union College in 1813 having entered the sophomore class when only fifteen. He studied medicine for a couple of years, turned to the Andover Theological Seminary obeying an inner call, but was forced by need of support to return to Union College as a tutor until 1821 when he was called to the First Baptist Church of Boston which he served for five years. No sooner had he accepted a recall to Union College than he was elected in 1827 president of Brown University, a post he held with such far-reaching effect on both the university and the community as to make his name ever remembered. Union College conferred on him an honorary D.D. in 1827, as did Harvard in 1829, adding an LL.D. in 1852.

President Wayland revised the entire structure of academic life at Brown. From the textbook method of instruction he turned to the analytic method with such effect that it was often repeated that Justice Story (fig. 16) as professor of the Harvard Law School claimed that he could always recognize a graduate of Brown by his "power of seizing upon the essential points of a case and freeing it from all extraneous matter." But Wayland did not stop here.

As the university grew in numbers and fame, so the reputation of its president made him an outstanding if not the outstanding educator of his day. Yet with all his university duties he took a large part in the civic life of Providence. During the last score of years of his life it is said that he held a weekly Bible class, the attendants all being convicts. As author of a plan for free public schools in Rhode Island, he also devised a public school system for Providence. He is recorded as having been the author of over seventy publications. He resigned as president in 1855, spent a year and a half as pastor of the First Baptist Church in Providence, and lived in retirement until his death in Providence in 1865. One of his last public acts was the moving address he made to the inhabitants of Providence and members of the university who gathered outside his residence on receipt of the sad news of the assassination of President Lincoln. Where else could they have found the words to comfort them? Such was Francis Wayland, fourth president of Brown.

27.

F. Wayland
Pres.t of Brown Univ.ty
Providence R.I.

Professor F. Wayland President of Brown University at Providence R.I.
taken in New York 8th April 1840.

76
Isaac Parrish, M.D. 1811–1852
Philadelphia, May 10, 1843

Isaac Parrish, like his father, was born in Philadelphia and attended the Friends Academy. He studied medicine under his father and received his M.D. from the University of Pennsylvania in 1832. During his last year of study he interned at the Blockley Hospital. When Philadelphia was struck with an epidemic of cholera in 1832, Dr. Joseph Parrish, who had a wealth of experience with epidemics, was made chief physician of the cholera hospital and Isaac was fortunate in being appointed as his assistant. Upon the organization of the Wills Eye Hospital in 1833–34, Isaac Parrish was elected one of its surgeons and served at the hospital the rest of his life, for the first eight years in close association with his father. He instituted the first course in ophthalmic surgery in 1839, was an early advocate of ether and chloroform, and enjoyed a large private practice. Prison reform and Negro education were advanced by his efforts, and he took a generous interest in many other philanthropical causes. Like so many of his contemporaries, he contributed articles to many medical journals and was an officer of the Medical Society and College of Physicians, in every way a worthy successor to his father. He must have received some pleasure from being paired with Edouart's posthumous profile of his father.

77
Joseph Parrish, M.D. 1779–1840
Taken posthumously from description, May 10, 1843

This likeness of Dr. Joseph Parrish is, of course, imaginary. Cut on the same day as that of his son Isaac, it can be presumed that the description must have come from the son and that perhaps he accepted the profile as an approximate likeness. The signature above the silhouette is no doubt that of old Dr. Parrish, probably clipped from some papers owned by his son. The information about his death appears to be in Edouart's hand.

Parrish was born in Philadelphia, attended the Friends Academy, and in 1802 began the study of medicine under Dr. Caspar Wistar, receiving his M.D. from the University of Pennsylvania in 1805. Throughout his career he was closely associated with the various hospitals in Philadelphia, enjoyed a large practice, and earned the respect of the community for his learning and skill. At the outbreak of the yellow fever epidemic in 1805, he was appointed resident physician at the emergency hospital established by the Board of Health. A few years later when typhoid fever became epidemic in 1812, he broke tradition with his predecessors, notably Dr. Rush, by abandoning bleeding as a specific, with notably favorable results. From 1807 to 1829 he served on the staff of the Pennsylvania Almshouse and the Pennsylvania Hospital. He was an officer of both the College of Physicians and the Medical Society and president of the Board of Managers of the Wills Eye Hospital from 1833 until his death. For his services during the cholera epidemic of 1832 the city presented him with an inscribed silver pitcher. As an ardent abolitionist it was a happy coincidence that he attended John Randolph of Roanoke in his last illness, during which the dying man made his will in which he freed his slaves. Dr. Parrish was only too glad to be able to testify to Randolph's testamentary capacity, of which there was some question, so that the will might be probated.

He was survived by eleven children, two of his sons, Isaac and Joseph, being physicians.

27½

Isaac Parrish M.D.
5 mo. 10th 1843.

Jos. Parrish
ob.t 3rd m.o (March) 18th 1840 in his 61st year

Dr. Joseph Parrish taken from description
Philadelphia 10th May 1843

One of the Surgeons of
Wills Hospital Philad.a
Isaac Parrish M.D. 5th Month 10th 1843.

Late Surgeon of the Penn.a
Hospital &c &c
Dr. Joseph Parrish taken from description
Philadelphia 10th May 1843.

78

H. Cunningham
Saratoga, July 1840

General Cunningham of Poughkeepsie stands on
the field of battle beside the wreck of a cannon,
one wheel off, cannon balls scattered about, an
encampment, tents, and men near by and a fortress in the distance, flag flying. But he is not
dressed for battle and stands as though about to
be decorated for bravery beyond the call of duty.
Apparently even Edouart did not know his first
name, which has also escaped us.

28.

W. Cunningham 1840.
Poughkeepsie. N.Y.

Col. H. Cunningham Poughkeepsie N.Y.
Saratoga N.Y. 1840.

Charles Caldwell, M.D.   1772–1853
Louisville, Kentucky, May 11, 1844

Dr. Caldwell's name comes to light in unsuspected fields and always with credit to him. Though his formal education was limited, by age twenty-three he already had translated Blusenbach's *Elements of Physiology* and was the author or translator of many other medical works. He can be found as editor of *Port Folio* following Nicholas Biddle (fig. 271), writing articles and reviews of books of poetry. He wrote the sketch of Dr. Rush that appeared in *Delaplaine's Repository* in 1813. Though he leaned toward the pulpit, he turned to medicine and studied under the great men of the day at the University of Pennsylvania. For a short time he held a commission in the army during the Whisky Rebellion in western Pennsylvania in 1794. He was a founder of the Medical Department of Transylvania University at Lexington, Kentucky, from which his son Dr. Thomas L. Caldwell (fig. 50) received his medical degree. He had such a reputation for learning that in 1821, with $10,000 of state funds, he went to Europe to purchase books for the Transylvania library and accumulated a large and rare collection, coming largely from the libraries of eminent French physicians who had been ruined by the French Revolution. By this means the Transylvania medical library became one of the great medical libraries in the country. After almost twenty years in Lexington he moved to the more progressive city, Louisville, became the first professor at the Louisville Medical Institute, where he remained until his retirement in 1849. He was an advocate of mesmerism, the theory of spontaneous generation and animal heat, and the unity of the human race. As an ardent proponent of phrenology, once described as "the apostle of phrenology in the West," it is told of him that as an aid to the diagnosis of his patient's ailments, he felt the bumps on their craniums and prescribed accordingly. We may smile at this today, but Dr. Caldwell was not a crank, and his more than two hundred publications, books and articles, establish him as one of the outstanding physicians of his day.

28½.   Charles Caldwell M. D.
                                        Louisville May 11th 1844
                                        Jefferson County Kentucky
                                        Louisville 11th May 1844

Chas. Caldwell MD of Louisville Jefferson Cty
Louisville 11th May 1844

80
Romeo Elton, D.D.   1790–1870
Saratoga, August 3, 1840

Biographical dictionaries describe Elton as a
clergyman. He was ordained as pastor of the Second Baptist Church in Newport, Rhode Island,
in 1817, where he served for five years, followed
by three years in charge of a church in Windon,
Vermont. But at age twenty-five his ecclesiastical
life seems to have ended. In 1825 he was appointed
professor of Greek and Latin at Brown University, from which he had graduated in 1813, and
after spending two years in Europe qualifying
himself for the position, he filled it with distinction for sixteen years. These were the years of Dr.
Elton the professor of classics. He then moved to
Exeter, England, in 1845, where he lived for
twenty-two years, followed by two years at Bath.
During this time he devoted himself to writing,
the notable work of this period being his *Life of
Roger Williams, the Earliest Legislator*. This was
Dr. Elton the scholar. He returned to America in
1869 and spent his remaining days in Providence,
Newport, and Boston. By his will he bequeathed
$20,000 to Brown to establish a chair of natural
philosophy, and a similar amount to Columbia
for a chair of intellectual and moral philosophy.
These were the legacies of Dr. Elton the philanthropist.

Edouart displays the learned and beloved professor of the Latin and Greek languages and literature in the act of explaining an obscure passage of Virgil or perhaps Homer to his students
who stand just out of our view.

Romeo Elton,
Prof. of the Latin & Greek
Languages & Literature in
Brown University,
Providence, R.I.
Saratoga Aug. 3, 1841.

Romeo Elton, Prof. Latin & Greek
Brown University, Providence R.I.
Saratoga 3d August 1841

81
Henry Placide   1799–1870
New Orleans, January 13, 1844

A theater-goer in the 1840s in New York would never have missed a chance to attend the Park Theater to see its greatest and most popular actor, Henry Placide. He was considered not only the best Polonius but *the* Polonius. As Sir Peter Teazle, Sir Anthony Absolute, Sir Harcourt Courtly, and Lord Ogleby, he was unexcelled. From 1823 when he joined the Park Theater until it burned in 1848, he was its greatest attraction, playing, so it is recorded, over five hundred characters. A brief appearance in London was a failure, but in New York he was always on the crest of the wave. He had a sort of eccentric humor and could play a part in the most trivial farce or the most sedate and serious drama. After the destruction of the Park Theater, of which he had been manager, he joined the company at Burton's Theater for a short period to its considerable advantage. His last performance was in 1865, after which he returned to his home in Babylon, New York, where he died.

His talent, to be sure, was inherited. His father, Alexander Placide, of French birth, was an acrobat, dancer, actor, and manager and for a time appeared at Sadler's Wells. His mother was the daughter of James Wrightman, who had for years been prompter at the theater in Drury Lane. His brother, Thomas, was a popular comedian, and his three sisters each had a stage career. Henry, having, as it is told, made his first appearance on the stage at the age of nine, had a successful career of some fifty-seven years.

29½.

Henry Placide.
of the Park Theatre
New Orleans
13th January 1844 — New York.

Henry Placide Actor Park Th. N.Y.
New Orleans 13th Jan'y 1844.

82

Jacob Medary   d. 1847
[Saratoga], July 9, 1840

Little is known of Jacob Medary though it is apparent he was an important influence in Columbus, Ohio. In all likelihood the original form of his name was Madeira. From William T. Martin's *History of Franklin County*, published in Columbus in 1858, we learn only that Medary was a newspaper publisher and that in 1836 he bought the *Ohio Monitor*, which had been established in 1816, from Judge David Smith, one of its original owners. The *Monitor* was then either discontinued or merged into the *Hemisphere*. Similarly, the *Western Hemisphere*, a weekly Jackson Democratic paper, commenced in Columbus in 1832, was sold to Jacob Medary and another. It was about this time that Medary's brother Samuel was elected state printer. In 1845 Jacob was appointed postmaster for Columbus, a post he held until his death.

In his profile of Medary, Edouart displays the tall, handsome, and no doubt successful Democratic newspaper publisher at what must have been the height of his career, and at a time when he could describe him as "adjt. Genl. of the Militia of the State of Ohio."

30

Jacob Medary,
Columbus, Ohio. — July 9, 1840.

Jacob Medary

83
Alexander C. Gibson
Saratoga, July 19, 1843

It must have come naturally to Gibson to write under his signature, "Mayor of Schenectady." He was first elected in 1840, served in 1841, 1843, and 1844. Saratoga was an obvious and convenient place to go for a holiday, and Edouart, with his eye always open and looking for prominent subjects, wasted no time. Mayor Gibson, hat in hand, is perhaps acknowledging a popular greeting or about to tell the visitors to the spa some of the virtues of Schenectady.

30th

Alex. C. Gibson
Mayor of Schenectady
Saratoga July 19. 1843

bay

Alex. C. Gibson Mayor of
Saratoga 19th July 1843 Schenectady N.Y.

84

John Arnold Rockwell   1803–1861
Norwich, Connecticut, May 4, 1840

Many a lawyer yearns to become a judge. Here we see Rockwell the lawyer just after his election to the county court of New London County. He was a graduate of Yale of the class of 1822 and practiced law for years in Norwich. For two years, 1838–39, he served in the state senate, in 1840 became judge of the county court, and in 1845 was elected to Congress, where he served two terms. As a congressman he was chairman of the Committee on Claims and was the principal originator of the Court of Claims to which, after leaving Congress, he principally confined his law practice. In the course of this practice he was obliged to learn Spanish and as a result was able to publish the standard treatise on the Mexican law relating to mines and real estate. *Appleton's Cyclopaedia of American Biography* recounts that one of the measures he introduced while in Congress was for commuting the spirits ration in the navy to its equivalent in money, though it is not disclosed how many availed themselves of this privilege.

31

John A. Rockwell
Norwich Conn. May 4. 1840

Judge John A. Rockwell
Norwich Conn. Ut
May 4th 1840.

85
Stephen Olin, D.D. 1797–1851
Saratoga, July 17, 1843

If ever there was a man who surmounted his phys-ical weaknesses it was Stephen Olin. Graduation with honors from Middlebury College, Vermont, in 1820 was at the expense of his health. He gave up his intended career in the law to recuperate in South Carolina, where he became an instructor at Tabernacle Academy in Abbeville, joined the Methodist Episcopal church, and for three years served the church in Charleston until his health failed again. This time he went to Georgia and was elected professor of ethics and belles lettres at Franklin College, a position he held until 1833, in the meantime having been ordained an elder by Bishop McKendree.

Randolph-Macon College, Mecklenburg Coun-ty, Virginia, called him as its first president in 1834, but by 1837 his health had once more broken down. This time his cure was obtained by three years spent in Europe and the Holy Land with his wife, a tour which not only restored his health but produced his 1843 *Travels in Egypt, Arabia Petraea, and the Holy Land*, in two volumes. In 1842, his ability still recognized and his services in demand, he became president of Wesleyan Uni-versity, a post he occupied to his own credit and to the enduring benefit of the university until his death. He was offered the presidency of Genesee College but declined it.

He was a noted educator and preacher, always in demand and extraordinarily popular. His scholarship and theological attainments earned him an honorary D.D. from Middlebury College in 1832, from Wesleyan and the University of Alabama in 1834, and an LL.D. from Yale in 1845. Ill health sent him abroad again in 1846. In Flanders he took part in the Evangelical Al-liance Conference in August of that year, and af-ter speaking at the launching of the missionary ship *John Wesley* in September, he embarked on a thirty-five-day passage home in a sailing vessel. Apart from his many published works, some post-humous, he is remembered for his great work in establishing Wesleyan University on the firm foundation it has enjoyed ever since.

31½

Stephen Olin
Wesleyan University
Middletown
Conn
Saratoga July 7, 1843

Rev. Stephen Olin
President of Wesleyan University, Middletown
Conn

86
Joseph Lyman   1767–1847
[Location unknown], May 4, 1840

The old adage "It's an ill wind blows nobody good" can well be applied to Lyman, and in his case it was a strange but understandable indictment of the time. He was the son of a Northampton, Massachusetts, farmer. A childhood accident fractured his skull, and his resulting delicate health convinced his family that he would never make a farmer. As an alternative they gave him an education. He studied under his pastor, the Reverend Solomon Williams, and then graduated from Yale in 1783. After studying law under Caleb Strong of Northampton, he was admitted to the Massachusetts bar in 1787 and practiced in Westfield for seven years, then returned to Northampton. There he was clerk of the county courts until 1810 and judge of the common pleas and of probate, which later office he held until 1816, the court of common pleas having been abolished in 1811. His last post, that of sheriff of Hampshire County, he assumed in 1816 and held until 1845, two years before his death.

He served in the state legislature, in the Massachusetts convention for revising the constitution, and as a member of the Hartford Convention. At his death the two surviving members of the Hartford Convention were Judge Wilde (fig. 328) of the Supreme Court of Massachusetts and the Honorable Harrison Gray Otis of Boston. He was twice married and the father of eleven children. A devoted member of the Unitarian Society of Northampton, he was beloved of his townsmen. His portrait is said to have been painted by Chester Harding. After twenty-four years in the office it is not surprising that he signed himself "Sheriff of Hampshire, Massachusetts."

32.

Joseph Lyman Sheriff of
Hampshire Massachusetts
May 4th 1840.

Joseph Lyman Sheriff
of Hampshire Massachusetts
4th May 1840.

87
Jacob De La Motta 1789–1845
Saratoga Springs, July 12, 1844

A reader of the *City Gazette* in Charleston, South Carolina, in October 1826 would have learned of the establishment of the South Carolina Institution for Correcting Impediments of Speech under the guidance of Dr. Jacob De La Motta. Although it is not clear what method was used to effect a ready cure for stammering, it was perhaps mesmerism or hypnotism. Dr. De La Motta was born in Savannah of Jewish descent, graduated from the medical school of the University of Pennsylvania in 1810. Two years of practice in Charleston were followed by two years of service as surgeon in the Second Regiment of Artillery. When honorably discharged, he practiced for several years in New York and was active in the County Medical Society and College of Physicians and Surgeons.

He was an active Mason, a popular after-dinner speaker, and interested in politics, though not a successful candidate for office. After a few years in New York and Savannah he returned to Charleston in 1823, where he spent a busy and fruitful life, active in all branches of his profession, commissioner of the Poor House, secretary of the Literary and Philosophical Society, assistant commissioner of health. For twenty years he conducted one of the leading pharmacies in Charleston, known as Apothecaries Hall. He is well described in the title of Thomas Tobias's 1963 article in the *American Jewish Historical Quarterly* as "The Many-Sided Dr. De La Motta." His many interests and pleasant conversation must have made him welcome at Saratoga.

88
James McHenry, M.D. 1785–1845
Philadelphia, October 6, 1842

Dr. McHenry studied for the ministry in his native Ireland but turned from it because he was a hunchback, as his silhouette reveals. His choice became medicine, and for some years he practiced in Larne, county Antrim, and in Belfast. He emigrated to the United States in 1817 with his wife and son and finally settled in Philadelphia, where for eighteen years he carried on a varied career in medicine, as a merchant, politician, poet, novelist, editor, and critic. In 1843 his friend President Jackson appointed him American consul at Londonderry, a position he held until his death.

He is best known for his colorful, humorous Irish poetry, though he published widely. *The Pleasures of Friendship*, his first book of verse published in America, was followed by *The Wilderness; or, The Youthful Days of Washington*. Years later his epic in blank verse, *Antediluvians; or, The World Destroyed*, suffered from a most unfavorable review in *Blackwood's*. For a time he edited the *American Monthly Magazine*, in which he displayed his fondness for Pope and scorn for Wordsworth, Coleridge, and Byron, for which he was thoroughly taken to task. He appears in Edouart's silhouette at about the end of his literary career and only shortly before returning to Ireland.

32½

Jacob De La Motta
M.D. James McHenry M.D.
Charleston S.C.
Aged 55. July 12th 44. Aged 56 Oct 6, 1842
Saratoga

Jacob. De La Motta MD of Charleston S.C.   James McHenry MD
Saratoga Springs 19th July 1844.   Philadelphia 6th Octob 1842.
56 Years of age

89
Burton Hepburn   d. 1843
Saratoga Springs, July 24, 1840

Colonel Hepburn signs himself in 1840 as "late of Georgia," and better might it have been for him had he never returned. But he did, with results which we learn from a newspaper clipping from an unknown paper containing an article entitled "Awful Tragedy in Columbus, Georgia." The writer states that he knew Hepburn well and that "he had a great deal of talent—some eccentricities—but was, taking him all in all, an honorable man." It is unfair at this distance in time and with no other knowledge of the man to question the strength of this statement. The article continues with two anonymous letters dated January 5, 1843, from which we quote:

Our town was early this morning thrown into a great excitement by what would be called in your city an awful tragedy. Col. Burton Hepburn is no more; he met his death this morning by the hands of Daniel McDougald, the former president of the Planters' and Mechanics' Bank, now of The Insurance Bank of this place. The circumstances of the case as far as can be correctly ascertained, are these:—Hepburn came out purposely to have a settlement with McDougald respecting some cotton transactions of old date, involving some $20,000 which McDougald has heretofore refused to settle. Hepburn stated to his friends that unless the thing was settled within two days, one or the other of them must die; which McDougald hearing, prepared himself to meet him, being also informed, through an anonymous letter, that Hepburn intended to assassinate him in the street. Hepburn proceeded this morning, about eight o'clock, to McDougald's office and on M'D. opening the door he stated that he had come to give him (what, God knows) : as he was stopped at these words, and pushed back by Mr. McDougald, and shot dead. This is McDougald's statement; he expired in less than five minutes, without speaking a word. . . . The coroner's jury returned a verdict of justifiable homicide, which would, however, in your city [have] been looked upon as a wilful murder.

The reporter commented: "Of General Daniel McDougald we have never heard aught against his character. What an awful result." The tall handsome figure of the colonel as he appeared to Edouart, must have made an easy target for the general.

90
Burr Harrison McCown   1806–1881
Lexington, Kentucky, June 1, 1844

Much of the available information concerning the Reverend Burr H. McCown comes from records in the possession of the Filson Club of Louisville, Kentucky. McCown was a native of Bardstown, Kentucky, and though is said by some to have been educated at St. Joseph's College, a Roman Catholic institution in Bardstown, is declared by others equally authoritatively to have received his early education and familiarity with Greek and Latin from the Presbyterian divines, the Reverends Joshua Wilson and James Blythe. Be that as it may he did receive a sound classical education, taught school at an early age in Bardstown, and for eleven years, until 1842, held the chair of Greek and Latin in Augusta College, the first college ever established in this country by the Methodist Episcopal church. By this time he had left the Presbyterian church, unable to accept its Calvinistic teachings, and had joined the Methodist church. In 1842 he joined the faculty of Transylvania University, in its classical department, but in 1847 on the division of the Methodist church he withdrew and returned to the Presbyterian church, where he ministered for twenty years. For some years he taught in a private school which he had founded near Anchorage, Kentucky.

His life was beset with theological difficulty. Rumored to have been educated by the Roman Catholics, he turned to the Presbyterians, then the Methodists, then back to the Presbyterians and finally, being at heart an Arminian, he returned to the Methodist church, where he died a member in 1881. We see him, facing Dr. Cross, when he was professor of languages, albeit dead ones, Latin and Greek, at Transylvania University.

91
James Conquest Cross, M.D.
Lexington, Kentucky, May 23, 1844

One of the earliest notices we have of Dr. Cross is that he was a colleague of Dr. Cobb (fig. 49) on the faculty of the Medical College of Ohio, in Cincinnati, in the 1820s and 1830s, where he taught materia medica. In 1839 he subscribed $500 for the benefit of Transylvania University, Lexington, Kentucky, having in 1837 become professor of the institutes and medical jurisprudence at its medical college and in 1838 dean of the medical faculty. He held these positions until about 1844 and died not long after.

He was born in the county of Lexington, was a brilliant student in his youth, graduated from Transylvania University, and was always ambitious to become a member of its faculty. It is said he received his appointment there through the influence of the Reverend Nathan H. Hall, a trustee, but against the judgment of other members of the board. Though of ability and learning, he suffered from a lack of mental balance, which effectively prevented his attaining prominence. When taken by Edouart and paired with the Reverend B. H. McCown, whom he must have known, he was at the end of his career on the faculty of Transylvania University. He never quite lived up to his challenging middle name.

33½- Rev. B. H. McCown.
Prof. Lang. Transylⁿ Univ
Lexington June 1844.

Jacob C Cross M.D.
Lex. KY
May 23ʳ 1844.

Revᵈ B. H. McCowy Prof. Lang. Transdⁿ University
Lexington 1ˢᵗ June 1844.

Jas. C. Cross M.D. of Lexington K.Y.
23ᵈ May 1844.

92
Robert Gilmor 1774–1848
Saratoga, August 11, 1840

Gilmor, as a leading citizen of Baltimore, was a figure one would expect to encounter at Saratoga in 1840. A patron of the arts, as a successful merchant and banker, he accumulated one of the finest collections of paintings, engravings, and statuary of his time in this country. He was educated in Baltimore and later in the Netherlands and France, leading to his being a partner in the shipping firm of Robert Gilmor & Sons from 1799 to 1830. He is said to have been a founder and shareholder of the Bank of Maryland. He took a hand in the construction of a powder mill at Gwinn's Falls, which was blown up in the War of 1812, and established a company in 1807 to procure supplies of merchandise from Calcutta and China. But he was also a man of strong social and civic interests. President of the Academy of Science, one of the founders of the old Library Company (later merged into the Maryland Historical Society), president of the Washington Monument Association in Baltimore, he became the center of social life in that city, where he died in November 1848.

34.

Robert Gilmor

Baltimore 11 Aug. 1840

Baltimore 11 Aug. 1840

93
Nathan Bourne Crocker, D.D.
1781–1865
Saratoga, August 18, 1843

Dr. Crocker was a principal influence in the Episcopal Diocese of Rhode Island in the first half of the nineteenth century. From 1803 until his death, excluding only three years absence for reasons of health, he was rector of St. John's Church, Providence. Bishop Bass ordained him deacon in Boston in 1803, and Bishop Moore of New York raised him to the priesthood in Trinity Church, New York, in 1808. He was a part of, and in larger part responsible for, the growth of the Episcopal church in his state, being almost solely responsible for the establishment of St. Paul's Church in Pawtucket. President of the Standing Committee for many years, delegate to nineteen triennial conventions of the Episcopal church (at the last of which he died, in 1843), for fifty-seven years a fellow of Brown University and fifteen years its secretary, as a mark of respect and gratitude his fellow citizens and colleagues had his portrait painted by the New York artist Daniel Huntington and hung in Rhode Island Hall, which had been built under the aegis of President Wayland (fig. 75). He stands a head taller than his junior and undoubted friend Professor Goddard.

Dr. Crocker was born in Barnstable, Massachusetts, the ancestral home of the Bournes, his mother's family.

94
William Giles Goddard   1794–1846
Saratoga Springs, June 29, 1843

It was quite natural that Edouart would have placed Professor Goddard in conversation with Dr. Crocker, of whose church he was long a warden. Goddard's career in Providence was exceeded in length, both early and late, by that of Dr. Crocker. Goddard, a native of Johnston, Rhode Island, graduated at Brown University in 1812. After a short stint at the study of the law under the Honorable Francis Blake of Worcester, his health caused him to remove to Providence in 1814, where for eleven years he was editor of the *Rhode Island American*. He held the professorship of moral philosophy and metaphysics, and then of belles lettres, for a total of seventeen years, until his health failed him. As a member of the Board of Trustees of Brown, after years of service he became its secretary. His services to his community in the cause of religion, education, philanthropy, and the interpretation of the Constitution were legion. His *Political and Miscellaneous Writings*, edited by his son Francis W. Goddard, was published in 1870. His memory is perpetuated in a memorial discourse published in 1846 by President Wayland (fig. 75). Of his address in 1843 on the new constitution of Rhode Island, President Wayland, in Walter C. Bronson's *History of Brown University* (1914), is reported to have said, "I do not remember any commentary upon the nature of our free institutions, which, in so few pages, contains so much that is of permanent value."

34½. Dr. Crocker
         of Providence R.I.

William G. Goddard,
Saratoga Springs,
June 29, 1843

Revd Dr. N. B. Crocker DD
Providence R.I. Saratoga Aug 18th 1843

Wm G. Goddard
late Prof.r of Belles lettres at
Brown's Univ.y Providence R.I.

95
Grenville Mellen   1799–1841
New York, August 17, 1839

An obituary notice of Mellen headed "A Poet
Gone" calls him "one of the sweet bards of our
country," but such a reputation his writings,
lacking humor and depth, have been quite unable
to support. In his brief biographical sketch in the
Dictionary of American Biography, his friend
John Neal is quoted as saying of him that "he
dealt too much in mystery—the mystery of language, not of thought." He was the eldest son of
Chief Justice Mellen of Maine, a graduate of Harvard College in the class of 1818, and for a few
years practiced law. But his bent was poetry and
journalism. For a while he contributed poems and
articles to the *United States Literary Gazette*, the
Atlantic Souvenir, and the *Legendary*, as did his
fellow townsman Longfellow at the same time.
The loss within a year of his infant daughter and
his wife left an inevitable mark on his career. After 1836 he lived in New York with the editor
Samuel Colman. Under his signature above his
silhouette there is written in another hand his
latest accomplishments: "Author of the 'Martyr's
triumph,' Buried Valley & other Poems etc. etc. &
editor of Colman's Monthly Miscellany." There
seems to be no reason for his being paired with
Ingraham unless it is their common acquaintance
with Longfellow.

96
Joseph Holt Ingraham   1809–1860
Washington, June 17, 1841

Longfellow, in his journal in 1846, as quoted in
Samuel Longfellow's *Life of Henry Wadsworth
Longfellow* (1886–87), wrote: "In the afternoon
Ingraham the novelist called. A young, dark man,
with soft voice. He says he has written eighty
novels, and of these twenty during the last year;
till it has grown to be merely mechanical with
him. These novels are published in the newspaper. They pay him something more than three
thousand dollars a year." This was five years after
Ingraham stood for Edouart's silhouette, by which
time he had published many of his blood and
thunder tales such as *Lafitte; or, the Pirate of the
Gulf* and many others which had tremendous
success.

Ingraham was born in Maine, went to sea before the mast, and had some involvement in a
South American revolution, which may have fed
fuel to the fires of his early tales. It is scarcely
possible to discuss all his published works, they
were so numerous. For a brief period he was connected with Jefferson College at Washington,
Mississippi, which provided the excuse for his
later using the title of professor. After establishing a school for young women at Natchez in 1849,
he turned to theology and was ordained priest in
the Episcopal church in 1852, serving as rector of
St. John's, Mobile, Alabama, and Christ Church,
Holly Springs, Mississippi. During these years he
produced his greatest works, the trilogy *The
Prince of the House of David* in 1860, *The Pillar
of Fire* in 1859, and *The Throne of David* in 1860,
all designed as a sort of biblical fiction to attract
the attention of those not familiar with the Bible
to the wonderful events there related. These three
books enjoyed enormous popularity. Shortly after
the last was published, Ingraham died as a result
of the accidental discharge of a gun in his own
vestry.

35.

Grenville Mellen. —

New York. 17th August 1839.

Author of the "Martyr's triumph"
Buried Valley & other Poems &c. &c.
& editor of Colman's Monthly Miscellany.

J H Ingraham
Natchez. Miss ppi
June 17/41.

Grenville Mellen Poet.   J H Ingraham of Natchez Miss
New York 17th August 1839   Washington 17th June 1841.

97
William McIlhenney c.1779–1854
Philadelphia, March 14, 1843

McIlhenney graduated A.B. from the University of Pennsylvania in 1797 and three years later was admitted to the bar. For a time he was "Consul of Venezuela," as he describes it. He was also librarian and secretary of the Athenaeum of Philadelphia for thirty-four years, from 1820 until his death. He must have been not only a familiar figure but one much respected in Philadelphia. In his later years he became a great admirer of Comte, whose philosophy he assiduously studied.

98
C. P. Bronson
Saratoga, August 9, 1843

We know of Bronson not much more than he himself tells us—as he puts it, he was professor of oratory. Apparently he was an itinerant lecturer on elocution. Two letters from him survive in the Gratz Collection of the Historical Society of Pennsylvania. One, written in Philadelphia, is concerned with tickets and reservations for his lectures there. Perhaps this suggests that they were popular. The other, written in Cincinnati, is directed to the editor of the *Cincinnati Times* and relates to advertising his lectures. His presence at Saratoga may have been by popular request, or it may simply have represented his desire to find an audience for his lectures. Edouart seems to show him as though delivering an oration or instructing Consul McIlhenney how to do so.

35th Wm McIlhenney Secy Athenm.
March 14. 1843 Consul of Venezuela.

C. P. Bronson
Prof. of Oratory &c.
Saratoga Aug. 9th
1843

C. P. Bronson Prof of Oratory &c.
Saratoga 9th Augt. 1843.

Wm Mc Ilhenney Secretary Athenœum
and Consul of Venezuela Philada 14th March 1843.

C. P. Bronson Professor of Oratory &c.
Saratoga 9th Augt. 1843.

99
John Williamson Nevin, D.D.
1803–1886
Saratoga, August 20, 1840

Nevin, through no fault of his own but as a child of the times, was caught up in the doctrinal controversy which divided the Presbyterian church in the 1830s. His early education had been at Union College, Schenectady, New York, from which he graduated in 1821. Here he had come into contact with George W. Doane (fig. 245) and Alonzo Potter, later Episcopal bishops. One class ahead of him was William H. Seward (fig. 2), later governor of New York. In his own class was John Proudfit (fig. 105), later to become professor at Rutgers, and on the faculty was that incipient giant Francis Wayland (fig. 75), later president of Brown University. Ill health delayed Nevin's entry to Princeton Theological Seminary until 1823. In 1830 he assumed a professorship in Western Theological Seminary at its organization at Allegheny, Pennsylvania. Ten years at this post produced a surprise call to a professorship at the Theological Seminary of the German Reformed Synod at Mercersburg, Pennsylvania, an appointment he acknowledged beneath his signature inscribed over Edouart's silhouette. His change of affiliation from Presbyterian to the Reformed church resulted in controversy, followed by a pamphlet campaign. Nevin translated the German address of Dr. Philip Schaff to the Mercersburg seminary and undertook to defend himself for his stand on tradition and the sacraments. At this time he wrote his *Mystical Presence and History and Genius of the Heidelberg Catechism*. While at the seminary he was also acting president of Marshall College until his retirement in 1853 for reasons of health. He returned as lecturer from 1861 to 1866 when the college was merged with Franklin College to become Franklin and Marshall College, of which he was president until his resignation by reason of age in 1876, after which he lived in retirement until his death. He played a leading part in what came to be known as the "Mercersburg theology" and was largely responsible for the liturgy devised for the Reformed church in 1867 which was long in use.

36.

John W. Nevin, Prof of Divinity
in the Theol. Sem. of the German Ref. Synod
Mercersburgh, Penn.

Saratoga 20th Augt 1840.   *John W. Nevin, Prof of Divinity*
in the Theol. Sem. of the German Ref. Synod

100
Simeon Baldwin
Saratoga, July 31, 1844

Judge Baldwin's silhouette is missing. Probably
over the years it worked loose and fell out of the
volume. But his signature remains and his own
statement that he was late a judge of the Superior
Court of Connecticut, was eighty-two and one-
half years old, and, as Edouart adds beneath the
blank space, had been a member of Congress from
1803 to 1804. He must have been born about 1761
or 1762. His position on the bench would make
him an appropriate visitor to Saratoga and a
natural companion to Judge Hedding in Edouart's volume. It is a pity he could not have been
paired with his son (fig. 241), whose silhouette
was cut the very same day in Saratoga. No doubt
someone still has the duplicate which Edouart
invariably cut.

101
William Hedding
Saratoga, July 26, 1843

Judge Hedding was one of the fourteen children
of James Hedding, a farmer of Pine Plains, New
York. William and his brother Elijah were the
more prominent of the family, Elijah (1780–
1852) being a noted preacher and bishop of the
Methodist Episcopal church in Addison County,
Vermont. Hedding identified himself "First Judge
of Clinton County," which gives us a fair indica-
tion that he was a man of consequence, well borne
out by his confident stance, hat in hand, head up,
in Edouart's silhouette, in company with Judge
Baldwin.

36½ Simeon Baldwin.
Late a Judge of Sup. Ct. of Conn.t 82½
Saratoga July 31. 1844.

William Hedding
First Judge of Clinton
County
Saratoga Springs
July 26th 1843

Simeon Baldwin.

William Hedding.

Simeon Baldwin Late Judge Sup. Ct. Connet.
and member of Congress 1803 44.
Saratoga 31st July 1844.

82½ of Age.

Wm Hedding. First Judge of
Saratoga July 26/43. Clinton Co.

102
John Power 1792–1849
New York, October 23, 1840

Father Power was one of New York's most beloved Roman Catholic priests of his day, though he never received from Rome the preferment his friends thought he deserved. He was born in county Cork, Ireland, where he received his classical training and for a while taught at the diocesan seminary. In 1819 he was asked by the trustees of St. Peter's Church in New York to become pastor of that church, a position he held with honor until his death thirty years later. He was an eloquent preacher, an astute politician, and an idol of the Irish of New York, whose interests he always supported. He edited a *Laity's Directory* in 1822, compiled his *New Testament by Way of Question and Answer* in 1824, and *True Piety* in 1832, all prominent Roman Catholic publications in their time. Twice his name was sent to Rome as a candidate for the see of New York, or as coadjutor, but each time he was passed over, first for Bishop Dubois and later for Father John Hughes (fig. 104). Hughes, however, recognized his worth, and in 1839 named him vicar general of New York, a title he acknowledges below his signature as he stands before Edouart, apparently bestowing his blessing on the faithful of the three churches in the distance, which appear from their architecture to be Roman Catholic, Congregational, and Anglican. He presents a fine figure, and his profile confirms his Irish descent.

John Power
Vicar General
of New York &
Rector of St. Peter's
Church, Barclay
Street.
New York October
23rd A.D. 1840

John Power ... Genl. of N.Y. and Rector of St. Peter's
New York ... Church Barclay St.

103
Marmaduke Burrough, M.D.
1797–1844
Philadelphia, October 31, 1843

Dr. Burrough received his M.D. at the University of Pennsylvania in 1820. Despite his degree he appears to have taken a larger interest in the diplomatic service and the natural sciences. He was consul at Lima in 1827—perhaps *Lima* is the word Edouart was reaching for—and from 1829 to 1830 at Calcutta. On his return from Calcutta in 1830 he brought with him "a living Rhinoceros," whose freight was said to have cost 400 rupees, exactly twice what Burrough's passage cost. Either the voyage or the Philadelphia climate proved too much for the large creature, for in December 1830 it was reported that Burrough gave to the Academy of Natural Sciences of Philadelphia a "stuffed skin and mounted skeleton of a Rhinoceros." In November and December of the same year he presented to the academy 109 skins of birds of India, a *Plotus melanogaster* (which translated literally is a "blackbellied fish"), a *Bos grunniens*, as Linnaeus described it, and a cashmere goat.

During his consulship at Vera Cruz, Burrough collected skulls for Dr. Samuel G. Morton (fig. 177), author of *Crania Americana*, and ancient pottery for the American Philosophical Society, to which he was understandably elected in 1833. He died at Mount Holly, New Jersey; his walking stick still lies on the mantelpiece of the office of the Philosophical Society's librarian.

M. Burrough.

Oct 31. 1843.

Dr. M. Burrough M.D.
late consul to   Philadelphia 31st Oct. 1843

104
John Joseph Hughes 1797–1864
New York, October 22, 1840

The son of a small farmer, brought up in the most modest circumstances, having emigrated to Pennsylvania at the age of twenty, Hughes became one of the leading Roman Catholic churchmen in this country. Having earned his living as a gardener while studying theology, he was ordained priest in 1826. From that moment he became a man to be reckoned with. As pastor of St. John's Church in Philadelphia, he built the new church which was to become the leading Roman Catholic church in that city. He also entered the lists against the antiquated system of trusteeism and was instrumental in having laws passed allowing real property to be held in the name of the bishop and his appointees. Founder of the *Catholic Herald* in 1833, he entered into debate with the Presbyterian minister John Breckenridge in the *Herald* and the *Presbyterian* over the relation of Roman Catholic and Presbyterian doctrine to civil and religious liberty.

At last his preferment came. Rome named him coadjutor bishop of New York, and in 1838 he was consecrated titular bishop of Basileopolis, succeeding to the see of New York in 1842, and in 1850 when New York was created an archdiocese he became the first archbishop. In New York he disposed of trusteeism, salvaged St. Patrick's Church from mismanagement, and many years later, in 1858, laid the cornerstone of St. Patrick's Cathedral on Fifth Avenue and Fifty-fifth Street. He was never idle. Under his guidance were founded the Sacred Heart Academy in Manhattanville, Manhattan College, and St. John's College. His unsuccessful struggle to get public funds for parochial schools has a familiar ring today and made him the target of "no popery" groups which invaded the Irish wards of the city.

At the request of John Quincy Adams (fig. 172) and John C. Calhoun (fig. 161) he preached before Congress in 1847 on "Christianity, the only source of Moral, Social and Political Regeneration." During the Civil War he supported the Union, though he was forced to defend his position, not being an abolitionist. At the request of Lincoln and Seward (fig. 2) he went to Europe to explain the Union's cause. By his persuasive oratory he quelled the draft riots in New York. His writings were voluminous, but he considered them as designed on the spur of the moment to meet each emergency as it arose and opposed their publication. However after his death Lawrence Kehoe edited *The Complete Works of the Most Rev. John Hughes* in two volumes in 1865.

He was one of the first and greatest of a long line of distinguished New York Roman Catholic prelates. The tall gentle figure revealed by Edouart in 1840 does in no way suggest the activist and controversial archbishop.

38.

+ John Bishop ℞℞℠℃ +
New York Oct 22

John Hughes
Bishop of Basileopolis, in Asia Minor
Coadjutor and administrator of the
Diocese of New York 22. Oct 1840.

105
John Proudfit, D.D.   1803–1870
Saratoga, August 14, 1843

Dr. Proudfit describes himself as "Prof. of Greek
& Lat. Lit." at Rutgers College, New Jersey. The
college profited from his learning from 1841 until
1859, at which time he retired and devoted himself to the church and other philanthropic activities until his death. The son of a clergyman,
he was born in Salem, New York, graduated at
Union College in 1823, from which he received a
D.D. in 1841, and, after studying theology at
Princeton Theological Seminary until 1824, became pastor of the Reformed church in Newburyport, Massachusetts, for six years. Seven years
as professor of Latin at New York University led
to his call to Rutgers. He was well read, wrote
articles for reviews of the day, and founded the
New Brunswick Review, which had merit but
lacked finances. William H. S. Demerest in his
History of Rutgers College, 1766–1924 (1924) says
of Dr. Proudfit that he "lived in the house now
known as the Vail house at the corner of Livingston Avenue and New Street and he was a familiar
figure, riding horseback." He was a member of
the second of four generations of his family which
produced clergymen.

Edouart caught him at the commencement of
his long career in classical literature at Rutgers,
when, like many of his colleagues, he visited
Saratoga.

Aug. 14. 1843

J. Proudfit. Prof. of
Greek & Lat. Lit.
Rutgers New Jersey

J. Proudfit Profsr of Greek and Latin Litr
Rutgers Coll. New Jersey Saratoga 14th Augt 1843

106
Columbus O'Donnell   1792–1873
Saratoga Springs, August 11, 1840

The descendants of General O'Donnell, whose
title stems from the state of Maryland, are legion
and many are worthy successors to their progenitor. Son of an Irish immigrant, he was educated
at St. Mary's College in Baltimore under the aegis
of the Fathers of the Oratory of Saint Sulspice. In
1813, under the age of twenty-one, he married
Eleanora Pascault, daughter of the marquis de
Poleon. At the time she was only fourteen years
old, and the strange and unfamiliar names of the
witnesses to the marriage, recorded in the archives
of the Old Cathedral at Baltimore, may suggest
that the affair was an elopement. Be that as it
may, they lived happily together for over half a
century and their children married well, with the
Hillen, Lee, Iselin, Carroll, and Jenkins families.

Columbus was able and successful and succeeded in magnifying his large inheritance from
his father, John O'Donnell. To list his prominent
activities is no simple task: for fifteen years president of the Baltimore Water Company, for thirty
years a director of the Union Bank of Baltimore,
connected with the administration of the Baltimore & Ohio Railway, and one of the commissioners that had a hand in the development of
Druid Hill Park. His father's estate on the banks
of the Patapsco River was absorbed by the Canton
Company, of which Columbus was head, and ultimately developed into Baltimore's industrial
and shipping operation. Streets and wharves bear
the family name. For thirty-seven years he was
president of the Baltimore Gaslight Company,
which chose Peale's Museum in Holliday as the
first building in Baltimore to be illuminated by
gas, a choice which benefited the museum, as
people flocked to it to view the new wonder. He
survived his wife by three years and was blind for
the last five years of his life. An account of his
death, published May 25, 1873, noted that he was
"one of the wealthiest and most honored citizens
of Baltimore." Small wonder that when at Saratoga he was captured by Edouart.

39.

Columbus O'Donnell
Baltimore August 11 1840

Columbus O'Donnell

107
Joseph Henry 1797–1878
Philadelphia, May 30, 1843

In 1835 President Jackson advised the Congress of a bequest of upwards of $500,000 from the Englishman James Smithson to the nation, to establish an institution at Washington "for the increase and diffusion of knowledge among men." John Quincy Adams (fig. 172) was appointed chairman of a House special committee to administer the fund. In 1846 the Smithsonian Institution was established as a learned organization, and Joseph Henry became the first secretary, the choice having been left to a Board of Regents who sought a man not only who was distinguished as an investigator but who possessed judgment, character, and wide interests. Henry was the natural choice, and he set a standard as the first secretary, from 1846 to 1878, thirty-two years, which has served as an example to his successors. Weather reports and prediction of storms were instituted by him. He became president of the Light House Board, a member of the American Philosophical Society, president of the American Association for the Advancement of Science, and of the Philosophical Society of Washington.

Yet his career prior to the establishment of the Smithsonian Institution was almost as distinguished. Born in Albany, New York, he clerked in a village store, was apprenticed to a watchmaker, and was a youthful playwright and stage manager. His accidental reading of a book on natural science was for him a turning point. He entered the Albany Academy, served as a surveyor in laying out roads in western New York, and in 1826 became professor of mathematics and natural philosophy in the Albany Academy. And then, by one of those coincidences with which the world abounds, he discovered the now familiar fact of the induced current at about the time that Farraday announced the same discovery. There was no jealousy involved. Each discovery was independent of the other and Farraday published his first. At that time, 1832, Henry was elected to the professorship of natural philosophy in the College of New Jersey at Princeton. There he continued with his researches in the field of electricity and earned a reputation as a scholar with the capacity and imagination to investigate new fields of scientific inquiry, all of which led to his choice as the first head of the Smithsonian Institution. After his death in Washington, the sculptor William Wetmore Story, son of Justice Joseph Story (fig. 16), modeled a bronze statue of him to his memory.

108
Nathan (or Nathaniel) William Cole, M.D.
Burlington, New Jersey, June 5, 1843

Dr. Cole was one of the founders of the Burlington County Medical Society, and his name stands first on its roll of members. Though he studied medicine at the University of Pennsylvania, he did not receive its medical degree until 1829, after several years of practice in New Jersey. Details of his life are few. In 1832 he delivered before the State Medical Society the first address that was formally presented to the society, "The Importance of Medical Science." Some years later, in 1846, he was a delegate to the American Medical Association. It is not unlikely that his scientific interests may have prompted Edouart to pose him on the same page with Henry.

39½   *May 30th 1843*

Joseph Henry

Professor of
Nat. Phil. Col.
of New Jersey

Natll. Wm. Cole M.D.
Burlington N Jersey
June 5th 1843

Joseph Henry. Professor of Natl. Phil.
Philad: 30th May 1843. Coledge of New Jersey

Dr. Nathl. Wm. Cole **ND**
Burlington New Jersey 5th June 1843.

109
Edward Norris Kirk, D.D.
1802–1874
New York, January 18, 1840

"The Chrysostom of American revivalists," as Kirk was called in Frank G. Beardsley's *History of American Revivals* (1912), was a native New Yorker, grew up with relatives at Princeton, where he graduated from the College of New Jersey in 1820, and turned to the law. Upon his "conversion" two years later, he entered the Princeton Theological Seminary and in 1826 received his license to preach. Two years later we find him supplying at the Second Presbyterian Church in Albany during the illness of its pastor. But his revivalist, evangelical, uncompromising preaching was not acceptable to his congregation, numbering among them Martin Van Buren (fig. 230), B. F. Butler (fig. 43), and W. L. Marcy (fig. 6). In 1829 he was installed as pastor of the Fourth Presbyterian Church, organized by friends. For eight years he labored there, delving deeply and successfully in revivals, missions, temperance, and antislavery movements.

His reputation preceded him and in 1842 he was in charge of the Mount Vernon Church in Boston, which he served with all his evangelical fervor for more than thirty years. Edouart took his likeness shortly after his return from a trip abroad to recover his health, and during a high point in his evangelistic preaching.

Rev. Edward Norris Kirk. May 8. 1840.

40.

Rev. Edward Norris Kirk _____ Secretary of the Evangelical Society
New York 18th Jan'y 1840

110
Alexander McClelland, D.D.
1796–1864
[Saratoga], August 18, 1843

Despite the notations above and below Dr. Mc-
Clelland's silhouette, it is clear that it was taken
in Saratoga, the very same day as that of Dr.
Crocker (fig. 93). Dr. McClelland would have been
an acceptable visitor to Saratoga as an ornament
in the pulpit and as the distinguished professor of
biblical literature in the theological seminary of
the Reformed church in New Brunswick, New
Jersey. A native of Schenectady, he was graduated
at Union College in 1809, and by 1815 was pastor
of the Rutgers Street Presbyterian Church in New
York. For seven years, until 1829, he was professor
of rhetoric, logic, and metaphysics in Jefferson
College. Then he became associated with Rutgers
College, where for many years, until his retirement, he was professor of Oriental languages and
literature. He published several theological works.
William H. S. Demerest's *History of Rutgers College* (1924) says of him that "when he died the
church lost one of our greatest intellectual lights,
Biblical literature one of its proudest ornaments,
and the pulpit an acknowledged master of sacred
eloquence."

111
John Ludlow, D.D.   1793–1857
Philadelphia, May 30, 1843

His innate modesty led Dr. Ludlow to limit his
signature above his silhouette to name, place, and
date. Others could describe him as the seventh
provost of the University of Pennsylvania, a post
he held to his credit for eighteen years. A graduate
of Union College in 1814, he soon became pastor
of the Reformed Dutch Church of Albany, New
York, and within a few years had the unusual opportunity of declining election to three institutions of learning. He was a brilliant preacher and
lecturer and one of the few men of his day to lecture at the Smithsonian Institution during the
secretaryship of Joseph Henry (fig. 107), whom he
must have known well.

40.½

Alex McClelland
New Brunswick N.J.
Aug 18 1843.

John Ludlow
Philᵃ May 30ᵗʰ
1843

Alex McClelland DD.
Professor of biblical literature in the
theological seminary N. Brunswick N.J.

John Ludlow DD President of the Univ
of Pennsylvania
Philadelphia 30th May 1843.

112
Robert Gould Shaw   1776–1853
Saratoga, August 8, 1840

It may well have been the hard life of his youth in Gouldsborough, Maine, where he was born in 1776, that brought out the best in young Shaw and enabled him to make his way in the world with very little of the advantages of education and happy family life. When his father died, he was sent to Boston and was apprenticed to his uncle William Shaw. When he came of age and completed his apprenticeship, he went into business for himself, forming the house of Shaw, Barker & Bridge, which did a thriving auction and commission business. In 1805 he went to England in the *John Adams* and for two years engaged in buying and shipping out merchandise of various sorts. By 1810 he was a general merchant on his own account, owned many vessels, and gradually accumulated a large capital and became one of Boston's most prominent merchants.

As a devoted Mason he came to the rescue of the Grand Lodge of Massachusetts by purchasing the Masonic temple during the lodge's hard times and later selling it back at cost. Twice a representative to the General Court, he was also president of the Massachusetts Society of the Cincinnati. He married Elizabeth William Parkman, who bore him seven sons and four daughters, most of whom survived him. He is remembered for his generous philanthropy both during his life and under the terms of his will. At the time he was in Saratoga he was president of the Boston Bank.

113
Samuel Hubbard 1785–1847
[Saratoga], August 13, 1845

Although the place of taking Judge Hubbard's silhouette is not mentioned by Edouart, the silhouettist was in Saratoga on August 13, 1845, when he cut the likeness of J. B. Christian (fig. 231).

Judge Hubbard, who looks every inch the jurist he was, received his appointment as justice of the Supreme Judicial Court of Massachusetts from Governor Davis (fig. 317) in 1842. He held that position until his death, conducting himself with an impartiality and wisdom that made him one of the most respected members of the bench. Though a Bostonian by birth and a descendant of Harvard men, he nevertheless graduated from Yale in 1805. For five years he practiced law in Biddeford, Maine, then moved to Boston, where he practiced the rest of his career, in the early years as a partner of Charles Jackson (fig. 262). Like most busy, successful men, he had time for civic duties. Seven terms in the General Court, trustee of Phillips Academy at Andover, member of the Corporation of Dartmouth College, president of the Society for the Promotion of Temperance, and an active membership in the Bible Society, show the breadth of his interests. His first wife, Mary, was the daughter of Gardiner Greene, reputed to be the wealthiest man in Boston. He married secondly Mary Ann Coit, widow of the Reverend Henry Blatchford. By his first marriage he had four daughters and one son; by his second he had five sons and one daughter. His descendants are now legion.

114
Edward King 1794–1873
Philadelphia, May 27, 1843

Judge King in Edouart's grouping is apparently explaining one of his decisions to Judge Hubbard. Although their silhouettes were cut at different times, it is more than likely that they were acquainted, if not personally, surely by reputation.

King, a Philadelphian by birth, was well educated though he did not attend college. He received his legal training from Charles Chauncey and was admitted to practice in 1816. His early and vigorous interest in politics made him one of the leaders of the Democratic party in Pennsylvania and probably contributed to his becoming clerk of the orphan's court in 1824. His elevation to president judge of the court of common pleas in 1825 came as a surprise to many of his colleagues, but he soon proved himself preeminently qualified for the post. He served for over a quarter of a century and was without an equal in the administration of criminal justice. Upon his retirement the governor named him to a commission to revise the state criminal code. The commission's recommendations, largely a product of his works, were promptly adopted by the legislature. Outside of his legal profession he was a member of the American Philosophical Society and for some years president of the trustees of Jefferson Medical College.

41½

Sam: Hubbard
Justice of the
Sup. Judcourt of Mass.
Aug 13. 1845

Edward King. President
Judge 1. Dist Penna
May 27 1843

Edward King. Presid. Judge 1st Dist Penn.
Philadelphia 27th May 1843.

115
Ezra Meech   1773–1856
Saratoga Springs, August 20, 1840

The six-foot-five-inch, 370-pound Ezra Meech modestly signed his silhouette without giving himself a title, though his two-year stint as chief justice of Chittendon County Court in Vermont enabled Edouart to entitle him "Judge."

Meech was born in New London, Connecticut, moved with his family when but a youth to Hinesburgh, Vermont, where his education stopped at the district school level. He was a hunter and trapper, associated in the fur trade with John Jacob Astor, and conducted a store and farm in Shelburne. During the War of 1812 he supplied the American army with provisions, and at its conclusion was active in the timber business in Canada. He was elected to the state legislature in 1805 and 1807 and to Congress in 1819–21 and 1825–27. His election to the Chittendon County Court came in 1822 and 1823. Four times he was an unsuccessful Democratic candidate for governor of Vermont; in 1840 he was a presidential elector on the Whig ticket. His farm of several thousand acres is said to have supported a flock of 3,000 sheep and 800 oxen. He enjoyed the reputation of being one of the best trout fishermen in the country.

Ezra Meech Shelborn[?] Vermont 20 1840 42.

Judge Ezra Meech
of Shelborn, Vermont
Aug.t 20. 1840.
Saratoga Springs

116
Matthias Bruen   1776–1846
Saratoga, August 23, 1844

Matthias Bruen is shown by Edouart as he appeared aged seventy-eight, only two years before his death, and his profile gives the appearance of age. He was born in Newark, New Jersey, where he married Hannah, the daughter of Benjamin Coe, and moved to New York early in the nineteenth century. Here he became associated with Thomas H. Smith, the famous tea merchant, initially as his bookkeeper. The tea store was looked on as a wonder of the city, a city block in length, located on South Street near Dover Street. Smith also had stores in Perth Amboy, Bruen's residence for some years, and here his ships landed their cargoes of tea. The failure of the firm, of which Bruen was an assignee, owing the United States government upwards of three million dollars, was not, however, disastrous for Bruen. A compromise with the creditor resulted in Bruen's making some two million dollars, from which he subsequently settled sums on the children of Thomas Smith. He had six children of his own, two of his sons becoming successful businessmen. Bruen, while en route to Buffalo in 1846, died at the Delavan House in Albany. This famous temperance hotel had been built by Edward C. Delavan (fig. 23), who may well have been known to Bruen, either through his business or as a visitor at Saratoga.

117
Benjamin Wood Richards
1797–1851
Philadelphia, May 29, 1843

Richards was born at Batso, New Jersey, where his father was the proprietor of the Batso Iron Works. He graduated from Princeton in 1815, moved to Philadelphia, and in 1821 married Sarah Ann, daughter of Joshua Lippincott. Having thus "married the boss's daughter," in 1822 he became a partner in the house of J. & W. Lippincott, commission merchants, an association which lasted thirty years. He was mayor of Philadelphia from 1829 to 1832 when he was succeeded by John Swift (fig. 226). President of the Blind Asylum, member of the American Philosophical Society, trustee of the University of Pennsylvania, President Jackson appointed him a director of the United States Bank, and of the Mint. It was during his one term in the state legislature in 1827 that he procured the first appropriation of state funds for the establishment of public schools in Philadelphia, a fact which prompted Simpson in his *Lives of Eminent Philadelphians* to record that the popular periodicals of the day remarked that "thousands and thousands yet unborn will bless the name of Richards."

42½.

B.W. Richards Philad^a.
Mayor of the City 29 to 1832.   May 29. 1843

M. Bruen of New Jersey
Saratoga 23 Augt 1844.

Bⁿ W. Richards Mayor of the City of Phil^a.
1829 to 1832.
Philadelphia 29th May 1843.

118
Samuel Rossiter Betts 1786–1868
Saratoga, August 25, 1843

The confrontation of Judge Betts with Chancellor Walworth, as shown by Edouart, was surely a meeting of old friends. Each was at the height of his career, and though their profiles were cut at different dates they must often have met as we now see them.

Betts, born in Richmond, Massachusetts, a graduate of Williams College in 1806, studied law in Hudson, New York, and was admitted to practice in 1809. The War of 1812 cut short for a time his practice just beginning in Monticello, for he enlisted in the army and after a short time was appointed judge advocate by Governor Tompkins. When hostilities were ended he served a term in Congress and was for a few years a circuit judge of the New York Supreme Court. His ability and worth were recognized by President John Quincy Adams (fig. 172), and in 1826 he became a judge of the United States District Court for the Southern District of New York. Forty years on that court established for Judge Betts an enviable reputation. He was the authority of the day on admiralty law, dealing in later years with the large number of cases arising out of the Civil War, problems of prizes, blockade, neutrality, contraband, and the like. He codified the maritime laws, established new and practical procedures, and his *Admiralty Practice*, published in 1838, was a valuable contribution to his profession. He died in New Haven, Connecticut.

119
Reuben Hyde Walworth
1788–1867
Saratoga, August 29, 1840

Succeeding Chancellor Kent (fig. 15), Walworth became the last chancellor of New York. Born in Bozrah, Connecticut, and having worked on his father's farm in Hoosick, New York, until he was seventeen, Walworth studied law in Troy and was admitted to practice in 1809. He commenced his profession in Plattsburgh. The War of 1812 interrupted his career as it did so many others, but he gained distinction in several engagements with the enemy at Plattsburgh. He was in Congress from 1821 to 1823, when he became, as had Judge Betts, a circuit judge of the Supreme Court of New York. Then in 1828 he succeeded Kent as chancellor, a position he maintained with enthusiasm and diligence, although it has been stated that one-third of his decisions were reversed by the Court for the Correction of Errors. When President Tyler (fig. 258) proposed Walworth to fill a Supreme Court vacancy, it is reported in the *Dictionary of American Biography* that Thurlow Weed wrote that Walworth was "recommended by many distinguished members of the Bar of the State *merely because they are anxious to get rid of a querulous, disagreeable, unpopular Chancellor.*" His name was tabled. Upon retirement from office in 1848, he directed his attention away from judicial matters to genealogy, producing the monumental two-volume *Hyde Genealogy* in 1864.

His interest to us, however, is the part he played in the life of Saratoga Springs. While circuit judge of the district and later as chancellor, Walworth established at Pine Grove, his estate at Saratoga Springs, a modest courtroom by covering a wooden box with a carpet, placing upon it an arm chair and a high, long-legged desk. Here for many years counsel came to argue motions in chancery, and here was an arena in which tourists could catch a glimpse of what was called "real life drama." Among those who appeared as lawyers before this country court were O'Conor (fig. 252), Butler (fig. 43), Seward (fig. 2), and Webster (fig. 164). But Pine Grove became also a social mecca, thronged in the season by those of social or professional standing. Among such lions, those preserved in Edouart's gallery include Van Buren (fig. 230), Marcy (fig. 6), Granger (fig. 183), Kent (fig. 15), Story (fig. 16), Stone (fig. 235), Miss Sedgwick (fig. 141), Delavan (fig. 23), General Scott (fig. 120), Wool (fig. 340), President Wayland (fig. 75), and Archbishop Hughes (fig. 104). Here the mighty were entertained, and here, late in November 1867, the last chancellor died.

R Hyde Walworth Chancellor of
the State of New York
Saratoga Springs 29th August 1840

Sam R R Betts U. S. Judge
South. Dist. of N. York
Saratoga Aug 25" 1843

43.

Sam R R Betts U. S. Judge 1st Dist. N.Y.   R. Hyde Walworth Chanc.
South 25th Aug 1843   Saratoga 19th Aug 1840   H.M. Ldy

120
Winfield Scott   1786–1866
Saratoga, August 25, 1840

To detail the military exploits of General Scott would require a description of almost every battle fought by the United States Army from the time of Jefferson to that of Lincoln. Six feet five inches in height and 230 pounds in bulk, Scott was a born soldier and leader. A Virginian by birth, he attended the College of William and Mary but did not complete his course. Intending for the law, the unpleasantness between the *Leopard* and the *Chesapeake* led him to seek a commission, and as a lance corporal he saw his first action. Suspended for one year on being court-martialed for remarks about his superior General Wilkinson, he returned to serve under General Hampton, was promoted to lieutenant colonel in 1812, and was captured by the British at the battle of Queenstown in 1812. He fought the British bravely and with distinction and was awarded a gold medal for his bravery at Lundy's Lane, where he took a bullet in his shoulder, later removed by Dr. Gibson (fig. 181). He drafted the first American drill regulation, was given command in the Black Hawk War in 1832, and conducted the campaign against the Creek and Seminole Indians in Florida in 1835. His restoration of peace along the Canadian border in 1838 led Van Buren (fig. 230) to direct him to conduct some 16,000 Cherokees west, beyond the Mississippi. In 1841, on the death of General Macomb (fig. 251), Scott became Commander in chief of the United States Army, and he captured Vera Cruz during the Mexican War in 1847. In 1856 he was an unsuccessful candidate for president, being overwhelmingly defeated by Franklin Pierce.

The only nickname that was ever applied to him was "Fuss and Feathers," some of which are visible in his profile. He was bitterly disappointed not to attain the presidency, but his service to his country cannot be forgotten. He took a principal part in ending two wars and settling boundary and Indian disputes, and was the founder of America's professional army. As he was constantly on the battlefield we tend to forget that he married Maria Mayo of Richmond, Virginia, in 1817 and had seven children; but no son survived childhood. General Scott died at West Point, a fitting point of departure for a great soldier.

44.

Winfield Scott, 1840.

Genl. W. Scott —
Major Genl. of the U.S. Army
Saratoga Augt. 25 1840.

121
Robert Anderson   1805–1871
Saratoga, August 20, 1840

Anderson, a graduate of West Point in 1825, served under General Scott (fig. 120) in the Black Hawk and Florida wars, while conducting the Indians to the West, and in the siege of Vera Cruz. His great claim to be remembered is for his brave and considerate action in Charleston harbor at the outbreak of the Civil War. He successfully withdrew from Fort Moultrie to Fort Sumter and did not give up the latter until after thirty-six hours of bombardment, resulting in a complete reduction of the fort. He struck his colors and withdrew with about seventy men, with the honors of war. Failing health brought an end to his active military career, but in 1865 he was given the honor of raising again the flag over Fort Sumter, four years from the date on which he had lowered it. He published a translation from the French of *Instructions for Field Artillery* and *Evolutions of Field Batteries*, and was instrumental in organizing the Soldiers' Home in Washington.

4 4½

Robert Anderson
Asst. Adjt. Genl.

Capn. Robert Anderson. Assistant adjt. Genl. U.S.A.
Saratoga 20th August 1840.

122
Gardiner Greene Howland
1787–1851

123
Samuel Shaw Howland   1790–1853
Saratoga, August 10, 1840

Edouart correctly caught the relationship between the Howland brothers by portraying Samuel looking over his older brother's shoulder. They were born in Norwich, Connecticut, descendants of John Howland, who came to this country on the *Mayflower*. Their father moved to New York when they were young and brought them up in his business as a merchant and shipowner. By 1816 the brothers had formed the firm of G. G. & S. Howland. They bought frigates from the Greeks and, on the failure of the house of Bayard & Company, took its place in the commercial world. They carried on an active commerce with Latin America, ran packets to Venezuela and to Pacific points. They were closely involved in the New York & Harlem Railroad,

and by 1845 their wealth was in excess of half a million. In the decade from 1830 to 1840 they were reputed to have had the largest business of any firm in New York City. Walter Barrett in *The Old Merchants of New York City* (1863) describes the cargoes of the Howland ships as "everything, from a cambric needle to a hoop pole. Ironwares, bars, steel, provisions, salt, brandies—in small barrels to go on mules' backs—wines, bales of domestics, fireworks, Chinese crackers, gunpowder, muskets, lead, spelter, costly flaming crimson and scarlet crape shawls, crockery ware, and in fact a country store on a mammoth scale." Their obituary notices are said to have dwelt more on business success than upon any charitable qualities they may have possessed.

45

Yrs truly,
G.G. Howland

Saml S. Howland
of New York
Saratoga Springs
1st Aug
1840

G.G. Howland
of New York

Samuel S. Howland
Saratoga 10th Augt 1840.

124
James Mease, M.D.   1771–1846
Philadelphia, May 28, 1843

Mease received his medical degree in 1792 at the first commencement held after the Medical School of the College of Philadelphia and the University of Pennsylvania were united. He practiced in Philadelphia, but his interests spread further afield than the limits of his profession. He was a member of the Philosophical Society, the Agricultural Society and first vice-president of the Philadelphia Athenaeum. He twice had yellow fever while serving as a physician during epidemics—in the second instance, under the care of Dr. Rush, being bled to the quantity of 162 ounces; yet he was Dr. Rush's physician during his last illness. He lectured on pharmacy, had a vineyard of 3,000 plants, and because of his antiquarian interest in preserving old buildings and landmarks was called "the first American antiquarian."

The scope of his interests can be gathered from the titles of some of his published works: *Medical Lectures and Essays, Thermometrical Observations as Connected with Navigation, A Geological Account of the United States*. He married Sarah, daughter of Pierce Butler, and his sons changed their names to Butler to secure their inheritance. One of them married the actress Fanny Kemble.

James Mease M.D.
Philad. May 28. 1843.
Born 11th August 1771.

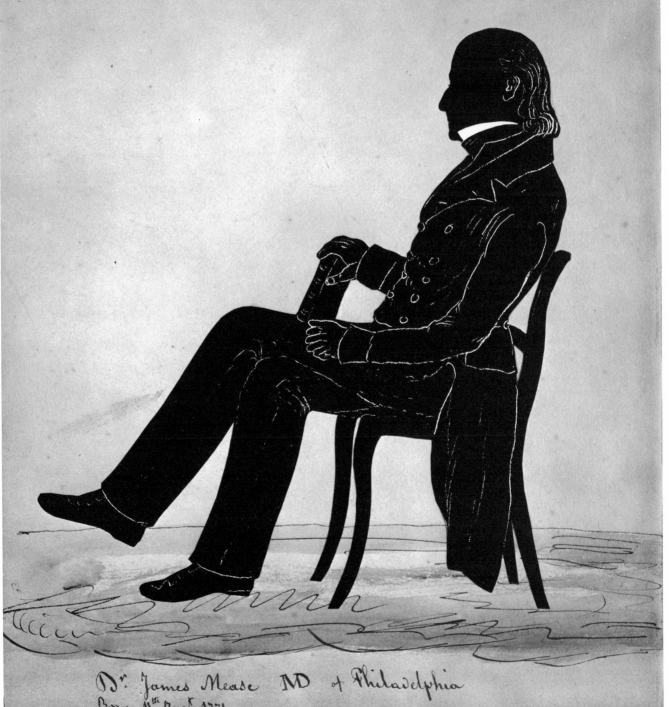

Dr. James Mease MD of Philadelphia
Born 11th Aug. 1771.

125
Silas Moore Stilwell 1800–1881
[Saratoga], August 20, 1840

Stilwell will be remembered as the author of an act bearing his name passed in New York in 1831 by which imprisonment for debt was abolished—at a time when there were three thousand persons in prison for debt, many for sums of less than one hundred dollars. Ellis Lewis (fig. 149) was engaged in the same pursuit for Pennsylvania. Stilwell's early career was checkered. As a surveyor he went to Tennessee in 1814 and was elected to the legislature. He then removed to Virginia, was admitted to the bar in 1824, and served as a member of the House of Delegates. Returning to New York in 1828, he served three terms in the assembly and was an unsuccessful candidate for lieutenant governor on Seward's ticket. He became president of the board of aldermen and was acting mayor of New York City at the time of the great fire of 1835. He was offered a cabinet post by President Harrison (fig. 233), which he declined, and then accepted from President Tyler (fig. 258) appointment as United States marshal for the Southern District of New York. During most of this period he continued his practice of the law and wrote several volumes on banking and financial topics. For many years he contributed articles to the *New York Herald* under the pen name Jonathan Oldbuck. When his wife, Caroline (daughter of the wealthy New York merchant Norsworthy), died, he turned to spiritualism, where it can be hoped he found comfort.

126
Samuel Turell Armstrong
1784–1850
Saratoga, August 23, 1844

It was Armstrong's success as a bookseller and publisher that led to his influence in public affairs. He published Buchanan's *Researches in Asia* and Scott's *Commentary on the Bible*, both of which were financial successes. He was active in the life of Boston. Twice a state representative and once a senator, he served as lieutenant governor under Levi Lincoln and John Davis (fig. 317); when Davis became a United States senator in 1835, Armstrong served as governor for the balance of his term. During his term as mayor of Boston in 1836, the Common was enclosed on three sides by an iron fence. His intention to leave his considerable fortune to charity was thwarted by his sudden and unexpected death.

It was Armstrong who as a deacon in the Old South Meeting discovered in the tower of the church John Winthrop's manuscript of the third volume of his *History of New England*—a fact which alone will long keep his name alive.

46.

Silas M. Stilwell
New York City,
Augt. 20th 1840.

James C. Armstrong
acting Govr. of Mexco. 1835

Silas M. Stilwell   Col. of the James C Armstrong
Counsellor at Law   Saratoga 23d Augt 1844.

127

John Moss   1774–1847
Philadelphia, November 5, 1842

John Moss emigrated from London at the age of
scarcely twenty and became an astute businessman
even though not educated in the tradition of
Philadelphia's sons. Glass engraver, shopkeeper,
with the assistance of his wife he succeeded in becoming a merchant owning ships in trade with
Europe and dealing in much Philadelphia real
estate. He and his brother owned residences on
Spruce Street. Prominent in city affairs, he is said
to have erected before the Water Works in Central Square a fountain of a nymph carved by
William Rush, which was afterward reproduced
in bronze in Fairmount Park. Through his efforts
copies of lions carved by Canova for the tomb of
Pope Clement XIII in St. Peter's were also later
removed to the Philadelphia Museum of Art in
Fairmount Park. His success and prominence as a
citizen of Philadelphia, without the bulwark of
formal education, made him a figure who attracted
the attention of the silhouettist, whose profile of
the sixty-eight-year-old merchant is eloquent and
convincing.

46 ½

John Moss of Philadelphia
5th Novemb. 1842.

John Moss of Philadelphia
5th Novemb. 1842.

128
Erastus Root   1773–1846
Saratoga, September 2, 1840

Though born in Hebron, Connecticut, Root graduated from Dartmouth College in 1793, studied law, was admitted to the bar, and commenced practice in Delhi, New York, a fact he communicates by describing himself beneath his signature as of Delhi. His life was that of a political lawyer and can be easily outlined in a list of the offices he held. He was several times elected to the state assembly, where he served for eleven years; he was Speaker of the House for three years, state senator for eight years, and a member of Congress for a similar period. At one point in his career he was postmaster at Delhi. In 1822 he was elected lieutenant governor though he failed in his attempt to be reelected. He was one of those who joined the opposition and effectually contested the election of John Adams to the Fourteenth Congress. One of the ablest politicians of his day, he was an ardent Democrat and a disciple of George Clinton.

47.

Your obed^t Ser^t
Erastus Reed
Delhi 2 Sept. 1840

Genl Erastus Reed ... 4 Sept. 1840.

129

John Chapman Cresson   1806–1876
Philadelphia, May 13, 1843

It fell to Frederick Fraley (fig. 130) to write for
the American Philosophical Society the obituary
notice of John Chapman Cresson, late vice-president of the society, from which we learn of his
life. As a Philadelphian he was educated at
Friends' Academy and at the University of Pennsylvania. His first significant step on the ladder
of opportunity was when in 1836 he was made
superintendent and engineer of the Philadelphia
gas works, which important and highly responsible position he held for twenty-eight years. After
filling the chair of mechanics and natural philosophy in the Franklin Institute for thirteen years,
he became president of the institute, a post he
served in until 1863. He was vice-president of the
Pennsylvania Institute for the Blind, trustee of
the University of Pennsylvania, vice-president of
the Philosophical Society, a commissioner and
chief engineer of Fairmount Park and president
of the Mine Hill and Schuylkill Haven Railroad.
These are examples of the usefulness to his community of this valued inhabitant of the city, who
was understandably much beloved by his contemporaries.

130

Frederick Fraley   1804–1901
Philadelphia, May 13, 1843

It was not without forethought that Edouart
posed Fraley and Cresson together in friendly
converse. They were old trusted and tried friends,
and brothers-in-law, Fraley having married Cresson's sister.

Fraley's career was one that almost touched
three centuries. Born in the last year of Jefferson's
first administration, he survived to see Theodore
Roosevelt succeed to the presidency. His term of
service to the institutions he served so faithfully
during his long life must be reckoned by decades.
For sixty-eight years he was a member of the
Board of Trade and for fourteen its president. He
served as a trustee of the University of Philadelphia for forty-eight years; and, as a founder of the
Franklin Institute, he was for seventy-seven years
an active member. He was a member of the Common Council of Philadelphia, a senator for a term
at Harrisburg, president of the Schuylkill Navigation Company, director of Girard College; no post
of usefulness to his city was ever turned down.
As a leading member of the Philosophical Society,
of which he was president from 1880 until his
death, he served, in 1843, on the Committee of
Arrangements for the Centennial Celebration of
the Society, and, almost unbelievably, in 1893 he
presided at the 150th anniversary of the founding
of the Society. He lived through dramatic times
and after ninety-seven years died in the "un-
impaired enjoyment of his mental faculties,"
mourned by all who were privileged to know him.

J. C. Cresson Prof. Nat. Phil.
May 13 1843

F. Fraley. Prest.
Am. Fire Ins. Compy.
Philada. May 13. 1843.
Member Senate Penna.
1840
Philadelphia 13th May 1840

J. C. Cresson Professor of Natl. Philosophy
Philada. 13th. May 1843. Franklin Institute

Frederick Fraley Senator of Penna. 1840
Secretary of American fire Insce. Co.
Philadelphia 13th. May 1843.

131
Gardiner Spring, D.D.   1785–1873
Saratoga, August 1840

Dexter's *Biographical Sketches of the Graduates
of Yale College* gives us a review of Dr. Spring's
life, which, after he settled down, was single pur-
posed. Born in Newburyport, Massachusetts, he
graduated at Yale College in 1805 and practiced
law until 1809 when the spirit moved him to enter
the ministry. For eight months he studied at Andover Theological Seminary and in 1810 was ordained and installed in the Brick Presbyterian
Church in New York, for a few months as colleague of the aged John Rogers. This charge became his life's work, and for sixty-three years he
devoted himself to his ministry, declining offers
of the presidency of Hamilton and Dartmouth
colleges. His flock grew, he wrote volumes of
theology, supported the Union during the war
and was influential in effecting the union of the
two branches of the Presbyterian church. His
works were published in ten volumes. By his first
wife, Susan Barney of New Haven, he had seven
sons and eight daughters.

He was surely one of those we would expect to
have visited Saratoga, for by 1840 he had been
pastor of the Brick Church for thirty years, and
Edouart catches him either reading his book of
worship or, perhaps, as though preaching in the
old church on Beekman Street.

48.

Gardiner Spring
Aug: 1840
Brick Presbyn Church
New York.

Revd Dr Gardiner Spring. Brick Presbterian Church New York
Saratoga New York Aug 1840

132
John Benge
Washington City, April 24, 1841

Edouart had a knack for selecting prominent people whose profiles he might preserve. In the fall and early winter of 1838 the Cherokee Nation left their homeland in Tennessee for settlement in Oklahoma. After a final Council at Rattlesnake Springs, Tennessee, the first detachment of 1,103 Cherokees left on October 1, 1838, under the eagle eye and convoy of Winfield Scott (fig. 120). One of the principal officers of this group was John Benge, a descendant of the red-haired chief Berch, who had fought for Cherokee freedom almost fifty years before. The journey was a severe one, requiring crossing the Cumberland Mountains under harsh and unfavorable weather conditions. Benge, who was the son of a trader of the same name who had married a Cherokee woman despite his having a wife in the settlements, obtained a reputation for his efforts in the resettlement and with the title of captain was a delegate of the Cherokee Nation in Washington in 1841. It is unlikely that his name appearing to the left above his silhouette is his signature. More likely the abbreviated notation to the right represents his writing, the *Ch* standing for Cherokee, the other characters being more cryptic.

48½

Capt John Benge
    of the Cherokee Delegation
Washington City 24th Apl 1841.

Ch ftr

Capt John Benge of the Cherokee de
Washington City 24th April 1841.

133
John Ross   1790–1866
Washington City, April 22, 1841

John Ross, whose name as chief of the Cherokee
Nation was Kooweskowe, was the son of a Loyalist Scotsman and a woman who was a Scot but
one-fourth Cherokee. He grew up in Tennessee
and in 1809 was a member of a mission to the
Cherokee Nation, which at the time had removed
to Arkansas. In 1812 he fought in the battle of
Horseshoe Bend against the Creeks, and by 1817
was a member of the national council of the Cherokee. He helped draft their constitution of 1827
and was principal chief of the nation from 1828
to 1839. He opposed their removal westward, but
in 1838–39 led them to their new home, uniting
the eastern and western tribes under one government of which he was chief from 1839 until his
death. He tried to keep his people out of the
Civil War, but for a while was allied with the
Confederacy. He married first a full-blooded
Cherokee and after her death a white woman,
Mary Bryan Staples, a Quaker of Wilmington,
Delaware, who died in 1865. He died in Washington while on a mission to arrange the Cherokee
treaty of 1866. There is no doubt that he earned
the respect and confidence of the Cherokee Nation. Pasted into Edouart's book of silhouettes,
alongside that of Ross peering over his tribal empire, is a clipping from an unidentified newspaper,
dated September 1843, describing the hostilities
between the Cherokees and Osages and adding,
"John Ross, we understand, keeps a daily body
guard of from one to two hundred armed Cherokees about him."

49.

Jn̄ Ross Principal Chief of the Cherokee Nation
Park Hill C. N. West. Washington City Apl 22d 1841.

John Ross Principal Chief of the Cherokee Nation Park Hill
Washington City 22d April 1841. E. W. West

134
David Varn   d.1843
Washington City, June 17, 1841

Varn, according to what appears after what may well be his signature (it is not Edouart's hand), was treasurer of the Cherokee Nation and was the third prominent Cherokee whose likeness Edouart took in the spring of 1841. According to the newspaper clipping pasted into Edouart's book, Varn "died at his residence at the Saline on the 2d ult., of wounds inflicted upon him by a lawless mob" on the eighth of August. Underneath the clipping in Edouart's hand is written "2d. Septber. 1843," probably intended as the date of death rather than the date of the newspaper. Further history of Varn has escaped us.

135
G. F. Morris
Washington City, June 17, 1843

Washington during the early 1840s was constantly visited by Indian chiefs and officers seeking settlement of their many claims and voicing their objections to mass immigrations. Morris was undoubtedly one of them. He describes himself, and it is repeated by Edouart, as from North Carolina, Cherokee County. The Cherokee had long held lands in North Carolina and as early as 1833 Ross (fig. 133) had been in negotiations with the government in relation to the proposed acquisition of those lands. The part, if any, played in that controversy by Morris is not known. It was during these years that Charles Bird King, the well-known Newport and Washington artist, painted so many of his portraits of Indian chiefs who then crowded into Washington.

49½

David Varen Treasurer of the
Cherokee Nation Washington City
17th June 1841

G. F. Morris N.C. cherokee county

2d Septber 1843.

David Varen Treasurer of the Cherokee Nation   G. F. Morris N.C. cherokee county
Washington City 17th June 1841.   Washington City 17th June 1843

136
Willis Hall   1801–1868
Saratoga Springs, August 19, [1840]

A graduate at Yale in 1824, admitted to the bar
in 1827, Hall practiced law in Alabama for four
years and in New York from 1831 to 1838. Then,
after a year in the assembly, he was appointed attorney general of the state of New York, a position
he was able to hold for only one year, during the
success of the Whig party. For some years he lectured on law at Saratoga, where Edouart caught
him and where he was one of the interesting per-
sonalities of the resort. He was elected for one
more term to the assembly, but poor health forced
his early retirement. He was opposed to the nomination of General Taylor for the presidency,
being a Clay supporter, and retired from public
life. The high point of his career was his becoming attorney general, and this he remembered and
recorded after his signature though he had only
held the office for a short time.

137
Laura Dewey Bridgman   1829–1889
Boston, June 29, 1843

Look carefully at Edouart's touching profile of this fourteen-year-old girl, dressed for her age, long pigtails and holding her sewing in her hand. She was by then deaf, dumb, and blind, destitute of the sense of smell and nearly so of that of taste. Her contact with the world was her sense of touch. Born in Hanover, New Hampshire, at the age of two scarlet fever deprived her of sight and hearing. In her early youth her mother taught her what she could about the house she lived in, and how to knit and sew. By a stroke of fortune, in 1837 her condition came to the notice of Dr. Samuel Gridley Howe, husband of Julia Ward Howe, who was superintendent of the Perkins Institution for the Blind, founded by Thomas Handasyd Perkins (fig. 220). Through Howe's patience, perseverance and imagination, she learned the names of familiar objects by means of raised letters and gradually learned not only a manual alphabet but one formed by the raised letters. By degrees, over the years, she learned arithmetic, gained some understanding of geography, and developed a religious sense, finally joining the Baptist church to which her family belonged. In 1852 she returned home from the institution but after a short time became homesick for the routine of her life there and went back. There she spent the rest of her life in peace and happiness, making regular annual visits to her parents as long as possible. She could cook and sew and joined in teaching the children at the institution as she had been taught herself. Charles Dickens in his *American Notes* mentions how impressed he was with her knowledge and ability. It may well be that with the advanced methods in use in modern times she could have been taught to speak. Her writing was quite legible.

What was accomplished with Laura was one of the marvels of the day, the credit going not only to her own gentle and inquiring nature but especially to Dr. Howe. In his will he made provision for her which took care of her for the rest of her life. Her journal and letters are preserved at the Perkins School, and several biographies of her have been written. In Edouart's volume are four double-column pages from the *New World*, the date not shown, giving a detailed account of Laura's early life.

Sydney Smith is reported to have acknowledged Dr. Howe to be a "second Prometheus" and at his memorial service in 1876 Laura was understandably looked on as the "silent orator" on the occasion. Photographs of her show her wearing glasses, probably to conceal her sightless eyes.

Laura Bridgman

South Boston 2. July 1842

Laura Bridgman Born in Hanover New Hampshire on the 21st Decemb. 1829.
Blind, deaf and and dumb, destitute of smell and nearly so of taste,
Taken in the Perkins institution for Blind at Boston 29th June 1843.

138
George S. Gibson 1800–1872
Saratoga, July 13, 1844

Though Dr. Gibson's silhouette was taken later than that of the bulky mayor of Baltimore, they undoubtedly knew each other, and it was natural for Edouart to pair them together. Gibson, born in Virginia, was educated in England and Holland, returning to America in 1818 or 1819, where he became a pupil of Dr. Macouley. He graduated at the University of Maryland in 1823 and succeeded to Dr. Macouley's practice. During his forty years of practice in Baltimore he held many active positions in his profession. He became a member of the medical and chirurgical faculty of the university in 1829 and was treasurer in 1836. For a time he was attending physician at the Maryland Hospital for the Insane. He retired in 1862 and died in Baltimore.

139
Solomon Hillen, Jr. 1810–1873
Saratoga, August 16, 1843

Mayor Hillen was clearly a man of ability. In 1843 when his imposing profile was cut by Edouart, he was only thirty-three years old, yet in the middle of his term as mayor of Baltimore. He was born in Baltimore on the Hillen family estate and was able to graduate at Georgetown College in 1827. He chose the law as his profession, was admitted to the bar, and practiced in Baltimore. He was state representative for a term ending in 1838, whereupon he was elected a member of Congress, where he served until 1841. He was a young and vigorous politician, and no sooner did he retire from Congress than he succeeded in becoming mayor of Baltimore, a position he held from 1842 to 1845. Thereafter he resumed his law practice until his retirement. He died in New York City but was buried in Greenmount Cemetery, Baltimore.

George S. Gibson MD.
Baltimore
Saratoga
13th July 1844.

Sol. Hillen Jr.
Mayor of the
Aug 16th 1843. Baltimore

51.

Geo Gibson MD Balti
Saratoga

Sol. Hillen Junr Mayor of Baltimore
Saratoga 16th Augt 1843.

140
Sarah Josepha Buell Hale
1788–1879
Philadelphia, October 17, 1842

When Sarah Hale sat to the silhouettist in 1842, her career as an author, editor, and feminist was firmly established. Widowed at the age of thirty-four, with five children, she turned to writing for support. Her husband's Masonic friends helped her publish her first book, *The Genius of Oblivion*, a volume of verse, in 1823, but it was her two-volume novel *Northwood: A Tale of New England*, which appeared in 1827, that made her widely known. The Reverend John L. Blake, the principal of Boston's Cornhill School for Young Ladies, was impressed by her work and offered her the editorship of his proposed new women's magazine to be called *Ladies Magazine*. She accepted and in 1828 moved from Newport, New Hampshire, to Boston, where she remained thirteen years.

She was born in Newport, New Hampshire, the daughter of Captain Gordon Buell, a Revolutionary officer. Her early youth was marked by misfortune, her father failing in business and her mother and sister dying, all within two years. Then she married a young and able lawyer, David Hale and enjoyed eleven years of happy home life, completing her education with her husband's help, reading aloud with him every evening. In later years she credited all of her literary and editorial success to her husband's patient devotion to her education. Her aim was the improvement of women, in manners, dress, and education, and her articles and books often remind us of the modern books of etiquette, or home and housekeeping journals. But Sarah was public spirited, too. She was instrumental in developing a women's group who raised the last $50,000 required to complete the Bunker Hill Monument. As a result of her long campaign, Lincoln finally established Thanksgiving Day as a national holiday.

Her great opportunity came in 1837 when the Philadelphian Louis Antoine Godey, editor of *Lady's Book*, which he had founded in 1830, determined to persuade Sarah Hale to join his publication as editor. To further his purpose he bought *Ladies Magazine*, combined it with *Lady's Book*, and induced Sarah to become its editor. She agreed but did not leave Boston for Philadelphia until 1841 after the graduation of one of her sons from Harvard. She remained as editor of *Godey's Lady's Book* until 1877. During the years *Godey's* columns included such authors as Poe, Irving, Lowell, Longfellow, Emerson, and Bryant. Her best-known work is her *Woman's Record*, which was published in 1850 and contained biographical sketches of over two thousand women. While she published or edited upwards of sixty books, the titles of a few will serve to illustrate her field of interests: *Traits of American Life, Complete Housewife, New Household Receipt Book, The Bible Reading-Book, The Letters of Lady Mary Wortley Montague*, and innumerable novels, gift annuals, books of poetry, one including "Mary Had a Little Lamb." In all her ninety-one years she was scarcely ever without active literary employment and easily earned her place in *Notable American Women*. Her forty years' association with Godey was marked with friendship and productivity, and *Godey's Lady's Book* under her editorship acquired the largest circulation of any American magazine of its time. She died in Philadelphia, "serene in the consciousness," as stated in her sketch in the *Dictionary of American Biography*, "that she had labored faithfully to elevate her country-women by providing for them in her periodical 'a beacon-light of refined taste, pure morals, and practical wisdom.'"

5 1/2.

Sarah Josepha Hale
Philadelphia
Oct. 22. 1842 -

Mrs Sarah, Josepha Hale   Author of "Northwood Flora's interpreter," - Ladies Wreath -
Philadelphia 17th Octob. 1842.   the Good House Keeper &c.&c. and Editor of the Lady's Book,

141
Catherine Maria Sedgwick
1789–1867
Saratoga Springs, August 16, 1842

Miss Sedgwick's first book, *A New-England Tale*, was published anonymously in 1822 and attained immediate success. Following it with *Redwood* in 1824 and *Hope Leslie* in 1827, she established her reputation and popularity in the literary world and for the next thirty years produced innumerable articles and books, many still remembered today, *The Linwoods; or, Sixty Years Since in America*, *The Poor Rich Man and the Rich Poor Man*, *Letters from Abroad to Kindred at Home*, written after her return from a trip to Europe, and, of course, her last novel, *Married or Single*, designed to take the sting out of the term *old maid*.

She was born in Stockbridge, Massachusetts, daughter of Theodore Sedgwick, and grew up in well-to-do educated surroundings. She became a staunch Unitarian and was a disciple of William Ellery Channing (fig. 237). She lived at various times in Albany and New York City, but finally made her home in Stockbridge, while her brother lived in Lenox, thereby making the Berkshires the center of the social and cultural life of western Massachusetts. Though in all her writings she sought to develop the moral and social advancement of her public and championed social reform, her only notable public activity was as the founder in New York of the Woman's Prison Association. She was unquestionably the most popular woman writer before Harriet Beecher Stowe. Edouart shows her, as she must often have appeared, with pen and paper in hand, just after the publication of her *Letters from Abroad*.

C. M. Sedgwick.
Stockbridge.
16th August
'42

Miss Catherine Maria Sedgwick of Stockbridge (Saratoga Springs 16th Augt. 1842.

142
Lydia Maria Francis Child
1802–1880
New York, July 20, 1841

Author, reformer, and abolitionist, Lydia Francis was born in Medford, Massachusetts, where she attended Miss Swan's Seminary and profited from the advice and help of her brother Convers, a Harvard man, later professor in the Harvard Divinity School. After a few years teaching school, she lived with her brother and his wife in Watertown, where she wrote her first novel, *Hobomok*, an Indian and white woman love story, taught school, and continued to write. Her tales were well received; she won access to the Boston Athenaeum and Boston's literary circles. Marrying David Lee Child in 1828 marked a turning point in her career. He was improvident but an ardent reformer, and to his interests she joined her own, often supporting him by her writings, *The American Frugal Housewife*, *The Mother's Book*, and the like. Inspired by William Lloyd Garrison, she joined the antislavery movement and published *An Appeal in Favor of That Class of Americans Called Africans*, which became an influential abolitionist work. Athough its unpopularity in other circles discouraged the sale of her more popular books, the work attracted the attention of Dr. Channing (fig. 237). She became editor of the *National Anti-Slavery Standard* in New York for several years and then returned to Wayland, Massachusetts, where she spent the rest of her life. She offered to nurse John Brown while he was a prisoner at Harpers Ferry. Brown countered with the request that she help his family, which she did. Governor Wise and Mrs. J. C. Mason, wife of the author of the 1850 fugitive slave law, rebuked her, the governor courteously, Mrs. Mason by threatening her, however impotently, with damnation.

Her numerous works, novels, and articles on serious and sentimental subjects established her firm reputation as one of the leading female authors of her day. She and Sarah Child and Catherine Sedgwick were certainly the outstanding literary members of their sex in the mid-nineteenth century. A volume of her letters was published posthumously with an introduction by Whittier and an appendix by Wendell Phillips.

Upon receipt of her counterpart of her silhouette from Edouart, she wrote to him thanking him for his "beautiful shadow of an insignificant subject" framed and mounted "with such laborious care and tastefulness," adding, "Really your shadows are almost alive." Edouart preserved the letter in his volume.

52.

L. Maria Child. Feb. 11. 1802.
New York, July. 1841

Mrs Lydia Maria Child
New Yk 20th July 1841

Mrs Lydia Maria Child
New Yk 20th July 1841

143
William H. Maxwell
Saratoga, August 25, [1840?]

It is not entirely clear who this silhouette portrays. We have found no William H. Maxwell, but there was a Hugh Maxwell whose activity and attainments could well have drawn him to Saratoga and recommended him to Edouart. Hugh Maxwell was a Scotsman by birth, born in 1787; he died in 1873 in New York. After graduating at Columbia College in 1808 he was admitted to practice in New York and in 1814 was appointed assistant judge advocate general of the United States Army. Elected district attorney of New York County in 1819, he served for twenty years. In this capacity he gained considerable renown in the Barker and Eckford conspiracy trials. It was not long after his victory in these trials that we would expect to see him at Saratoga basking in his success. He returned to private practice in 1839, where he was a leader of the bar, and in 1849 was appointed collector of the port by President Taylor, a post he held during two administrations. At his death he was the oldest member of the Saint Andrew's Society. But was Hugh Maxwell the "Wm. H. Maxwell" we see in Edouart's shadow?

Wm H Maxwell

53.

Wm H. Maxwell Counsr at Law
of New York

144
James Ewing Cooley   b.1802
Saratoga Springs, August 2, 1842

Cooley, the head of the well-known book auction
firms of Cooley, Kesse & Hill and Cooley & Bangs,
appears in Saratoga Springs in the first flush of
success following the publication of his *Americans
in Egypt*, reviewed in the *New World* of New
York on August 6, 1842. It is termed "a magnificent octavo of 600 pages, and containing 100 illustrations . . . most beautifully printed and handsomely got up by the house of Appleton & Co. of
this City." Cooley had married the sister of William H. Appleton, which might account for the
choice of publishers. The review continues: "It
commences with the author's voyage from Athens
to Alexandria, and closes with his preparations
to set out for Cairo to visit the Holy Land. . . .
The book is one of the most amusing and entertaining that we have had in our hands for a very
long time, and we predict for it a large sale,
through numerous editions." David H. Finnie in
*Pioneers East, the Early American Experience in
the Middle East* (1967) says of Cooley's book that
it was "a very successful book," but that it was
"pretty awful" and had been described as the
"first of the 'funny school' of American travel-
writing, a vein which Mark Twain exploited
so successfully a generation later in *Innocents
Abroad*."

Cooley later became a state senator, then moved
to Florence, Italy, where he lived for some years
until his death.

53.½.

J. E. Cooley
Saratoga Springs Aug.t 2d 1842

James E. Cooley, Author of the American in Egypte

Saratoga Springs 2d Aug.t 1842.

145
George Pope Morris   1802–1864
Saratoga Springs, August 2, 1842

General Morris, or "the Brigadier," as he was often called, acquired his title from his services in the New York State Militia. By profession he was a journalist, author, and poet. He was born in Philadelphia, worked in a printing office, and as a youth of fifteen moved to New York and started his literary career by contributing articles to the *New York Gazette* and the *American*. He established the *New York Mirror* in 1823 and soon became associated with Nathaniel P. Willis. In 1842 the old *Mirror* was discontinued, and he and Willis formed the *New Mirror* and then the *Evening Mirror*. Late in 1845 he was the founder of the *National Press*, which became the *Home Journal* a year later and which with Mr. Willis he edited for the rest of his life. His books include a volume of prose sketches, *The Little Frenchman and His Water Lots* (1839), *Briarcliff* (1825), and the libretto of Charles E. Horn's opera *The Maid of Saxony*.

But it is as a song writer, perhaps in his time America's greatest song writer, that he will be remembered and he attained wide popularity. Who does not recall "Woodman, Spare That Tree" and "Near the Lake," said by Poe to be a composition of which any poet might be proud. It has been many times repeated that a member of the House of Commons in a speech favoring protection quoted from "Woodman, Spare That Tree," the allusion being that the tree was the British Constitution and Sir Robert Peel the woodman about to cut it down.

In an article on Morris in the April 1845 issue of Philadelphia's *Graham's Magazine*, his friend Willis wrote: "Morris is the best known poet of the country by acclamation not by criticism. . . . Morris's ear is at the level of most other people's and his poetry flows out by that door. . . . As to the man—Morris my friend—I can hardly venture to 'burn incense on his moustache,' as the French say—write his praise under his very nose —but, as far off as Philadelphia, you may pay the proper tribute to his loyal nature and manly excellences." Recalling some of the sentimental verses so popular in that age it is perhaps appropriate to quote the opening lines of Morris's popular "My Mother's Bible":

> This book is all that's left me now!—
> Tears will unbidden start—
> With faltering lip and throbbing brow,
> I press it to my heart.
> For many generations past,
> Here is our family tree;
> My mother's hands this Bible clasp'd;
> She, dying, gave it me.

Geo. P. Morris.
Saratoga Springs
Augt. 2d. 1842.

General Geo. P. Morris — Editor of N. Y. k Mirror
taken in Saratoga Springs 2d. Augt. 1842.

146
George Thompson
Philadelphia, April 29, 1843

Thompson, whose profile reveals the strength of
character required for his position, signs himself
"Warden" of the "Eastern State Penitentiary,"
which was in Philadelphia and which had been
authorized by the legislature and constructed in
1821 as the State Penitentiary for the Eastern District of Pennsylvania. Alfred Trumble's *In Jail
with Charles Dickens* (1896) gives an interesting
and revealing glimpse of Dickens's experience at
the penitentiary, his reactions to the inmates he
saw, and the factual details of their lives and
crimes before and after Dickens's visit. His re-
action was more sentimental than thoughtful,
and Trumble leads us to believe that all in all
the Eastern State Penitentiary, at about the time
Thompson was warden, was a well-run and hu-
mane institution. Richard Vaux (fig. 173), who
was president of the board of inspectors and must
have been well acquainted with Thompson, compiled a history of the institution from its early
days. Details of Thompson himself have proven
elusive.

54½

George Thompson. Warden of the
Eastern State Penetentiary of Penn
Philadelphia Apl 29th 1843.

147
Henry Clay 1776–1852
Washington, March 10, 1841

Here stands Henry Clay, whose profile is so familiar and who needs little introduction to any student of American history. He was twice elected to the Kentucky legislature and for fourteen years was Speaker of the House of Representatives of the United States with the record of not having had one decision reversed. Carl Schurz wrote in his biography of him that he was the "greatest of the speakers." He was United States senator on four occasions, declined more offices of distinction than most mortals ever attain to: that of minister to Russia under Madison, secretary of war and minister to England under Monroe, and secretary of state under Harrison (fig. 233). He survived three duels and was thrice an unsuccessful candidate for the presidency: in 1824 when John Quincy Adams (fig. 172) was elected and chose him as his secretary of state, in 1832 when Jackson won the election, and in 1844 when Polk was successful. On his leaving the office of secretary of state the day before Jackson's inauguration, it was said of Clay that during his term as secretary more treaties between the United States and foreign nations had been signed than during all the preceding years under the constitution.

We see him standing here to Edouart, less than a week after Harrison's inauguration, scarcely three weeks before Harrison's death, having just declined the office of secretary of state and yet, at the moment, the acknowledged leader of the Whig party. He appears as though in the midst of the delivery of what he thought was his last farewell to the Senate, under the administration of President Tyler (fig. 258). Edouart inserted in his volume a copy of the farewell address, which concluded:

And now in retiring as I am about to do from the Senate, I beg leave to deposit with it my fervent wishes, that all the great and patriotic objects for which it was instituted, may be accomplished—that the destiny designed for it by the framers of the Constitution may be fulfilled—that the deliberations now and hereafter, in which it may engage for the good of our common country may eventuate in the restoration of its prosperity, and in the preservation and maintenance of her honor abroad, and her best interests at home. . . . May the blessings of Heaven rest upon the heads of the whole Senate and every member of it; and may every member of it advance still more in fame, and when they shall retire to the bosom of their respective constituencies, may they all meet there that most joyous and grateful of all human rewards, the exclamation of their countrymen, "well done, thou good and faithful servant."

55.

H. Clay of Ashland.

Hon.ble Henry Clay of Ashland K.Y
Senator of Kentucky
Washington 10th March 1841.

148
Joseph Marion Hernandez
1793–1857
Washington, April 13, 1841

Born in St. Augustine, a citizen of Spain, Hernandez became an American citizen upon the organization of Florida as a United States territory in 1822. As a former prominent Spanish citizen, he became the first delegate to Congress from the new territory in September 1822. He was soon to become the presiding officer of the territorial house of representatives. At the outbreak of the war against the Florida Indians he became brigadier general of the Volunteers, then entered the service of the United States and was in command of the expedition which in 1837 captured the Indian chief Osceola. This secured his appointment as brigadier general of the Mounted Volunteers where he rendered distinguished service in the trouble with the Indians near Mosquito Inlet. After an unsuccessful attempt to obtain a seat in the Senate in 1845 as a Whig candidate, he moved to Cuba and was engaged as a sugar planter until his death near Matanzas, where he was buried. Edouart apparently caught him in Washington during his military career, when he could sign himself "Brigr. Genl. F. M. [Florida Militia]," not long before his attempt to obtain a seat in the Senate.

55½.

Brigadier Genl. Joseph M. Hernandes.
Florida Militia. Washington 13th April 1841.

149
Ellis Lewis 1798–1871
Saratoga, August 15, 1843

As a member of the Pennsylvania legislature in 1831, Ellis succeeded in doing for Pennsylvania what Stilwell (fig. 125) had done that same year for New York, procuring passage of a bill eliminating imprisonment for debt and thereby abolishing the debtor's prison. Ellis's career began as a printer, apprenticed to John Wyeth of Harrisburg, but all the while he studied law and in 1822 was admitted to practice. Full of ambition, an active Democrat, he became deputy attorney general and in 1833 attorney general of the state. His temperament and ability were recognized, and before long he was appointed by Governor Porter (fig. 163) president judge of the Eighth Judicial District, then in due course was elevated to the supreme bench of the state and ultimately became its chief justice. He served with such distinction that at the end of his term he was renominated. He declined the honor, however, and retired to private life. He was the author of an *Abridgment of the Criminal Law of the United States*, published in 1848. His most prominent decision as judge, and one noted by Edouart on the page opposite his silhouette, was that delivered in *Commonwealth* v. *Armstrong*, in which he held against clerical interference with a parent's right to direct the education of his children. He received an LL.D. from both Jefferson College and Transylvania University and, because of his familiarity with medical jurisprudence, an honorary M.D. from the Philadelphia College of Medicine.

150
John Allen Collier 1789–1873
Saratoga Springs, August 20, 1840

Collier was one of the distinguished products of the first law school in the United States, Tapping Reeve's law school at Litchfield, Connecticut, where he studied after graduating from Yale with honors in 1803. He early moved to Binghamton, New York, where he became its leading citizen, married three times, raised a family, and carried on a successful career as a lawyer. He became the first district attorney of Broome County in 1818 and subsequently served in the Congress as a representative from New York for two years. He controlled a large share of the legal business in Binghamton, acquired a fortune and the devotion of his fellow citizens. Not long after he stood to Edouart in prosperous profile, he became comptroller of the state of New York. In a letter to his family written some time before his death and quoted in the *Biographical Review . . . the Leading Citizens of Broome County, New York* in 1894, he wrote modestly but gratefully: "Having received the unbought honors of the world with abundant personal comforts, never knowing hunger or want, holding a high rank in my profession, enjoying a long life of perfect health, possessed of a reasonable share of this world's goods, have I not great and abundant cause for thanksgiving in being as much blessed and favored above the average of my fellowmen?"

56

John A. Collier

Ellis Lewis
President Judge of August 20, 1840
2d Judicial District Co. Penna.
Saratoga Aug 15th 1843.

Ellis Lewis President Judge   John A. Collier Counsellor at Law
of 2d Judicial Dist & late Attorney   Saratoga Springs 10th July 1840.
Genl of Penna. Saratoga Aug 15th 1843

151
Samuel Norris 1796–1866
Philadelphia, April 22, 1843

Caught in a casual pose talking with a Philadelphia friend, Norris, newly elected president of the Common Council of Philadelphia, makes a fine figure. He held the post for at least two years. He is said to have attended the University of Pennsylvania and to have withdrawn to enter the counting house of Joseph Lewis. Norris was director of the Athenaeum of Philadelphia in 1828, president of the board of directors from 1863 to 1865, and a member of the committee on building the hall in 1845.

Edouart was busy in Philadelphia at this moment, having within a few days cut likenesses of the governor (fig. 163), the mayor (fig. 226), the recorder (fig. 173), the high sheriff (fig. 162), and Commodore Barron (fig. 34), to name a few. We can only wish we knew as much about City Council President Norris as we feel sure Senator Fox did as he stood beside him that spring day.

152
Joseph Mickle Fox 1779–1845
Philadelphia, April 22, 1843

Lawyer and landowner are two words that describe Senator Fox, whose life was active and honorable but not marked by any great events. For the curious it can be noted that he was the first person to introduce coffee to the district of Foxburg, where his lands were situated. As the eldest of thirteen children, he bought from the trustees under his father's will something in excess of 13,000 acres of land in Clarion County, for which he is said to have paid $11,400. In 1820, when he was practicing law in Bellefonte, Centre County, Pennsylvania, he married Hannah Emlen. Several years later he moved to his lands at the junction of the Allegheny and Clarion rivers, where the town of Foxburg was later established. At that time the land was occupied largely by Pennsylvania Dutch farmers, with the nearest post office sixteen miles distant. In later years a post office was established on Fox's own land, and he served as postmaster. For part of a term he served as state senator to fill a vacancy.

He had only one child, a son, Samuel, who lived on the family lands during the summer, but occupied the old family mansion in Philadelphia the rest of the year. Sidney G. Fisher, the Philadelphia diarist, notes that his niece Mary married young Samuel Fox a few years after his father's death; that at the time Samuel was worth about $60,000 and his widowed mother $50,000, and that sixty or seventy persons were at the wedding.

Saml Norris.
April 22d. 1843.

Jos: M. Fox
22 April 1843

Samuel Norris Presidt. of City Council
Philadelphia 22d. April 1843.

Jos. M. Fox Counsellor at Law
Philada. 22d. Ap. 1843. and Senator of Pennsylva State
in 1829

153
Samuel Jarvis Peters   1801–1855
New Orleans, August 19, 1840–February 7, 1844

There appears to be confusion as to the date of Peters's silhouette, but it must have been in 1844 that the shade was cut. Edouart was active in Saratoga during the month of August 1840, and equally active in New Orleans in February 1844, e.g., Chinn (fig. 325), Johnson (fig. 320). The 1844 date is Edouart's; the 1840 is Peters's, but its significance is obscure.

Peters, a Canadian by birth, settled in New Orleans at the age of twenty. With imagination, energy, and ambition he became a leading figure of New Orleans and is remembered as "the father of the public school system." Paved streets, well-surfaced side walks, and safely designed levees occupied his attention. With James Caldwell he developed New Orleans and built the St. Charles Hotel and the Merchants' Exchange. But it is for his influence in establishing the public school system, and especially for the Samuel J. Peters Junior High School, that his name will survive in New Orleans history.

He was president of the Chamber of Commerce, and though his friends hoped he could obtain a post in President Taylor's cabinet, all he received was the position of collector of the port.

Saml. J. Peters
New Orleans.
Aug 19. 1840.

57.

Saml. J. Peters
N. Orleans Feb 7th 1844—

154
George W. Jones
Philadelphia, April 20, 1843

The president of the Guardians of the Poor of Philadelphia and Districts resided in 1843 at 40 Almond Street. He was a merchant and broker, and his store was at Second and Chestnut streets. We can guess from his profile that in 1843 he was a middle-aged gentleman. His middle name remains unknown but was possibly Washington. He may, then, have been the father of the George Washington Jones of Virginia, born in 1806, who became a congressman and trustee of the Tennessee Hospital for the Insane, dying in 1884. One thing is certain, he fell under Edouart's eye and was thereby joined to a noble throng whose shadows are here preserved.

155
William Smith Stockton   1785–1860
Philadelphia, April 22, 1843

Stockton was born and died in Burlington, New Jersey, but he spent much of his life in Philadelphia. He married first in 1807; twenty-one years and six children later he married again and fathered nine more children. Influential in establishing the Methodist Episcopal church, he edited for several years the *Wesleyan Repository* and wrote a book on the Temperance Movement as well as editing the *Life of John Wesley*, in ten volumes. For seventeen years he was superintendent of the Philadelphia Almshouses, where he succeeded in abolishing such antiquated forms of harassment of the poor as the treadmill, punishment by shower-bath, the whip, chaining the insane, and the like. To Edouart he must have appealed as an outstanding member of the community carrying out his duties with tireless and unselfish devotion. He was a member of the well-known and prolific Stockton family, descendants of Richard Stockton of Cheshire, England, who settled on Long Island in the middle of the seventeenth century.

57½

George W. Jones President
of the Guardians of the Poor
of the City of Philadelphia
and Districts.

W J Stockton
Supt Philad. Alms House
Ap. 22, 1843

George W. Jones Presidt of the Guardians
Phil. 20th April 1843 of the Poor of the City of Phila & Districts

W. J. Stockton Superintendt of the Phila
Philad. 22d April 1843. Alms House

156
J. H. Ostrom
Saratoga Springs, August 19, 1840

Ostrom has been difficult to identify. In volume
4 of Cuyler Reynolds's *Hudson-Mohawk Valleys
Genealogical and Family Memories* (1911), there
is a long genealogy of the Ostrom family which
gives many statistical details but no date which
matches the death date in 1845 at age fifty-one as
stated in Edouart's volume. There was a John Ostrom said to have been born in 1764 and to have
died in 1845. He served in the militia under General Van Rensselaer and later settled in Montgomery and became the progenitor of a large
family. The record states that he had a son John
born in 1797, who died 1843, who married three
times but had no issue, and who lived in or near
Schenectady. No further details are given.

58.

J. H. Ostrom
Saratoga Aug.t 19. 1840

Died at Poughkeepsie aged 51 years
on the 16.th Aug.t 1845.

Major Gen.l J. H. Ostrom
1840.

157
Daniel James, M.D.
Saratoga Springs, August 13, 1842

What little we learn of Dr. James appears on Edouart's silhouette. His presence in Saratoga implies some social or professional position of standing; and his being paired with the mayor of Utica, and being himself from Utica, suggest that he might have been Mayor Kirkland's personal physician. His profile, stance, and cane all suggest that in 1842 he was an elderly man.

158
Joseph Kirkland   1770–1844
Saratoga Springs, August 13, 1842

General Kirkland, aged seventy-two when he stood to Edouart, must have been a contemporary of Dr. James though he had not yet taken to a cane. He was a successful lawyer, father of twelve children, and by 1842 had been for several years a member of the state assembly, district attorney for the Sixth District of New York, member of Congress, and the first mayor chosen under the new charter of Utica, a post to which he was reelected in 1834 and in which he served during the cholera epidemic. His title of "General" derives from early service in the state militia but is supported by his confident bearing. Edouart, ever on the lookout for clippings of his subjects, preserves General Kirkland's death notice, in which he is described as "one of the oldest and most respected inhabitants" of Utica.

58 ½.

Daniel James.
Utica August 13th 1842

J. Kirkland
Utica Augt 13 1842

Death of Gen. Joseph Kirkland.—The death of this gentleman, the first Mayor of Utica, N. Y., and one of the oldest and most respected inhabitants of that city, occurred on the 2d inst. Gen. K. was 74 years of age.

2d february 1844.

Dr. Daniel James MD. of Utica N.Y.   Genal J. Kirkland of Utica N.Y.
Saratoga Springs 13th Augt 1842.

159
Daniel Carroll   1756 or 1764–1849
Washington City, March 8, 1841

That Daniel Carroll of Duddington was an old
gentleman when he sat to Edouart is evident not
only from his profile but from his signature—but
there seems to be some question as to how old.
He is usually said to have been born in 1756,
which would have made him eighty-five years old
in 1841. Yet the monument over his grave in
Mount Olivet Cemetery recites "Obt. May 9th
1849, Aged 84", which would advance his birth
to 1764.

Perhaps his principal claim to distinction is
the fact that the United States Capitol and the
Mall lie on lands acquired from him, 1,774 acres,
of which the Mall was in excess of 200 and not
considered to be worth much, being, as was said,
"a waste of land." After the establishment of the
federal city, Carroll built himself a substantial
home on the very edge of the city limits—in fact
it encroached to such an extent on the road laid
out that L'Enfant had it torn down and for years
a controversy raged as to how much compensation
Carroll should receive. He later controlled a large
brick kiln, built many houses and a hotel in the
city, gave the land on which St. Peter's Church
was built, and in every way was a generous and
public-spirited citizen.

At the first election of the city council in 1802,
Carroll received the most votes and became chairman; he served in several capacities in that body.
He had been a delegate from Maryland to the
Continental Congress, had signed the Articles of
Confederation, and was a representative to the
Congress from 1784 to 1791. As a commissioner
for surveying the District of Columbia, he was
one of those who voted for moving the seat of
government to the banks of the Potomac. His
later years were devoted to looking after his large
estates. His old mansion, known as Duddington
Manor, descended in his family and was de-
molished in 1886. Portraits of him exist, one by
Healy and one long said to have been by Stuart.
Carroll's own portrait of Washington by Stuart
now belongs to the Metropolitan Museum of Art
in New York.

59

Dan.l Carroll of Dud.n
March 8
1841

Daniel Carroll of Dudington   Washington City 8th March 1841.

160
John Bouvier 1787–1851
Philadelphia, April 13, 1843

For more than a century, scarcely a single lawyer
in the country has not had occasion to use or own
Bouvier's *Dictionary*, published in 1839 under the
title *A Law Dictionary Adapted to the Constitution and Laws of the United States of America,
and of the Several States of the American Union.*
For this work his name will not be forgotten. But
he had a busy life on the side. Born in the south
of France, he came to Philadelphia in 1802. The
early death of his father precipitated him into
business, first the printing business in Philadelphia and then editing and publishing the *American Telegraph* in Brownsville. He took up the
study of law, made an analysis or abridgment of
Blackstone's Commentaries, was admitted to the
bar in 1822, and returned to Philadelphia to practice. In his early years of practice he sensed the
need for a lawyer's dictionary and commenced to
compile one. He continued actively in practice,
was recorder of Philadelphia in 1836, and by 1838
an associate judge of the Court of Criminal Sessions. His dictionary appeared in 1839, received
immediate and wide approval, and quickly went
through three editions, a fourth being *in limine*
at the time of his death. His last publication was
his four-volume *Institutes of American Law,* published in 1851. He signs himself modestly, above
his shade, "Author of Am. Law Dictionary," and
would be no doubt pleased to know that to an
American lawyer the name *Bouvier* is synonymous
with *dictionary*.

59 1/2.

J Bouvier

Author of Am. Law Dictionary,

Philad. April 13. 1843.

Judge John Bouvier Late Recorder of Ph.
Author of American Laws District. Phil 13th April 1843.

161
John Caldwell Calhoun   1782–1850
Washington, March 8, 1841

Edward Everett once said: "Calhoun, Clay, Webster! I name them in alphabetical order. What other precedence can be assigned them?" Philosopher, statesman, member of Congress (1811–17), secretary of war under President Monroe (1817–25), vice-president under Adams (1825–29) and for a further term under Jackson (1829–32), secretary of state under Tyler (1843–45), United States senator (1832–43, 1845–50), a man of the highest principles and oratorical ability, his great cause, "nullification," or "states' rights," as it came to be called, was doomed to disappointment. He was unequivocally loyal to the South, and a supporter of slavery. On his deathbed his last words were, "The South, the poor South."

A graduate of Yale in 1804, he was one of the great lawyers who obtained their legal education at Tapping Reeve's law school in Litchfield, and was admitted to practice in Charleston, South Carolina, in 1807. His first great stand in Congress was his recommendation of a declaration of war in 1812 and his efforts to carry it out with success. To Alexander J. Dallas (fig. 232) he was "the young Hercules who carried the war on his shoulders," and he was able to stand up to Webster (fig. 164) and hold his own in debate.

We see his tall figure and bushy locks as he stood to Edouart the same day as old Daniel Carroll (fig. 160), only a few days after the inauguration of President Harrison (fig. 233). His life's record is too well known to be further detailed, but it is of interest to note that Edouart's volume includes so many of the greatest statesmen of those days in America: John Quincy Adams (fig. 172), Clay (fig. 147), Webster (fig. 164), Tyler (fig. 258), Harrison (fig. 233), Van Buren (fig. 230). He had an eye for prominence and his skill found ready acceptance by all he approached. His silhouette of Calhoun is proof of his extraordinary ability to catch a characteristic likeness.

60.

J.C. Calhoun
S.C.

John C. Calhoun Senator
for S. Carolina
Washington 8th March Fort Hill
1841

162
William Augustus Porter
1821–1886
Philadelphia, April 21, 1843

Sheriff Porter attained his high post at the age of twenty-two, less than a year after his admission to the bar. His jaunty stance contrasts with the dignified pose of his father, the governor of Pennsylvania, who doubtless had a hand in his son's sudden rise. The younger man was a graduate in 1819 at Lafayette College, of which his uncle, George B. Porter, was a founder and for twenty-five years president. By his career, William showed that his father's confidence in him was not misplaced. In 1856 he became city solicitor of Philadelphia and two years later a judge of the Supreme Court of Pennsylvania. Later in life he served from 1874 to 1876 as judge of the court of *Alabama* claims in Washington.

His writings include an *Essay on the Law Pertaining to the Sheriff's Office* in 1845, numerous contributions to the *American Law Magazine* and the *Law Journal*, and in 1855 a biography of Chief Justice John B. Gibson (fig. 195), about which S. Austin Allibone's *A Critical Dictionary of English Literature* (1870) noted that "Chief-Justice Gibson deserved a Memoir; and Mr. Porter has done well to write it."

163
David Rittenhouse Porter
1788–1867
Philadelphia, April 21, 1843

Named after his father's friend, the great scholar Dr. David Rittenhouse, Porter was kept from entering Princeton College when its buildings were destroyed by fire. For a while he studied law while acting as assistant to his father, the surveyor general, but gave up that profession and entered into the iron business in Huntingdon County, Pennsylvania, and raised horses and cattle. He became a member of the state assembly in 1819, made influential friends, and before long was appointed clerk of the courts of Huntingdon County, recorder of deeds, and register of wills. His great interest was the betterment of the state, and by his efforts in this behalf he became a state senator in 1836, and governor of the state in 1838, a post he held with great distinction for the maximum time allowed, retiring in 1848. His efforts to complete certain public works, canals, and railroads and maintain the credit of the state won him acclaim, as did his influence in putting down the riots of 1844. He was noted for his excellent appointments of judges, including Edward King (fig. 114) and Ellis Lewis (fig. 149). He retired to his profitable iron business, and with his friend General Sam Houston of Texas planned a railroad from Texas to the Pacific, which the commencement of the Civil War thwarted. He died in Harrisburg, greatly lamented.

The Porters, together as we see them, were distinguished members of a distinguished Pennsylvania family.

60½.

Wm A Porter
Sheriff of Philada Co
21st April '43

David R Porter
Governor of Pennsd
21 April 1843

Wm A Porter High Sheriff of Philada Co ..
Philadelphia 21st April 1843.

David R. Porter
Governor of Pennsylvania State
Philadelphia 21st April 1843.

Daniel Webster   1782–1852
Date and place unknown

Although Webster's silhouette is neither dated nor signed (the signature being on a separate slip of paper), there are other silhouettes of Webster by Edouart, one done at Saratoga, August 20, 1840, which we presume is the duplicate of this, though all we have found is a notice of it in a catalog. It is curious that with his practice of getting the signature of almost all his subjects, Edouart seems to have failed in the case of Webster. Included in the volume is a long six-column report (undated) attributed to the *New York Herald*, although it appears to be from a Boston newspaper, titled "Daniel Webster's Great Speech, Delivered on the occasion of meeting his friends at Faneuil Hall, Boston, Yesterday," shortly after the death of President Harrison (fig. 233). This would be consistent with an 1840 date for this shade.

For those whose memory holds fast the career of the godlike Daniel, who Sydney Smith said was "a Cathedral in himself," and who Van Wyck Brooks characterized as having "an eye as black as death and a look like a lion's," we need only recall that he was a representative in Congress from 1823 to 1827, a senator from 1827 to 1839, secretary of state under Presidents Harrison, Tyler, and Fillmore. The great phrases from his argument in the *Dartmouth College* case, his closing words in his second reply to Hayne, ring in the ear of all students of American history of any age. His personal life and financial transactions have raised eyebrows, probably with justification, but there is no question that he was the greatest American orator of all. This is one reason why there were probably more portraits painted of Webster than of any other American save Washington.

D. Webster bt.

Hon.ble Daniel Webster

165
Robert H. Collyer, M.D.
Boston, May 17, 1842

It is with great skill that Edouart has caught the action in this view of Dr. Collyer putting Monsieur de Bonneville "in the Mesmeric or Magnetic State." Edouart had previous notice that the hypnotist was in Boston and asked him if he would sit for a profile in the very act of exhibiting his powers.

Collyer wrote to the silhouettist on May 16, 1842, from Boston.

Monsieur Edouart,
It is extremely gratifying to me, in being able to accord with your polite invitation to sit for my Silhouette profile in the attitude of *Mesmerization*, which mighty truth must e'er long occupy the attention of every philosophic mind, as it offers an analysis of all those hitherto mysterious and inexplicable phenomena known in dreaming, ecstacy, hallucination, exaltation, ap-

166
Monsieur de Bonneville
Boston, May 17, 1842

paritions, forebodings, accordance of ideas in different persons, fascination or charming, curing of the king's evil, spiritual emancipation from all living bodies, called spheres,—the ——se of love, hatred or indifference at first sight etc; which laws have —— been known by their effects, and have been used by the designing and crafty in past ages for the subjection of the ignorant multitude.—

> I remain yours
> with much Respect
> Most truly &c.
> Rob. H. Collyer

The piercing hypnotic eye is clearly there, and de Bonneville has succumbed to it and is seen "in the Mesmeric or Magnetic State." But of Dr. Collyer and de Bonneville we have been able to find no further trace.

61/2

Robt H. Collyer

Boston, May. 17th 1842

Dr. Robt H. Collyer MD putting Monsr de Bonneville in the Mesmeric or Magnetic State
Boston 17th May 1842.

167
Peter A. Lorillard   1763–1843
Saratoga, August 25, 1840

To escape persecution in the eighteenth century, the Lorillard family, French Huguenots, fled their native land first to Holland and then to this country, where they settled in Hackensack, New Jersey. Peter married Maria Dorothea, daughter of Major Schultz, in 1789 and had five children who all married well. For several generations they held a high place in the business and social community. Our subject, who stands as though on his estate in Hackensack, went into the tobacco business with his brother George, formed the firm of P. & G. Lorillard in 1810, and amassed a fortune in tobacco and New York commercial real estate. The firm of P. Lorillard has been a familiar name for generations, synonymous with financial success. Alongside Edouart's silhouette is pasted a clipping dated in Edouart's hand "22d. May 1843" reading: "Another Millionaire Gone.—Peter Lorillard, reported one of the wealthiest citizens in New York, died a day or two ago, in the 80th year of his age."

On the same day he cut Peter Lorillard, Edouart cut silhouettes of Lorillard's daughter Mrs. John Wolfe and her daughter Miss M. Lorillard Wolfe. In July 1844 he cut the profile of G. L. Renalds, Lorillard's grandson—but none of these was considered by Edouart as worthy of inclusion in this volume.

Peter Lorillard

62.

Peter Lorillard of New York   Saratoga 25th Augt 1840.

168
T. W. Schmidt
Saratoga, July 31, 1844

No clue to Schmidt has turned up other than what appears under his silhouette, that he was consul of Prussia and consul general of Baden. The fact his signature does not appear suggests that he may have made a quick visit to Saratoga, that Edouart did not know his first name and never had the opportunity to secure his signature.

169
Steen Anderson Bille   1797–1883
Philadelphia, April 6, 1843

Bille describes himseelf in 1843 as "Chargé d'affaires of Denmark." He was the son of that Danish admiral Steen Bille who took part in the blockade of Tunis in 1796 and later in the battle of Copenhagen in 1801. Our subject was born in Copenhagen, served in the French army in the campaign of 1823, and was made minister of marine and rear admiral in 1852. Between terms he visited this country as chargé d'affaires and was singled out by Edouart. A year later Edouart found another foreign diplomat to share the page with Bille. During the years 1845–47 Bille was in command of the Danish corvette *Galathea* on a scientific expedition around the world, the results of which were published in three volumes in 1849–51. The voyage offered the opportunity to fly the Danish flag around the world, but Bille had to strike his flag at the fort in Tranquebar, India, which had been sold to the English East Asiatic Company for two million Danish kroner, having become too expensive to maintain. Admiral Bille died in Copenhagen.

62½

Steen Bille
Chargé d'affaires
of Denmark
Philad.ª April 6ᵗʰ 1843

J.W. Schmidt. Consul of Prussia
New York   and Consul Gᵉⁿ of Baden
Saratoga 31ˢᵗ July 1844

Steen Bille Chargé d'affaires of Denmark
Philadelphia 6ᵗʰ April 1843.

170
William McKendree Gwin
1805–1885
Saratoga, August 26, 1840

Distinguished in both Mississippi and California, the son of a well-known Methodist minister of Tennessee, the Reverend John Gwin, William had been named after Bishop McKendree, one of the first American Methodist bishops. He prepared for the law, but after seeing in action the great men of the bar in Tennessee, he decided it was not his calling. He turned to medicine, receiving a degree at Transylvania University at Lexington, Kentucky, in 1828. After a short but successful practice in Clinton, Mississippi, he retired from medicine upon being appointed marshal of the Southern District of Mississippi by President Jackson. The post was important and lucrative, and he filled it to the satisfaction of his sponsor. As a congressman from Mississippi in 1840, he was a strong adherent of Calhoun (fig. 161). For financial reasons he did not run for a second term but accepted President Polk's appointment to superintend the construction of the new customs house in New Orleans.

Calhoun had always told Gwin what a future lay ahead for California, and on the election of President Taylor Gwin went west and took an active part in organizing the new state government. From 1850 to 1861 he served as United States senator from California and is alleged to have established the California mint and to have instigated the survey of the Pacific coast. Twice arrested during the Civil War on charges of disloyalty, he went to Paris to interest Napoleon III in colonizing Sonora, Mexico, with southerners, but the scheme did not materialize. He then retired from public life and many years later died in New York. He was a man of extraordinary energy and ambition and was engaged in important political activities in widely different circumstances. His widely extended career is suggested by the title of a recent biography by Lately Thomas, *Between Two Empires: The Life Story of California's First Senator* . . . (1969).

63.

Wm M Gwin
Marshal of the Southern
District of Mississippi
Vicksburg Mississippi

171

John Fanning Watson   1779–1860
Philadelphia, April 1, 1843

Edouart's dating of this silhouette August 1, 1843, is clearly an oversight, as he was then in Saratoga. We can assume Watson's date of April 1 to be the correct one. Curiously enough Edouart erred twice in his inscription, misdescribing Watson's first notable book as "Annals of Pensylvania & Penna.," intending "Philadelphia."

In addition to (or perhaps in spite of) a long career of thirty-three years as cashier of the Bank of Germantown and twelve years as secretary and treasurer of the Philadelphia, Germantown & Norristown Railroad, Watson was a thorough-going, devoted antiquarian and historian. For a few years after 1809 he published *Select Reviews of Literature and Spirit of the Foreign Magazines*, which, when he sold it, became the *Analectic Magazine and Naval Chronicle*. Then in 1830 came his *Annals of Philadelphia*, 800 pages of early history and reminiscences of the city, much of it obtained from answers to a form of questionnaire he devised and distributed as widely as possible. Two years later in the same vein were published his *Historic Tales of Olden Time, Concerning the Early Settlement and Advancement of New-York City and State*. These were followed by other antiquarian publications. He was a founder of the Historical Society of Pennsylvania, which benefited from collections of manuscripts, portraits, and curiosities procured through his efforts. And to him goes the credit for the erection of appropriate monuments over the graves of many prominent Pennsylvania citizens. We see him in a scholarly pose, just after he had published a second edition of his *Annals of Philadelphia* in 1842.

63½.

John F. Watson
Author of Annals of Philad & Penn^a
& of Facts & Occurrences of olden time
of New York City & State —
Philad^a April 1843

John F. Watson. Author of the Annals of
Pensylvania & Penn^a and of the facts and occur. of old
times of New Y^k City and State. Philad^a 1st Augt 1843

John Quincy Adams 1767–1848
Washington City, March 11, 1841

The sixth president of the United States needs no introduction to Americans, but Edouart preserved a newspaper account of him that gives a splendid summary of his career. The article is headed "From Washington (Correspondence of the Herald) Congressional Sketches" and is dated in Edouart's hand "April 1842," when he was in Boston. The account is a long one and we quote only a few sentences.

John Quincy Adams, now a member of the House of Representatives, has filled so large a space in the public eye for so long a time, and his history is so well known by the people of this country, that it will be superfluous in these short sketches to give anything more than a succinct synopsis of his career. He entered the public service forty-eight years ago, and has been in constant employment ever since. In 1791, he was appointed Minister to the Netherlands. In 1796 Minister to Portugal. In 1797 Minister to Prussia. In 1803 he was elected a Senator and remained in that body until 1809 at which time he was sent as Minister to Russia. On his return in 1811 he was appointed a Judge of the Supreme Court of the United States [which he declined]. In 1813 he was sent as one of the Associate Ministers at the Treaty of Ghent. In 1815 he received the appointment of Minister to England, and while abroad in 1817 was selected by Mr. Monroe as his Secretary of State, in which office he continued until his elevation to the Presidency in 1825. In 1832 he took his seat in the Lower House of Congress, where he has been a prominent member continously from then to the present day.

Adams recorded the making of this silhouette in his diary: "Mr. Edouart is a Frenchman," he wrote on March 11, 1841, "who cuts out profiles in miniature on paper and came and took mine. He says he has a collection of them 8500 in number. . . . He gave me a full length profile of President Harrison, in the attitude of delivering his inaugural address." A few weeks later, June 11, 1841, he continued: "In the Evening Mr. Edouart the man of shades, came and left with me full length profiles of . . . President Tyler, and myself." On a later occasion Adams called on Edouart and saw his collection of shades of distinguished men of the country "assembled together and standing in one hall in relative positions to each other, forming a very pleasant tableau and many of them striking likenesses." President Harrison's silhouette (fig. 233) was cut on February 20, twelve days before his inauguration, President Tyler's (fig. 258) on April 16, only ten days after his inauguration. What Edouart delivered to Adams were undoubtedly counterparts of what we see in this volume.

To conclude, from Edouart's newspaper clipping on Adams:

It is sad to think that a mind so gifted, so stored with knowledge, attained by unremitted study during a great portion of a century—an intellect so active, so lofty and sagacious—statesmanship so wise and courageous—must, in the order of nature, so soon cease to be. . . . I sincerely concur with the worthy captain of one of our steamboats, who said to me the other day, "Oh, that we could take the *engine* out of the old Adams, and put it into a new *hull*."

John Quincy Adams
11. March 1841.

John Quincy Adams Ex President
Washington City 11th March 1841

173
Richard Vaux   1816–1895
[Philadelphia], April 20, 1843

The post of recorder of the city of Philadelphia was but one of the many rungs on Vaux's lofty professional ladder. Following a short diplomatic career he settled in Philadelphia. After three attempts he was elected mayor of Philadelphia; he was for many years trustee and for three years president of Gerard College and became grand master of the Pennsylvania Grand Lodge of Masons. His great interest was penology, and for a time he was inspector of the Eastern Penitentiary, later publishing two books on the subject. A brief sketch of his life in the *Dictionary of American Biography* states that he started the custom of wearing of gowns by the judiciary, which was finally adopted by the Law Association "with no enthusiasm, and mainly to secure relief from Mr. Vaux's importunity." Perhaps this remark is a clue to the origin of the statement made about him by the Philadelphia diarist Sidney George Fisher. Fisher writes on February 28, 1844, an account of the death and the previous trial of Nicholas Biddle (fig. 271) arising out of the suspension of the Bank of the United States. Criminal charges were levied, and a trial followed with the public thirsty for punishment. Fisher wrote one comment on Vaux. "He [Biddle] was committed for trial by Vaux, the recorder, a silly, extravagant, violent radical & *mob pet*, the son of the man whom Mr. Biddle had persecuted, and who gloated over his downfall with all the rapture of gratified revenge." Yet, in Scharf and Westcott's *History of Philadelphia*, it is written of him that "he has led an active political life of over forty years, and yet no one can point to an act of his and say that its motive was not as stainless as the Arctic snow."

174
Ovid Frazer Johnson   1807–1854
Philadelphia, March 31, 1843

For twelve years, from the age of twenty-six, Johnson served as attorney general of Pennsylvania and must have been well acquainted with Vaux, the city recorder. Johnson was born near Wilkes-Barre, in Luzerne County, and after studying law under John N. Conyngham his early practice was in Wilkes-Barre. Having obtained some notice as a political writer, he published, during the governorship of Joseph Ritner, a political satire bearing the title *The Governor's Letters*. His death at the age of forty-seven occurred in Washington.

Richard Vaux
Recorder of the City of Phila.
April 20/43.

Ovid F. Johnson
Attorney Genl. of Penna.
Philad. March 31. 1843.

Richard Vaux. Recorder of the City of Phila.
20th April 1843.

Ovid F. Johnson Attorney Genl. of Pennsylvania
Philadelphia 31st March 1843.

175
William Campbell Preston
1794–1860
Washington, February 17, 1841

Colonel Preston, as he was called, was born in Philadelphia, where his father was serving as a congressman, but he was in all other respects a South Carolinian. He was a defender of slavery and the "gag rule" and of states' rights, a nullifier, and an early supporter of Calhoun. He inherited his eloquence from his great-uncle Patrick Henry and used it to good advantage during his two terms in the state legislature and eight years as a United States senator from South Carolina, becoming a brilliant and imposing speaker. He had studied law under William Wirt in Richmond and had practiced with profit for several years at Columbia. In later life he was for several years president of the University of South Carolina, from which he had graduated in 1812. Despite his advanced age and ill health, he contributed to the advancement of the university and rendered devoted and valuable service, albeit his administration was marked by riots and rebellions.

The diary of Sidney George Fisher contains Fisher's opinion of Preston in 1834: "He is however a man of no ordinary talents, tho not at all of the first order, or to be ranked for a moment with such men as Webster or Calhoun." A few years later Fisher heard Preston argue the great *Presbyterian Church* case and found him brilliant and eloquent. He compared his performance with that of Horce Binney: "Binney is a Tuscan or Doric temple, simple & elegant, massy and plain; Preston a Gothic Cathedral, grand, strong and vast; but encrusted with rich and fanciful decoration and lighted by windows of painted glass."

At his death, Preston endowed the Columbia Library with a gift of his own library of some three thousand volumes.

65

Wm Preston Senator South Carolina Washington 9th February 1841

176
George McClellan   1796–1847
Philadelphia, March 25, 1843

Dr. McClellan and his colleague Dr. Morton are quite naturally paired by Edouart, who cut their shades on consecutive days. They are perhaps shown discussing the imminent resignation of the faculty of the Medical Department of Pennsylvania College, a creature of McClellan's founding.

Born in Woodstock, Connecticut, graduated at Yale in 1816, Dr. McClellan's career can be divided between his institutional and his medical activities. He was a principal founder of the Jefferson Medical College in 1826 and was its professor of surgery until 1838 when, for reasons never clearly known and probably the result of personality differences, all the professorships were vacated by the trustees and a new faculty founded which excluded Dr. McClellan. Disappointed but not daunted, he founded the Medical Department of Pennsylvania College, at Gettysburg, which continued usefully until 1843 when, due to financial reverses for which Dr. McClellan was not responsible, his leadership terminated.

His medical career was outstanding. He attended the medical lectures at the University of Pennsylvania, received his M.D. in 1819, and commenced an outstanding career, performing many well-known and many entirely new operations with outstanding success as a result of his skill and his courage in the innovation of new processes. He is said to have acquired the largest practice as a surgeon in the country, and was renowned for operations for cataract, for lithotomies, and for extirpations of the parotid gland, though Dr. Gibson (fig. 181) accused him of falsehood for claiming to have many times accomplished the last. His *Principles of Surgery*, published posthumously, evidences his vast knowledge of and experience in the subject. His son John H. B. McClellan became a distinguished surgeon and another son, George B. McClellan, became the well-known Civil War general.

177
Samuel George Morton, M.D.
1799–1851
Philadelphia, March 24, 1843

Dr. Morton, a contemporary and colleague of Dr. McClellan and a distinguished physician, was best known as a naturalist. He published many scholarly articles in the learned journals of natural science, "An Analysis of Tabular Spar from Bucks County" in 1827, "A Synopsis of the Organic Remains of the Cretaceous Group of the United States" in 1834, and at the same time two medical works on anatomy and consumption. Over the years he formed a collection of skulls about which Louis Agassiz remarked that there was nothing like it elsewhere and that it was alone worth a journey to America. From his work in this field he published his two great volumes, *Crania Americana* in 1839 and *Crania Aegyptica* in 1844. From these he was led to the conclusion that the human races were of diverse origin, a theory which involved him in bitter controversy with many people, especially the clergy and the Reverend Dr. John Bachman of South Carolina, who considered his belief an attack on the authority of Scripture.

His early study of medicine was under Dr. Joseph Parrish (fig. 77). He received his medical degrees from the University of Pennsylvania in 1820 and the University of Edinburgh in 1823. His scientific interests led him to become a member of the Academy of Natural Sciences, of which he was president in 1849. He was also a member of a number of foreign medical and scientific societies. He died after a short illness in 1851.

65½.

Go M Clellan   Samuel George Morton MD
Prof. of Surgery   Prof. Anat. Med. Dept.
Penns. College   Penns. College. 1843
March 25. 1843.   March 24

George McClellan   Samuel George Morton MD
Prof. of Surgery Penns. Coll   Prof. Anat. Medca Dept. Pennsylvania Coll.
Philadelphia 25th March 1843.   Philadelphia 24th March. 1843.

178
James Tallmadge   1778–1853
Saratoga, August 12, 1844

A founder of the University of the City of New York (now known as New York University) and its president for twelve years, a founder of the American Institute of the City of New York and its president for most of the years from 1832 until his death, General Tallmadge, as Edouart caught him in 1844, looks every inch the lawyer and prominent public figure he was. He was born in Dutchess County, New York, graduated from Brown University (then Rhode Island College) in 1798, was a member of Congress from 1817 to 1819, and defended Jackson's practice in the Seminole Indian question. In his earlier life he had been interested in farming in Dutchess County and for a time served as the printer to Governor Clinton. He took an active part in the state constitutional conventions of 1821 and 1826 and served as lieutenant governor from 1826 to 1827. On a trip to Russia he favored one of his great interests, the encouragement of domestic production, by taking a lead in introducing a knowledge of American manufacturing processes, especially relating to cotton manufacturing. He married his second cousin Laura Tallmadge. One daughter alone survived him, marrying Philip Van Rensselaer, proprietor of the Metropolitan Hotel, at which General Tallmadge died in 1853.

179
Nathaniel Pitcher Tallmadge
1795–1864
Washington, March 25, 1841

Just what the family connection was between Senator N. P. Tallmadge and General Tallmadge is not clear, but Edouart must have known of it when he paired the two together, though their shades were cut three years apart. Senator Tallmadge was born in Chatham, New York, graduated at Union College 1815, studied law under General Tallmadge, and, after admission to the bar in 1818, practiced with him for several years. He was elected to the assembly from Dutchess County in 1828 and to the state senate in 1829, and was a United States senator from 1833 to 1844 when he resigned, his seat being filled by Daniel S. Dickinson (fig. 45). President Tyler (fig. 258) appointed him governor of Wisconsin Territory in 1844, a post he held only a year or so when he returned to Fond du Lac to practice his profession. He turned to spiritualism in his later years. His publications were principally speeches and an introduction and appendix to Charles Linton's *Healing of the Nation*, published in 1855. He died in Battle Creek, Michigan.

66.

N. P. Tallmadge

of New York

March 25th 1841.

Gen. James Tallmadge Late L.G. N.Y.S.
President of American Institute N.Y.
Saratoga 13th Aug 1844.

Hon. N. P. Tallmadge
Senator for State of N.Y.
Washington 25th March 1841.

180
William Edmonds Horner, M.D.
1791–1853
Philadelphia, March 7, 1843

Dr. Horner was a prominent anatomist and the author of the first text on pathology published in America. In his youth he was a frequent visitor at Judge Bushrod Washington's mansion while at school at Dumfries. Born in Warrenton, Virginia, he early took to the study of medicine and, after a short spell as surgeon's mate in the army during the War of 1812, resumed his medical studies and graduated at the University of Pennsylvania in 1814. His evident knowledge and skill in his dissection and operation led Dr. Caspar Wistar to offer him a post in the Medical Department of the University of Pennsylvania, which was continually held open to him first by Dr. Dorsey, then by Dr. Physick until his resignation, at which time Horner became professor of anatomy and dean of the Medical Department. This office he held for upwards of thirty years. In later life he embraced Roman Catholicism and was instrumental in founding St. Joseph's Hospital. At his death he bequeathed to the university all his specimens and dissecting instruments and apparatus, perhaps among them the very one he holds out to Dr. Gibson for inspection and comment.

He visited Judge Washington two days before his death, and upon the decease of the judge's widow only four days later in her carriage near Philadelphia, her body was brought to Dr. Horner's house until arrangements could be made for its removal to Virginia. As Henry Simpson records in *Lives of Eminent Philadelphians*, Dr. Horner, recalling Mrs. Washington's kindness to him as a youth twenty years before, expressed his gratitude at being able to give a respectful asylum to her remains, though but for a moment, and to contribute to the comfort of those who were with her.

181
William Gibson, M.D.   1788–1868
Philadelphia, March 7, 1843

Dr. Gibson was a noted surgeon, scientist, scholar, and traveler. He was one of twin boys born in Baltimore, educated both at St. John's College, Annapolis, and Princeton. His medical degree was received from the University of Edinburgh, where he studied under the great surgeon Sir Charles Bell. For a few years he was professor of surgery at Baltimore and in 1819 he succeeded Dr. Physick, sharing the chair of surgery with Dr. McClellan (fig. 176), with whom he did not often get on. This position he held until 1855, three years after which he retired to Newport, Rhode Island. He died at Savannah, Georgia.

His early experience included examining many wounded soldiers returning from the battle of Coruña. He was also present and slightly wounded at the Battle of Waterloo. He it was who successfully removed a bullet from General's Scott's (fig. 120) shoulder and who tied the common iliac artery for the first time in America (although the case terminated fatally, the example had been set). His greatest feat and one which displayed his surgical courage was the performance of the Caesarean section twice upon the same woman, in both cases successfully for mother and child. He published on medical subjects and on his travels. Dr. Samuel D. Gross (fig. 299) in his *Autobiography* published in 1887, writes of Dr. Gibson: "It is said that one should not speak ill of the dead. Far be it from me to do so; but I cannot ignore the fact, known to most of his contemporaries, that Gibson was not an amiable man." Perhaps this deficiency can be gleaned from Edouart's view of Dr. Gibson, in a two-handed argument with Dr. Horner over a bit of anatomy just removed from a patient whose silhouette we could wish had been taken at the same time and preserved.

66/2.

W. E. Horner M.D.
Prof. Anat.y Univ. Penns.a
March 7th 1843

Wm Gibson M.D. Prof. Surg.
University of Penn.a
Philad.s March 7th 1843

Dr. W. E. Horner M.D.
Prof.r Anat.y Univ.o Penns.a Philadelphia 7th March 1843.

Dr. Wm Gibson M.D Prof. Surg. Univ. Penn.a

182
John (or Jonathan) Meredith
c.1784–1872
Saratoga, August 12, 1843

Meredith practiced law for years in Philadelphia, the place of his birth. Few details of his life have come to light, though J. Thomas Scharf's *Chronicles of Baltimore* (1874) tells us that in 1816 he was appointed an insolvent commissioner to examine applicants and grant provisional relief. By 1831 he was considered a lawyer of great prominence both on the lecture platform and in private circles. Scharf wrote of him that "living an honorable, upright life, in death he was crowned with the respect and esteem of all who knew him." He was at the height of his career, aged fifty-nine, when he stood to Edouart.

183
Francis Granger   1792–1868
Washington, June 12, 1841

As he stood before Edouart in 1841, as postmaster general appointed by Harrison (fig. 233), a post he held for a short period under Tyler (fig. 258) until the break between the president and the Whig leaders, Granger was following in the steps of his father, Gideon, who had held the same office under both Jefferson and Madison. He was a Yale graduate, 1811, and commenced his law practice in Canandaigua, but politics was his real love. He became a member of the state's lower house and was a supporter of Governor Clinton. Twice he was an unsuccessful candidate for governor. As an anti-Mason he was nominated for vice-president but not elected, though he did serve two terms in Congress. The slavery question and the proposed annexation of Texas proved to be stumbling blocks in the way of his continued friendship with Seward (fig. 2) and Thurlow Weed. At the time Granger presided over the Whig convention in 1850, upon the adoption of a vote praising Seward, Granger and his conservative group withdrew and held their own convention—the Silver Grays, as they were called, after the fine head of hair of their leader. At this time Granger returned to private life, except for a short appearance in 1861 as a member of the peace convention on the appointment of Governor Morgan.

Granger was a man who made friends easily, a man of great intelligence and ready wit, and he was on terms of intimacy with the political leaders of his day, Webster (fig. 164), Clay (fig. 147), Preston (fig. 175), and Everett. He died at Canandaigua having survived his father by only five days.

J. Meredith
Saratoga
12th August 1843.

Th: Granger
12 June 1841.

67

John Meredith Couns. at Law
of Baltimore Saratoga 12th Augt 1843.

Francis Granger Post Master Genl
Washington 12th June 1841.

184
William John Duane   1780–1865
Philadelphia, February 15, 1843

Colonel Duane, who won his title for services near Philadelphia during the War of 1812, is another of the many lawyers and political figures of Pennsylvania caught by Edouart. He was born in Ireland, and in his youth, when his father was a reporter in London, the young lad made a point of listening to debates from the gallery of the House of Commons. When his father moved to Philadelphia, young Duane worked for his newspaper, the *Aurora* (to which Jefferson is said to have attributed his own election), and before long became interested in public affairs, studied law, and was admitted to practice in 1815. He became a member of the Pennsylvania House of Representatives and at various times was chairman of the Committee on Roads and Inland Navigation and the Committee on Banks. For a brief spell he was secretary of the treasury on the appointment of President Jackson but was dismissed when he refused to withdraw government funds from the United States Bank without congressional knowledge. He later published a defense of his position. He made no claim to the title when he signed Edouart's silhouette; it was Edouart who described him as "Late Secretary of Treasury." Like his father, he had long been a close friend of Stephen Girard. He was his lawyer in the acquisition of his coal lands in Schuylkill County (said by 1928 to have become worth $30 million) and became his executor, serving for a time as a trustee of Girard College.

He married Deborah Bache, grand-daughter of Benjamin Franklin and sister of Benjamin Franklin Bache, the father of Dr. Franklin Bache (fig. 189). To add to a genealogist's confusion, Benjamin Franklin Bache's widow married for her second husband Colonel Duane's father. We can wonder why Edouart never found an appropriate figure to pair with Colonel Duane, who is apparently waiting patiently for a companion.

672

Wm J. Duane Esq[r]
Philadelphia Feb[r] 15th
1843
late Secret[y] of Treasury.

185
Francis Lieber   1800–1872
Washington, July 9, 1841

Few men, in or out of Edouart's volume, have had a more eventful career than Francis Lieber. He stands before us in middle life, just having published the greatest of his innumerable works, his two-volume *Manual of Political Ethics* in 1838–39, to be followed immediately by *Legal and Political Hermeneutics*, which was cited with strong approval by such as Kent (fig. 15) and Clay (fig. 147), and then by his best-known work, widely used as a college textbook, *On Civil Liberty and Self-Government*. Dr. Lieber's life to this moment was indeed varied and unusual. Born in Berlin, his youthful study of medicine interrupted by the Napoleonic wars, in which he served under Blücher at Waterloo and was seriously wounded at Namur, he early fell under the influence of Friedrich Jahn and his gymnasia and patriotic societies. Several times imprisoned on suspicion of political intrigue, he became involved in the Greek War of Independence, made his way back to Rome, and became a member of the household of the Prussian ambassador, the great Niebuhr. With the degree of Doctor of Philosophy from Jena he made his way to England and finally, in 1827, to Boston. There he edited the *Encyclopaedia Americana*, published in thirteen volumes, and lectured widely on history and politics. He had a leading hand in devising the constitution of the newly formed Girard College and before long was called to the chair of history and political economy at the University of South Carolina, where he remained twenty years. Although feeling isolated from the center of political activity, he continued his prolific writing. In 1856 he assumed the same chair at Columbia and four years later was professor of political science at the law school.

His vast knowledge of military history, spiced by his own experience, led him to be consulted by the government; in 1862 he produced his famous *Guerilla Parties Considered with Reference to the Laws and Usages of War* and *A Code for the Government of Armies*, which was revised to become what was subsequently known to the American army as "General Orders No. 100." His legal, military, and literary works are too many to mention, but it is curious to note that he wrote a paper on the vocal sounds of Laura Bridgman (fig. 137), the blind deaf mute, compared with elements of phonetic language.

His was the idea of an organization of worldwide legal and historical scholars to codify international law, and after his death such societies were founded in several countries—the precursors of the conferences at The Hague. In Elihu Root's *Addresses on International Subjects*, it is told that at a meeting of the American Society of International Law on the fiftieth anniversary of Lincoln's propounding General Orders No. 100, an address delivered by the president in memory of Dr. Lieber and his extraordinarily eventful and productive career closed with the remark: "If our Society at once national and international, were about to choose a patron saint, and the roll were to be called, my voice for one would answer 'Francis Lieber.'"

Francis Lieber
Washington July 9. 1841.

author of Political Ethics.

68.

Francis Lieber
Author of Political Ethics

186
William Hawley d.1845
Washington City, June 12, 1841

During the War of 1812 Hawley was captain of
a company of volunteers, and rumor reports that
he resigned rather than go to the front on being
ordered to do so. Be that as it may, he was a distinguished clergyman and rector of St. John's
Episcopal Church, Washington, across Lafayette
Square from the White House. The church was
designed by Latrobe and completed in 1816, at
which time Hawley was called as associate rector
succeeding as rector the next year on the resignation of Dr. Wilmer. Hawley continued as rector
until his death in 1845 as recorded on Edouart's
page. Descriptions of him in Hagner's "History
of St. John's Church" published in *The Records
of the Columbia Historical Society* (1909) accord
well with Edouart's silhouette. He wore knee
breeches, long stockings, Geneva bands, and a
shovel hat, and at times certainly carried an um-
brella. He is said to have worn a black silk gown
when preaching and black gloves with one finger
split open to enable him to turn the pages of his
sermon. John Quincy Adams (fig. 172) took ex-
ception to Hawley's disapproval of the election
of a Unitarian as chaplain to the House of Representatives, which is not perhaps surprising for
Adams. But Hawley was a popular and able
preacher and carried on friendly relations with
his Roman and Presbyterian brethren, and his
death was greatly regretted. He lies beneath the
chancel of St. John's, and a marble memorial tab-
let preserves his memory.

68.½.

Revd. Wm. Hawley Rector St. John's Church Washington City
June 12. 1841.

☞ The Rev. Mr. Hawley, rector of St. John's
Church, Washington City, died on Thursday
morning. 26th Jany 1845

Revd. Wm. Hawley, Rector of St. John's Church. Washington City
12th June 1841.

187
Chauncey Allen Goodrich
1790–1860
[Saratoga], August 27, 1841

Goodrich the lexicographer, professor, and Congregational minister was born in New Haven, where he spent most of his life and where he died. A Yale graduate of the class of 1810, he was ordained and settled as pastor of the Congregational Church at Middletown, but only for one year. He held the chair of rhetoric and English literature at Yale from 1817 to 1839, declining the presidency of Williams College, to which he was elected in 1820. From 1839 until his death he was professor of pastoral theology at the Yale Divinity School, of which he was a generous benefactor. He was editor of the *Christian Quarterly Spectator* and wrote *Elements of Greek Grammar: Lessons in Greek Parsing*, but his greatest work was as a lexicographer.

He married Julia Frances, daughter of Noah Webster, the philologist, and he was entrusted by his father-in-law with preparing an abridgment of the dictionary, bringing it up to modern standards. This was done under his supervision by Dr. Joseph E. Worcester and was considered a valuable contribution to the science of lexicography. In a biographical sketch of Dr. Worcester in the 1888 edition of his own dictionary, this work on Webster's dictionary is mentioned: "In 1829, he [Dr. Worcester] was induced by the publisher of Dr. Webster's large American Dictionary, reluctantly, and not until the persuasive powers of the publisher, to use his own expression, had been 'severely taxed in securing the desired result,' to prepare an abridgment of the work." In 1847 Goodrich published a well-received second edition of Webster's dictionary and died while preparing a complete revision of it.

188
Jacob Abbott   1803–1879
[Saratoga], August 25, 1841

Two generations ago no one would have to be reminded who Jacob Abbott was. "The friend of children" he was called. Who was not familiar with "Little Rollo," the hero of twenty-eight volumes of Rollo books with such titles as *Rollo at Work, Rollo at Play*? They were the most popular books of the time for children in an age when children were offered only the most priggish and prissy fare. Samuel G. Goodrich (fig. 46) tried to fill the gap with his "Parley Books," like Abbott's, moralistic though entertaining tales and, as has often been said, not unlike Thomas Day's British classic *Sanford and Merton*. Abbott continued his writing until he had produced over two hundred volumes.

He was born in Hallowell, Maine, graduated at Bowdoin College in 1820, studied theology at Andover Seminary, and for a few years was professor of mathematics and natural philosophy at Amherst. In 1828 he married, moved to Boston, and founded the Mount Vernon School, one of the early institutions devoted to the education of women. In 1839 he moved to Farmington, Connecticut, and occupied himself almost entirely with his literary efforts. His first major work, *The Corner Stone*, preaching a practical Christianity, aroused the British Tractarians, and Newman's "Tract No. 73" of *Tracts for the Times* was published in 1835 attacking it. Abbott when in England shortly afterward was able to convince Newman that his work was not heretical, and Newman subsequently modified "Tract No. 73." Abbott died in Farmington but was buried in Mount Auburn Cemetery, Cambridge.

69.

Chauncey A. Goodrich
Yale College

Jacob Abbott
Boston Augs 18 1841

Aug 27
1841

Chauncey A. Goodrich
Professor in Yale College
New Haven Conn

Jacob Abbott author of the corner stone
the young Christian

189
Franklin Bache, M.D.   1792–1864
Philadelphia, February 4, 1843

Benjamin Franklin's grandson Franklin Bache, born in Philadelphia, inherited his grandfather's inquiring mind. After graduating at the University of Pennsylvania in 1810 and obtaining his M.D. in 1814, he spent three years in the army as surgeon. After eight years' practice he became physician to the Walnut Street Prison and professor of chemistry at the Franklin Institute for six years, professor of chemistry at the Philadelphia College of Pharmacy, and from 1841 to his death professor of chemistry at Jefferson Medical College. Not only did he practice and teach, but he also wrote notable medical works. With his close friend and biographer Dr. George B. Wood, with whom he converses in Edouart's shadows, he wrote the *Dispensatory of the United States of America* in 1833, a 2,000-page volume which by 1890 had gone through sixteen editions. Among his many medical publications was a translation of a *Memoir of Acupuncturation*, a description of the experiences of the Frenchman Julius Cloquet.

He was a member of many medical societies and president of the American Philosophical Society; at the time of his death he was president of the Deaf and Dumb Asylum.

190
George Bacon Wood, M.D.
1797–1879
Philadelphia, January 20, 1843

Dr. Wood was another of the great Philadelphia physicians of the nineteenth century. After graduating at the University of Pennsylvania, he studied medicine under Dr. Joseph Parrish (fig. 77) and then in succession held most of the important medical posts in Philadelphia. Professor of chemistry in the Philadelphia College of Pharmacy, professor of materia medica and pharmacy in the University of Pennsylvania, and professor of the theory and practice medicine at the same place. He was president of the American Philosophical Society for twenty years and from 1848 until his death president of the College of Physicians of Philadelphia. Not only did he collaborate with Dr. Bache on the monumental *Dispensatory of the United States*, but he wrote a *Treatise on the Practice of Medicine* that went through many editions, and a number of historical works dealing with medical subjects and institutions. He died, as he had lived, in Philadelphia, without issue, leaving his enormous collection of specimens and plants and funds to establish a botanical garden, as well as generous legacies, to the university, its hospital, and the College of Physicians. Dr. Hartshorne, reading to the American Philosophical Society a long memoir of Dr. Wood following his death, fervently closed with the words: "May his memory, and the influence of his example, never pass away from amongst us!"

69½.

Franklin Bache.   Geo. B. Wood, M.D

Philada Feb. 4. 1843.   7

Professor Franklin Bache M.D.   Dr. George B. Wood MD Professor of the Univ. of Pen.
of Chemistry Phila 4th feb.ry 1843. Jefferson Med. Coll. Philadelphia 20th Jan.y 1843.

191
Duff Green   1791–1875
Baltimore, March 20, 1841

General Green, as he was sometimes called, was
a Washington journalist of some note; and though
he shifted sides rather freely, he wielded considerable influence. He rose to captain in the War
of 1812 under General Harrison (fig. 233). After
being a surveyor and land speculator in Missouri
he was admitted to the bar and developed a large
practice.

He was a member of the Missouri convention
gathered to form a state government and became
a state senator in 1833 as well as editor of the *St.
Louis Enquirer*, which supported Jackson in 1824.
In 1825 he purchased the *United States Telegraph*
in Washington, of which he was editor until 1835,
opposing Adams (fig. 172), supporting Jackson
and later, turning against him, supporting Clay
(fig. 147) and Calhoun (fig. 161) in 1836. He was
an informal representative of Jackson in various
courts of Europe, and in 1843 Calhoun, as Tyler's
secretary of state, sent him to Mexico to negotiate
for the acquisition of the territories of Texas,
New Mexico, and California. In business he developed vast coal and iron lands in Virginia and
Maryland, engaged in railroad building in Tennessee and Georgia, and after the war engaged in
organizing several smaller railroads. A large block
of houses he owned in Washington where the Library of Congress now stands was known as Duff
Green's Row. His papers and letters are in the
Library of Congress and the University of North
Carolina Library. His great interests were industrial development of the South, protection of its
political rights, and a free and independent press.
In his old age his tall figure, long white beard,
and cane made him a striking and stately figure,
which is apparent in Edouart's handsome shade.

Duff Green
Baltimore
March 20th 1841

70.

Genl Duff Green
Baltimore
March 20th 1841

192

Aaron Kitchell Woolley   1800–1849

Lexington, Kentucky, May 23, 1844

Judge Woolley, born in Springfield, New Jersey, became one of the most distinguished and successful lawyers of Fayette County, Kentucky. He led his class at West Point, studied law under Richard Biddle, brother of Nicholas Biddle (fig. 271), and practiced for a time at Port Gibson, Mississippi. In the summer of 1827 he married Sally, the daughter of the lawyer Robert Wickliffe, became his partner, and inherited his large and lucrative practice. In the state legislature he represented Fayette for two years in the lower house and for four in the senate, after which he served five years as circuit judge. For ten years he was professor of law at Transylvania University. He was a candidate for the convention of 1849 to revise the state constitution but died of cholera a few days before the election.

70.½

A. K. Woolly L. L. D.
Lexington Ky 23d May 1844.

193
Samuel Wilkeson   1781–1848
Washington, April 15, 1841

Though his early life was spent on a farm, without any formal education, Wilkeson's achievements are outstanding. He had ambition, imagination, and the ability to manage people. Beginning his business career as a builder and shipping man, he supplied General Harrison (fig. 233) with transports for his troops during the invasion of Canada in the War of 1812. He then settled in Buffalo, was a strong advocate of the construction of the Erie Canal, and saved the day by constructing a suitable harbor for a terminus for this canal. This it was that effectively established the city of Buffalo as a viable commercial town and earned Wilkeson the epitaph "Urbem Condidit." He was elected to the state senate in 1824 and served it and the Court for the Correction of Errors for six years. He became mayor of Buffalo in 1836.

He was opposed to outright emancipation but was a member and for a time president of the American Colonization Society and was instrumental in sending many freed slaves to Liberia. His son wrote of him in the *Publications of the Buffalo Historical Society*, "This man was a king among men." A portrait of Judge Wilkeson belonging to the Buffalo Historical Society reveals the same prominent Roman nose that cast its shadow for Edouart.

Wilkeson Buffalo new yar
15th April 1841   71

P. Wilkeson Judge Buffalo N. Y!
Washington 15 April 1841.

194
Henry Baldwin, LL.D. 1780–1844
Philadelphia, November 2, 1842

Judge Baldwin, born in New Haven, graduated at the top of his class at Yale in 1797, and from then on, except for occasional financial reverses, his career was upward. After studying law under Alexander J. Dallas (fig. 232), he set up practice in Pittsburgh and was soon its leading lawyer and a leading citizen. In 1812 he entered Congress and served three terms, during which he was made chairman of the Standing Committee on Manufacturers, where he made himself popular in many quarters as a strong supporter of protection. In 1830, following the death of Judge Bushrod Washington, he was called from private practice by President Jackson to take Washington's place on the Supreme Court. Horace Binney and John Bannister Gibson (fig. 195) were also under consideration. Duff Green (fig. 191) opposed Baldwin in the *United States Telegraph*, but his nomination was confirmed, whereupon Yale granted him an LL.D.

Although Baldwin was an admirer of Marshall (fig. 196), on whose Court he sat for five years, their views were philosophically opposed, resulting in Baldwin's writing a large number of dissenting opinions. To Baldwin's view the Constitution was the creation of the people of the several states and not of the United States as a whole. Perhaps his most important decision was in the case of *McGill* v. *Brown*, decided in 1833, involving testamentary bequests for charitable purposes. He suffered from an eccentricity and, in his last years, weakness of mind, and his personal affairs went to pieces. At his death it was necessary for his friends to raise a subscription to cover the costs of his burial.

In view of their rivalry for Washington's seat on the Court, it is interesting to see Edouart pair Baldwin and Judge Gibson, and we can muse over their conversation together in the shade.

195
John Bannister Gibson, LL.D. 1780–1853
Philadelphia, January 19, 1843

Judge Gibson ranks high among Pennsylvania judges. His widowed mother put him through Dickinson College under the handicap of very limited means. He turned promptly to the law and soon made a way for himself. In 1812 he became judge of the Court of Common Pleas for Tioga County and in 1816 was appointed to the Supreme Court of Pennsylvania. Eleven years later he succeeded Judge Tilghman as chief justice. In 1838 he made the only mistake of his career, and one he carried in his conscience long after. At that time the new Constitution provided for a term of years for judges instead of life appointments, and the terms were to expire at intervals of three years in order of seniority, the first in January 1839. Judge Gibson resigned as chief justice and was immediately reappointed by Governor Ritner, by which means instead of holding the shortest term, three years, he obtained the longest, fifteen years. In mitigation of the action it has been said that his associates proposed it, but it was plainly an injudicious step which he long regretted. Nevertheless he presided over the court for twenty-three years until the Constitution was again changed, at which point he was reelected to the new court but not as chief justice. At his death, Chief Justice Black, in concluding a panegyric on the old judge, said: "The profession of the law has lost the ablest of its teachers, this court the brightest of its ornaments and this people the steadfast defender of their rights, so far as they were capable of being protected by judicial authority."

71½

Henry Baldwin One of the
associate Justices of the Supreme
Court of the United States
2 November 1842 —

John B Gibson
Chief Justice of Pennsylvania
19 January 1843

Judge Henry Baldwin one of the associate Justice
of the Supreme Court of the U.S. Philadelphia 2d Nov. 1842.

Chief Justice of the Supreme Ct. of Pennsylvania
John B. Gibson Phila 19th Jany 1843.

196
John Marshall 1755–1835
Posthumous

Chief Justice Marshall, the third and greatest chief justice of the United States, held that high office for thirty-five years, until his death. He it was who firmly established the Constitution as the superior law of the land. "It is a proposition too plain to be contested," he wrote in his opinion in *Marbury* v. *Madison*, "that the Constitution controls any legislative act repugnant to it. . . . A legislative act contrary to the Constitution is not law." This philosophy runs throughout his opinions. His career is well known: for six years he was in the military service; he was a member of the Virginia House of Delegates, carried on a distinguished practice of the law at Richmond, and was a member of the state convention called to ratify the Constitution in 1788; with Pinckney and Gerry he was a member of the famous XYZ mission to France; and at the last moment of John Adams's presidency he was appointed chief justice. He presided over the trial of Aaron Burr, wrote the opinion in the *Dartmouth College* case, which for a time at least protected corporate charters from amendment by legislative action of the granting authority. His decisions are legion and many would be familiar if named. In his old age he was a member of the Virginia Constitutional Convention of 1829–30, the so-called Last Meeting of the Giants painted in session by Catlin. He was the first chief justice to die in office.

Edouart's silhouette is of course posthumous and is taken from one of many cut in 1830 by William Henry Brown, the well-known New England silhouettist. What it does point up is Edouart's evident desire in this one volume to include the important people of the day, and Marshall certainly stands high on that list.

red code of Virg.
J. Marshall

Chief Justice of U.S.
J. Marshall
Washington

197
Jonathan Knight, M.D.   1789–1864
Saratoga, August 20, 1844

To Dr. Knight goes the credit for first employing digital compression for the cure of aneurysm. It is told that in 1848, after forty hours of treatment administered by relays of his young assistants at the Yale Medical School, relieving each other in turns at brief intervals, the aneurysm disappeared. This was an important experiment but only an incident in a long and useful career. For fifty years Dr. Knight held a chair in the Yale Medical School, at which he was one of the first physicians. From 1813 to 1838 he was professor of anatomy and for the following quarter of a century professor of surgery, and throughout that half-century he maintained an active private practice.

Born in Norwalk, he graduated at Yale in 1808, was a tutor at Yale, and then to equip himself to serve in the Yale Medical School studied for two years under Dr. Rush at the Pennsylvania Medical School. As one of the most prominent physicians of the day he became president of the American Medical Association. He died in New Haven of peritonitis. He stands before Edouart as though lecturing, while behind him we see Dr. Ely in the act of preaching.

198
Ezra Stiles Ely, D.D.   1786–1861
Philadelphia, January 19, 1843

A three-day trial before the New York Presbytery in 1814 arising from a strong anti-Hopkinsian statement resulted in the unanimous and honorable acquittal of Dr. Ely and enabled him to assume the position of pastor of the Third or Pine Street Presbyterian Church in Philadelphia. Twenty years of service there enabled him to sign himself in 1843 as formerly of Philadelphia. In 1834 he moved west to found Marion College in Marion County in northern Missouri, to which he contributed generously and where for a time he served as professor of polemic theology. But hard times in 1837 and his own financial reverses brought the enterprise to an end. His wife died in 1842, shortly before he stood to Edouart, and by 1844 he returned to Philadelphia to become pastor of the First Presbyterian Church of Northern Liberties, where he served for seven years, until he suffered a stroke under which he lingered until his death. He was a generous supporter of the Jefferson Medical College in Philadelphia, and stated clerk and moderator of the Presbyterian General Assembly. He published many sermons and theological works, one with the cheerful title *Endless Punishment*.

72½.

Ezra Stiles Ely,
D.D. of Missouri,
formerly of Philᵃ. Pᵃ.
at Philadelphia

J. Knight MD Profᵣ of Surgery Yale Coll Dr Ezra Stiles Ely DD of Missouri formerly
Saratoga 20ᵗʰ Augᵗ 1844.   Philᵃ 19ᵗʰ Janʳʸ 1843,   of Philadelphia

199
Roger Jones 1789–1852
Washington City, March 20, 1841

Bravery on the field of battle was the mark of
Roger Jones. He was brevetted major in July
1814 for distinguished service at the Battle of
Chippewa, lieutenant colonel in September on
the recommendation of General Scott (fig. 120)
for gallant conduct in the sortie from Fort Erie
and in the Battle of Niagara, colonel in 1824 for
ten years' faithful service in one grade, brigadier
general in 1832 for the same reason, major general
in 1848 for meritorious conduct if not for playing
the leading hand in the Mexican War. And in
1825 he was appointed adjutant general of the
army, a commission he acknowledges under his
signature in Edouart's view of him, sword at side,
cockaded hat in hand, as though accepting the
honors he had so brilliantly earned. In John
Frost's *The American Generals* (1860) it was said
of him: "Above all is the country largely indebted
to him for his exertions during the Mexican War.
. . . It will not therefore be considered hyperbol-
ical to assert, that no small share of the efficiency
of our armies is the result of the skilful administration of Adjutant General Jones."

73

Genl. R. Jones.
Adjt. Genl.
March
20th 1841.

Gal Rogers Jones adjt Gal U.S. Army
Washington City 20th March 1841.

200
Robert Mendenhall Huston, M.D.
1795–1864
Philadelphia, May 4, 1843

Dr. Huston is clearly making a point with his colleague Dr. Dunglison about the bottle he holds in his hand, but we, unfortunately, cannot overhear the conversation. Huston's life was single-purposed—the practice and teaching of medicine. A product of the Medical Department of the University of Pennsylvania, for three years he was professor of obstetrics and diseases of women and children (is that a baby's bottle he holds in his hand?) in Jefferson Medical College, followed by sixteen years in the chair of materia medica and general therapeutics. He published many of his medical addresses and edited the American edition of Churchhill's *Theory and Practice of Midwifery*. His standing as a physician is borne out by his being able to sign himself "President of the Phila. Med. Society."

201
Robley Dunglison, M.D.
1798–1869
Philadelphia, January 16, 1843

Dunglison, "the Father of American Physiology," was born and trained in England, practiced in America, and had the privilege of serving his sponsor Thomas Jefferson. It was Jefferson who in 1824 invited Robley to a professorship of medicine in the Medical Department of the University of Virginia, which he occupied for nine years. He treated Jefferson, Madison, Monroe, and Jackson. In John Dorsey's *The Jefferson-Dunglison Letters* (1960) Dunglison's diary is quoted as saying: "Mr. Jefferson had more inspiration, Mr. Madison excelled perhaps in judgment," and as for Monroe, "he made a much less favorable impression in regard to his intellectual powers than Mr. Jefferson or Mr. Madison." Dr. Dunglison held the chair of materia medica and therapeutics in the University of Maryland for three years and then for thirty-two years he was professor of the Institutes of Medicine in Jefferson Medical College, Philadelphia.

As president of the Institute for the Blind, he was instrumental in developing the printing of books in raised letters. His great works, the standards, were *Dunglison's Medical Dictionary* and *Human Physiology*. In *The Jefferson-Dunglison Letters*, Sir William Osler is quoted as saying that Jefferson did a good work when he imported Dunglison from London, that he brought a good reputation to Jefferson Medical College, and that "after all, there is no such literature as a dictionary," and that the twenty-three editions of *Dunglison's* was a testimony to its usefulness. He added, however, that the *Physiology* was the book of Dunglison's full of joy for the student, not only for its knowledge but because there were "so many more trimmings in the shape of good stories."

73½

Robert M Huston,
President of the Phila. Med. Society,
Professor of Materia Medica
in Jefferson Medical College of Phila.
May 4. 1843

Robley Dunglison
Jan.y 16. 1843.
Professor of Institutes of Med. &
Jefferson Medical College.
Phila.

Dr. Robert M Huston MD.
Pres. Phila. Medical Society. and.
Professor of Materia Medica &c. in Jefferson Coll.
Philadelphia May 4. 1843.

Dr. Robley Dunglison MD.
Professor of Institute of Medicine in Jefferson
Philadelphia 16th Jan.y/43 Medical College
Phila.

202

Ferdinand Rudolph Hassler
1770–1843
Washington, March 21, 1841

The Swiss-born son of a watchmaker, Hassler became the first superintendent of the United States
Coast Survey. But his life was frustrating to him.
He emigrated to America in 1815 with a land
company to form a Swiss colony in the South,
bringing with him his library of several thousand
volumes and some scientific instruments. The settlement scheme failed, but in Philadelphia Hassler, with his mathematical and geodetic training,
discovered kindred spirits in the American Philosophical Society.

When Jefferson procured the passage of an act
authorizing a survey of the coasts of the United
States, Hassler was put in charge of the venture.
Yet progress was slow, the scheme was held in
abeyance, and for two years Hassler served as
professor of philosophy and mathematics at Union
College, then went to London to obtain appropriate instruments for surveying. The War of
1812 delayed him, but he returned to the United
States in 1815 and commenced work on the survey.
Changes in the law intervened to delay his work;
for a while he took to farming and then was appointed by Jackson as superintendent of weights
and measures. Not until 1832 was the survey
reestablished. He did not live to see the task completed, but his work was carried out with the
highest scientific standards and laid the foundation for the future progress of the coastal survey.
The story is told that he and Woodbury (fig. 225)
could not agree on his salary and the matter was
referred to Jackson, who at Hassler's request for
$6,000 replied that that was as much as Mr. Wood-
bury, secretary of the treasury, received. E. S. C.
Smith in *Union Worthies* (no. 13, 1958) quotes
Hassler as replying: "Plenty Mr. Woodburys, plenty Mr. Everybodys for Secretary of de Treasury,
vone, vone Mr. Hassler for de head of de Coast
Survey." He won the $6,000. As some justification
for such a boast we have the statement of President
Nott of Union College on learning of his death:
"We have not such another man to die." His successor said of him that "he was a man like the
work itself, in advance of the times."

F. R. Hassler 21 Mars 1841

74

obt. 19t. Novemb. 1843
Philadelphia

F. R. Hassler Survey Genl. of the Coast of the U. States
Washington 21t March 1841.

203
Joaquin Cesar de Figaniere e Moraõ
1798–1866
Philadelphia, March 6, 1843

It is not difficult to distinguish which of these two ministers is foreign and which American. He who is described by Edouart as "Ministre de Sa Majesté très fidèle aux Etats Unis d'Amérique" is every inch a visitor to our shores. He seems to stand patiently listening to his American counterpart, perhaps not understanding all that is being said but well able to defend faithfully His Majesty's interests.

He had been chargé d'affaires of Portugal from March 1835 to June 1838, was minister resident of Portugal on December 30, 1840, and by 1854 was envoy extraordinary and minister plenipotentiary of Portugal. In 1843 he lived on Thirteenth Street above Pine Street; and he had trouble with his coachman whom he dismissed twice for disrespect and intemperance, as he wrote in 1847 to Manuel Carvallo.

De Figaniere was the author of "An Account of a Remarkable Accumulation of Bats," which appeared in the Smithsonian Institution's *Annual Report* of 1863. This was an amusing account of the measures taken to rid his house at Seneca Point, near Charleston, Maryland, of an infestation of bats, the house having been uninhabited for some years. After trying several orthodox measures, the minister and his family resorted to wooden paddles with which they killed the bats as they emerged from their sleeping places at dusk. He reported that in a few nights they killed 9,640 bats in the main house alone. The bodies were added to the manure pile and used to fertilize the flowers. Thus, he wrote, "in some degree, they served to compensate us for the annoyance to which we had been subjected." The minister died at Brooklyn, New York.

204
Daniel J. Desmond   d.1849
Philadelphia, December 16, 1842

By training Desmond was a lawyer, but little is known of his early life. By 1843, when he resided at 99 Spruce Street, he was vice-consul of Austria; consul general of Rome; consul general of the Pontifical States, according to Edouart; vice-consul of Portugal, where he succeeded John Vaughn; consular agent of Tuscany; and in 1849 also consul of Sardinia and Sicily. At home he was secretary for foreign correspondence for the Historical Society of Pennsylvania from 1844 to 1849, a post he must have been eminently fitted to fill. Hampton L. Carson in his *History of the Historical Society of Pennsylvania* (1940) states that Desmond did "much to resuscitate the Society at the crisis of its sinking spell."

Something of Desmond can perhaps be discovered from the several books he gave to the American Philosophical Society, including "a large German Atlas," which might, he said, "fill up some chasm in your Catalogue of Foreign works in the same subject." Another was his own translation, published in 1837, of Paul de Kock's comic sketches *The Good Fellow*. He gave a copy of his own *Annual Address of the Philodemic Society of Georgetown College . . . July 28, 1831*, its theme being the progress of liberty in the world, the rise of free institutions; and it "inculcated the diffusion of knowledge, the love of country, and the practice of virtue, as the best safeguards of liberty." In preparation, doubtless, for the proper discharge of his duties as Portuguese vice-consul, he borrowed in 1841 or 1842 from the Philosophical Society's library a New Testament in Portuguese and a Portuguese grammar, dictionary, and book of exercises. Here was a public servant who took his responsibilities seriously.

74 1/2.

O Sons. de Viganière et Morão   Daniel J. Desmond
                                            16th December 1842

Ministre de Sa Majesté très fidèle
aux Etats Unis d'Amérique   Portugal
Philadelphie 6 Mars 1843.

Daniel J. Desmond.
Consul General of the Pontifical States
de Viganière e Morão
Ministre de Sa Majesté très fidèle   and Counsellor at Law, Philad.
aux Etats Unis d'Amérique   Portugal
Philadelphie 6 Mars 1843.

205
Chin Sung
Washington, February 10, 1841

The charming silhouette of Chin Sung is one of the two in this volume signed by Edouart and gives us a clue to identifying the handwriting on many of the other silhouettes.

Chin Sung has, happily, written for us a description of himself in his own language. For our own convenience it is translated as follows on a slip of paper interleaved in the volume:

The Chinese characters written by Chin Sume are as translated by Doct. Peter Parker, Missionary to China
"Chin Sume who was born at Peking, emigrated to the Province of Canton—respectfully writes his name—
"Chin Sume translates it as follows:
Peking
Chin Sume
came
Canton
and placing his hands
on his breast
bows with profound
respect"

Dr. Parker's inscription clearly reads "Sume" and Edouart's equally clearly "Sung." Perhaps Edouart's spelling was simply phonetic.

Chin Sung, however, is not bowing as Parker's translation states; he is rather pointing upward. The inscription has been translated in recent times, 1975, to read as follows:

From Pekin
Arriving Canton Province
and Macao
Mr. Ching Sung
Portrait

Always chatting
with his friends
and looking at the moon
recites a poem.

The gifted reader may be able to produce another version, but unlikely one more politely poetic.

興友常談望月

吟詩

北京省生到廣東羊城澳門陳松相

augⁿ Edouart, fecit 1841.

Chin Sung of China
taken in Washington
Feby 10ᵗʰ 1841.

206

Paul Beck, Jr. 1760–1844
Philadelphia, October 7, 1843

In 1787 worth four thousand pounds, in 1797 sixty thousand pounds, at his death in 1844 Paul Beck was possessed of a million and a quarter dollars, yet, as has been said of him, his wealth was acquired not by extortion but by his skill and acumen as a merchant. The uses to which he put it occasioned neither envy nor hostility, but rather gratitude.

Son of an immigrant German, apprenticed to a wine merchant at the age of fourteen, Beck's financial star was ever in the ascendancy and he died one of Philadelphia's wealthiest merchants, having long served his city with unselfish devotion.

He was warden of the port, tried unsuccessfully to restore William Penn's design for a magnificent quay along the Delaware River, reconnected the Chesapeake and Delaware bays by a canal, was a founder and patron of the Pennsylvania Academy of the Fine Arts, treasurer of Christ Church Hospital, a benefactor of the Deaf and Dumb Asylum, and president of the American Sunday School Union.

We see him as an old gentleman at the close of his life, resigned and patient and no doubt with his conscience at ease from having carried more than his share of his city's burdens.

7 4 1/2.

Paul Beck

The death of Paul Beck, jr., Esq., a wealthy merchant
of Philadelphia, is announced.

22d December 1844.

Paul Beck 84 y.rs of age Philadelphia 7th Octob. 1843

207
Justin Perkins 1805–1869
Saratoga, August 27, 1842

Perkins, "the Apostle of Persia," as he was called, spent his boyhood on a farm in West Springfield, Massachusetts. He took his degree at Amherst in 1829, studied theology at the Andover Theological Seminary, and in 1833 was chosen by the American Board of Commissioners for Foreign Missions to take the gospel to the Nestorians of Persia. With his wife he reached Constantinople in December, Tabriz in August 1834, and finally settled at Ooroomiah (Oroomich or Urumish) in 1835. Here he established some seventy schools for boys and girls and trained students to read the Scriptures. His notable work was to translate the Bible into the Nestorian dialect of Syriac and to establish a printing press in 1840. He returned to America in 1842 and, aided by the bishop of the Nestorians, whom he brought with him, succeeded in arousing great interest in his missionary efforts. He returned to Persia, where he continued his missionary work until 1869, when in ill health he returned to die at Chicopee on the last day of the year. His books, other than his Syriac translations, were *A Residence of Eight Years in Persia* and *Mission Life in Persia*.

Unlike his usual practice, Edouart seems to have procured Perkins's signature and that of his companion on separate pieces of paper which he then pasted into his volume, that of Perkins being pasted on the opposite page.

208
Mar Yohannan
Saratoga Springs, August 27, 1842

What a social lion the bishop of Ooroomiah, Mar Yohannan, must have been at Saratoga that August 1842! There can be little doubt that he bolstered Justin Perkins's pleas for assistance for his missionary efforts. From Perkins's *A Residence of Eight Years in Persia*, we learn that the bishop lived in the best house in his village, Gavalân, that his father was a priest, and that it was the bishop who had been Perkins's friend and guide in Persia and who had taught him the Syriac language. Under a woodcut full-face view of the bishop in that book, there appears the bishop's signature, almost identical with what he has written above his shade, and then there is printed the bishop's very telling question: "How can you make books for us in your country, when you do not know our language?" Between them they effectively answered that question.

W. L. Stone, in his *Reminiscences of Saratoga* (1875), writes that Chancellor Walworth's dwelling, The Grove, "has known the portly form of Joseph Bonaparte in tights, and the squat figure of Mar Yohannan in multitudinous folds of cloths." He must have made a splendid spectacle.

Alongside these two figures Edouart included several newspaper clippings—one, dated October 1842, advises that "the celebrated Nestorian Bishop, Mar Yohannan, who has been received everywhere in this country with distinguished honor, sailed from Boston on Wednesday on the barque Emma Isadore, for Smyrna." The other, dated September 1843, describes the "Terrible Massacre" of Nestorian Christians by the "Savage Turks."

75

Mar Yohannan. Bishop. of Oovoomiah.
Persia

ܡܪܝ ܝܘܚܢܢ ܐܦܣܩܘܦܐ ܕܐܘܪܡܝܐ܂

Saratoga Springs 27th August 1842.

Rev. Justin Perkins

Miss to Persia Saratoga 27 Aug 1842

Mar Yohannan Bishop of Oovoomiah
Persia

209
William Ramsey   1803–1858
Philadelphia, January 19, 1843

Edouart was clearly impressed with the height of Ramsey, so much so that he mentioned it, 6 feet 3½ inches, which was indeed considered tall in those days.

What Ramsey tells us himself in the legend, written in Marathi, to which he points is: "In the country of America there was a city. Its name was the city of Thomson. There was a merchant there. His name was Sir Ramsey. He had two children, a daughter and a son. The son's name was William. At the age of twenty-seven he left his country and arrived at Bombay. And there he lived among the Hindu people for five years. Then he returned to his native land."

Ramsey was born in Thompsontown, graduated from Princeton in 1821, and attended the Princeton Theological Seminary from 1823 to 1826. He was ordained by the Presbytery of Huntington, Pennsylvania, in 1827 and carried on missionary work in Southwark, Philadelphia, from 1826 to 1830. The *Philadelphia City Directory* lists his address as 409 South Front Street as late as 1834. He is listed as an agent for the American Board of Commissioners for Foreign Missions in 1835 and 1836, which may have been part of the time he was in Bombay. The fact that he is also recorded as having been pastor of the Cedar Street Presbyterian Church in Philadelphia from 1837 to 1857 would leave only the years 1830 to 1835 for his term in Bombay. The Presbyterian Historical Society of Philadelphia has two paintings of Ramsey and one of his wife.

75/2

अमेरीके मुलुखांत एक नगर
होता, त्याचें नांव थॉमसॉन नगर
होता, त्यांतील एक व्यापारी होता
त्याचें नाम रामसी साहीब –
होता, त्याला दोन लेकरें होतें
कन्य व पुत्र ॥ पुत्राचें नांव –
वीलीयाम होता. जेव्हां तो सत्त
वीस वर्षे हॉऊन त्याचा देष सो
डून मुंबाईला पोंचला. आणी
तेथे हिंदुलॉकांमध्ये पांच वर्ष
राहिल. नेतर आपला देषांत
फीरून आला ॥

(मुंबाई Bombay)

पाद्री रामसी साहीब
सन: २०. १८४३

پادرس رامسی صاحب
۱۸۴۳

Revd. William Ramsey
Philadᵃ Jany 20th
1843.

Revd. William Ramsey Late Missionary at Bombay
Philadelphia 19th Jany 1843. Ætat 3 ½ m. India

210
James DePeyster Ogden   1790–1870
Saratoga, July 28, 1841

An old merchant of New York City, of whom there was none more eminent, was James D.P. Ogden, as he signed himself. In 1805, aged but fifteen, he was a clerk with Van Horne & Clarkson, shippers and importers, of 129 Pearl Street, only a step from the docks of the East River. By 1820 he was in business for his own account and for forty years he carried on an active mercantile life. He traveled abroad, and while in Liverpool he acted as United States consul under President Jackson. He deplored the Civil War, was friendly toward the South, but was wholeheartedly opposed to secession. William Barrett, in *The Old Merchants of New York* (1863), was his great admirer and urged his choice as mayor of the city. Descended from families prominent in the settlement of New York, he was also the progenitor of prominent New Yorkers.

He stands proudly before Edouart, at the social center of the East Coast of the country, and at the peak of his mercantile career.

211
Charles Augustus Davis   1795–1867
New York, October 1, 1839

Here we see another of the old merchants of New York. Davis was one of the partners of Davis & Brooks, who were actively engaged in the iron business and in the Mediterranean trade. But he was more than just a successful merchant—he was an able and witty writer on commercial and financial matters. His "Peter Scribes Letters" and "Major Jack Downing Letters," published in the *Daily Advertiser* and the *New York Express*, were received with interest and amusement but were to the displeasure of President Jackson, who was somewhat ridiculed by them. Jackson is said to have exclaimed that if he could have caught Davis he would have drowned him.

Davis was a great admirer of John Quincy Adams (fig. 172) and commissioned the artist Asher B. Durand to paint a replica of the portrait of Adams he had done for Luman Reed. Davis then gave the portrait to Charles Francis Adams's wife.

Although these two New York merchants were cut by Edouart on different dates, they must often have met in New York very much as they appear here, Davis the iron merchant and Ogden the importer.

76

Jas D. Ogden of New York
28 July 1841.

Cw Aug. J Davis
N. York 1 Oct. 1839.

Jas D. Ogden of New York
Saratoga 28th July 1841.

Chs Augs. Davis of N.York
1st Octob. 1839.

212

Joseph Michael Doran   1800–1859
Philadelphia, October 4, 1842

Judge Doran was caught by Edouart in Philadelphia just before the end of his three years on the
Court of General Sessions, and he rather enjoyed
the seat and the title. He was a graduate of the
University of Pennsylvania in the class of 1820
and was admitted to practice in 1824. Solicitor of
the District of Southwark in 1835, member of the
constitutional convention in 1837, Doran enjoyed
a comfortable practice, attaining his greatest successes in criminal cases. He was noted for his humor, which always added zest to his addresses to
juries. He was born and died in Philadelphia; and
only three of his eight children survived him, one
of whom, Joseph Ingersoll Doran, became a distinguished lawyer.

76½

J M Doran
Oct 4th 1842.
General Sessions.

Judge Joseph M. Doran   General Sessions Philadelphia
4th October 1842.

213
John Ellis Wool 1784–1869
[Troy, New York], October 3, 1841

Wool's shade of this date appears to have given us the slip but there is ample evidence it was once here. We have his signature, Edouart's notation, and the shadow cast on the terrace. But the likeness has evaporated.

Though he commenced life as a bookseller and was then lawyer, Wool's career was that of a gallant soldier constantly at the service of his country. He aided General Scott (fig. 120) during the removal of the Cherokees and was commissioned brigadier general in June 1841. He served in the Mexican War under General Zachary Taylor and years later, in 1861, succeeded General Butler in the command of Fortress Monroe. He was said to have had superior talent in the service as an organizer of troops. At his death at an old age in Troy, he left a generous bequest to Rensselaer Polytechnic Institute; and his widow erected a seventy-five-foot shaft to his memory with an inscription written by William Cullen Bryant: "This stone is erected to Major-General John Ellis Wool, the gallant soldier, the able commander, and the patriotic citizen, distinguished in many battles; and to Sarah Moulton, his excellent and worthy consort."

He was enormously popular in his day and a fitting member of Edouart's respository of great Americans. For his appearance two years later, in company with General Scott, see fig. 340.

214
George Mercer Brooke d.1851
Saratoga, July 28, 1843

No one seems to know just when Brooke the Virginian was born, but his brother Francis, the jurist, was born in 1763. Like General Jones (fig. 199), General Brooke was a gallant soldier constantly rewarded for bravery on the field of battle, on one occasion in the sortie from Fort Erie in the company of Jones.

He entered the service in 1808 and, having served continuously in the army—with time out for a moment's relaxation at Saratoga—he took a leading part in the war with Mexico in 1848 and was rewarded for his meritorious conduct. Fort Brooke, at the head of Tampa Bay, Florida, where he was once stationed, was named after him. He died in San Antonio, Texas. He and General Wool would have had much in common to discuss on Edouart's terrace.

John E. Wool
Brig: Gen.l U.S.A 3 October 1841

Geo. M. Brooke
Brig.d Gen.l U.S.a
Saratoga July 28st
1843

77.

Brig.r Gd.l John E. Wool
U.S Army

Geo. M. Brooke Brig.d Gen. U.S Army
Saratoga July 88th 1844.

215
Titian Ramsay Peale   1799–1885
Philadelphia, December 12, 1842

Titian Peale, the naturalist and artist, was, as described by Edouart in 1842, proprietor of the Philadelphia Museum, founded by his father, Charles Willson Peale. He had also just returned from a four-year turn as a naturalist on the staff of the United States exploring expedition to the South Seas under Captain Charles Wilkes. Here we see him as though showing his brother one of the many drawings he made on that expedition, which were later published in Cassin's *Mammology and Ornithology* in 1858.

Like all of his family, Titian, the youngest son, was an artist, but he exercised his talent almost exclusively in the delineation of animal life. He was the naturalist-artist on Long's expedition of exploration between the Mississippi and the Rockies, on Barrow's expedition exploring the Magdalene river in New Grenada; on both trips he drew numerous sketches and collected specimens for the museum. He drew plates for the first and fourth volumes of Lucien Bonaparte's *American Ornithology* and was a frequent contributor to scientific publications and a member of the American Philosophical Society. When the museum was sold, his wide interests led him to become an examiner in the United States Patent Office. At his death he was engaged in preparing a work on Lepidoptera illustrated with his own drawings. He painted a rather charming portrait of himself about 1850 which has inscribed on the back "T. R. Peale—by himself with a little help from his brother Rembrandt."

216
Rembrandt Peale   1778–1860
Philadelphia, December 15, 1842

Who doesn't know the so-called porthole portrait of Washington painted by Rembrandt Peale. When Washington sat to Charles Willson Peale in 1795, Rembrandt, aged only seventeen, painted alongside his father. From his painting, in later life, he developed what he considered the "certified" Washington, the porthole likeness of which he painted some seventy-nine replicas.

He was an able artist, studied under Benjamin West in England in 1802, painted portraits of distinguished Americans for his father's gallery, and aided in the establishment of the Pennsylvania Academy of the Fine Arts. Critics vie with each other in choosing Rembrandt Peale's "best" painting; his portrait of Washington and *The Court of Death*, which was suggested to him by Bishop Porteus's poem "A Death," rank high. Our choice would be the second portrait of Jefferson, painted in 1805, now belonging to the New-York Historical Society. But his portraits are legion and many are superlative examples of his art.

In 1814, emulating his father, he opened a "Peale's Museum" in Baltimore in what was the first building in that city to be illuminated by gas. This venture was sponsored by Columbus O'Donnell (fig. 106), president of the Baltimore Gas Light Company. He succeeded John Trumbull as president of the American Academy of Fine Arts in New York, painted and wrote late into his life, and died in Philadelphia aged eighty-three. He was probably the most talented and successful of all the artistic children of his versatile and beloved father, Charles Willson Peale.

77½ Titian R Peale
Philad.ª Dec.ʳ 12ᵗʰ 1842.

Rem: Peale
Rembrandt Peale.
Philad.ª Dec: 15. 1842

Titian R. Peale Prop. of Philadelphia Museum
12ᵗʰ Dec. 1842.

Rembrandt Peale Port. Painter
Philadelphia 15ᵗʰ Dec. 1842.

217
Josephine Clifton   1813–1847
Boston, May 5, 1842

The life of the tragedian Josephine Clifton was
itself in a way a tragedy. Her acting career, brilliant in its beginnings, lasted only ten years and
she died suddenly only a year after her marriage
to Robert Place, manager of the American Theater in New Orleans.

She was brought up in the home of Thomas
Hamblin, manager of the Bowery Theater, and
her debut on the stage at the Bowery is variously
described as in Otway's *Venice Preserved* as Belvidere, and in *Bertram* as Imogene. Her charm,
beauty, and talent made her an instant success.
She played Lady Macbeth at the Walnut Street
Theater in Philadelphia to universal approval
and delight. She is said to have been the first
American actress to "star" in England, where she
appeared at the Drury Lane Theatre as Belvidere.
She was almost a rival of Charlotte Cushman, but
she became obese, suffered great distress when an
old scandal about her mother was revived, and
was not seen again on the stage after 1846. Her
marriage was terminated by her death in only her
thirty-fourth year. Her profile is that of a young
woman of charm, and her signature is clear and
spirited. It was for her that N. P. Willis wrote the
tragedy she performed in so well, *Bianca Visconti*,
earning the affectionate title "the Magnificent
Josephine."

78

Josephine Clifton
Boston May 5th /42

Miss Josephine Clifton 5f 10 inch
Tragedian Boston 5th May 1842

218
Joel Jones   1795–1860
Philadelphia, October 4, 1842

Judge Jones is but another of the distinguished lawyers and jurists whose legal education was obtained at Tapping Reeve's law school in Litchfield, Connecticut, shortly after Jones's graduation from Yale in 1813, standing second in his class. With his family he moved to Pennsylvania, established himself in his profession at Easton, and acquired a large practice and high reputation for his learning and ability. Governor Wolf appointed him as one of three to revise the laws of Pennsylvania and then appointed him a judge of the District Court for the City and County of Philadelphia, of which at the end of ten years he became president judge in 1845. He was the first president of Girard College, but because of disagreement with his trustees served only eighteen months. In 1849 he was elected mayor of Philadelphia, as a Democrat, against John Swift (fig. 226). He then retired to private practice for the remainder of his life. He was a distinguished Greek and Hebrew scholar and a student of the Bible, his *Notes on Scripture* being published posthumously in 1861.

He stands amiably and politely before Judge Stroud, for whom he was certainly a match.

219
George McDowell Stroud
1795–1875
Philadelphia, October 17, 1842

Judge Stroud was a distinguished member of the United States District Court of Philadelphia, to which he was appointed in 1835. A graduate of the College of New Jersey (Princeton) with high honors in 1817, he was admitted to practice before the bar in Pennsylvania in 1819. His principal publication was *Sketch of the Laws Relative to Slavery in Several of the States* (1827). He spent in all some thirty-one years on the court. He sat with Judge Hare in the district court in the celebrated case *Bank of United States* v. *The Wilmington Railroad* and was in 1859 a pallbearer at the funeral of the seventy-nine-year-old Richard Rush, son of Dr. Benjamin Rush.

Joel Jones
Dist. Court.

Geom. Stroud Dist. Court
Philad: Oct. 17. 1842

Judge Joel Jones
Philadelphia 4th Octob: 1842.

Judge Geo. M. Stroud Dist. Court
Philadelphia 17th Octob. 1842.

220
Thomas Handasyd Perkins
1764–1854
Boston, February 11, 1842

Colonel Perkins is well described in the title of his
biography, published in 1971—*Merchant Prince
of Boston*. He was indeed a prince among merchants. Everything he touched turned to gold. His
fortune was made in the China trade and it was
reported to be in excess of $2 million. He grew up
within sound of the Boston Massacre and by-
passed a college education to commence his remarkable commercial career. As a prominent
member of the Federalist party, he was eleven
times elected to the state legislature and once bore
important dispatches abroad to London. He was
active in forwarding the completion of the Bunker
Hill Monument, albeit he had financial interests
in the Quincy quarry that furnished the stone and
the Quincy Railway, which transported it. But his
charitable interests were many and generously
supported by him. The Mercantile Library Association and the Boston Athenaeum were objects
of his beneficences. What will long keep his memory green is the asylum for the blind which bears
his name, now the Perkins School for the Blind.
He was one of the outstanding openhanded men
of Boston in his day, and his name lives after him.

79

J H Perkins
Boston Feb 11
1842

Col Tho. H. Perkins of Boston 11th Feby 1842

221
Charles West Thomson 1798–1879
Philadelphia, December 15, 1842

There was a day, only a century ago, when *The Gift, The Token, The Atlantic-Souvenir* were known and read avidly and enjoyed—the gift annuals. Who wrote for them? One answer is that prolific writer the Reverend Charles W. Thomson, Quaker-born Philadelphian turned Episcopalian, for sixteen years rector of the Episcopal church in York, Pensylvania. But his true calling was poetry. We see him in his clerical garb in 1842, before his call to York and at a time when what Edouart noted about him was that he was the author of *The Sylph and Other Poems*, published in 1828.

He was a popular writer in his day, a friend of Edgar Allan Poe, a book collector, and entitled to a place in American literature of the day. For many years he was closely associated with the Franklin Association of Philadelphia. A bibliography of his writings was compiled by Charles F. Hartman in 1921, in which it is stated that historians of literature had shamefully neglected him.

791/2

Chs. West Thomson. Author of the Sylph and other Poems
Philadelphia 15th Decemb. 1842.

William Cranch   1769–1855
Washington, April 14, 1841

Judge Cranch is the second of the midnight judges, appointed by President Adams as the sands of his presidency ran out, to appear before us in Edouart's company. His father had married John Adams's sister, and he himself had been a classmate of John Quincy Adams at Harvard, class of 1787. President Adams was perhaps exhibiting a human, if nepotistical, failing, but Cranch was well qualified for the post. He had already served as a commissioner of public buildings in Washington, and Adams had had a chance to observe him. His confidence was not misplaced. Cranch's term in the district court extended for fifty-four years, during fifty of which he was chief justice. His record for wise and correct decisions was unimpeachable. He was appointed chief judge in 1805 by Jefferson, which, in view of the then chilly relations between Jefferson and Adams, surprised everyone, Cranch most of all.

As reporter for the Supreme Court, succeeding Alexander J. Dallas, father of Commodore Dallas (fig. 232), he published nine volumes of reports containing many of Chief Justice Marshall's great constitutional opinions. Lewis in his *Great American Lawyers* quotes Cranch as remarking on the death of Decatur, the naval hero, at the hands of Commodore Barron (fig. 34) on the field of honor: "However fairly and honorably a duel may be fought, yet, if death ensues, it is, in the eye of the law, murder. . . . A doubt of the law may not be excited by the high and honorable standing of the parties, by the solemn pomp of funeral rites, or the universal sympathy of the nations." Cranch, in the words of a contemporary, was one who "by his integrity, zeal, uprightness and purity of character, has added a lustre to the whiteness of the judicial ermine."

80.

W. Cranch Ch. J. D. of Col.
14 April 1841. Æ. 72.

Wm Cranch Chief Justice District of Columbia
72 Y.s of age   Washington 14th April 1841.

223
William Darlington, M.D.
1782–1863
Philadelphia, November 1, 1843

Though Darlington was read out of the Society of Friends because of a voyage to India in 1806 as a ship's surgeon, his "Letters from Calcutta" appeared in the *Analectic Magazine* in 1819. With an M.D. degree from the University of Pennsylvania received in 1804, Dr. Darlington took his part in the medical profession of the day but was at heart, as in practice, a botanist. A few terms in Congress, president of the Bank of Chester County, Pennsylvania, clerk of the county, and membership in forty learned societies were as nothing to him compared to his scientific and botanical interest. *Flora Cestrica*, published in 1837 and describing the plants of Chester County, *Agricultural Botany*, 1847, and *American Weeds and Useful Plants* point out his field. He was called "the Nestor of American Botany," and many plants were named in his honor by naturalists in America and abroad. Yale gave him an LL.D. and Dickinson a Ph.D. His own collections of botanical works, with his herbarium, went to his own county museum. Not trusting to the partiality or sentimentality of friends or relatives, he wrote his own epitaph, which is inscribed on his gravestone in Oaklands Cemetery: *Plantae Cestriensis, quas dilexit atque illustravit, super tumulum eius semper floreant*—May the plants of Chester, which he loved and described, ever bloom over his grave.

224
Richard Cowling Taylor
1789–1851
Philadelphia, November 28, 1842

Taylor's great work *Statistics of Coal*, published in 1848, firmly established his reputation as a geologist and mining engineer, developed throughout his life in England and the United States. Born in Hinton, Suffolk, England, he exhibited his antiquarian bent in early life in his *A General Index to Dugdale's Monasticon Anglicanum*, a description of Norman ruins on his father's estate in Norfolk. He became a pioneer in the preparation of geological maps. Coming to this country in 1830, he entered into an exploration of the coal regions of Pennsylvania, the copper mines of Cuba, gold mines of Panama, and elsewhere. But *Statistics of Coal* excelled all. He became a member of the American Philosophical Society, and the Academy of Natural Science of Philadelphia, and a fellow of the Geological Society of London, which latter honor he records after his signature, "F. G. S."

80/-

Wm Darlington, M.D.
West Chester, Penna.
November 1, 1843.

Richd C. Taylor   F. G. S.
Philadelphia 28th Nov
1842

Richard C. Taylor. Fellow of the Geological Society of London
member of the American Philosophical Society of Philadelphia &c.
28th November 1842.

Wm. Darlington MD West Chester Penna
Philadelphia 1st November 1843.

225
Levi Woodbury 1789–1851
Washington City, January 22, 1841

Tapping Reeve, Litchfield's legal light, helped mark the way for Levi Woodbury, the budding lawyer and incipient jurist fresh from Dartmouth in 1809. Admission to the bar in 1812 was the first firm step on the career ladder of this young native of New Hampshire. By 1816 he was clerk of the state senate, judge of the Supreme Court of New Hampshire in 1817, governor of the state in 1823, and in 1825 was elected a United States senator as a Democrat, serving six years. Jackson appointed him secretary of the navy in 1831 and secretary of the treasury in 1834, succeeding Taney, where he served until the end of Van Buren's (fig. 230) term in 1841. Then followed another four years as senator, at the end of which the death of Justice Story (fig. 16) gave President Polk the opportunity to appoint him to the Supreme Court of the United States, on which he sat until his death.

He had long had what was called "Potomac fever" and was always available for nomination for the presidency, but, when closest to it, he died. We see him just before the end of his term as secretary of the treasury, seven years of controversy and frustration arising out of the uncertain financial policies of Jackson and Van Buren and the so-called Bank War. But if he was disappointed, his profile does not show it. It is rather a view of a man of substance looking bravely and hopefully to the future.

81

Levi Woodbury
22d January 1841.

Levi Woodbury, Secretary of Treasury
Washington City 22d Jany 1841.

226
John Swift 1790–1873
Philadelphia, April 25, 1843

Colonel Swift, bred to the bar, whose military title stems from the War of 1812, served his native city Philadelphia as mayor for over twelve years, 1832–41 and 1845–49. We see him here as he appeared between his terms as mayor. He was a man of courage and action, evidenced by his conspicuous service in the county prison during the cholera epidemic of 1832 (for which the city rewarded him with a "service of plate"), as well as by his success in quelling several riots, which he accomplished by leading the police himself. It is told of him in an account in "The Swift Family of Philadelphia," published in the *Pennsylvania Magazine of History and Biography* in 1906, that on one occasion, on learning of a riot in a jail, he went to the scene with a loaded pistol in each hand and "met the prisoners beginning to come down the steps. Promptly he shot the first man, wounding him, and then drove back the others and put down the turmoil." He died in Philadelphia and is buried in Christ Church burying ground.

But he was not all "blood and thunder." He was one of the committee in charge of the Military Birth Night Ball given on Washington's birthday in 1818, and was later chief marshal of the parade held at Philadelphia in 1824 in honor of Lafayette.

227
William Freret 1799–1864
New Orleans, March 5, 1844

It is not hard to imagine the conversation taking place between Colonel Swift, mayor of Philadelphia, and William Freret, mayor of New Orleans. Freret was the tenth mayor of New Orleans, and we see him just before the end of his second term. He was a popular city servant and exercised his influence in establishing a proper system of public schools. As a man of business he operated the Freret Cotton Press, one of the first enterprises of the kind in the city, designed to compress cotton for shipment abroad. In politics he was a Whig and a devoted friend of Henry Clay (fig. 147). During President Taylor's administration in 1850 he was appointed collector of the port, but within a year or two was dismissed by the Fillmore administration. It was generally felt that his removal arose from political considerations only and was both ill advised and unjust. He died in New Orleans and was buried in St. Patrick's Cemetery.

Mr Swift   April 25 1843

Wm Freret

New Orleans 5th March 1844

Philad. 25th April 1843, for 9 Years 1832.

Col. Jn. Swift Late Mayor of Philad City
Philad. 25th April 1843, for 9 Years 1832.

Wm Freret
Mayor of N Orleans — "
March. 5. 1844

228
Luther Bradish   1783–1863
[New York], October 22, 1840

Luther Bradish's first career was that of a lawyer. As a graduate of Williams College in 1804, he was admitted to the bar and exercised his profession for many years in pursuing for collection a large claim in South America, the West Indies, and England. At the request of John Quincy Adams (fig. 172), secretary of state, Bradish in his second career was led to Turkey as an unofficial diplomat to explore the possibilities of establishing American trade with the Levant. He made a most favorable impression wherever he went, though his mission was thwarted by the Greek revolution. He then pursued his travels in the East, visiting Egypt, Luxor, and Dendera.

Politically a Whig, he was a member of the New York State Assembly for six years. In 1838 he was elected lieutenant governor with Seward (fig. 2) as governor, and again in 1840 in the wake of the victory of President Harrison (fig. 233). Defeated in his bid for the governorship in 1842, Bradish retired to private life, where, as a third career, he devoted himself to literary and charitable objects. At his death in Newport, he was president of the American Bible Society and the New-York Historical Society, a gentleman of "stateliness of bearing" and "elegance of manners."

82.

L. Bradish
Lieut. Governor of
State of New York
Oct. 22nd 1840

Luther Bradish
Lieut. Governor
State of New York
Oct. 22nd 1840

229
Thomas Sully   1783–1872
Philadelphia, January 3, 1843

It would seem that all that need be said of the
subject of this silhouette, in a view so full of
grace and charm, is what Edouart himself wrote
below it, "Thomas Sully Painter." We can, however, remind ourselves that Sully was born in
Lincolnshire, England, and was brought to this
country at the age of nine. He studied for a short
time under Stuart, and for longer under West and
with Charles Bird King. From 1810 he lived
and painted in Philadelphia—over two thousand
paintings. We see him at his easel only shortly
after he executed his great portrait of Queen Vic-
toria, commissioned by the Society of the Sons of
Saint George in Philadelphia. After the death of
Stuart and Charles Willson Peale, Sully had no
substantial rival in this country. His forte, it has
often been said, is the graceful, and it was for his
pictures of women, the fair and lovely, that he was
perhaps most in demand.

Of the gathering of characters represented in
this volume, Sully painted at least nineteen: figs.
12, 180, 181, 194, 196, 201, 206, 216, 220, 232, 233,
234, 239, 243, 251, 257, 271, 274, and 332. He died
at the age of ninety, beloved and mourned.

82½

Thomas Sully Philadelphia Jan 3ᵈ 1843

Thomas Sully Painter

Thomas Sully Painter   Philadelphia 3ᵈ Janᵞ 1843.

Martin Van Buren   1782–1862
Washington City, January 21, 1841

The first four months of 1841 marked a high point in Edouart's career of cutting presidential silhouettes. In January he reproduced the retiring president, Van Buren, in unmistakable profile, confident and jaunty. In February, Harrison (fig. 233) was preserved, John Quincy Adams (fig. 172) in March, and Tyler (fig. 258) in April. The decorous Van Buren was defeated by Harrison by an electoral vote of 234 to 60, but the defeat does not appear in his shade. After his defeat he retired to Kinderhook, New York, his birthplace, and devoted his time to his estate, Lindenwald. Though he toyed with future chances of nomination to the presidency, he was ultimately and conclusively disappointed. During the Civil War he was, as long as nature allowed, a firm supporter of Lincoln.

As a youth he was admitted to the bar in 1803 and was a supporter of Jefferson. He was surrogate of Columbia County for five years, was elected to the state senate in 1812 and attorney general of the state in 1815. By 1820 he was in law partnership with Benjamin F. Butler (fig. 43). He took a seat in the United States Senate in 1821 and for some years was chairman of the Judiciary Committee. He gave his Senate seat up on the death of DeWitt Clinton to become governor of New York in 1828. In 1832, as Jackson's vice-president, he presided over the House which a year before had rejected him as Jackson's secretary of state. In 1836 he won the presidency against Harrison (fig. 233), Hugh L. White, and Webster (fig. 164). On his cabinet served Levi Woodbury (fig. 225) in the treasury, Benjamin F. Butler (fig. 43) as attorney general, and Joel R. Poinsett (fig. 243) in the War Department. His presidential term began and ended with a financial crash. Though not one to inspire enthusiasm, he was a gentleman and cultivated the society of gentlemen. He accepted defeat and disappointment graciously, had a keen sense of humor, and never suffered from the envy or distrust of friend or foe. His profile of January 1841, especially considering the circumstances of the moment, exudes cheer and confidence.

M. Van Buren Jany 21st 1841

84

Martin Van Buren President of the U. States
Washington City
21st Jany 1841.

231
John B. Christian 1794–1856
Saratoga, August 13, 1845

Christian, born in Kent County, Virginia, studied at the College of William and Mary in or about 1816. He became a member of the state legislature, and from 1832 to 1851 was a judge of the General Court of Virginia. During the last decade of his life he was a visitor of the College of William and Mary. He was buried at Oak Grove, New Kent County. His family connections are a genealogist's nightmare. His sister Letitia was the first wife of President Tyler (fig. 258), while Christian himself married Martha Semple, who was the daughter of Judge James Semple by his first wife, Anne Tyler, sister of President Tyler. As a result Tyler was Mrs. Christian's brother-in-law and uncle.

232
Alexander James Dallas 1791–1844
Philadelphia, January 21, 1843

Entering the naval service at fourteen years of age during Jefferson's administration, Dallas was appointed lieutenant when only nineteen. While acting under the command of Commodore John Rogers, he had the doubtful distinction (without fault of his own), in an action with the British man-of-war *Little Belt*, of returning her fire, thereby firing the first hostile gun that precipitated the War of 1812. He served under Commodore Chauncey on Lake Ontario and under Oliver Hazard Perry on Lake Erie. He took part in Decatur's expedition to demand indemnity from Algiers for depredation on American ships and later supported General Scott (fig. 120) in his efforts to contain the Seminole Indians in Florida. In 1843, while in command of the Pacific fleet, Commodore Dallas died on board his ship stationed in the roads at Callao, Peru, after thirty-nine years of service. His first wife, Henrietta, was General George C. Meade's sister; his second wife, Mary Byrd Willis, was a great-granddaughter of Mrs. Fielding Lewis, President Washington's only sister.

84½.

J B Christian Judge
of the Gen.l Court Virginia
Saratoga 13th aug.t 1845

A J Dallas
U.S. Navy
Ph.a 21 Jay - 43

Judge J. B. Christian of the Gen.l Court
Saratoga 13th Aug.t 1845   Virginia
Commodore Alexand.r J. Dallas U.S.N.
Philadelphia 21st Jan.y 1843. Ent.d 22d Nov.o 1805.

233
William Henry Harrison
1773–1841
Washington, February 20, 1841

When General Harrison resigned his command in 1814, it was said of him that "he was longer in active service than any other general officer, was perhaps oftener in action than any of them, and never sustained a defeat." Twenty-seven years later he was the ninth president of the United States for exactly one month, and the first to die in office.

During his military career he served in the 1790s under "Mad Anthony" Wayne with signal distinction. President Adams appointed him governor of the new territory of Indiana, created on the division of the Northwest Territory, and he held the post under both Jefferson and Madison. The year 1811 saw his great victory over the Indians at Tippecanoe, which earned him a resolution of gratitude from the legislature of Kentucky for his "cool, deliberate, skilful and gallant conduct," and which occasioned the great party rallying cry thirty years later, "Tippecanoe and Tyler too." Following Commodore Perry's victory on Lake Erie in September 1813, General Harrison, by his victory over the British on the banks of the Thames River, recovered Detroit and thereby won a congressional gold medal designed by Sully (fig. 229). He served in the Senate and as minister to the Republic of Columbia, but lost an appointment as minister to Mexico to Joel Poinsett (fig. 243).

His election to the presidency in 1840 was a great victory and his death a stunning blow to his supporters. He stands to Edouart not long after his election, shortly before his inauguration and perhaps for his last likeness. It was this likeness that Edouart gave to John Quincy Adams (fig. 172) on March 11, 1841.

85.

W. H. Harrison

President Wm H.^y Harrison   Washington 20th Feby 1841.

234

Samuel Jackson, M.D.   1787–1872

Philadelphia, January 17, 1843

Long one of Philadelphia's distinguished physicians, Dr. Jackson, or "Professor Jackson" as he was called to distinguish him from another of the same name, commenced his career in his father's apothecary shop but turned to a medical career with enthusiasm, became head of the Philadelphia Department of Health during the yellow fever epidemic, aided in founding the Philadelphia College of Pharmacy, and served as its professor of materia medica and pharmacy. In the University of Pennsylvania he held the chair of the Institutes of Medicine for twenty-eight years and was noted for his successful teaching methods. He published numerous medical articles and in 1832 wrote *The Principles of Medicine*, which was unfavorably reviewed by Dr. Charles Caldwell (fig. 79). He married late in life and that his marriage was a happy one is attested to by Dr. Samuel Gross in his *Autobiography* (1887) when he tells us that Professor Jackson was a martyr to neuralgia and "often told his class that there was no remedy so efficacious for the relief of that disease as the soft and gentle touch of a lovely woman's hand."

Samuel Jackson M. D.
Philad.a Jan.y 17th 1843

Dr. Samuel Jackson MD Professor,
Philadelphia 17th Jan.ry 1843.

William Leete Stone   1792–1849
New York, April 21, 1840

Colonel Stone's great contribution to history was his lecture series at the New-York Historical Society in 1838, which resulted in the creation of the New York State Historical Agency, under which documents in Holland and England relating to New York were collected or copied and gathered in the New York Colonial Documents Collection. But in his day he was principally known as a newspaper editor, having edited for many years the *New York Commercial Advertiser*, which was always regarded as a sort of political barometer. In his earlier days at Hartford he and Wainwright (fig. 40) and Goodrich (Peter Parley; fig. 46) had jointly edited the literary magazine *The Knights of the Round Table*. Beyond his career of writing, Colonel Stone was appointed minister to The Hague by President Harrison (fig. 233) but was almost immediately recalled by President Tyler (fig. 258).

An interesting event in his career was the libel suit brought against him by Fenimore Cooper for an unfavorable review of *Home as Found* and the *History of the Navy of the United States*. Stone had not written the review but quite properly assumed responsibility for it. The extent of literary criticism allowed in a review had not yet been settled, and the case was one of first impression. The lower court decided in favor of Cooper, but on appeal to the Court for the Correction of Errors, at that time the state senate, Chancellor Walworth (fig. 119) with a majority reversed the lower court, but not until after Stone's death. Stone married Susannah Wayland, sister of the president of Brown University (fig. 75). At the time Edouart cut his profile he was basking in the sunlight of his *Life of Joseph Brant*, published only a short time before.

William L. Stone
author of life of Brant

88

Col. Wm L. Stone.
Editor Comal advert

236

Caspar Wistar Pennock, M.D.
1799–1867
Philadelphia, March 20, 1843

It must have been a handicap for a doctor in Philadelphia to carry the given names Caspar Wistar, and it was surely an odd coincidence that Pennock married Caroline, daughter of Caspar Wistar Morris. Genealogists will enjoy the added confusion that Pennock's daughter married W. H. Morris.

Pennock was a graduate of the Medical Department of the Pennsylvania Hospital. He specialized in and edited an important work of Bouillard on the diseases of the heart. For the last ten years of his life he was debilitated by an unusual form of paralysis. Pursuant to his request, at his death an autopsy was performed and published in the *Transactions of the College of Physicians of Philadelphia* in 1867, and a year later was translated into French as "Le cas du Docteur W. Pennock, ou contribution's à l'histoire de la sclerose en plaques disséminées," so that in a sense it could be said that the good he did lived after him. He appears before us in his rocking chair only shortly before the onslaught of his strange paralysis.

C. Wistar Pennock M.D
Philada 20th March
1843.

Dr. C. Wistar Pennock ND   Philadelphia 20th March 1843.

237
William Ellery Channing
1780–1842
Boston, March 17, 1842

Dr. Channing, the founder of the American Unitarian Association, hardly needs introduction. He appears to us at his desk writing a sermon only six months before his death, which was proclaimed in one newspaper clipping preserved by Edouart as a "public calamity—A great man has Fallen in Israel." A graduate of Cambridge (England), 1798, he was ordained in 1803 and installed as minister of the Federal Street Church in Boston, where he officiated until his death. A noted preacher, involved against his best wishes in the "Unitarian controversy," he eventually became the leader and spokesman. He wrote widely, especially on Milton, Bonaparte, and Fenélon, and devoted his energies toward the abolition of slavery. Seven volumes of his writings were collected and published, and several biographies. His apologist in Edouart's newspaper obituary says of him, "Milton was the Channing of his own time, and Channing was the Milton of ours." The same writer noted, not very broad-mindedly, that Milton as a political moralist was "known only through the prejudice of his principal biographer, the ignorant, illiberal, rancorous Dr. Johnson: a writer who made a merit of defaming or depreciating all the ablest and purest advocates of English liberty, whose pedantry and false taste have done no little harm to English literature." Such are the limits to which theological differences lead some people. Dr. Channing would not have expressed himself so harshly about Dr. Johnson, however difficult he found it to swallow the Trinity.

87.

Wm E. Channing
Boston March 17 1842

Revd. Dr. Wm E. Channing.
Boston 17 March 1842.

238
Edward Hutchinson Robbins, M.D.
1792–1850
Saratoga, August 17, 1844

A great-nephew of Thomas Hutchinson, the last governor of the Massachusetts Bay Colony, Dr. Robbins was a graduate of Harvard College in the class of 1812 and of its medical school in 1815. He married Ann Coffin in 1818. His medical career seems to have been spent in Boston, which he acknowledges beneath his signature.

239
Peter Stephen (Pierre Etienne) Du Ponceau 1760–1844
Philadelphia, January 15, 1843

Du Ponceau appears before Edouart in his eighty-third year, but his stance in profile exhibits the spirit and vigor he displayed to the last, despite approaching blindness and increasing deafness. Born in the Ile de Ré, France, he early abandoned his family's design for him to take orders. He was for a while secretary to the philologist comte de Gebelin, came to America in 1777, and within a year became aide-de-camp to Baron Steuben. He became a citizen in 1781 and before long acquired a high reputation as a lawyer, appearing often before the United States Supreme Court. His advice was always in demand on matters of civil and foreign law, and he wrote and translated books on the subject. In addition he became a learned philologist and wrote much concerning philology into his old age. A member of the Royal Institute of France and of most of the learned societies in America, he was also president of the American Philosophical Society.

He had a great love of Pennsylvania; in Simpson's *Lives of Eminent Philadelphians* it is told that Du Ponceau's "Discourse on the Early History of Pennsylvania," delivered before the Philosophical Society in 1821 when he was its president, prophetically stated:

Pennsylvania once realized what never existed before, except in fabled story . . . during the first century of our social existence. I well remember them, those patriarchal times, when simple yet not inelegant manners prevailed everywhere among us; when rusticity was devoid of roughness, and polished life diffused its mild radiance around, unassuming and unenvied; when society was free from the constraint of etiquette and parade; when love was not crossed by avarice or pride; and friendships were unbroken by ambition and intrigue. This was the spectacle which Pennsylvania offered even in the midst of the storms of the Revolution; and which she continued to exhibit until a sudden influx of riches broke in upon the land, and brought in its train luxury, more baneful than war. . . . We are gradually returning to those moderate habits, which we never should have abandoned.

But this was over a hundred and fifty years since.

87.1/2

E. H. Robbins, M.D. Peter S. Du Ponceau
Boston. Saratoga 17 August Philad. 15 January
1844. 1843.

E. H. Robbins MD of Boston Mass.
Saratoga 17th Augt. 1844.

Peter S. Du Ponceau
Philadelphia 15th Jany. 1843.

240

James Kirke Paulding   1778–1860
Washington, January 21, 1841

It was at the end of his term as secretary of the navy under Van Buren that Paulding stood before Edouart in Washington. His naval career had spanned a quarter of a century, eight years as secretary to the Board of Navy Commissioners, fifteen years as navy agent for New York, and three as secretary of the navy. For this service he does not stand out in the public memory. He is remembered best (and without research, perhaps not well remembered) as a prolific author—before, during, and after his public career. In his youth he and his sister's brother-in-law, Washington Irving, who became a lifelong friend, published jointly the periodical *Salamagundi; or, The Whim-whams and Opinions of Launcelot Langstaff, Esq. and Others*, which enjoyed a brief popularity. He wrote a popular *Life of Washington*, books on slavery, genre pictures of the Dutch of New Amsterdam, satires on Scottish writers, novels, and historical tales. His best-known work is *The Diverting History of John Bull and Brother Jonathan*, and although everyone can recite the Peter Piper jingle, few recall that it first appeared in Paulding's *Koningsmarke; or, The Long Finne*, in 1823.

Though forgotten today, Paulding was a beloved figure in his later years at his country residence Placentia in Putnam County, where as a gentleman farmer he continued writing up to his last days. Not long after he stood to Edouart, Paulding accompanied Van Buren (fig. 230) on a trip to the South, to New Orleans and other parts of the country he had not seen before, including a visit to Poinsett (fig. 243) in South Carolina and one to Jackson at the Hermitage. Edouart misread Paulding's middle initial as "H."

J. Paulding.

Jany 21st 1841.

J. H. Paulding. Secty of the Navy
Washington 21st Jany 1841.

241
Roger Sherman Baldwin 1793–1863
Saratoga, July 31, 1844

Governor Baldwin must have been a welcome figure at Saratoga that summer of 1844. A graduate of Yale, 1811, he was another of the sons of the Litchfield law school and had been a member of the New Haven Common Council, had served in the state senate and General Assembly, and now was governor of the state of Connecticut. But his career continued. As a Whig, he was for many years in the United States Senate in the days when Webster (fig. 164), Clay (fig. 147), Calhoun (fig. 161), and Seward (fig. 2) were members. In an obituary notice written by Governor Harrison of Connecticut it was said of him: "In any forum, anywhere,—in the Superior Court at Washington, or in Westminster Hall or at any other bar, where our system of jurisprudence is understood as practiced—Gov. Baldwin would have been regarded, not merely as a skillful practitioner, but as a man entitled to rank among the great lawyers of his day."

One of his greatest legal battles, ending in victory, was his defense of the captives of the *Armistad*, Negroes brought in slavery from Africa to Cuba and who, when on the way to be sold, overpowered the captain and his crew and were in turn captured off the shore of Long Island, arrested, and charged with murder and piracy. The case was lost in the lower court, but on appeal in the Supreme Court in which Baldwin was associated with John Quincy Adams (fig. 172), he was successful and the Africans won their freedom.

Governor Baldwin's father stood for his silhouette in Saratoga the same day as his son, and it was included in this volume, designated here as fig. 100, though it has unfortunately slipped out. It would have been gratifying to see the two generations of distinguished lawyers standing together.

242
Charles Paine 1799–1853
Saratoga, June 30, 1843

Governor Paine, great-grandson of Robert Treat Paine, was Vermont's youngest governor, serving from 1841 to 1843 and then declining to run for reelection. A lifelong resident of Northfield, Vermont, he became its greatest benefactor. He gave the land on which the Northfield Academy was built, built the Congregational church at Depot Village, devised to the Roman Catholic congregation the land on which its church was built, and was a patron of the University of Vermont.

In his early years he was engaged in managing his father's woolen mills and in farming and stock breeding. His great contribution to Northfield and indeed to Vermont was the construction of the Vermont Central Railroad, which he promoted and encouraged, and of which he became president. It was not a financial success, but at Paine's death it was said in a eulogy of his career, referring to the railroad, "There is his monument."

The last years of his life were devoted to promoting a railroad to the Pacific, and in the course of his travels to that end, he became ill in Waco, Texas, where he died. His devotion to Northfield will always be kept alive for the citizens of that town by the lofty granite shaft erected to his memory in Elmwood Cemetery, itself one of his many benefactions.

88½

Roger S. Baldwin
New Haven, Conn.t
Saratoga July 31st 1844

Charles Paine
Northfield
Vermont
Saratoga
June 30. 1843

Roger S. Baldwin Governor of Connecticut
New Haven   Saratoga 31st July 1844

Charles Paine Esqre
Governor of Vermont

243
Joel Roberts Poinsett   1779–1851
Washington, January 25, 1841

Secretary of war in the cabinet of President Van
Buren (fig. 230) was the highest political office attained by Poinsett, but he was a man of many
parts and great ability. Born in Charleston, South
Carolina, he studied abroad and as a man of
means traveled widely through Europe and was
offered a commission in the Russian army by the
czar, which he declined. President Madison sent
him to South America to investigate and report
on the revolutionary activities underway there.
While in Chile he was able to rescue several
American merchant vessels which had been seized
off Peru by the Spanish authorities. He served in
the South Carolina state legislature and in Congress. He was sent to Mexico in 1822 and appointed by President John Quincy Adams (fig.
172) as the first minister to Mexico in 1825 because of his wide knowledge of Spanish-American
affairs. He championed the cause of Mexican independence and was in favor of emancipation of
the Irish Roman Catholics.

His most valuable services to the country were
rendered as secretary of war when he took the lead
in improving the army's field artillery and the
states' militias, and also played a hand in removing 40,000 Indians west of the Mississippi. A man
of many scientific interests, he gave to various institutions valuable collections of natural history
specimens. His interest in botany is perpetuated
by the popular poinsettia, a Mexican flower he
first introduced into this country and which bears
his name.

J R Poinsett
January 25 1841

89

Hon Joel R. Poinsett,
Secy of War. U.S.
Washington Jany 25, 1841

William Short   1759–1849
Philadelphia, February 3, 1843

As "80 of age" Edouart describes Short, and indeed he was, though another decade lay ahead of him. A Virginian, a 1779 graduate of the College of William and Mary, Short was secretary of legation to Jefferson in Paris and was sent by Jefferson, and his diplomatic colleagues Adams and Franklin, to negotiate at The Hague a commercial treaty between Prussia and the United States, which he did. He had a firm command of French and was warmly received wherever he went. When Jefferson returned to America, Short as chargé d'affaires spent two years attempting to arrange commercial treaties with France. He suffered a bitter disappointment when Jefferson became president, for the post he coveted, that of minister to France, went to Gouverneur Morris. In 1793 he went to Madrid with William Carmichael to negotiate treaties relating to boundary lines between Florida and Mississippi, questions of navigation on the Mississippi, and other commercial matters. Just on the verge of completing the treaty he was again disappointed by having Thomas Pinckney sent to conclude it. After his return to the United States he was appointed by Jefferson minister to Russia, but the Senate rejected his nomination. Through with politics and diplomacy, he returned to private life, settled in Philadelphia, and lived out his life looking after his own substantial affairs. He never married. A large number of his valuable and informative state papers are preserved in the Library of Congress.

89 1/8.

W. Short
Philadelphia Feb. 3. 1843

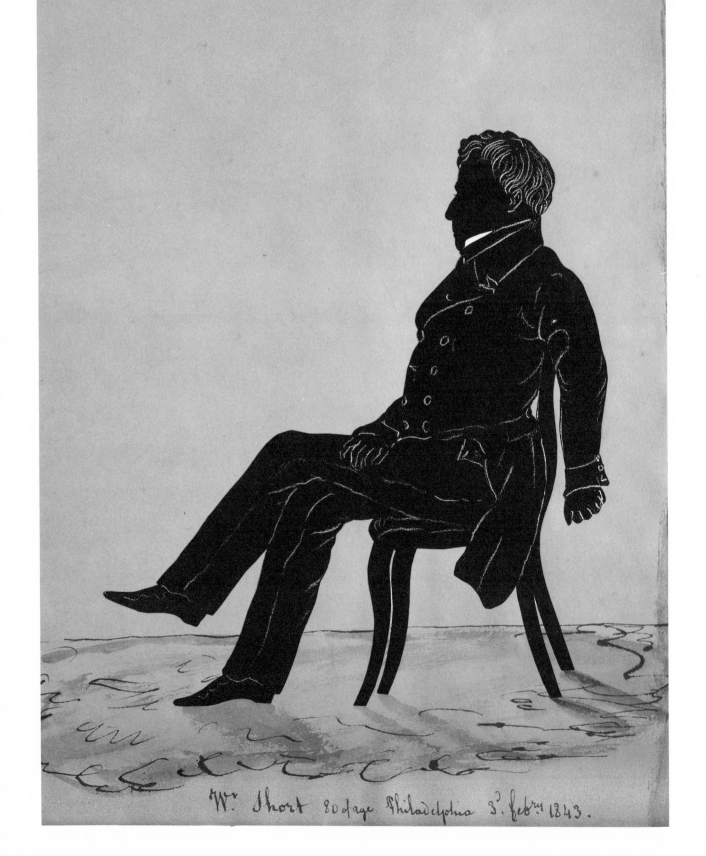

Wᵐ Short 80 d age Philadelphia 3 febᵘ 1843.

245
George Washington Doane
1799–1859
Burlington, New Jersey, June 8, 1843

Bishop Doane, in the prime of life, appears as if in the act of bestowing his episcopal blessing on the faithful committed to his charge in New Jersey. He was the sixth student at the General Theological Seminary and was ordained priest in 1823 by the great Bishop Hobart, whom he served as assistant at Trinity Church, New York. For a couple of years he taught rhetoric and belles lettres at Washington (now Trinity) College and then served as rector of Trinity Church, Boston, until elected bishop of New Jersey in 1832. He was consecrated by Bishops William White, Benjamin T. Onderdonk (fig. 39), and Levi Silliman Ives. To support himself he also served as rector of St. Mary's, Burlington, New Jersey, throughout his episcopate until his death. He was a leader in the Oxford movement and defended Newman's "Tract No. 90" of *Tracts for the Times* which eventually brought the movement to a head and precipitated Newman's turning to Rome. He was a strong sound churchman and did much to strengthen the Diocese of New Jersey. He was not only a brilliant preacher but also a hymnologist, writing, for example, "Softly Now the Light of Day" and "Fling Out the Banner." His son William became bishop of Albany, but his son George Hobart, ordained in the Episcopal church, forsook it and went over to Rome, forcing on his father the sad duty of deposing him.

90.

G.W. Doane, Bishop of New Jersey
7 June 1843

The Right Hon.ble the Bishop of New Jersey 8 June 1843 G.W. Doane

Wilmington N. Jersey 8. June 1843.

246

Joseph Francis Duggan
1817–after 1879
Philadelphia, November 7, 1843

Duggan, born in Dublin, was a pianist and composer of songs, operas, and instrumental music. He taught in Philadelphia, Baltimore, and Washington and was a professor in the Philadelphia Musical Institute in 1841. He went to Paris in 1844 and finally settled in London, where he lived after 1845. He was lighthearted, cheerful, and humorous and was a friend of the illustrator Felix C. Darley. In a letter to Darley in the Gratz Collection at the Historical Society of Pennsylvania, he told Darley that he could be found at home "wrapt in pious meditation and perhaps tobacco smoke." The letter went on to suggest that Darley's sister provided her brother's friends with very strong drink indeed—so strong that Duggan protested, mildly.

Joseph L. Duggan Prof. of Music
Philadelphia 7th Novemb. 1843.

247
Josiah Quincy 1772–1864
Boston, January 5, 1842

Josiah Quincy, the second of three generations of the name, graduated from Harvard College at the head of his class in 1790 and forty years later was president of Harvard. He was an ardent Federalist, elected to the Massachusetts state senate in 1804 and to Congress the following year, where he served for eight years, becoming the minority leader. Losing his seat by opposing the War of 1812, he returned to private life, but only for a short time. Again state senator, he was finally elected mayor of Boston from 1823 to 1827 during which period he transformed the city. He introduced water and sewage systems, reorganized the fire departments, built the Quincy Market, entertained Lafayette during his triumphal return to America when he laid the cornerstone of the Bunker Hill Monument.

He served Harvard as its sixteenth president for sixteen years, during which the law school was established, Gore Hall, the most magnificent collegiate library in the country, built, and the astronomical observatory completed. As an able historian he wrote *A History of Harvard University*, *The History of the Boston Athenaeum*, *Memoir of the Life of John Quincy Adams*, and others. History records him as one of the Hundred Boston Orators, and he was noted for his brilliant and witty informal after dinner speeches. It is recorded in James S. Loring's *The Hundred Boston Orators* (1852) that in celebrating the completion of the great granite Quincy Market, Judge Story (fig. 16) proposed, "May the fame of our honored Mayor prove as durable as the material of which the beautiful market house is constructed," and that "quick as light" Mayor Quincy responded, "That stupendous monument of the wisdom of our forefathers, the Supreme Court of the United States; In the event of a vacancy may it be raised one Story higher." On leaving Harvard he retired to private life, was an active and valued member of the Massachusetts Historical Society, the American Academy of Arts and Sciences, and the Boston Athenaeum, and in his ninety-second year was a public and strong supporter of the Union and Lincoln. Without question he was one of Boston's outstanding public servants.

248
Josiah Quincy, Jr. 1802–1882
Boston, January 10, 1842

Josiah Quincy, Jr., was a true son of his father, before whom he stands respectfully. A graduate of Harvard in the class of 1821, he took up the practice of the law and was inevitably led to politics. He served as president of the Boston City Council from 1834 to 1837 and as president of the state senate in 1842 when we see him. But it was as mayor from 1845 to 1849 that he emulated his father and brought lasting improvements to the city. The greatest and the one he is remembered for was bringing Cochituate water to Boston. The ground-breaking took place in August 1846, performed by the mayor, his aged father, and the venerable John Quincy Adams (fig. 172). The name of the water supply was changed from Long Pond to Cochituate. Two years later the arrival of the water was celebrated on Boston Common, where the mayor spoke and James Russell Lowell's ode for the occasion was sung by schoolchildren. At a signal the water was turned on and a column six inches in diameter shot up to a height of eighty feet amid shouts, ringing of bells, and firing of cannon and sky rockets. It was said of Quincy, "He has written his name in water, yet it will last forever." His well-known book *Figures of the Past* was published the year of his death.

91.

Josiah Quincy
President of
Harvard College
5. Jan.y 1842.

Josiah Quincy Jr
10. Jan.y 1842.

Josiah Quincy
Taken in Boston
5. Jan.y 1842.

Presid.t of Harvard Univ.y
Cambridge Mass.

President of the Senate H.e Mass.
Boston 10.e Jan.y 1842.

249
William Bradford Reed 1806–1876
Philadelphia, January 11, 1843

William Reed at the time we see him was at the height of one of his three careers, that of lawyer, to which he had added two years in the Pennsylvania Assembly, one in the senate, and one as attorney general of the state on the appointment of Governor Ritner. He had also spent several months in Mexico City with Joel Poinsett (fig. 243) in an effort to negotiate with the Panana Congress. Soon he was to make a reputation for himself as district attorney of Philadelphia.

His second career was as a diplomat, where he rendered valuable service in concluding the Treaty of Tientsin in 1858, which furthered the opening up of China and improvements in American trade. On his return to the United States he resumed private practice, but his opposition to the Civil War caused him to lose most of his practice.

In his third career he published many books, including the *Life and Correspondence of Joseph Reed* (his grandfather and the great patriot), 1847, and *Life of Esther deBerdt*, 1853. He contributed many articles to the *American Quarterly* and the *North American Review*, and was an editor of the *New York World*. As a labor of love he edited the posthumous works of his brother who stands behind him. Sidney George Fisher, the diarist, wrote in December 1869 that Reed had embezzled $30,000 from an English client and his own sister, adding, "No one is much surprised, for his father did the same thing and his own character for integrity and truth has never been high. . . . What he did, is done by thousands of men in business every day, who escape disgrace merely by success. . . . In the opinion of the public, the crime is detection."

250
Henry Hope Reed 1808–1854
Philadelphia, January 2, 1843

Henry Reed, William's younger brother, was a scholar and man of letters. At the age of seventeen he had graduated from the University of Pennsylvania with honors. He tried the law as a profession but it did not suit. An assistant professorship of literature at the university was quickly followed by the chair of rhetoric and English literature, which he occupied with great credit until his death.

He was especially noted for his profound attachment to Wordsworth and published selections of his poems and proposed an American edition of Wordsworth's complete works. Others of his works include his edition of Thomas Arnold's *Lectures on Modern History*, Lord Mahon's *History of England* . . . , and the poetical works of Thomas Gray. His lectures charmed his students and won for him such popularity that they were published posthumously by his brother William and passed through several editions. In 1854 he visited Europe accompanied by his wife's sister, where he was warmly received both in England and on the Continent. Fate intervened during his return. He set sail on the *Arctic* and a week out in the fog his ship collided with a French vessel and sank with the loss of Reed and some three hundred passengers. Accounts of the tragedy report that he was last seen sitting on the deck with his sister-in-law, sadly but calmly awaiting the inevitable.

91.½

William B. Reed.
Philad: January 11. 1843.

Henry Reed
Prof.r of Eng. Literature
University of Penn.a
Philadelphia.

Wm B. Reed Counsellor at Law.
Philadelphia 11th Jan.ry 1843.

Henry Reed Prof.r of English Literature
University of Pennsylvania
Philadelphia 2d Jan.ry 1843.

251
Alexander Macomb   1782–1841
Saratoga, August 25, 1840

No one more deserved promotion to general-in-chief of the army in 1828 than Major General Macomb, though the choice was disputed by General Scott (fig. 120) and General Gaines (fig. 288). But President Adams (fig. 172) and General Jackson both decided in his favor, not only for his extraordinary successes but for his length of service. His subsequent career was not very active—concluding a treaty of peace with the Indians during the Seminole war of 1839 and commanding the funeral escort at President Harrison's funeral. Within a couple of months thereafter he died, lamented by his friends and associates at arms. Edouart displays him holding the fort in all his regalia, scarcely a year before his death.

Born in what was considered the West, Detroit, he was educated in New Jersey and at an early age entered the military service, by ability and diligence working his way up so that by 1812 he was appointed a colonel. For his distinctive service at Niagara and Fort George he was raised to brigadier and put in charge of the region bordering on Lake Champlain, there setting the stage for his playing the lead in the decisive battle of Plattsburg. Sir George Prevost had at his command the flower of the British forces, those who had met and tasted victory under Wellington and at San Sebastian and Bayonne. But in General Macomb they met their match at Plattsburg. On September 11, 1814, Macomb administered a decisive defeat to the British for which he received a magnificent sword from the state legislature, the freedom of the city of New York in a gold box, and from Congress a vote of thanks and a gold medal struck for the occasion and emblematical of his glorious victory. He holds his place in the military history of the United States as the victor at a great and decisive battle.

Alex.r Macomb.
Gen.l in Chief of the
U. S. Army. taken at Saratoga
Aug.t 25th 1840.
ob.t 25th June 1841.

252
Charles O'Conor 1804–1884
Saratoga, August 25, 1843

O'Conor, an Irish Roman Catholic, was a Democrat who aspired to office but never attained it. He failed to be elected lieutenant governor of New York in 1848 but did serve as United States attorney for the Southern District of New York for a little more than a year. But from his admission to the bar in 1824 until his retirement to the Island of Nantucket in 1881 with his library of 18,000 volumes, he devoted his life to the practice of the law and won an extraordinary reputation for ability and learning. His career can best be understood by mention of the great trials in which he was involved. To list a few: the Parrish and Jumel will cases involving millions of dollars; the Lispenard will case in 1843, which he might appear to be arguing before Edouart; the case that brought down Boss Tweed; and the Forrest (fig. 293) divorce suit. He defended Jefferson Davis as his senior counsel when he was tried for treason and went bail for him with Horace Greeley and others. He was remembered as one who "would not suffer in comparison with the greatest lawyers of any nation at any time."

253
Justin Butterfield 1790–1855
Saratoga, August 23, 1843

When Butterfield visited Saratoga in 1843 he had only recently become United States attorney for the District of Illinois, a post he held through the entire terms of the Harrison and Tyler administrations. Upon becoming president, Taylor appointed Butterfield commissioner of the land office, a post he held through the Fillmore administration. But his real claim to fame was his enviable position as the unchallenged leader of the Chicago bar. Though born in Keene, New Hampshire, graduated from Williams College, 1817, and having practiced first in Watertown, New York, and then New Orleans, where he established his reputation, Butterfield, "the Oracle of Cook County, Illinois," carried on his lucrative practice in Chicago for twenty years. He it was who, with Senator Douglas, secured for Illinois the land grant which subsidized the Illinois Central Railroad, whose earnings eventually were the financial salvation of the state.

As the leading lawyers of their states, Butterfield and O'Conor must have had much in common to share that August in Saratoga, where they stood to Edouart only two days apart.

92½

Chas O'Conor
Atty of New York.
Saratoga. Aug 25. 1843.

Justin Butterfield
U. S. Atty Dist Illinois
Saratoga. August 23a. 1843.

Saratoga 23 Augt 1843

92½

Chas O'Conor Attorney at Law.
New York. Saratoga 25th Augt 1843.

Justin Butterfield U.S. Attorny
Dist. Illinois
Saratoga 23 Augt 1843

254

Duncan Lamont Clinch   1787–1849
Washington, April 4, 1841

General Clinch, a native son of North Carolina, spent his life between distinguished military service and the care of his plantation. He was active in the War of 1812 and in the Seminole Indian wars and served a short term in Congress. Thrice married, by his first wife he had five sons and three daughters, their daughter Elizabeth becoming the wife of General Robert Anderson (fig. 121), the hero of Fort Sumter; and one of his grandsons, Duncan C. Heyward, was twice governor of South Carolina. Clinch County, Georgia, near the border of Florida, was named after General Clinch. By 1841 when Edouart cut his silhouette he had resigned his commission and had retired to his plantation.

D. L. Clinch   4 April 1841

93

Genl D L Clinch U.S. Army
Washington 4 April 1841.

255
John Nicholson   1787–1848
Saratoga, August 30, 1843

Nicholson was a native of Philadelphia but was
for forty years a citizen of New Orleans. In his
youth he had enlisted shortly after his arrival in
New Orleans as a sergeant in Captain Ogden's
Company of Dragoons organized for the defense
of the city. He was cashier of the Bank of Carrollton, a suburb of New Orleans, a post he held when
in Saratoga in 1843, holding in his hand, perhaps,
a statement of the bank's condition. That he was
a humanitarian is attested to by a eulogy written
by the Boy's Orphan Asylum at his death and
printed in the *Daily Picayune* on May 20, 1848, a
few lines of which make the point.

> Thou too art gone, our friend!
> Death! Archer insatiate!
> Couldst thou not have aimed thy shaft at others,
> The weary and the care-worn, the useless or the vile,
> And spare one friend of the orphans and the destitute?
> But 'tis thus ever.

He was an officer of Christ Church Cathedral and
was buried in the Girod Street Cemetery in New
Orleans.

93½

John Nicholson

John Nicholson
Carrollton Bank N. Orleans
Saratoga Augt 30. 1843

256

George Bomford 1782–1848
Washington City, March 20, 1841

To Colonel Bomford the country was indebted
during the War of 1812, he being the foremost
authority on the manufacture of ordnance and
ordnance stores. He served as assistant engineer
engaged in the fortifications of New York harbor
and the defenses of Chesapeake Bay, and he invented the bomb-cannon called the "Columbiad"
in honor of Joel Barlow's epic poem. He became
the first chief of ordnance of the army, a title he
records under his signature, and was later an inspector of arsenals, ordnance, arms, and muni-
tions of war. Joel Barlow bequeathed his estate
Katorama to his niece Mrs. Bomford, who transformed it into a veritable botanical garden to
which many prominent inhabitants of Washington often came. Bomford died on a trip to Boston to inspect the casting of some new weapons.
Though a public-spirited citizen, able speaker,
and writer, he stands first in our memory as the
ordnance expert of his time.

G. Bomford
Col. of Ordnance

G. Bomford Col 4 Ord
Washington City 20th March 1841

257

Charles Chauncey 1777–1849
Burlington, New Jersey, June 9, 1843

Chauncey, a great-grandson of the president of Harvard by that name, was born in New Haven, graduated at Yale in 1752, and turned to the law as his profession. On the advice of his father's friend Chief Justice Ellsworth, he moved to Philadelphia to practice law, where he prospered for nearly forty years, devoting himself to his clients' interests only and seeking no civil or judicial office. His principal public activity outside his own practice was as a member of the convention to revise the Constitution of Pennsylvania. Yale honored him in 1827 with an LL.D. degree. He died at Burlington. This is one of the few silhouettes Edouart did not have signed by the subject. Fisher wrote of Chauncey that he was "remarkable for gentlemanly manners and the scrupulous neatness and elegance" of his appearance as much as for his "legal learning, skill and eloquence."

94½.

Cha. Chauncey Esqr. Counsellor at Law. Burlington N. J.
June 9th 1843

John Tyler 1790–1862
Washington City, April 16, 1841

Edouart lost no time in obtaining this profile likeness of John Tyler, tenth president of the United States. At his home in Williamsburg, Tyler received word from the members of Harrison's cabinet, significantly addressed to him as vice-president, of the death of President Harrison on April 4, 1841. He sped to Washington, made it very clear what the succession was to be, that he was president, and was sworn in on April 6, the first president so to obtain the office. Ten days later, in the midst of his bitter party fight with Clay (fig. 147) and the rest of the cabinet (saving Webster; fig. 164), he found time to stand to the silhouettist. This was undoubtedly a counterpart of the likeness Edouart presented to John Quincy Adams (fig. 172) two months later. Before the end of his term Tyler had obtained passage of a new tariff law, a uniform bankruptcy law, a treaty with Great Britain setting the northeastern boundary of the United States, and finally a joint resolution in favor of annexing Texas.

These accomplishments did not fall to Tyler's lot by chance. He had been admitted to the bar in 1809 and was successively member of the Virginia House of Delegates for seven years, member of the United States House of Representatives for five years, governor of Virginia for two years, nine years a senator, and vice-president for a moment. He was twice happily married, having by his first wife four daughters and three sons, and by his second, five sons and two daughters.

As P. A. Bruce wrote in *The Virginia Plutarch* in 1929, Tyler was one of the outstanding instances in the history of Virginia of a class of men England used to produce, namely, "the statesman of birth, talent, and inherited fortune, who devotes most of his time to the occupations of public life. . . . Throughout, he played a useful and honorable part in the history of his community, his state, and his country."

John Tyler

John Tyler, President of the U.S.
Washington City 16th April 1841.

259
Le Chevalier Fidencio de Bourman
Philadelphia, March 6, 1843

Our fine tall handsome foreigner left no doubt
that he was not an American. His spelling of
"Philadelphie" and "le 6. Mars" and his crisp
delicate profile all suggest the polished European
diplomat. It is from Edouart, who never found
a companion silhouette suitable for the chevalier,
that we learn he was in fact "Capitaine de Cavalerie et Secretaire de la legation d'Espagne aux
Etats Unis d'Amerique." From January 2 to August 5, 1849, he was chargé d'affaires for Spain in
the United States. There can be little doubt that
with his fine figure and stance he cut a swath
through Philadelphia's diplomatic field.

95½.

Le Chev.^r L. Bourman

Philadelphie Ce 6.me Mars 1843.

Le Chevalier de Bourman
Capitaine de Cavalerie et Secretaire
de la legation d'Espagne aux Etats Unis
d'Amerique. Philadelphia 6.^h March 1843.

260
John Henderson   1795–1857
Washington, February 17, 1841

The first word we hear of Henderson, who was
born in New Jersey, is that he was flatboating on
the Mississippi River and in his leisure time reading Blackstone's *Commentaries*. Blackstone led
him to the law, the Mississippi River to Natchez,
New Orleans, and Pass Christian. He became a
successful lawyer, a member of the Mississippi
state senate, and for six years a United States senator. Daniel Webster (fig. 164) is reputed to have
said of him that he was the greatest land lawyer
in the country.

He joined the cause of the young Republic of
Texas and supported annexation. And he aided
at great personal expense General Narcisse Lopez
in his expedition to Cuba on behalf of the op-
pressed Cubans against Spain. For this he was
indicted for violating the neutrality laws, arrested,
and tried; but with a jury holding out eleven to
one for acquittal, the government dropped the
case. Henderson then retired to private life and
died in Pass Christian. The Cuban government
erected a monument in Havana in recognition of
those Americans who lent support to the Cubans
in their struggle for independence, and on this
memorial Henderson's name is carved. It was as
senator from the state of Mississippi that Henderson appeared before Edouart in Washington in
1841.

96

John Henderson
State of Mississippi
Feby. 17. 1841

John Henderson Senator from
Washington 17th Feby 1841

261
William Peter 1788–1853
Philadelphia, November 12, 1842

From his birth in Cornwall, England, to his coming to this country in 1840, aged fifty-two, Peter had led a long and active life. A graduate of Christ Church, Oxford, 1803, he was called to the bar at Lincoln's Inn, 1813, was justice of the peace and deputy lieutenant for Cornwall, member of Parliament, and a man of letters. His first wife, by whom he had ten children, died in 1836, whereupon he moved to America and devoted himself to letters. It was not until 1840 that he was appointed British consul to Pennsylvania and New Jersey and moved to Philadelphia, where he spent the rest of his life. He was an accomplished scholar and poet and a prolific writer, his last work being a translation of the *Prometheus* of Aeschylus. In Philadelphia he married for his second wife Mrs. Sarah King, the widow of Edward King, son of the Honorable Rufus King of New York. She was in her own right a woman of great distinction. She established in Philadelphia, with the continued support of Sarah Joseph Hale (fig. 140), the School of Design for Women, and in Cincinnati, after the death of Mr. Peter, the Ladies Academy of Art, which became the Art School of Cincinnati. She then submitted to Roman Catholicism, made nine pilgrimages to Rome, and founded many sisterhoods and convents in the Archdiocese of Philadelphia and Cincinnati.

When Consul Peter appeared before Edouart, it was as a widowed scholar, though only a few months before his second marriage. Fisher, the Philadelphia diarist, wrote of Peter: "He is an English gentleman of good family . . . and an agreeable, well-bred, cultivated person. He has received great attention here and enjoys society, eating and drinking more than any man I ever knew."

96½.

William Peter.

William Peter British Consul Philadelphia 12 Nov. 1842.

262
Charles Jackson   1775–1855
Boston, December 20, 1841

In 1841 Judge Jackson had been off the bench for eighteen years and practicing law and fulfilling his public duties in gradual retirement. Born in Newburyport, he had studied law under the Honorable Theophilus Parsons, as had John Quincy Adams (fig. 172). Admitted to the bar in 1796, he soon attained the summit of his profession, acquiring what was said to have been the most lucrative practice ever before known in Massachusetts. Then Governor Strong called him to the state supreme court, where he served with fidelity for ten years until required by health to retire to private life. He was one of the Americans appointed to revise the general statutes of the commonwealth, an overseer of Harvard College, and the author of *Pleading and Practice in Real Actions*. In his biographical sketch in the *Dictionary of American Biography* it is said that "a contemporary estimate of Jackson's character takes the form of a rating scale with 7 representing the highest degree. It runs: law knowledge, 7; political knowledge, 2; classical knowledge, 1; talent, 5; wit, 0; integrity, 7; practice, 7." There is no doubt he was a useful and valued citizen of Boston, where he died. His daughter married Dr. Oliver Wendell Holmes.

263
John Mason Williams   1780–1868
[Boston], May 6, 1842

Judge Williams was born in either New Bedford or Taunton, Massachusetts, and was graduated at Brown in 1801. He practiced law in New Bedford from 1804 to 1816, and in Taunton after 1816. Associate justice of the circuit court of common pleas from 1819 to 1821, of the court of common pleas from 1821 to 1839, he then held the office of chief justice for the following five years. Twelve years of practice in Boston, which included eight as a commissioner of insolvency, made him ready to retire to New Bedford. There he died twelve years later, aged eighty-nine. Brown honored him with an LL.D. in 1842, and Harvard did the same three years later. In New Bedford he was held in high esteem by the members of his profession.

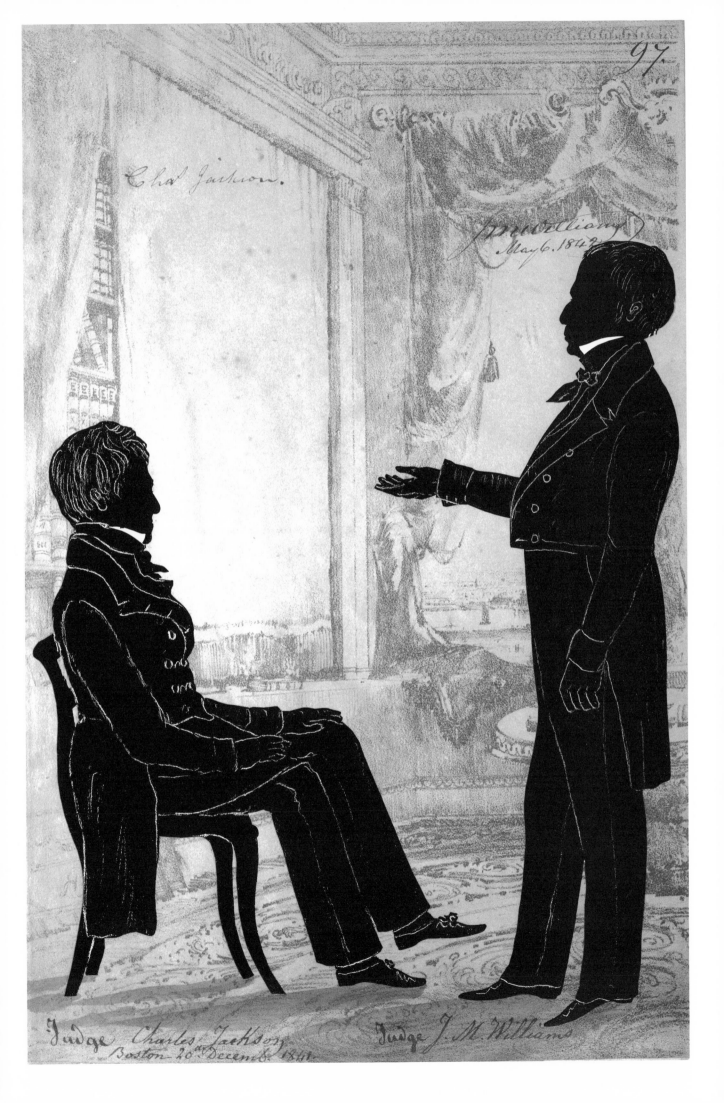

97.

Chas Jackson.

Judge J. M. Williams

Jno Williams
May 6. 1842

Judge Charles Jackson.
Boston 20th Decemr 1841

Judge J. M. Williams

264
L. de la Forest
Philadelphia, January 6, 1843

We can almost hear Monsieur "Le Consul gènèral de France" as he wrote his title and added the date "le 6. Janvier." It is Edouart who tells us that his consulate was in New York. He had been consul at Charleston and was living in Philadelphia in 1824, but his name does not appear in the *Philadelphia City Directory* for the years 1843–45.

265
Baron d'Hauterive
Philadelphia, December 5, 1842

Presumably these two French consuls met on state affairs in Philadelphia, and Edouart, always on the lookout for prominent figures, was able to capture both and place them in friendly converse. The baron's method of dating is a familiar European variation, "5 Xbre 1842." He was resident as consul at Philadelphia as late as 1843. On December 12, 1842, Edouart cut silhouettes of other members of the baron's family, described as the "Baronne," Auguste, Maurice, and Marie, but their shades perhaps were not considered appropriate to be preserved in this volume. In the Academy of Natural Sciences of Philadelphia there is a letter dated 24 June 1843 from Guizot to d'Hauterive thanking him for sending a report by Mr. Cornu on the improvements made in the United States in the construction of steam engines. In 1847 the baron was listed as an honorary member of the Historical Society of Pennsylvania.

97.⅟₃ Philadelphie, le 6. Janvier Philadelphie 5 x.ᵇʳᵉ 1842.
1843. Le Consul général de France M.ᵒⁿ d'Hauterive
L. Delaforest

L. de la Forest Consul G.ᵃˡ of France Baron d'Hauterive French Consul
6ᵗʰ Jan.ʸ 1843 at New York. Philadelphia 5ᵗʰ Decemb. 1842.

266
Cavaliere Rocco Martuscelli
1801–1853
Washington, October 28, 1840

The Chevalier Martuscelli, who identifies himself as "Consul Général de Naples aux Etats Unis d'Amérique" with a cheerful flourish, is described in Hough's *American Biographical Notes* as "envoy extraordinary from the court of Naples." He died in New York, where he had served as chargé d'affaires for fourteen years.

98.

Si Chev. Martuscelle
Consul Général de Naples aux États
Unis d'Amérique 28. Oct.re /40.

Le Chevalier Martuscelle Cons.l Gén.al
Washington 28 Oct.r 1840 of Naples.

267

T. Holmes, M.D.
Philadelphia, January 6, 1843

The identity of Dr. Holmes is a mystery.

98½

J. Holmes.

Phil. 6th Jan. –43.

J. Holmes MD
Philadelphia 6th Jany 1843.

268
John Stryker   d.1885
Saratoga, August 20, 1841

Senator Stryker was for many years one of the leading lawyers and prominent citizens of Rome, New York, where he practiced most of his life. He lost his father at the age of seven and was brought up by his mother at Whitestone, Oneida County. As a Democrat he served in the state legislature and became clerk of the court and for ten years judge of the probate court. He ran for Congress in 1867 to fill the seat vacated by Roscoe Conkling when he was elevated to the Senate, but was roundly defeated. He was survived by two sons and three daughters.

As a successful lawyer and president of the Old Bank of Rome, he built the family house which after his death was occupied by his son Thomas, born in 1847, who became in his own right a leading industrialist of Rome.

99

John "Stryker State Sen" New Y.
of Rome Saratoga 20th Aug 1841.

269
Edmund P. Banning, M.D.
Saratoga Springs, August 5, 1843

We discover little of Dr. Banning save that he was, as he wrote, a doctor and, as Edouart tells us, "of Pittsburgh, Penna." A handwriting expert could no doubt tell us something of his character from the distinctive flourishes in his hand. He appears to be serious and intelligent and is clearly making a point, perhaps to his medical students in Pittsburgh.

270
Andrew Comstock, M.D.   b.1795
Philadelphia, January 4, 1843

Comstock, the professor of elocution and lecturer on oratory, wrote many books on his subject, one of which, *System of Elocution*, was in its sixteenth edition by 1854. In a preface to the eighth edition, published in Philadelphia in 1846, appear eight pages of recommendatory notices, which we can read with pleasure today. They range in date from 1837 to 1845, and the number of them written in 1842 and early 1843 suggest why Dr. Comstock came to Edouart's attention. The *Pennsylvania Law Journal* wrote in December 1842, "Although a treatise on elocution cannot be regarded as a law book, the subject of vocal delivery is so nearly connected with the practice of the law, that we willingly accord to this volume a notice in our *Journal*." A long and favorable notice followed. Dr. W. E. Horner (fig. 180), who attended Dr. Comstock's Gymnasium on August 10, 1837, wrote that one of his pupils who only a week before "had been a most unpleasant stammerer, was then heard to recite publicly with great care and fluency, with a full intonation." To the Philadelphia *North American* in 1841 it was "a good system for breaking up the stiff jaws of a speaker, and rounding the sharp angles in his uncouth gestures." The *Saturday Evening Post* reported in December 1841 that "no man, perhaps, in the United States understood so well how to cure stammering as Dr. Comstock." The *Law Journal* had a telling argument in favor of Dr. Comstock's work: "How many a jury has thought a speaker's argument without force, because his manner was so; and have found a verdict against law and against evidence, because they had been charmed into delusion by the potent fascination of some gifted orator!" Dr. Comstock at least offered "equal opportunity."

99½

Andrew Comstock, M.D. Author of A System of Elocution, & Teacher of Elocution & Curer of Stammering. Philadelphia, Jan. 4, 1843.

Doct E. P. Banning
Saratoga Aug⁵ 1843

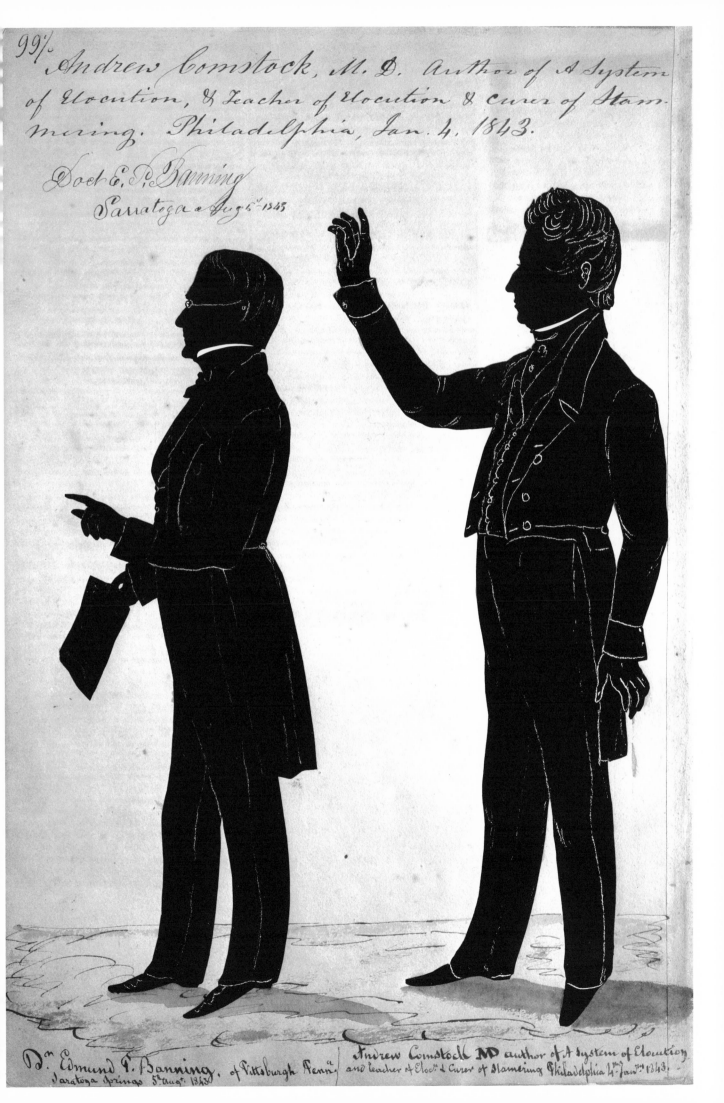

*Dr. Edmund P. Banning, of Pittsburgh Penn*ᵃ
Saratoga Springs 5ᵗ Augᵗ 1843.

Andrew Comstock MD author of A System of Elocution and Teacher of Eloc⁺ & Curer of Stammering Philadelphia 4ᵗʰ Janʸ 1843.

271
Nicholas Biddle 1786–1844
Philadelphia, January 12, 1843

Graduation from the College of New Jersey at Princeton as valedictorian, with honors, at the age of fifteen was a propitious start of a career. Admission to the bar, a few years as editor of *Port Folio*, the only literary journal of repute in the country, and election to the state legislature in 1810 continued the rise. But Biddle's public career, marked by both success and failure, began on the reincorporation of the United States Bank, of which he was one of twenty-five directors appointed by President Monroe, and in 1822 he became the president. All went well until the "Bank War" which started under President Jackson. When the bank's charter, which expired in 1836, was not renewed, the government withdrew millions of dollars, ruined the bank, and caused a depression over the entire nation. Biddle was blamed, censured, persecuted, committed for trial by Richard Vaux (fig. 133) for embezzlement, but saved by the court's sustaining a technical objection. He retired to his estate Andalusia on the Delaware River, which became a seat of intellectual and social life. Entries in Sidney George Fisher's diary give some popular opinions of Biddle's career. In Fisher's opinion Biddle could not have obtained a fair trial in the light of the corruption of the court and the attorney general. "Mr. Biddle," he wrote, "represented the money power of the country; he wielded millions and the influence which they commanded . . . he was the personification of the Almighty Dollar." But Fisher did not believe him guilty of any act of personal dishonesty. Of Biddle's funeral he wrote: "Was glad to hear that it was very numerously attended by people of condition and responsibility, about 300 being present . . . a few years ago it would have been made a public affair. Still, however, that so many are left to do him reverence shows a consciousness by the public that the censure and harsh judgments passed by society on his conduct were excessive and that the services he rendered to the country, the talents he exhibited and the works he achieved were not forgotten."

100.

U Biddle
Philᵈ Janⁿᵍ. 12. 1843

Nicholas Biddle Late Govʳ. of U.S Bank
Philadelphia 12ᵗʰ Janʳʸ 1843.

272
Calvin Blythe
Philadelphia, May 1, 1843

Blythe, caught in a fine stance by Edouart, does not appear in the standard reference books relating to Philadelphia. He was a lawyer, and his presence in Edouart's volume probably stems from the fact that from 1843 to 1845 he was collector of customs of Philadelphia, a federal appointment, his duties being to levy duties on imported goods. Apparently no appropriate companion was found to occupy the blank space on his page.

Calvin Blythe

Phila May 1st 1843

Calvin Blythe Coll. of the Port of Philadelphia
Philadelphia 1st May 1843

273
George Morell   1786–1845
Troy, New York, September 23, 1841

When Judge Morell stood to Edouart in Troy, he
must have been on vacation. Since 1832 when he
was appointed a judge of the United States Court
for the Territory of Michigan, he had lived in
Detroit. In 1837 when Michigan was admitted
into the Union, he was appointed a judge of the
state supreme court, and in 1842 its chief justice,
a post he held until his death.

Born in Lenox, Massachusetts, he graduated
from Williams College in 1807, studied law in
Troy, was admitted to the bar in 1810, and settled
in Cooperstown until called to Michigan. In politics a Democrat, he presided as judge with dignity and was distinguished for his learning and
industry. That month in Troy, Edouart cut some
eighty silhouettes of local personages, but Judge
Morell is one of the few he considered entitled to
a place in this volume.

101.

Judge Geo. Morell of Supn Court Detroit Michigan
taken in Troy 23d Sept. 1841.

274
Peter Vivian Daniel 1784–1860
Saratoga, August 16, 1843

A personal and political friend of President Jackson and a supporter of President Van Buren (fig. 230), Daniel profited accordingly. A lawyer of Stafford County, Virginia, member of the House of Delegates and of the Executive Council from 1812 to 1835, for many years lieutenant governor, he earned his political reward when Jackson appointed him judge of the United States district court, where he served until 1841. In that year, upon the death of Justice Barbour, he received from President Van Buren what was characterized as a "midnight" appointment to the Supreme Court of the United States, before Barbour was buried. Daniel was an able lawyer, a loyal party man, and a careful if not brilliant judge. He supported the Dred Scott decision with language that would be unacceptable today. Two scholarly works on his career have appeared. In Leon Friedman and Frederick L. Israel's *Justices of the United States Supreme Court, 1789–1969* (1969) it is said of Daniel: "He maintained his original principles while many men around him were trying to adjust theirs to changing times. . . . 'Principled anachronism' might have been an appropriate caption for his epitaph."

275
Walter Bowne c.1770–1846
Saratoga, August 16, 1843

For three terms state senator as a staunch Democrat, for eleven years, 1820–31, grand sachem of the Tammany Society, he became mayor of the city of New York in 1828, holding that office for four years. During his term as mayor the population of New York City reached 200,000. Not long after his term, Congress appointed him one of a commission to erect the New York Customs House on Bowling Green. He was a successful merchant engaged in the hardware business and died at his residence in Beekman Street a wealthy man. Bowne and Daniel, both Democratic politicians enjoying the rewards of their party, must have found much in common that day in August 1843 when they were together in Saratoga.

101½.

P V Daniel
Justice of the Supreme
Court of the United States
Saratoga Aug 16. 1843.

Walter Browne

Walter Browne
Mayor of N. York from 1829 to 1833.
Saratoga Aug. 16. 1843.

Peter V. Daniel
Justice of the Supreme Court of the U.S.
Richmond Va
Saratoga Aug 16. 1843.

276

Oliver Caswell   1830–1896

[Boston, June 29, 1843]

Young Oliver was the son of a ferryman at James-town, Rhode Island, and had been deaf, dumb, and blind since the age of three. He was sent to the Perkins Institution at Boston in 1841, four years after Laura Bridgman (fig. 137) had been brought there by Dr. Howe. Laura was one year older but three or four years more advanced in learning finger language, and she and Oliver were at once attracted to each other. Laura spent much time in helping her young friend, and the Perkins Institution possesses a touching portrait of the two together as she guides his fingers over the embossed page. Anna Gardner Fish wrote of the portrait in her *Perkins Institution and Its Deaf-Blind Pupils, 1837–1933* (1934). "His face is uplifted, as if the thought behind the words were dawning upon his mind." So Edouart depicts the lad as he tests the tines of his fork. The silhouette was presumably taken at the Perkins Institution at the same time as that of Laura Bridgman.

Oliver remained at the institution until 1856, when he returned to Rhode Island. Nothing has come to light as to his later life, but his nephew presented to the institution, as a symbol of gratitude for its great work, the watch his uncle Oliver had carried.

ver Caswell. 13 Y. of age. Blind, deaf and dumb. See his history here annexed.

277
Leonard Bacon   1802–1881
Saratoga Springs, August 27, 1841

Pastor of the First Church in New Haven, Congregational, usually called the Center Church, for forty-one years until 1866, then professor of revealed theology and lecturer on ecclesiastical polity and American church history at the Yale Theological Seminary, Dr. Bacon was one of the great proponents and supporters of Congregationalism in New England. The son of a missionary, he had graduated at Yale in 1820 and at Andover Theological Seminary in 1824 and one year later entered into his life's career.

For some years he edited the *Christian Spectator* and founded the *Independent*. He served as moderator in the dispute arising around the Beecher-Tilton controversy. Taking a strong stand against slavery, he supported the American Colonization Society in New England. Hamilton College honored him with an S.T.D. and Harvard with an LL.D. It was entirely appropriate for Edouart to have paired Dr. Bacon with Dr. Taylor and more than likely the two Center Church ministers were vacationing together.

278
Nathaniel William Taylor
1786–1858
Saratoga Springs, August 27, 1841

Dr. Taylor was a product of President Dwight of Yale, under whom he became steeped in Calvinistic theology of the kind modified by the Edwardses. He was an able preacher and was called to the Center Church in New Haven in 1812. There he remained until 1822 when he became professor of didactic theology on the organization of the theological school at Yale; he continued in that position until his death. He was succeeded at the Center Church by Dr. Bacon. Professor Goodrich (fig. 186) was long a colleague of Taylor's. As a leading exponent of "the New Haven theology," the liberalism of his age, Taylor was bitterly opposed by other divines of the day but was nevertheless one of the most influential in his particular calling or branch of the faith. Many of his works were published anonymously and related to the theological controversies of the day. At his funeral service, Dr. Bacon characterized his preaching as "those solid and massive discourses, full of linked and twisted logic, yet giving out at every point sharp flashes of electric fire."

102.

Leonard Bacon Yale Coll*
New Haven 27th Aug* 1841.

taken at Saratoga Springs

Nath*. W. Taylor Yale Coll*
New Haven 27th Aug* 1841.

279
Joseph Nicolas Nicollet   1786–1843
Philadelphia, May 8, 1843

Nicollet, astronomer, mathematician, and explorer, came to America in 1832 as a result of financial misfortunes in France. As a youth in France he was a mathematical prodigy, taught school at the age of nineteen, and became librarian of the observatory in Paris, where he worked with Laplace and discovered several comets. His career continued as professor of mathematics at the College Louis-le-Grand until the failure of his financial speculations.

Arriving in America in 1822, he went from New Orleans to Saint Louis and was soon engaged in exploration, particularly in the southern states, where he explored the great basin tapped by the sources of the Red, Arkansas, and Missouri rivers. Later still he explored the Mississippi to its source and learned much of the Chippewa Indians. Joel Poinsett (fig. 243), when secretary of war, recognized the value of the discoveries and materials collected by Nicollet and engaged him in further exploration, through which he prepared and supplied the government with many valuable maps. In his search for the source of the Missouri River he was accompanied by John C. Frémont.

We see him four months before his death and a week after he and his companion had attended in Albany a meeting of the Association of American Geologists and Natural History of which Rogers was president. Perhaps some geographer will recognize the map Nicollet holds in his hand—the word in the upper right-hand corner appears, tantalizingly, to be simply "Map."

280
Henry Darwin Rogers   1808–1866
Philadelphia, May 8, 1843

The most important geological work to have appeared in America by the mid-nineteenth century was Rogers's geological survey of Pennsylvania, published in Edinburgh, the title of which gives evidence of the wide field he covered: *The Geology of Pennsylvania: A Government Survey; with a General View of the Geology of the United States, Essays on the Coal Formation and Its Fossils, and a Description of the Coal-Field of North America and Great Britain; with Seven Large Maps and Numerous Illustrations on Copper and Wood.*

He had been professor of chemistry and natural philosophy at Dickinson College, lecturer on geology at the Franklin Institute, and professor of geology at the University of Pennsylvania. He completed a survey of New Jersey in 1840 and commenced his work on Pennsylvania. State funds ran out in 1842, but he continued on his own. In the end, in 1855 he took his report to Edinburgh to be printed, finding the work could be done more advantageously there, and it appeared in two volumes in 1858. While abroad he received the appointment of regius professor of natural history in the University of Glasgow, where, except for a short return to America, he spent the rest of his life. Although some of his scientific conclusions have been proven wrong, nevertheless his *Geology of Pennsylvania* is a monument of geological scholarship of the day.

102½.

J. N. Nicollet
Philadelphia May 8th 1843.

Henry D. Rogers
Philadelphia
May 8t 1843
Prof. of Geology. Univ. of Penna.

Monsieur J. N. Nicollet
Astronome, Géog. &c, &c,
Philadelphia 8th May 1843.

Obt 11th Septber 1843.

Henry D. Rogers Professor of Geology
University of Pennsylvania
Philadelphia 8th May 1843.

281
Albert Collins Greene   1791–1863
Boston, May 30, 1842

Born in East Greenwich, Rhode Island, Greene turned early to his chosen profession, being admitted to the bar in 1812 and becoming at once active in the state militia and in public affairs. In 1821 he was elected major general of the militia. During his career he represented his community in the state legislature and his state in the United States Senate. He was a member of the state's General Assembly for seven years, for five as its speaker; attorney general of the state for eighteen years; state senator for four years; and United States senator for six. By his first wife, Catherine, daughter of William Greene, he had seven children, four of whom survived him. We see him at the close of his long term as attorney general and shortly before becoming United States senator.

282
Horace Mann   1796–1859
Boston, January 8, 1842

At the height of his professional career as a lawyer (a product of the Litchfield law school) and statesman, after six years as state representative and four as state senator—the last as president of the senate—Horace Mann resigned all his political prospects to become secretary of the newly created Massachusetts State Board of Education, remarking, "Let the next generation be my client." For twelve years, 1837–48, he held the post and during that time revolutionized the school system, raised the salaries of teachers, and took a large part in establishing the first public normal school in America. His twelve annual reports to the school board and the legislature are models of their kind for effectively arousing public interest in the problems of education. Of his tenth report the *Edinburgh Review* noted: "This volume is indeed a noble monument of a civilized people, and if America were sunk beneath the waves, would remain the fairest picture and record of an ideal commonwealth."

Upon retirement from the secretaryship, Mann was elected to Congress, to fill the vacancy caused by the death of John Quincy Adams (fig. 172), as a strong antislavery Whig. In 1852 he was defeated as a candidate for governor of Massachusetts and accepted the presidency of the newly established Antioch College, which then suffered serious financial losses, anxiety for which probably hastened Mann's death. The great educator, a graduate of Brown with honors in 1819, was buried in Providence. His first wife, whom he had married in 1830, the daughter of President Messer of Brown, had died childless in 1832. He was survived by his second wife and three children.

103.

Atto. Genl. of Rh. Island
May 30, 1842.

Horan Mann
Janry. 11, 1842.

Albert C. Greene Atty Genl. R.I.
Boston 30th May 1842.

Horace Mann
Boston 8th Janry. 1842.

283
Charles Frederick Gove 1793–1856
Saratoga, August 30, 1843

Judge Gove received his law degree from Harvard Law School in 1820 and commenced practice in Goffstown, New Hampshire. He rose rapidly; clerk of the House of Representatives in 1829, four years a member of the House, five years a state senator and one its president, five years attorney general, and from 1842 to 1848 circuit judge of the court of common pleas. All accounts of him attest to his high character and energy but frail constitution and an irritability that perhaps impaired his usefulness. In Charles H. Bell's *Bench and Bar of New Hampshire* (1899), the tale is told that one day he directed the sheriff to remove from the courtroom the next man who coughed. Silence reigned. That evening a stranger appeared at the local hotel suffering from an incessant cough. "I can tell you how you can cure that," said a bystander. "You just go down to the court house, and there is a little wizened-faced judge there who'll put a stop to that cough of yours in less than five minutes,—a sure cure!"

Upon retiring from the court in 1848 Judge Gove held the office of superintendent of the Nashua & Lowell Railroad until his death.

284
Andrew Salter Woods 1803–1863
Saratoga, August 30, 1843

Judge Woods was said to have been the first native of Bath, Maine, to enter the legal profession. With a degree from Dartmouth he studied law under Ira Goodell, becoming his partner and quickly acquiring a high reputation. After twelve years of practice, he was appointed an associate justice of the Supreme Court of New Hampshire in 1840, and its chief justice in 1855. Then a revision of the laws of the state legislature threw him out of office. He returned to private practice in Bath, where he enjoyed a profitable career until his retirement because of illness. Dartmouth recognized his distinction as a jurist by awarding him an LL.D. in 1852. What a pleasant coincidence that Edouart should have had these two New Hampshire jurists under his scissors the same day.

303½ Charles F Gove
one of the Justices of the
Court of Common Pleas for
the State of N. Hampshire
Saratoga Aug.t 30th. 1843

Andrew S. Woods
one of the Associate
Justices of the Superior
Court of the State of
New Hampshire
Aug.t 30th 1843

Charles F. Gove. Justice of C.t of Comm. pleas
Saratoga 30th. Aug.t 1843.   State of New Hampshire

Andrews S. Woods, associate Justice of the Sup.e C.t
State of New Hampshire Saratoga 30th. Aug.t 1843.

285
Benjamin Lincoln
Saratoga Springs, August 25, 1841

Lincoln, a member of the New Bedford Fire Department in the first decade of the nineteenth
century, became lieutenant colonel of the First
Regiment of the militia in 1817. Colonel Lincoln
directed the Washington's birthday celebration
in New Bedford in 1809, and during the War of
1812 the local military units of New Bedford were
under his command. By 1815 he was brigadier
general, and on June 4, 1819, became major general. He married Trepha Lincoln, daughter of
William and Rebecca Lincoln of New Bedford.
It is not clear just what his relationship was to
General Benjamin Lincoln, the Revolutionary
soldier. His profile suggests that by 1841 he had
given up the physical activities of a soldier.

104.

Gen. Benj. Lincoln
New Bedford Mass. August 25 1841

Gal. Benj. Lincoln
of New Bedford Mass. Saratoga Spr. 25th Augt 1841

286

Josiah Harlan 1799–1871
Philadelphia, March 17, 1843

"Mokurrib ul Khakan Unees ul Dowlah B'hader" —Companion of the Imperial Stirrup, and Nearest Friend of the Empire, the Brave—"Look on me ye mighty and despair." So we can address General Harlan. At the age of twenty-four he entered the employ of the East India Company, served as a surgeon in the first Burmese war, journeyed to North India, and became the aide-de-camp to Dost Mahommed Ameer of Kabul. His intrigues led him to journey to the Afghan capital disguised as a dervish to start a revolution in Afghanistan. For seven years he was in the service of Maharajah Runjeet'h Singh, prince of the Punjab, and for a time was governor of the province of Googerath. Under instructions from the Runjeet'h he was able to bribe the brother of the ameer of Kabul in order to avoid a war. Later he aided Dost Mohammed Khan in defeating the Sikhs in the battle of Jamrud in 1837, where he profited from having trained the Afghan infantry in European military tactics. The following year he commanded a force sent into Tartary to chastize the prince of Kundooz, a venture which convinced Harlan that Balkh, in ancient Bactria— whence Alexander the Great traveled—would be the route for every threat to India. As Harlan wrote in his *Memoir of India and Afghanistan* (1842), after describing the passage between Kabul and Bulkh: "Should the result lead to, or facilitate the views of national glory, which the history of Russian policy shows us the never tiring and aggrandizing diplomacy of the north sustains, the consequences attending this great enterprise, may, and probably will, prove an entering wedge for the destruction of the Indo-British empire, the disintegration of that arrogant and audacious power which wields at this moment an universal sway; of Great Britain, whose preeminence is the jealousy of the Christian world; of England, King of Kings." Prophetic words!

General Harlan, the soldier-adventurer, retired to Philadelphia in 1841, published his memoirs in 1842. In his fine uniform and with a fund of tales of war and intrigues, he must have been in constant demand. He married in 1849, served in the Army of the Potomac during the Civil War, and moved to San Francisco, where he died.

104½. Philadelphia
March 17th 1843

General Harlan
Late aid de Camp
to Dost Mahomed
Ameer of Cabul —

Genl Harlan. Late aid de Camp to Dost Mahomed
Philadelphia 17th March 1843. Ameer of Cabul

287
Myra Clark Gaines 1805–1885
Washington, March 20, 1841

The diminutive Myra stands before her second husband, whom she had married only two years before, holding in her hand what appears to be the notice of lectures they were to deliver before the Saint Louis Mechanics Institute on November 17, 1840. His is entitled "A Lecture on National Defense by Steam Power," and hers, "The Address of Mrs. Gaines on the Horrors of War, Delivered on the Same Occasion."

But the "Horrors of War" were as nothing compared to Mrs. Gaines's lifetime effort to establish herself as her father's legitimate daughter and recover as her rightful inheritance real estate in the city of New Orleans valued at upwards of $35 million. Her father, Daniel Clark, a reputed bachelor, formed a connection with a Frenchwoman of beauty during the absence of her reputed husband in Europe. Myra was one of two daughters born of the alliance. Brought up by friends of her father in Philadelphia, Myra discovered in 1830 papers relating to her birth. In 1832 she married W. W. Whitney, who pursued the discovery, joined with his wife in bringing suit to recover her father's vast holdings that had passed under an 1811 will. The lawsuit was classic; Whitney did not survive its conclusion, nor did her second husband, General Gaines. In 1883 she received a judgment in excess of $2 million, but appeal was taken. She had exhausted her resources and died before the entry of a final judgment freed her mother's name from stain and awarded substantial sums to her own estate.

288
Edmund Pendleton Gaines
1777–1849
Washington, March 20, 1841

General Gaines, twenty-eight years older than his third wife, was perhaps better qualified to discuss "National Defence by Steam Power" than his wife to address the Mechanics Institute on "The Horrors of War."

He was born in Culpeper County, Virginia, and early in 1799 received the rank of ensign of the Tenth Infantry. His was a military career. He was collector of the port of Mobile in 1805, and a year later, under order from President Jefferson, he captured Aaron Burr. He testified at his trial, for which, on Burr's acquittal, he discovered he had made many enemies. Conspicuous for his bravery and agility at Chrysler's Field in 1813, engaged in the defense of Fort Erie a year later, he was wounded while repelling the British veteran army and earned a congressional gold medal and the thanks of the nation. He took part with Jackson in the Creek and Seminole wars. In his latter years he was in constant and bitter strife with the War Department, General Scott (fig. 120), and General Macomb (fig. 271). For his action in the Mexican War, calling out troops without authority, he was court-martialed, but was acquitted. His wife's lawsuit must have been a welcome change from the controversies of his official career.

105.

Edmund P. Gaines ⟩ Born 20 March
United States Army ⟩ 1777
March 20. 1841

Myra Clark Gaines
March 20th 1841.

Mrs. Myra Clark Gaines wife of Genl. Edmd. P. Gaines Born 20th March 1777
Washington 20th March 1841 United States Army

289
Thomas Mayne Reid   1818–1883
Philadelphia, October 29, 1843

Mayne Reid, as he was called, was born in county Down and emigrated to this country in 1840, first to New Orleans, where he served variously as storekeeper, Negro overseer, schoolmaster, and actor, and then, in 1842, to Philadelphia. There he took up and pursued his true interest, writing novels, mostly romantic, adventure tales for boys. He became acquainted with Edgar Allan Poe, wrote for *Godey's Lady's Book* under the pseudonym "The Poor Scholar," and was for a time correspondent for the *New York Herald*. As an adventurer he served as a captain in the Mexican War, receiving a wound that plagued him the rest of his life. In 1849 he went abroad to take part in revolutionary activities, but he was too late. In London he published his first novel, *The Rifle Rangers*, and then produced over the years some fifty volumes of romance and excitement, much of it founded on his own experiences.

He returned to America in 1867, founding the *Onward Magazine*, but after a short time returned to England, where he died. His wife, Elizabeth Hyde, whom he had married in England at age fifteen, and the subject of his novel *The Child Wife*, claimed kinship with the family of the earl of Clarendon. Of his many works, a considerable number were translated into French. In a notice appearing in the *Athenaeum* in 1857, it is said of him, "Now-a-days, in place of lectures, the world of little folks has its race of story-tellers who are 'boys with the boys' and are nonetheless efficient from being cheerful. Among these the Captain [Reid] is at the head of the company, and right worthily does he perform the office." His silhouette, taken at the start of his literary career, is indeed that of a young man of spirit.

105½.

Tho Mayne Reid

Philadelphia
Sunday Oct 29th
1843

290
Euphrasie Borghese
Saratoga, August 10, 1841

The prima donna Euphrasie Borghese had performed at many prominent theaters before her
visit to Saratoga. Edouart describes her as "Prima
donna, des Theatres Italiens de St. Charles, de
Naples, de Venise, de la Havane et du Theatre
Royal de l'opéra Comique de Paris." This suggests that her voice was as attractive as her profile.
On August 8, Edouart had cut the silhouette of
Edouard Borghese, perhaps Euphrasie's husband
or brother. The music she holds in her hand reveals an aria designed for a soprano; the notes are
clear but the words are tantalizingly, no doubt deliberately, indistinct.

A student of the opera in the nineteenth century
could perhaps supply our young prima donna's
history. She must have been a charming enter-
tainer at Saratoga.

Euphrasie Borghese [signature, top]

106.

Euphrasie Borghese — *Prima donna des Theatres Italiens de St. Charles de Naples, de Venise de la Havane et du Theatre Royal de l'Opéra Comique de Paris. Saratoga 10th Augt. 1841.*

291
Montroville Wilson Dickeson, M.D.
Natchez, Mississippi, April 24, 1844

Dr. Dickeson appears as an M.D. in Natchez in 1844. A decade later we can find him, as a professor of natural science, the director of the City Museum in Philadelphia, which opened in 1854. The museum originated as a commercial enterprise, only moderately successful, in the building of the old Second Universalist Church. The first floor was arranged for the display of curiosities of natural history and science, pictures and portraits; the second floor was used by the City Museum Theater. Dr. Dickeson with his wide interests was a member of the American Association for the Promotion of Science, the Historical Society of Pennsylvania, the Academy of Natural Science of Philadelphia, and the Ethnological Society of New York and was a fellow of the Royal Society of Antiquaries of Copenhagen. In 1859 he published in Philadelphia *The American Numismatical Manual.*

292
William L. Jones, M.D.   b. c. 1800
Natchez, Mississippi, April 24, 1844

Information concerning Dr. Jones has been hard to come by. His signature above his silhouette gives his initials as "W.L." or possibly "W.S." This question apparently plagued the takers of the United States census and his local tax office. The Adams County (City of Natchez) personal tax rolls of the day list a W. S. Jones, the 1850 census records record a "William La. Jones." In 1850 he was recorded as age fifty, born in Maryland, as was his wife, Eliza, then age thirty-eight, and their four children. He also appears to have lived in Natchez from 1840 to at least 1852 and in his latter years the personal tax rolls credit him with the ownership of thirteen slaves, which suggests that he had a successful medical practice.

106:

M. W. Dickeson MD · W L Jones M D.

Natchez April 24 1844.

Natchez April 24 /44

M. W. Dickeson MD
Natchez Miss. 24th April 1844.

W. L. Jones MD
Natchez 24th April 1844.

293

Edwin Forrest   1806–1872
Boston, April 25, 1842

Forrest, the tragedian, was the first American-
born actor of prominence. Born in Philadelphia,
he first appeared on the stage at the age of fourteen. His first great public appearance was in 1820
as Othello at the old Bowery Theater in New
York, where he gained instant success. In England
in 1836 he played Spartacus in the tragedy *The
Gladiator* at the Drury Lane Theatre, and from
there he went on to fame, playing, among others,
Macbeth, Othello, and King Lear to large audi-
ences in England and America. While in England
he married Catherine, the daughter of John Sin-
clair, the popular singer, but the marriage was a
catastrophe. When Edouart caught him he was
at the peak of his career.

He was a rival of the actor William Macready.
After exchanges of hisses at several performances,
a repetition at the Astor Place Opera House in
1849 incited the famous Astor Place riot in which
twenty-two persons were killed and thirty-six
wounded, leaving, as was said, a black shadow on
the reputation of Forrest from which he could
never quite emerge.

About 1850 he built an imitation feudal castle
on the Hudson, ultimately sold to a convent. That
year his wife brought suit for divorce, he counter-
claimed, and the trial lasted off and on for two
years. Mrs. Forrest was represented by Charles
O'Conor (fig. 252), who succeeded in winning the
verdict, clearing the name of his client and securing a handsome alimony. The suit attained such
publicity that at its conclusion Forrest was able
to play the part of Damon at the Broadway
Theater for sixty nights to an unprecedented audience. But his career gradually petered out. Fisher,
the Philadelphia diarist, wrote of him that he had
had a great run in London, "but I do not like
him, he is too violent, rants and distorts his features too much, and sadly oversteps the modesty
of nature." This criticism is tempered by Fisher's
next sentence, "I detest the theatre."

107.

Edwin Forrest

Boston 25 April 1842

Edwin Forrest Tragedian
Boston 25th April 1842.

Henry Tooley   1773–1848
Natchez, Mississippi, April 24, 1844

It has not proven possible to confirm Edouart's description of Tooley as "M.D." He was a native of Tennessee and for many years a prominent citizen of Natchez, as magistrate, mayor, and president of the board of county police. He was a member of the Methodist church for sixty years and for fifteen years a preacher. As a dilettante in astronomy, he contributed meterological information to the *American Almanac*. As a student of Hebrew, he made some progress in a translation of the Bible from the Hebrew, which even in his day would seem to have been a work of supererogation. He was called "the Father of Temperance" at Natchez, but no concomitant roster of his progeny appears. He reveals a strong profile and the handwriting of a man of education. He was the first grand master of Freemasonry in Mississippi.

107½-

Dr H. Tooley MD Born 27th June 1773. Natchez 24th April 1844. Miss.

295
David Butler, D.D.　1763–1842
Troy, New York, September 16, 1841

Less than a year before his death, the Reverend Dr. Butler stood to Edouart in his old-time clerical garb, knee breeches and tailcoat, in the city of Troy, where for thirty-seven years he had faithfully and affectionately served his flock as rector of the Episcopal church, St. Paul's. He was one of the few who could boast of being ordained both deacon and priest by the venerable Bishop Samuel Seabury, the first Episcopal bishop in America.

He was born in Harwinton, Connecticut, and for five years served as rector of St. Michael's Church in Litchfield. From there he removed for a few years to Reading until he received his call to Troy in 1804. He was a High Churchman and a successful though not brilliant preacher. Washington College (later Trinity) gave him an honorary D.D. in 1832. He died beloved by his parishioners and survived by a large family. His funeral sermon was preached by his old friend Bishop Doane of New Jersey (fig. 245). When he stood to Edouart all he could sign was his name, in the shaking hand of an octogenarian. It was the silhouettist who added his title and other descriptive words.

Revd Dr David Butler Epis-
St Paul's Troy.
16.th September 1841.

DIED,
On Monday the 11th inst., at his late residence in Troy
the Rev. DAVID BUTLER, D. D., aged 80 years. July 1842

July 1842

Revd Dr David Butler
Rector of St Paul's Episcopal
Troy 16 September 1841.

296

Henry Lockett   c.1800–1854
New Orleans, April 12, 1844

Henry Lockett was a prominent member of the community of New Orleans in 1844. He had been police commissioner of the Second District of New Orleans from 1828 to 1838 and served as alderman for the same district from 1838 to 1846, under two terms of Mayor Freret (fig. 227). He was an Episcopalian and at his death in 1854 was buried in the Girod Street Cemetery of New Orleans.

108½...

A. Lockett
New Orleans Aprl. 12. 1844

New Orleans 12th April 1844

H. Lockett *Alderman and H. Serv.*
New Orleans 12th April 1844

297
Morgan Lewis 1754–1844
[New York, March 1841]

General Lewis, Governor Lewis, Chief Justice Lewis, by whatever title, was one of the oldest of Edouart's sitters. The date of the occasion, as will appear later, may well have been in 1841. Lewis bridged two centuries. The son of Francis Lewis, a signer of the Declaration of Independence, Lewis graduated at the College of New Jersey (Princeton) in 1773 and studied law under John Jay. With the advent of war, he took his part, served gallantly, and held the rank of colonel under General Gates in the action at Bemis's Heights at Saratoga. After the war he resumed practice of the law, entered the state legislature, became judge of the court of common pleas, attorney general of the state, judge of the Supreme Court of New York, and in 1801 its chief justice.

In 1804 he was elected governor of the state and served one term. In the War of 1812 he was with General Dearborn at Niagara, and he captured Fort George. After the war, having married into the Livingston family, he lived in retirement looking after the family estates. As grand master of the Order of Freemasons in the United States, president of the New-York Historical Society and of the New York branch of the Order of the Cincinnati, he was always in demand for patriotic orations. In Edouart's volume there is included a delightful newspaper account, dated at Saratoga Springs, August 15, 1839, of an excursion of twenty carriages of the elite of Saratoga setting out from the United States Hotel, led by General Lewis, "now in the enjoyment of a green old age," to view the site of the Battle of Bemis's Heights. Henry Clay (fig. 147) and N. P. Tallmadge (fig. 179) were of the party, but the old Revolutionary officer was the lion. When they reached the bridge where Burgoyne surrendered, the general called out, "This is the place—there's the two knolls—here the shot poured in hot and heavy." Edouart was not in Saratoga during the summer of 1839, but he cut Clay's and Tallmadge's silhouettes in Washington in 1841. One of them might well have given him the clipping and persuaded him to seek out the opportunity to take the general's profile in New York. The article was written by J. G. Barnard, chief engineer of the American army in the field, who was in the carriage expedition to Bemis's Heights, and whose silhouette Edouart cut in 1844. He may have supplied the clipping.

The old general was tremendously popular, and his funeral in New York drew an enormous throng of people. It is told that as the coffin left the general's house, an aged man turned to his companion "who as well as the former appeared to be themselves some of the brave hearts of oak of the olden time" and said, "There goes the last march of the General." "Yes," replied the other, "but it's to headquarters."

Morgan Lewis, born
16th October 1754.

109.

Died Sunday April 7
1844

Major Genl Morgan Lewis Born 16th Octr 1754

298
Thomas W. Colescott, M.D.
Louisville, Kentucky, May 14, 1844

Dr. Colescott's trail is hard to pick up at the ends though we can track him down in middle life. From the Louisville *Directory* it appears that he was a physician resident in Louisville from at least 1843 to 1863, often boarding with others, suggesting that he was unmarried. He was junior warden of Mount Moriah Lodge No. 106 in 1848 and 1849, and for a long time attending physician and surgeon at the Louisville Marine Hospital, later the Louisville City Hospital. He was one of the editors, with Dr. L. P. Yandell (fig. 61), of the *Western Journal of Medicine and Surgery*, the oldest medical journal in the West and by far the most widely circulated. He was concerned with, or at least took an interest in, some medical politics and wrote an article, "Anonymous Pamphleteers," for the *Western Journal* in April 1843. The *Filson Club History Quarterly* in its October 1966 issue contains an article, "The Early Printers of Louisville," which includes the name of T. W. Colescott with the date 1843. This is perhaps merely in connection with his editorship of the *Western Journal*. He stands before Edouart with the distinguished biographer Dr. Gross, whom, of course, he must have known well.

299
Samuel David Gross   1805–1884
Louisville, Kentucky, May 14, 1844

Dr. Gross was unquestionably one of Philadelphia's most distinguished citizens of his day and one of America's most famous physicians. His industry and accomplishments knew no bounds.

At the age of twenty-three he graduated at Jefferson Medical College in its third graduating class. By 1833 he had commenced his career as a teacher, which lasted forty-nine years. He was demonstrator of anatomy at the Medical College of Ohio, professor of pathological anatomy at the Cincinnati Medical College, for sixteen years professor of surgery in the University of Louisville, and from 1856 to his death professor of surgery at his alma mater. And all the while he was writing, translating, and editing. His *Elements of Pathological Anatomy* (1839) was the first book in English on that subject. His *System of Surgery* (though a century later superseded) became a monument, passing through many editions and translations. He founded two medical journals, was a member of numerous medical societies at home and abroad, and was president of the International Medical Congress of 1876. Oxford gave him a D.C.L. on its one thousandth commencement in 1872, and Cambridge an LL.D. the same year—the University of Pennsylvania not until the year of his death. Unsurpassed as a surgeon he could boast that he "never lost a patient on the table." Aside from the numerous and valuable model works, standards of their day, his *Lives of Eminent American Physicians and Surgeons of the Nineteenth Century* is a mine of biographical information often not elsewhere obtainable.

His colleague W. W. Keen said of him that his life could be summed up in a few words: "Daily labor in his profession, editorial labor without cessation, article after article in journals, address after address, twenty-six annual courses of lectures on surgery to thousands of students, labors without ceasing till he wrapped the drapery of his couch around him and calmly passed away."

109½ Th. W. Colescott. M.D.
Editor Western Journal of Med. &
Surgery.
Louisville, Ky.

May 14. 1844.

S. D. Gross, M.D.
Professor of Surgery. Louisville
Medical Institute.
Louisville
May 14, 1844

Th. W. Colescott MD
Editor Western Journal of Med. & Surgery
Louisville Kent.y 14th May 1844.

S. D. Gross MD Prof.r of Surgery
Louisville Medical Institute 14th May 1844.

300
Richard Henry Wilde   1789–1847
Boston, November 4, 1841

Here we see Wilde, the poet, congressman, and Italian scholar, hand on his breast, about to recite to J. B. Thomson, the educator, his youthful lyric of a quarter of a century earlier, "My Life Is like a Summer Rose." If only we could hear it—set to music by Sidney Lanier and praised by Byron. Of all his poems it is the only one to remain at all familiar.

He was born in Dublin, Ireland, and after his father's death in 1802 his mother moved to Augusta, Georgia, and made a marked success in educating her son. He was admitted to the bar in 1809, became attorney general of Georgia in 1811, served in Congress for eleven years, and, after traveling extensively, settled in Florence, Italy. He it is who is credited with the discovery in the Bargello of Giotto's portrait of the youthful Dante. On his return to Georgia he published in 1842, in two volumes, his *Conjectures and Researches Concerning the Love, Madness, and Imprisonment of Tasso*, which contained translations of many of the poems. Not long before his death he moved to New Orleans and was professor of constitutional law in the Law Department of the University of Louisiana.

After his death of yellow fever in New Orleans, he was twice reinterred, lastly in the "Poet's Corner" of the City Cemetery of Augusta.

301
James Bates Thomson   1808–1883
Saratoga Springs, July 5, 1843

Thomson's literary efforts may not sound romantic, but it is said of his *School Algebra* (1843) and *Arithmetical Analysis* (1854) that they had sales of upwards of 100,000 copies annually. Born on a farm in Vermont, he graduated at Yale in 1834 and was principal of an academy at Nantucket from 1835 to 1842. Perhaps it was from these years that he attained a not inconsiderable reputation as a conchologist. President Day of Yale persuaded him to publish an abridgment of *Day's Algebra*, and this led to his own arithmetical publications. He was for some years president of the State Teacher's Association of New York and spent his last years in Brooklyn. Hamilton College honored him with an LL.D. in 1853 and the University of Tennessee in 1882. He was commencing his educational work in New York at the time he vacationed at Saratoga and was cut by Edouart.

Rich.d Hen.y Wilde
4th Nov.r 1841.

James Thomson
5 July 1843

110.

Rich.d H.y Wilde Poet
of Georgia   Memb. of Cong from 1816 to 35
Boston 4 Nov.r 1841.

James Thomson of New York
Saratoga Springs 5th July 1843.

302
Gaspard Tochman
Saratoga Springs, July 27, 1842

Major Tochman, the "Polish Exile," stands to
Edouart as he had only a month before stood before the House of Representatives of New Hampshire, delivering one of his famous lectures on the
Polish revolution and the character, wrongs, and
prospects of the Poles. He was the nephew of the
great General Shrzynecki, commander in chief of
the Polish army, and told how he was with him
at Dobrc when the general with 8,000 Poles defeated 40,000 Russians, at Grochow when 50,000
Poles defeated 187,000 Russians, and later at
Ostralenka and Warsaw. At the end of the revolution he went to France and was vice-president of
the Polish Council until 1837 when he came to
America to write and lecture about his country
and to practice law.

He was living in Washington in 1861 but
moved to Montgomery, Alabama, in the service
of the Confederate army, to raise troops. He succeeded in raising a brigade of 1,700 men of whom
over 400 were of foreign birth. He was offered
command as a colonel, which he turned down, believing himself entitled to be made brigadier general. He filed a claim for expenses incurred in the
amount of $7,525, which was allowed.

But his heart was ever with his fatherland.
Above his name he wrote in Polish and English,
"Poland is not lost while we live," and he used to
recite the lines:

> Tell the North madman, Poland must be free;
> A Coeur de Leon to his inmost soul
> Is each true Pole—and all the world shall see
> That every freeman is at heart a Pole!

110½.

"Jeszcze Polska niezginęła, kiedy my żyjemy"

Poland is not lost while we live.

G. Tochman
a Polish Exile

Saratoga Springs, July. 27. 1842.

Major Gaspard Tochman Polish Exile
Saratoga Spring 27th July 1842.

303
Joseph Prescott 1762–1852
Saratoga, August 1, 1844

Dr. Prescott, in 1844 an old survivor of the Revolutionary War, was, as Edouart tells us, five feet eight inches tall, though the significance of the disclosure is not apparent. As a youth he entered the General Army Hospital as a student of Dr. Brown and subsequently became junior surgeon. He was in the action at Ticonderoga, stationed at Albany, Schenectady, and West Point, and took part in Sullivan's expedition against the Indians. His profile at the age of eighty-two is that of an old man, though he stood upright. The withdrawn lips suggest the loss of his teeth. At his death in his ninety-first year he was the only surviving surgeon of the Revolutionary army, vice-president and the only survivor of the original members of the Society of the Cincinnati of Massachusetts. He would have had many a memory to refresh with old General Lewis (fig. 297).

304
Benjamin Russell 1761–1845
Boston, April 11, 1842

Apprenticed to Isaiah Thomas at Worcester, his term being interrupted by service in the Revolutionary War, during which he was one of the guard at the execution of Major André, Russell was released at the age of twenty and became a journeyman printer. In Boston in 1784 he published the first issue of the *Massachusetts Centinel and the Republican Journal*, which by 1790 changed its name to the *Columbian Centinel*, a semiweekly journal which had no equal in its ability to influence public sentiment, and which continued in active publication under Russell for forty-four years. Stephen Higginson, John Lowell, Fisher Ames, Timothy Pickering, and George Cabot were active contributors. Russell's position as depositary of all foreign intelligence brought Louis Philippe and Talleyrand to his office while they were in Boston. During the early years of congressional activity, when the treasury was empty, Russell undertook at his own expense to publish the laws and other official documents, a service Washington later recognized by insisting that he accept payment in the amount of $7,000. For twenty-four years Russell was a member of the General Court of Massachusetts and for several years a senator and alderman of Boston.

Public-spirited and generous, with an eye for news and as a staunch Federalist, he made the *Centinel* the leading publication in New England. In his obituary notice preserved by Edouart, it was stated that "no man connected with the public press in this country was better known or more respected than Major Russell, and no man ever better deserved the universal regard which was entertained for him. He was a Federalist of the old school, and . . . gloried in it as among the highest honors he held."

111.

Benj. Russell
Born 13th September 1762; Boston, April 11, 1842.

Joseph Prescott born 6th Jany 1762.
Junior Surgeon in the Military Hospital
of the Revolution — of Massachusetts
Saratoga 1st Augt 1824

5 ft 8 inches
Dr Joseph Prescott Revolution! 83 yrs of age
Mass. Saratoga 1st Aug 1844.

Major Benj. Russell Revolution
Boston 11th April 1842. 80 yrs of age

305
Charles L. Schlatter
Philadelphia, November 28 or 29, 1842

Charles Schlatter was the engineer in chief of the state of Pennsylvania and resided at Harrisburg, as Edouart tells us and he himself indicates under his signature. Judges and physicians made up most of Edouart's crop of subjects in November 1842 in Philadelphia, although on November 28 he took the profile of Richard C. Taylor (fig. 224), the coal geologist, who must have been acquainted with Schlatter, the state engineer. Details of the career of the engineer in chief have escaped us.

111½

Charles L Schlatter
Novr. 28th 1842
Harrisburg
Pa:

Charles L. Schlatter Engr. in Chief
of the State of Pennsylvania . Harrisburgh
Philadelphia 29th Nov. 1842.

306
George Washington Whistler
1800–1849
Boston, January 12, 1842

At the time of his birth, five months after the death of President Washington, it was not surprising that Whistler's father, then an officer of the American army and commandant at Fort Wayne, should have named his son George Washington. Young George became a draftsman at the United States Military Academy, from which he graduated in 1819, was then assistant teacher of drawing at West Point, and in 1828 assisted in laying out the line of the Baltimore & Ohio Railroad. His railroad services included surveying and construction work for the Baltimore & Susquehanna, the Paterson & Hudson, and later the Boston & Providence line to Stoughton. He, his brother-in-law Major McNeill, and Captain William H. Swift were in demand as the leading American civil engineers.

When Russia was planning its railroads, a deputation sent to America selected Whistler as the best-qualified man for the job, and in 1842, only a few months after he stood to Edouart with his daughter, Whistler traveled to Russia. There he convinced the Russians to resort to the five-foot gauge used in America, and within seven years, at a cost of $40 million, some four hundred miles of the Moscow–Saint Petersburg Railroad were laid, much of the rolling stock and machinery being manufactured at Alexandroffsky under Whistler's supervision. For his services he received the decoration of the Order of Saint Anne. He did not survive the completion of the railroad, dying of a heart attack at Saint Petersburg aged only forty-nine. His daughter by his first wife faces him in Edouart's volume. By his second wife he had five sons, two of whom survived him, the more famous being the artist and etcher James Abbott McNeill Whistler.

What he accomplished in Russia was said by his biographer to have been a more Herculean labor than the building of the pyramid of Cheops.

307
Deborah Delano Whistler
c.1825–1908
[Boston], August 11, 1842

Deborah Whistler, also known as Dash, was in Russia with her father in Saint Petersburg and presumably had accompanied him when he left America late in August 1842. Perhaps her silhouette was cut on the eve of her departure. In 1844, in a petition for the sale of a minor's land, she is described as a "minor." She was the second child of Whistler by his first wife, who died in 1827. On October 16, 1847, Deborah married Francis Seymour Haden, etcher and surgeon and a friend of her half-brother James Abbott McNeill Whistler. Haden himself was an able etcher and founder of the Royal Society of Painter-Etchers, whose president he remained until his death in 1910. For his public service he was knighted in 1894 and made an honorary member of the Institut de France and the Académie des Beaux Arts. Four children were born of the marriage, a daughter and three sons. Lady Haden died in 1908 at their residence at Woodcote Manor, near Alresford, Hampshire. Both her husband and her half-brother, James, etched portraits of her reading by lamplight in 1858.

112.

George W. Whistler –
January 12ᵗʰ 1842 –

Miss Whistler
August 11ᵗʰ 1842

George W. Whistler
Civil Engineer & Railroad
Boston 12ᵗʰ 1842. Jany

Miss E. Whistler
August 11ᵗʰ 1842

308
Frederick Graff   1774–1847
Philadelphia, April 14, 1843

Who can remember wooden water pipes? Graff's first activity of any significance was as assistant engineer to H. H. Latrobe in constructing Philadelphia's first waterworks. The system to which he was an important contributor was the first steam-powered waterworks in the United States and raised the water from the Schuylkill River a total of eighty-six feet to reservoirs, from which it was distributed across the city through wooden pipes. As we now know, these proved inadequate. Graff devised the system of iron pipes, hydrants, and stopcocks, the use of which spread throughout the major cities of the United States. He picked Fairmount as the site of the new waterworks, superintended the construction, and was chief engineer and manager of the works until his death. Over 100 miles of mains were laid by Graff by the time Edouart cut his profile, and their success established his reputation. At his death, a monument in the shape of a Gothic canopy over his bust was erected in Fairmount, near the waterwheels, bearing the inscription: "To the memory of Frederick Graff who designed and created the Fairmount Water-works." He would have been proud to know that his son succeeded him as chief engineer of the Philadelphia water system.

309
Solomon White Roberts   1811–1882
Philadelphia, October 7, 1842

Roberts stood before the silhouettist as president of the Schuylkill Navigation Company, an office he held from at least 1842 to 1845. Curiously enough his biographical notices all state he held the office from 1843, but Edouart credited him with it from at least October 7, 1842. He was brought up by his uncle Josiah White of the Lehigh Coal and Navigation Company and was early engaged in railroading and the profession of civil engineer. He was employed by the state of Pennsylvania in the construction of the canal on the Conemaugh River and went to England to procure rails for the Philadelphia & Reading. He was intimately involved in the construction of the Portage Railroad over the Allegheny Mountains, including the 900-foot-long tunnel, the first railroad tunnel in the United States. This road was considered one of the wonders of the country. As an outstanding civil engineer, Roberts was a member of many learned societies and contributed articles to many scientific journals. Though his meeting with the engineer Graff on the pages of Edouart's volume was contrived by Edouart, it is not difficult to assume that they were well known to each other, both socially and professionally.

Fred.ᵈ Graff
Manager of the Fair Mount
Water Works, April 14/43

S.W. Roberts
Civil Engineer
Philadᵃ. Oct. 7. 1842.

The Courier

Frederick Graff Manager of the Fair Mount
Phila 14ᵗʰ april 1843   Water Works

Salomon W. Roberts President Schuylkil Navigᵗⁿ. Cᵒ. Phila
Civil Engineer   Philad. 7ᵗʰ Octob 1842.

310
Lemuel Shaw 1781–1861
Boston, June 16, 1842

Not since the days of Theophilus Parsons had Massachusetts known such a man as Lemuel Shaw. He can be described in a paragraph or in volumes, and his volumes of decisions still guide and inspire those learned in the law. Admitted to the bar in 1804, representative to the General Court for six years, senator for four years, after being selected he was persuaded by Daniel Webster (fig. 164) to accept the position of chief justice of the Supreme Judicial Court of Massachusetts. This post he held, indeed filled—pressed down and running over—for thirty years until age prompted his retirement. His wisdom was profound, his decisions precedents that the bar could lean on without fear, his influence unlimited. For Harvard he served fifteen years as overseer and thirty as a member of the corporation. His decisions are found in no less than fifty volumes. His name has become a legend. In politics he was a Federalist; among his cases that aroused the greatest interest was the famous trial in 1850 of Professor Webster for the murder of Dr. Parkman. As Mr. Thomas wrote of Shaw in his memoir for the Massachusetts Historical Society, "He was the servant of the law he was set to administer, and obeyed its mandates. With the most generous love of freedom and hatred of oppression, he stood unflinchingly by the Constitution he had sworn to support." Would that there were today more of his stamp!

311
Thaddeus Mason Harris, D.D.
1768–1842
Boston, January 14, 1842

Though urged by his mother to become a maker of saddletrees, Harris nevertheless persevered in his intention to enter Harvard College, which he did, graduating in 1787, after working his way through college by serving as a waiter in the commons. He studied theology at Harvard, where he was librarian for three years. In 1793 he was ordained pastor of the First Church in Dorchester, which was considered Unitarian, and there he served until 1839. He was a learned and scholarly man and took an active part in arranging Washington's papers in 132 volumes and aiding Jared Sparks in preparing them for publication. In 1813 Harvard conferred on him the honorary degree of D.D.

From 1837 until his death he was librarian of the Massachusetts Historical Society and for a time an overseer of Harvard. He wrote numerous discourses and longer works concerned with Masonry, theology, history, and biographical memorials. In his biographical sketch in the *Dictionary of American Biography*, speaking of his tendency to burst into tears while preaching, his biographer noted: "Leonard Withington, writing under the name of John Oldbug, satirized him in the *Puritan* as Doctor Snivelwell."

Lemuel Shaw
Chief Justice of the
Sup. Judicial Court
of Massachusetts. Boston 16 June
1842

Rev. Thaddeus Mason Harris
Boston Jany 14. 1842 —

113

Lemuel Shaw Chief Justice of the
Boston 16th June 1842 Ine. C.

3d inst. of pneumonia, Rev Thaddeus Mason Harris.
D. D.

3d April 1842, Boston U.S.

312
Cornelius Conway Felton
1807–1862
Saratoga Springs, August 19, 1844

Professor Felton became the twentieth president of Harvard College and to the sorrow of his colleagues, and indeed all who knew him, survived in that high office only one year. He was of the class of 1827 at Harvard and spent his life in its service, as regent of the college and for a quarter of a century as Eliot professor of Greek literature. He wrote many volumes on Greek history and literature and classical studies in general, and translated many foreign works. His best-known works were published posthumously, *Greek, Ancient and Modern* (1867) being his famous series of lectures before the Lowell Institute and *Familiar Letters from Europe* (1864), an account of his last trip abroad. In Greece when he traveled he became known as "the American Professor." Beyond the confines of his college he was a regent of the Smithsonian Institution, a member of the Massachusetts Historical Society, and a fellow of the American Academy of Arts and Sciences. His brief term as president of Harvard was marked by his extraordinary interest in and knowledge of all facets of the institution, both faculty administration, and in the oversight of the students. To Edouart he was simply "Profsor. Cambge. Coll. Massts."

313
Alfred Hennen   1786–1870
New Orleans, January 25, 1844

By 1844 Hennen had been practicing law with profit and distinction in New Orleans for thirty-five years and was to continue to do so for another quarter century. Born in Baltimore, his youth was spent in Nashville, and he was a Yale graduate of the class of 1806. After admission to the bar he moved to New Orleans, where he lived out his life. He turned down several offers of a seat on the bench, preferring private practice. For some years he was professor of common and constitutional law in the University of Louisiana. During his active life he accumulated one of the largest private libraries in the South. Though in his early life a vestryman of the Episcopal church in New Orleans, after 1828 when he aided in the introduction of Presbyterianism into the city, he became and remained a ruling elder in the First Presbyterian Church until his death.

He was one of the company of cavalry which formed General Jackson's lifeguard when Louisiana was invaded in 1864; and he suspended his practice of the law during his two years' residence within the Confederate lines while New Orleans was occupied by United States troops. He married twice and was survived by nine children.

113.2

Alfred Hennen 25 Jany 1844 N Oleans

Cornelius Conway Felton,
Saratoga Sp'r 19th Saratoga Aug. 19. 1844.

Cornelius Conway Felton Profsor   Camb'r Coll Mass. Alfred Hennen Counsellor
Saratoga Sp'r 19th Augt 1844.   N Oleans Jan 25th 1844.

314
John Davis   1761–1847
Boston, November 20, 1841

Old Judge Davis sits before us only a few months
after his resignation as judge of the District Court
of the United States for the District of Massachusetts, to which he had been appointed by President Adams in 1801—forty years of the most distinguished service. And yet his active and useful
life extended long back into the previous century.
He was graduated at Harvard in 1781, the youngest delegate to the Massachusetts convention on
the adoption of the Federal Constitution in 1788,
and became the last survivor. State senator in
1795, comptroller of the United States Treasury
for one year on the appointment of President
Washington, he then became United States attorney for Massachusetts. His distinction as lawyer and jurist has not been exceeded in Massachusetts. Beyond his profession he was a profound
antiquarian: his notes to Morton's *New England
Memorial* are a monument to his learning; he republished Winthrop's *Lectures on Comets* and
Oliver's *Essay on Comets* in 1811, adding a sup-
plement on the comet of 1811 written by himself;
and he published *An Attempt to Explain the Inscription on Dighton Rock*, for many years an
archaeological curiosity of Massachusetts. For
Harvard he was fellow, treasurer, member of the
corporation, and overseer, and in 1842 his loyal
and valued aid was recognized by the bestowal of
Harvard's honorary degree of LL.D. Elected a
member of the Massachusetts Historical Society
the year of its foundation, 1791, he later served
for seventeen years as its president and was a member of both the American Academy of Arts and
Sciences and the American Philosophical Society.

He was born at Plymouth, "the hallowed spot
of New England history always dear to his heart,"
as his memoir in the Collections of the Massachusetts Historical Society attests.

Boston Nov 26, 1841

John Davis

315
Frederic William Hopkins
1807–1874
Saratoga, August 22, 1842

General Hopkins was at his happiest when in full dress uniform. He had, as it was said, a taste for military life, and as adjutant and inspector general of the state of Vermont, as he and Edouart remind us, holding the office from 1838 to 1852, he established a uniformed militia and was its life and soul. Rutland, Vermont, was always his home. By profession a lawyer, his practice was not very successful, and he abandoned it upon being appointed clerk of the supreme and county courts for Rutland County. We are told that he held the reputation of being the best county clerk ever to hold office in Vermont, and that his rules of conduct were "arrangement, order, system, accuracy, neatness, and dispatch," which rules, the writer can attest, are, alas, rarely observed by county clerks. Twice married, he was survived by four children.

316
Harvey Munsill   d.1876
Saratoga Springs, July 16, 1842

Judge Munsill's birth date has eluded us, but he was married in 1818 and therefore may be presumed to have been born at or about the turn of the century. From 1820 Munsill was predominantly identified with the public affairs of the town of Bristol, Vermont, and the roster of the offices he held and services he rendered justify the statement in H. P. Smith's *History of Addison County, Vermont* (1886) that "in the observance of all of the proprieties of life, he was a noble and impressive example. He died . . . full of years and covered with honor." Judge of probate of the New Haven District of Addison County for thirty-four years, justice of the peace for over thirty years, trustee of the United States deposit money from 1838 to 1852, state senator, deputy sheriff of Addison County for eight years, county commissioner for four years, selectman for three years, town agent for thirteen years, moderator of the town meeting for eleven years, master of the Libanus Lodge of Masons No. 47 from 1828 to 1866, holding the charter during the anti-Masonic movement, often presiding at political conventions whether Whig or Republican, such was the life of this worthy citizen of Bristol, Vermont, and such were the men who meant so much to the many small communities throughout America during its early days.

114.½

F. W. Hopkins
Adjt. & Insp. Gen. of the
State of Vermont
Rutland 22 Augt. 1842

Harvey Munsill
Bristol Vt. Judge Probate
July 16 1842

F. W. Hopkins adjt. & Inspr. Genl. of the State of Vermont
Rutland   Saratoga 22. augt. 1842.

Harvey Munsill Judge Probate
of Bristol Vermt.
Saratoga Springs 16th. July 1842.

317
John Davis   1787–1854
Boston, May 26, 1842

Governor Davis, paired or compared with lieutenant governor Hull, stands prominently forward. Honest John Davis, as he was nicknamed,
had a distinguished career, though he was often
overshadowed by those he found about him. A
Yale graduate of 1812 with honor, he studied law
in Worcester under Francis Blake and practiced
for a decade with success. Elected to Congress as
a Whig, he served from 1825 until January 1834
when he resigned to take office as the twelfth governor of Massachusetts. He had entered Congress
as a relatively unknown man without strong
party backing and was immediately thrown into
competition as well as comparison with the great
figures of the day, Webster (fig. 164), Clay (fig.
147), Calhoun (fig. 161), and John Quincy Adams
(fig. 172). Yet he stood up to Clay and strongly
favored a high protective tariff. From the end of
his second year as governor until 1841 he served
in the Senate, an opponent of Jackson and Van
Buren, and still favoring protection of American
industry. In 1841 and 1842 he was again governor
of Massachusetts, and from 1845 to 1853 served
again in the Senate. He opposed the War with
Mexico and the introduction of slavery into the
territories. He narrowly missed the Whig nomination for vice-president in 1844 because of his
opposition to slavery, but Clay was planning, in
the event of his own election, to make Davis his
secretary of the treasury. Cautious and circum-
spect, he earned a reputation for absolute integrity, practical judgment, and an understanding
of the wants of the people. His wife, Eliza, was
a sister of George Bancroft the historian, and his
three sons, John Chandler, Horace, and Andrew
McFarland, had distinguished careers.

318
George Hull   1788–1868
Boston, May 27, 1842

George Hull was a resident of the town of Sandis-
field, Massachusetts. Largely self-educated, he
spent most of his life running a large farm, pot-
ashery, and general store, and was for almost fifty
years postmaster. He served in the state legislature
in 1821 and 1826 and was a member of the governor's council and for one term a state senator.
From 1836 to 1843 he served as lieutenant governor under Governors Everitt, Morton, and Davis.

115.

John Davis
Boston – May 26th 1842

Geo. Hull
May 27./
–/42

John Davis Govenor of Mass.
– Boston 26th May 1842.

Geo. Hull Lt. Govr. of Mass.
Boston 27th May 1842.

319
Theodore Howard McCaleb
1810–1864
New Orleans, February 22, 1844

McCaleb's education left nothing to be desired: private tutors at Cold Spring Plantation, Claiborne County, Mississippi, Exeter Academy, a few years at Yale, reading law under Rufus Choate in Salem, Massachusetts. That left him fully prepared to succeed to his older brother's law practice in New Orleans. In 1841 President Tyler (fig. 258) appointed him United States district judge for Louisiana, the youngest federal judge ever appointed by a president. When he resigned at the outbreak of the Civil War he was the only federal judge in the South who, on resignation, was not commissioned a Confederate judge by President Jefferson Davis. One of his most famous cases was that of Myra Clark Gaines (fig. 287) against the City of New Orleans. He was professor of admiralty and international law at the University of Louisiana (now Tulane) from 1847 until his death, and president of the University from 1850 to 1862. Noted for his eloquence, he delivered a famous oration on the death of his friend Henry Clay (fig. 147) and one on the unveiling of the Clay monument on Canal Street. He was sought out by visitors to the city—Edouart found him—and entertained many strangers to the city including Macready, Thackeray, Chateaubriand, and de Tocqueville. In 1844 at the age of thirty-four we see him perhaps explaining a point of law to his fellow justice Isaac Johnson.

320
Isaac Johnson   d. 1853
New Orleans, February 16, 1844

Johnson's father had settled in Louisiana during the Spanish regime. Brought up as a lawyer, Isaac became popular and successful. As a Democrat he was a representative in the state legislature, a judge of the Third District, and in 1846 governor of Louisiana as successor to Alexander Morton. He took great interest in bettering the public school system and was influential in completing the state house and the penitentiary at Baton Rouge. During the Mexican War he aided General Taylor with troops called up upon learning of his need, by which he was enabled to capture Matamoros. At the end of his term as governor he returned to private practice and died suddenly at the Verandah Hotel in New Orleans.

115° Theo. H. McCaleb

Isaac Johnson
16th Feby. 1844 - N.O.

The Times

Theodore H. McCaleb
Judge Dist. court. U.S.
N Orleans Feb 22nd 1844

Isaac Johnson
New Orleans 16th Feb. 44.

Judge 3d District Ct.

321

Moses Whitney   1775–1859

Saratoga, August 13, 1842

General Whitney earned his rank after many years of faithful service in the Massachusetts militia. Without formal education, he was a self-made man and in the 1830s ranked among the men of wealth in Milton. Born in West Roxbury, he moved to Blue Hills, Milton, in 1787, apprenticed to a tanner. He became a successful tanner and owned a large tannery at Milton Village on the Neponset River. He acquired the Rising Sun Tavern, where he acted for twelve years as Milton's second postmaster. Later he bought the Paine estate that extended from the Old Plymouth Road to the Neponset River where he built a tan house and enlarged the wharf. There he carried on a lumber and woodworking business for many years. He was twice married and had five children by his first wife. He remained in active business in Milton for sixty years, not counting his apprenticeship, and died at his home on Milton Hill on Christmas Eve.

Moses Whitney
August 13 1842

116.

Gen! Moses Whitney of Mutton Hill
Saratoga Aug 13th 1842

322
Joseph S. B. Thacher
Natchez, Mississippi, April 30, 1844

Judge Thacher was brought up in Boston but moved to Natchez in the early 1830s. From 1833 to 1837 he was judge of the district criminal court and in 1843 was elected to the state supreme court, one of two Natchez men to be elected to the court in the last antebellum decades. Six years later he was defeated for the same office. An active member of the Washington Lyceum, the intellectual, literary society of old Natchez, he read to the society a paper entitled "The Philosophy of Law."

As an advocate of expansion in the 1850s he was arraigned before a federal grand jury on charges of violating the neutrality statutes, but the charges were dropped for lack of evidence, the *Natchez Courier* coming to his defense. In Natchez Judge Thacher held a reputation for being the author of literary essays of merit and is remembered as an advocate of education, science, and the fine arts.

323
Edward McGehee   1786–1880
New Orleans, February 22, 1844

Judge McGehee was one of those men who made a success of everything he put his hand to. Reared on a plantation in Georgia, he married Margaret L. Crosby in 1811 in Georgia and brought her to Mississippi on horseback. He aided in the completion of the West Feliciana Railroad, at a cost of $35,000 per mile, which reached Woodville, Mississippi, in 1837 and was the first railroad in the state. A founder of the Woodville Bank and one of the first cotton factories in the state in 1849, which he operated until its destruction by Federal troops during the war, he also founded Bethel Church and the Woodville Female Academy and supported generally churches and colleges in Mississippi and Louisiana. President Taylor offered him the secretaryship of the treasury, which he declined, but he later served as Taylor's administrator. He owned and operated a large plantation, and his slaves numbered over a thousand. He resided in his residence Bowling Green, built at great cost in 1835 and said to be one of the finest mansions in the South. It contained a large library which was destroyed by a Negro regiment after the war. He was interested in the colonization movement and thought seriously of planting a colony of his own slaves in Africa. Tradition, always superlative, speaks of him as the "state's most respected citizen."

916 ½

J. S. B. Thacher
Natchez, Miss —
April 30th /44 —

Edw.d M.c Gehee June 22 1843

E M.c Gehee

Woodville Miss

J. S. B. Thacher
Judge of Sup. C.t of Miss.
Natchez, April 30th 1844

Judge Edw.d M.c Gehee
Woodville Miss.
N. Orleans 22.d Feb. 1844

324

John Downes   1784–1854
Saratoga Springs, July 22, 1842

Commodore Downes's naval career is not belittled
when it is said to be like so many other careers of
the great sailors in our naval history. Midshipman in 1802, lieutenant in 1807, master commandant in 1813, captain in 1817, he fought against
the Tripolitan feluccas and captured the British
ships *Georgianna* and *Poltey* while serving under
Commodore Porter. Later he skillfully captured
the Algerian frigate *Meshuda*. At Quallah Battoo
(Sumatra) in 1832, in the first American action in
the Orient, he revenged the outrages committed
on the American ship *Friendship* by a decisive if
severe victory over the Malays which received
President Jackson's approval. His sea service
ended in 1834 and the rest of his life was spent on
shore duty which included ten years as commandant of the Charlestown Navy Yard and a few
years as port captain of Boston and lighthouse
inspector. He was an ornament of the town of
Canton, Massachusetts, where he was born and
lived for many years. He stands to Edouart, on
shore duty in civilian garb, but with his commands, or ships like them, in the background.
His son John attained the rank of commander in
the navy.

117

Commodore John Downes
U.S Navy
Saratoga Springs 22d July 1842.

325
Richard Henry Chinn   d.1847
New Orleans, February 14, 1844

Judge Chinn came from Kentucky, of a family preeminent as lawyers, planters, merchants, and soldiers. In 1832 he resided in Lexington, Kentucky. He married Betsey Holmes, by whom he had twelve children. From 1833 to 1837 he served in the Kentucky legislature as a representative from Fayette County and then removed to New Orleans. He died in Taensas Parish in 1847. Apparently he had not yet been appointed to the bench when Edouart met him, because he is described simply as counselor-at-law. His sister Agatha married in 1816 George Poindexter, governor of Mississippi. His daughter Eliza Chinn Ripley wrote the well-known source book *Social Life in New Orleans*, long out of print.

326
James Mason Elam   1796–1856
New Orleans, February 13, 1844

As was not unusual in the early days of the United States Navy, Elam entered the service at the age of twelve and by 1815 was on board Commodore Decatur's flagship at the siege of Tripoli, an action in which Commodore Downes (fig. 324) had a part. In 1818 after the disbanding of the navy at Norfolk, Elam moved to New Orleans, was engaged in the sugar business, and was an overseer, farmer, and magistrate until 1832 when he was admitted to the bar of Louisiana. He had a successful career as lawyer and died in Baton Rouge, where he had settled after his marriage in 1825 to Rebecca Chambers of Camden, South Carolina.

117½

R. H. Chinn   J. M. Elam
                              New Orleans
                              13 Feby 1844
        Feby 14. 1844.

R. H. Chinn Couns.r at Law.   J. M. Elam Counsellor at Law.
N Orleans 14th Feby 44.   New Orleans 13th Feby 1844.

327
Jeremiah Mason   1768–1848
Boston, January 6, 1842

"A giant in stature and a giant in mind," Henry Clay (fig. 147) said of Jeremiah Mason. C. H. Bell in his *Bench and Bar of New Hampshire* (1894) quotes Webster (fig. 164): "If you were to ask me who was the greatest lawyer in the country, I should answer John Marshall; but if you took me by the throat and pinned me to the wall and demanded my *real* opinion, I should be compelled to say it was Jere. Mason."

The sixth of nine children, Mason was born in Lebanon, Connecticut, graduated at Yale in the class of 1788, and was admitted to the bar of Vermont in 1791. By 1797 with a growing reputation he moved to Portsmouth, and his practice and fame grew with each passing year. Aside from a few years as attorney general of New Hampshire, a few terms in the United States Senate, and a term as president of the Branch Bank of the United States at Portsmouth, his active life was wholly devoted to the practice of the law. He was a trial lawyer unmatched in ability and imagination. Often on the opposing side from Webster, the two grew into fast friends. More than once Webster acknowledged his indebtedness to Mason for much of what he had learned from him in his trial practice. They were associated together in the *Dartmouth College* case, and Mason supplied many of the arguments which Webster was to use so effectively. Judge Story (fig. 16) dedicated his *Equity Pleading* to Mason in admiration of his talents. Tales of his successes and his facility in breaking down recalcitrant witnesses on cross-examination are legion. He was almost a legend. It was his extraordinary defense of the Reverend Ephraim K. Avery for murder, a cause célèbre, that saved Avery from the gallows.

In 1832 Mason moved from Portsmouth to Boston and in 1838 retired from active practice with a substantial fortune. He stands before Edouart in all his six feet six inches as he appeared in his retirement, probably discussing the art of cross-examination with Judge Wilde.

328
Samuel Sumner Wilde   1771–1855
Boston, May 13, 1842

When Judge Wilde resigned his office as judge of the Supreme Judicial Court of Massachusetts in 1850, he had held the position for thirty-five years, longer than any other judge had held such a position in the commonwealth except Judge Sewall. He was a colleague and intimate friend of Chief Justice Lemuel Shaw (fig. 310), usually joining with him in decisions of the court. But in the famous trial of Peter York for murder, Judge Wilde's lone dissenting opinion resulted not only in the governor's reducing a death sentence to life imprisonment but eventually in the overturning of the majority opinion and a change in the law. He served with a spotless reputation and marked ability and was in every way an ornament to the bench in Massachusetts.

Taunton, Massachusetts, was his birthplace, and he was a Dartmouth College graduate of the class of 1789. For some years he practiced law in Warren and Hallowell, Maine, and represented Warren in the Massachusetts legislature in 1788 and 1789. Twice a presidential elector, he was also a delegate to the Hartford Convention, where he was a recognized leader. He became the last surviving member of that convention. When Maine separated from Massachusetts, Wilde moved to Newburyport, where he lived until his wife's death in 1826, later making his home with one or another of his children. For his service on the bench the honorary degree of LL.D. was conferred on him by Bowdoin, Harvard, and Dartmouth. His resemblance in profile to the duke of Wellington, often commented on by his family, is suggested by Edouart's silhouette.

J.D. Wilde

Boston 6th January 1842.
Jeremiah Mason Council at Law

Judge J.D. Wilde of the Supreme Ct. Mass.
Boston 13th. May 1842.

329
Henry Adams Bullard   1788–1851
New Orleans, February 13, 1844

Many of Louisiana's great lawyers and judges were born elsewhere and found their way to New Orleans after reaching maturity. Such was Judge Bullard. Born in Massachusetts, graduated at Harvard in 1807, he was admitted to the bar in 1812, by which time he had mastered French and Spanish. With his language proficiency he was sought out by General Jose Alvarez Toledo as his military aide and secretary in his revolutionary expedition into Texas in 1813. Toledo was disastrously defeated at the battle of Medina, near San Antonio. Bullard found his way to Natchitoches, where, destitute and friendless, he settled down to practice law, his knowledge of French and Spanish standing him in good stead. In 1816 he married Sarah Kaiser, a native of Lexington, Kentucky, and by 1822 he was elected a judge of the district court of Louisiana. As a Whig he served three terms in Congress and was an associate justice of the Louisiana Supreme Court from 1834 until the new constitution remodeled the court in 1846. His twelve years of service on the court were interrupted only once when he served for a year as secretary of state of Louisiana. After leaving the court he taught law in the University of Louisiana and was president of the Louisiana Historical Society. Through his mother he claimed a connection to the presidential Adamses.

H A Bullard
N Orleans Feb. 13th 1844

N Orleans Feb 13. 1844

Thomas A Bullard
Judge of Supreme Court
N Orleans Feb 13. 1844

330
Robert Charles Winthrop
1809–1894
Boston, May 20, 1842

Descendant of John Winthrop, great-nephew of James Bowdoin, son of Lieutenant Governor Thomas Lindell Winthrop, Robert, who stands before Edouart, twirling his eyeglasses in his hand, graduated at Harvard College in 1828 and studied law under Daniel Webster. After admission to the bar he was elected to the General Court, serving three of his six years in that body as speaker. For ten years he was a member of Congress, serving again as speaker for three years. Upon the resignation of Webster from the Senate in 1850, Winthrop filled his seat for two years. He was president of the Electoral College of Massachusetts, which voted for General Scott (fig. 120), and was president of the commission chosen by the city of Boston to build a public library. He was a brilliant orator, full of wit and humor, and was selected to deliver the address on the unveiling of the Franklin statue in 1856 and the erection of the Washington Monument in 1848. A large part of his career was devoted to the pursuits of a scholar and gentleman of leisure. The tale is told in James S. Loring's *Hundred Boston Orators* (1852) that at the Boston railroad jubilee festival in the Common in 1851, holding up a map of Massachusetts "covered all over with railroad lines," Winthrop remarked, "They tell us here of a hundred and twenty passenger trains, containing no less than twelve thousand persons, shooting into our city on a simple ordinary average summer's day, with a regularity, and precision, which makes it almost as safe to set our watches by a railroad whistle, as by the Old South clock!" *Sic transit . . . .*

331
Abbott Lawrence   1792–1855
Boston, March 14, 1842

Lawrence, Massachusetts, perpetuates the name of Abbott and his brother Amos, merchants of Boston. Cotton and woolen mills thrived under Abbott's guidance, and vast amounts of materials were imported from England to feed the mills. He became the leader in the development of the New England textile industry. Later in life he dealt extensively in the China trade, with reluctance finally becoming a protectionist. He was a delegate to the Hartford Convention, a member of Boston's Common Council, and served two terms in Congress. President Taylor offered him a cabinet post which he declined, but he did serve two years as ambassador to the Court of St. James's. Noted and long remembered for his charity, he contributed generously to the Boston Latin schools, to the Boston Public Library, and to Harvard to found the Lawrence Scientific School. His likeness was preserved not only by Edouart; Hiram Powers took him in marble, and George P. A. Healy on canvas.

119.

Abbott Lawrence, to

Rob.ᵗ C. Winthrop. Boston March 14 - 1842

Boston. May 20. 1842.

Robᵗ C. Winthrop Memb. of Congress   Abbott Lawrence Memb. of Congress
Boston 20ᵗʰ May 1842   for Mass Boston 14ᵗʰ for Massachusett March 1842

Heman Allen   1779–1852
Saratoga Springs, September 1, 1843

"Chile" Allen, as he was called, a nephew of
Ethan Allen, was born in Poultney, Vermont, and
graduated at Dartmouth in 1795. As a lawyer he
served as sheriff of Chittenden County and later
as chief justice of the county court. After one year
as a representative to Congress, President Monroe
appointed him United States marshal for the District of Vermont, and then United States minister
to Chile, where he served from 1823 to 1828.
Edouart preserves his full title: "Envoy Extraordinary and Minister Plenipotentiary of the U.S.
of America to the Republic of Chile." On his arrival at Santiago, shortly after a report of Monroe's historic message, the Monroe Doctrine,
Allen received the first expression of the Chilean
government's gratitude for the recognition of the
independence of the republic and Monroe's declaration protecting it from European interference.
On his return from Chile, Allen became president
of the United States Branch Bank at Burlington
until the expiration of its charter, at which time
he removed to Highgate, Vermont, where he died.
His first wife, Elizabeth Hart, known as one of
"the seven graces of Stratford," was a sister-in-law
of Commodore Hull (fig. 333), a fact Edouart
noted at the foot of the silhouette.

Heman Allen

Saratoga Springs,
1. Sept.r 1843.

Heman Allen Brother in Law of Comodore Hull
Late Envoy Extraordinary and Minister Plenipotenciary
of the U.S of America to the Republic of Chile in 1823 to 1822.
Saratoga Springs 1st September 1843.

333

Isaac Hull   1773–1843
[Saratoga], July 28, 1842

Two well-known engagements established Hull's reputation above all the naval heroes of his day. In 1801 as first lieutenant and sailing master he handled the *Constitution* in a friendly race with an English frigate which lasted a whole day and cost the Englishman a cask of wine. He became captain in 1806 and was in command of the *Constitution* when she carried Joel Barlow as United States minister to France and carried bullion to Holland to pay interest on the debt owed by the United States. It was his escape from a British squadron in July 1812, after a sixty-hour chase, that saved the *Constitution*, evidenced his skill as a seaman, and brought him prominently before the public.

But his glory depends on the great engagement with the *Guerrière*. In 1812 when at port in Boston, Hull grew restless and without orders put to sea. Within a week he gave chase to a ship which proved to be the *Guerrière*. In the ensuing engagement Hull so handled his vessel that, withholding his fire until only half a pistol's shot distance between the two, he opened fire and in less than thirty minutes dismasted the *Guerrière* and left her in such condition that she had to be burned. Hull lost seven killed and seven wounded; the British fifteen killed and sixty-two wounded. The *Constitution* was so slightly injured that she won the title "Old Ironsides." On his return to port Hull was feted with wild enthusiasm; a banquet was given in his honor in Faneuil Hall; he received a sword, the freedom of several cities, and a congressional gold medal, and a full-length portrait by Jarvis was ordered by the city of New York; $50,000 was distributed as prize money among the officers and crew. But he had sailed without orders and if the result had gone against him he might have suffered far worse than Commodore Barron (fig. 34). Admiral Farragut said of Commodore Hull that he "was as able a seaman as ever sailed a ship." He was succeeded in his command by Commodore Bainbridge. As is indicated in the clipping Edouart placed beneath the commodore's silhouette, taken late in life, "he was the first man of any nation who took an English frigate in fair and single fight." He gave to his country thirty-seven years of distinguished and faithful service, afloat and ashore, and at his death in Philadelphia, his last words were, "I strike my flag."

119¾

Isaac Hull
U. S. N.
July 28th 1842

☞ Of the late Commodore Hull it is said, that he was the first man of any nation who took an English frigate in fair and single fight.

334
Thomas Seir Cummings 1804–1894
New York, December 20, 1844

At age seventeen Cummings was studying as a pupil of Henry Inman, the portraitist, with such success that in a few years they entered into partnership. By 1827 Inman retired from miniature painting, leaving Cummings in the field where he prospered. With other younger artists of the day Cummings suffered under the presidency of Trumbull at the American Academy. As a result he and S. F. B. Morse and others founded the New York Drawing Association, which later became the National Academy of Design. Of this society Cummings was treasurer from 1827 to 1865 and vice-president from 1850 to 1859. In 1831 he was elected by the National Academy as a professor in drawing and in 1861 Winslow Homer studied in his class. He was also one of the founders of the Artist's Sketch Club, whose members in 1842 founded the Century (later the Century Association) in New York.

Cummings followed Morse in the chair of the arts of design in the University of the City of New York. On the side, as a member of the National Guard of the State of New York, in 1838 Governor Seward (fig. 2) commissioned him a brigadier general. His important *Historic Annals of the National Academy of Design* was published in 1865. He held a high rank among the miniaturists of the day, painting portraits of many of his contemporaries. Born in Bath, England, he died in Hackensack, New Jersey.

335
James Hamilton Shegogue 1810–1872
New York, December 20, 1844

Although principally a portraitist, Shegogue also produced some landscapes and genre paintings. French by descent, born in Charleston, South Carolina, he commenced his career in New York. He studied abroad and painted a copy of Guido's *Aurora* in the Borghese Palace which impressed the Princess Borghese. A member of the old Sketch Club and of the Century Association, like his friend Cummings he was also a member of the National Academy, of which he became corresponding secretary in 1849. His portraits attracted attention, and his profession returned him a substantial income. In his later life, tiring of the noise of New York City, he moved to Warrenville on the banks of the Mount Hope River, where he resided until his death. It was typical of Edouart to have caught the two brother artists on the same day and to have placed them as they must often have been seen, in amiable and perhaps professional conversation.

Thomas S. Cummings

Decemba 20th 1844.

J. H. Shegogue

76 Franklin St.

Decr 20th 1844

Brigadier Genl Thomas S. Cummings.
Minr Painter
New York 20th Decemb. 1844.

J. H. Shegogue Portrait Painter

336
Thomas ap Catesby Jones
1790–1858
Washington, April 19, 1841

Commodore Jones's naval career began as a midshipman in 1805 under Hull (fig. 333) and Decatur at Norfolk. From 1808 until 1812 he was in service in the Gulf of Mexico in the suppression of the slave trade, piracy, and smuggling. In the attack on New Orleans in 1814 Jones with his flotilla of five small gunboats held off a far larger British fleet until he was seriously wounded. For his bravery he received high praise and a sword from Virginia. He was in command of a South Seas surveying and exploration expedition in 1836 and commander of the Pacific Squadron in 1842. At this time, mistakenly believing war existed between the United States and Mexico, he took Monterey, for which error he was temporarily suspended from service. President Fillmore remitted the suspension in 1853, but the commodore saw no further active service. Edouart caught him toward the end of four years of inactive service and shortly before he was put in charge of the Pacific Squadron. His profile reveals a look of impatience, understandable in a shore-bound naval officer.

120.

April 19th 1841

Thos. ap C. Jones U.S. Navy

Comodore Thos. Ap Catesby Jones
U.S. Navy.
April 19th 1841.

Washington

337
J. D'Evereux
Saratoga Springs, July 15, 1844

D'Evereux, described by Edouart as a general and as blind, has so far eluded identity. The D'Evereux family of Utica was a large family and there is little doubt he was one of them. In a strange sort of way Edouart conveys the impression in his silhouette that the old general was in fact blind; and as to his identity we, too, are blind.

338
Leslie Combs   1793–1881
Lexington, Kentucky, May 27, 1844

General Combs, perhaps at Edouart's request, stands before the blind General D'Evereux "dressed in Kentucky hunting shirt as Gen. Harrison was at battle of Tippecanoe." And he would have known well what Harrison (fig. 233) wore in those days, for it was he as a young man who carried vital information from General Winchester to Harrison at the time of the expedition for the relief of Fort Meigs. As a result, he was complimented by Harrison for his courage and ability to thread his way through hostile Indian country. After his three or four years of war service he entered the practice of the law and took an active role in politics as a Whig. He represented Fayette County in the legislature for nine years and was Speaker of the House in 1846. In 1851 after a valiant race for a congressional seat, he was defeated by General Breckenridge. In his old age he was a gallant figure and often the chief speaker at reunions of old soldiers of the War of 1812, of which he was one of the youngest, always speaking with admiration for his old hero Tippecanoe.

Lexington Ky
May 27/44
Leslie Combs

J D Everaux

Saratoga Springs 15th July 1844.

J. J. D'Evereux (Blind)

Col Leslie Combs
dressed in Kentucky hunting
Shirt as Genl Harrison was
at battle of Tippecanoe

339
Winfield Scott   1786–1866
Saratoga, September 7, 1843

General Scott, now commander in chief of the United States Army, presents a fine figure of a man and a general. We see him only a year or so before his exploits in the Mexican War. A brief sketch of the general appears alongside his earlier silhouette (fig. 120), taken in 1840.

340
John Ellis Wool   1784–1869
Saratoga, September 7, 1843

The 1841 likeness of General Wool is missing from Edouart's volume. This one shows him only two years older and appropriately in company with General Scott. For a brief sketch of Wool, see the account alongside fig. 213.

Winfield Scott
U. S. Army.
Saratoga Sep. 7, 1843.

September 7th 1843

120.62

John E Wool

Brig. Genl U.S.A.

Saratoga

Winfield Scott.
Commander in chief U.S.A.

Saratoga Sep 7th 1843

John E. Wool
Brigadier Genl U.S.A.

341
Charles Augustus Dewey
1793–1866
Saratoga Springs, July 30, 1844

Judge Dewey, whose father and grandfather were jurists, was a loyal son of Williams College, from which he graduated in 1811 with honor. He commenced his law practice in his native town, Williamstown; in 1824 he moved to Northampton. Immediately successful in practice, he also served several terms in the state legislature, and was from 1830 to 1837 district attorney for the Western District of Massachusetts. At the end of that term he was appointed by Governor Everitt as an associate justice of the Supreme Judicial Court, on which he served faithfully until his death, almost forty years later. For forty-four years he was a trustee of Williams College and received the honorary degree of LL.D. from Harvard in 1840. He was twice married, first to Frances Henshaw, and secondly to Caroline Clinton, sister of DeWitt Clinton. Three sons and three daughters survived him.

342
William Hyslop Sumner   1780–1861
Saratoga, July 30, 1844

Judge Sumner was born in Roxbury in the house formerly owned by Judge Robert Auchmuty, a loyalist, which was confiscated during the Revolutionary War. After graduating at Harvard in 1799, he studied law under John Davis (fig. 314) and commenced practice in 1802. He was aide-de-camp to Governors Strong and Brooks and in 1814 was sent to Maine to prepare for the expected invasion by the British. Some years later he was appointed by the secretary of war a member of a board of which General Scott (fig. 120) was president to report a plan for the organization of the militia. In 1831 he carried out a project in which he had long been interested, to acquire the balance of Noddle's Island and arrange for its use as part of the city of Boston, which he did. He wrote a memoir of his grandfather, Governor Increase Sumner, in 1854; *Reminiscences of Lafayette's Visit to Boston*, in which he had played a part; and *Reminiscences of General Warren and Bunker Hill*.

At the laying of the cornerstone of the Bunker Hill Monument in 1825, the soldiers who were to take part in the ceremony assembled in General Sumner's office to give satisfactory evidence of having participated at the engagement fifty years before. It was on this occasion that he learned from Amos Foster of Tewkesbury of the last words of General Warren when he fell. Foster reported Warren as saying, "I am a dead man; fight on, my brave fellows, for the salvation of your country." On the following Fourth of July at the statehouse celebrations General Sumner used these famous words in a toast. Thrice married, he died without issue.

120 bis 1/2

Elias A. Dewey
Justice Sup. Jud.
Court of Mass. —

Wm H. Sumner late
Adjt Genl of Mass.tts
Saratoga July 30. 1844

Judge Chs. A. Dewey Justice Supe Ct Mass. Adjt Gl of Mass. Wm H. Sumner
Boston   Boston
Saratoga Springs 30th July 1844.   Saratoga 30th July 1844.

343
Henry Alexander Scarmel Dearborn
1783–1851
Boston, December 20, 1841

Few persons who today pass through the Hoosac Tunnel in New York State know that its construction is due more largely to General Dearborn than to any other man. It was he who was able "to induce the people of Massachusetts to connect the Atlantic with the Hudson River." The Horticultural Society, of which he was the first president, and Mount Auburn and Forest Hills cemeteries of Boston all attest to his genius and energy. Born in New Hampshire, he was a graduate of the College of William and Mary in 1803 and before long was practicing law in Salem, Massachusetts, under Judge Story (fig. 16). In 1812 he became collector of the port of Boston and as brigadier general was in charge of the defenses of the harbor. A member of the Governor's Council, the state senate, and the Massachusetts Constitutional Convention of 1820, he was also adjutant general of Massachusetts from 1835 to 1843 and in this capacity stood proudly to Edouart.

In the midst of all his military, legal, and intellectual activities, he was one of the originators of the plan for building the Bunker Hill Monument and chairman of the building committee for many years. He was also mayor of Roxbury from 1847 to 1851. His writings cover wide fields as can be gathered from their titles: *Life of Jesus Christ, Life of Commodore Bainbridge, Life of the Apostle Eliot, Letters on the Internal Improvements and Commerce of the West*, as well as volumes on the Dearborn family.

344
Jonathan Chapman   1807–1848
Boston, May 3, 1842

Preparation for college at Phillips Academy in Exeter, a bachelor's degree from Harvard in 1825, study of law under Chief Justice Shaw (fig. 310), membership on the Boston City Council from 1835 to 1845, and holding the office of mayor of the city from 1839 to 1841 all conspired to make Chapman one of the most popular figures of Boston in his day. In an address in 1841 he spoke eloquently of the commercial importance to Boston of the opening in 1840 of the Cunard Line transfer between Boston and Liverpool and the opening of the new Western Railroad to the Hudson River, which passed through the Hoosac Tunnel, for which General Dearborn (fig. 343) was so largely responsible. It was Chapman who gave the great and popular speech at the dinner in honor of Charles Dickens on the occasion of his visit to Boston in 1843, an amiable and witty parody of the Pickwick Club.

Chapman's usefulness to the city, however, was to a large degree due to his conception of economy in governmental expenditures, quite in contrast to the lavish and profuse spending by Mayor Quincy (fig. 248) and to those before him. He was said to have been a "temperate advocate of the temperance cause." His death at the early age of forty-one was a loss to the city.

121.

adjut. Gal. of Massachusett.

H. A. S. Dearborn

Boston Dec. 20, 1841.

Jon. Chapman
May 3, 1842.
Bo

Hon. A. S. Dearborn Adjt Genl of Mass.
Boston 20th Decemb. 1841.

Jonathan Chapman.
Mayor of Boston 3. May 1842.

345
Thomas Butler   1785–1847
New Orleans, February 27, 1844

The Cottage, a century ago one of the most charming plantation houses in the South, built in West
Feliciana Parish about 1811, was the home of
Judge Butler, the congressman and lawyer. Born
and educated in Pennsylvania, Butler moved to
Mississippi Territory in 1807 and had an active
legal and political career. Parish judge in 1812,
judge of the Third District Court for several
terms, member of Congress for four years, Butler
was in private life an owner of profitable sugar
and cotton plantations. For a while he was president of the Board of Trustees of Louisiana College at Jackson and a member of the Pennsylvania
Society of the Cincinnati. Eight of his twelve
children reached maturity. He stands before
Edouart with dignity and confidence, fitting to a
judge of the Third District of Louisiana.

121?

Thomas Butler
New Orleans Feb.y 27.th 1844

Thomas Butler. Judge
New Orleans 27.th Feb.y 1844.

346

James Hosken
[Saratoga], August 3, 1841

The first keel laid expressly for an Atlantic steam-ship was that of the *Great Western*, of Bristol, England, which left for New York in April 1838 and arrived fifteen days later, traveling at an average speed of 210 miles a day. Her captain was James Hosken, lieutenant in the Royal Navy, and his arrival was the cause of widespread celebration. Fisher, the Philadelphia diarist, wrote of it, "This is a great event, fraught with many vast and invisible consequences. . . . As railroads have superseded mail coaches, so will steam banish canvas from the oceans." Hosken was feted in New York at a banquet attended by, among others, Webster (fig. 164), Governor Mason of Michigan, Bradish (fig. 228), Speaker of the House of New York, John Ridge of the Cherokee Mission, and Philip Hone (fig. 8). Captain Hosken, speaking, as he said, "as an officer of the British Navy," gave as a toast, "The Navy of the United States—may we never be brought into other than friendly collision," to which the response was, "England—may she ever respond to those feelings of friendship."

The *Great Western* was a vessel of 1,340 tons, and the fare was 35 guineas out and 30 returning. Her interior accommodations are glowingly described in Ithiel Town's *Atlantic Steam-ships* (1838):

No description can adequately convey the remarkable beauty with which the main cabin is ornamented. We verily believed ourselves transported to some of the glorious saloons of France while yet under the luxurious rule of Louis XIV. . . . None could ever have fancied for a moment that, in such a place, the horrors of sea-sickness could ever be felt or that any of the mighty inconveniences to which those who "go down to the sea in ships" ever prepare themselves to endure, would here be their lot, for everything reminded them of luxuries far greater than most of us enjoy at home.

Whether Bernard Mathews (fig. 63) was a fellow officer or successor to Captain Hosken is not known.

James Hoskin Lieut. RN.
"Great Western" Stm. Ship
3d August 1841.

122.

347
David Osgood, M.D.   1793–1863
Saratoga, July 25, 1844

Dr. Osgood graduated at Harvard in the class of
1813 and received his medical degree in 1816.
Known for his kindness and generous treatment
of sufferers, he was an unfailing friend to his patients. His medical career was spent entirely in
Boston. In 1839 on a visit to Europe he met the
German philosopher Dr. Hahnemann, who introduced him to the system of homoeopathy of
which he became a very successful practitioner in
Boston. One of his most celebrated patients was
the scholar and author Fredricka Bremer. Dr. Osgood married Mary Ann Elder of Portland,
Maine, in 1821, who survived him, but they had
no children. Edouart pairs him with Parker, the
temperance enthusiast, who seems to be offering
him the pledge. Did he sign it?

348
George Phillips Parker   1793–1856
Saratoga, July 27, 1844

One of the United Brothers of Temperance of
New York, the Boston-born Parker added a middle name after leaving college and contributed
generously from his ample means to support the
cause of temperance. He was so active in its cause
in 1844 that Edouart considered it appropriate
to preserve his likeness with a copy of the temperance pledge in his hand; or perhaps Parker
himself asked for it. Parker must have been well
acquainted with the great temperance leader
Marsh (fig. 30) and Delavan (fig. 23)—perhaps he
had even been a patron of Delavan House in Albany. If Parker had stood to Edouart two years
earlier, we would have expected him to be paired
with Delavan or Marsh. As it is, we can only spec-
ulate whether Parker was able to convince Dr.
Osgood to sign the pledge.

122.½

George Phillips Parker
Saratoga July 27. 1844

Saratoga 25ᵗʰ July 1844.

George Phillips Parker of the order
of United Brothers of Temperance N. Yᵏ.
Saratoga 27ᵗʰ July. 1844.

Dr David Osgood MD of Boston Mass.
5f. 10½

United brothers
temperance
pledge

Appendix

Index

Appendix

In order to put within the two covers of this volume as complete a list of Edouart's American silhouettes as possible, there is included here an offset copy of a catalogue (excluding cover pages) published without date, but after 1921, entitled *Catalogue of 3,800 Named and Dated American Silhouette Portraits by August Edouart (1789–1861) Silhouillist* [sic] *to the Royal Family of France and to H.R.H. the Duke of Gloucester.*

The list appears just as it was printed, without any attempt to correct its various errors. It is not complete, it mentions only a few of the silhouettes reproduced here, and it has many errors of date and spelling. But it is believed that it will be of value and interests to collectors and antiquarians and as a bit of social history supplementing the extraordinary group illustrated in this volume.

COMPLETE LIST OF 3,800 SILHOUETTE PORTRAITS OF AMERICAN CITIZENS TAKEN BETWEEN 1839–1849 BY AUGUST EDOUART DURING HIS TOUR IN THE UNITED STATES

Abbay, S. F. R., Port Gibson, Miss. (New Orleans, April 16, 1844).

Abert, Chas. (Washington, April 28, 1841).

Abbott, Jacob (Saratoga Springs, Aug. 28, 1841).

Abbott, Rev. Gorham D. (Boston, June 4, 1842).

Abbott, Rev. John S. C., of Nantucket (Boston, June 5, 1842).

Acke, James (New York, Nov. 1, 1839).

Adams, Harriet, aged 2½ years (New Orleans, April 10, 1844).

Adams, C. (New Orleans, April 10, 1844).

Adams, Benjn., 30, Pemberton Square (Saratoga Springs, July 31, 1841).

Adams, Mrs., 30, Pemberton Square (Saratoga Springs, July 31, 1841).

Adams, Atkins, of Fairhaven, Mass. (Boston, April 2, 1842).

Adams, Mrs., of Fairhaven, Mass. (Boston, April 2, 1842).

Adams, Bushwood (Phila., Sept. 20, 1842).

Adams, Francis M., constable (Boston, Aug. 24, 1842).

Adams, Rev. M., Pastor of Central Presbyterian Church (New York, May 11, 1840).

Adams, James, of Washington (Saratoga, Aug. 30, 1843).

Adams, Mrs., of Washington (Saratoga, Aug. 30, 1843).

Adams, Chas., New York (6 ft.) (Saratoga, July 24, 1844).

Adams, John Quincey, ex-Pres. (Washington, March 10, 1841).

Adee, Dr. Augustus A., U.S.N. (Saratoga Springs, Aug. 4, 1842).

Adee, David Graham, son of above (Saratoga Springs, Aug. 4, 1843).

Aguilar, Señor Gaspar de Bettancourt (port. au prima) (Saratoga, Aug. 20, 1844).

Agnew, Cornelius, of New York (Phila., Oct. 11, 1842).

Agnew, Alex. (New York, Oct. 11, 1842).

Agnew, widow of John, aged 96 years (New York, Oct. 18, 1842).

Agnew, Wm., New York (Saratoga, Sept. 29, 1844).

Agnew, M. I., New York (Saratoga, Sept. 11, 1843).

Ainslie, Miss Esther, 12, Dublin Street (Jan. 16).

Alden, Robt. S., of Maine (Boston, Nov. 10, 1841).

Alden, B. R., 1st Lieut., 4th Infantry (Washington, April 24, 1841).

Alder, Geo. Walterson (Washington, June 19, 1841).

Aleantara, Signor Pedro, Havana (New Orleans, June 9, 1844).

Alexander, Ashton, M.D. (Baltimore, Dec. 12, 1844).

Alexander, Chas. (Washington, April 17, 1841)

Alexander, A. L., Georgia (Saratoga Springs, Sept. 3, 1841).

Alexander, Caleb, of Battlebore, Vt. (Saratoga, Aug. 26, 1841).

Allan, Augustus L., Atty. at Law, 61 & 62, Wall Street.

Allen, Elisha H., Bandon M. (Washington, June 12, 1841).

Allen, Robt., 1st Lieut., 2nd Artillery (March 21, 1844).

Allen, Mrs. Caroline M., wife of Stevens Allen (Saratoga, Aug. 28, 1844).

Allen, Miss Eleona, of Gardiner, Maine (Boston, June 3, 1842).

Allen, Geo. A., Providence (Saratoga, July 31, 1843).

Allen, C. W. Allenwood, Miss. (New Orleans, March 10, 1844).

Allan, Augustus L., Atty. at Law, 61, Wall Street (New York, Oct. 10, 1840).

Allen, Mrs. Eliz., widow of (Boston, Jan. 11, 1842).

Allen, Rev. John, Member of Conference of Methodists (Boston, Feb. 21, 1842).

Allen, Rev. John, Member of Conference of Methodists (2nd port.) (Boston, Feb. 21, 1842).

Allen, Benjn., 18 years of age (Saratoga Springs, July 4, 1840).

Almy, Moses B., Providence (Saratoga Springs, Aug. 16, 1843).

Alocar, Señor E., de, Argentine Legation (Saratoga, July 8, 1840).

Altrocchi, Signor, Prof. of Music, New York, of Lodi, Lombardia, Italy (Saratoga, Aug. 9, 1844).

Amas, T. W. P., Prof. of Music, New York, of Lodi, Lombardia, Italy (Louisiana, March 11, 1844).

Ames, Col. G., Springfield, Mass. (Saratoga Springs, July 29, 1841).

Ames, Fredk., aged 9 months, born March 9, 1839 (New York, Dec. 20, 1839).

Amory, Chas. (Boston, Nov. 17, 1841).

Amory, Mrs. Chas. (Boston, April 10, 1842).

Amory, Chas. Copley (Boston, Nov. 16, 1841).

Amory, Susan Green (Boston, Nov. 16, 1841).

Amory, Baby (Boston, Nov. 16, 1841).

Anderson, Mrs., 241, Canal Street (see Craig) (New York, Aug. 28, 1839).

Anderson, Miss Helene, 5, Manor Place.

Anderson, Miss Jane, of County Perth.

Anderson, H. C. (2 ports.) (New Orleans, July 22, 1844).

Anderson, Peter, from Ireland, 241, Canal Street (New York, Aug. 28, 1839).

Anderson, Alex., Knoxville, Knox, Senator, Tennessee (Washington, March 8, 1841).

Anderson, Joseph H. G. of Phila., Leader of Band (Brass) in place of Frank Johnson (Saratoga, Sept. 1, 1844).

Anderson, W. S. (Jackson, March 7, 1844).

Andres, Miss Ruth (Troy, Sept. 10, 1843).

Andrews, Ferdinand, Boston (Saratoga, July 16, 1840).

Andrews, Mrs. Ferdinand, Boston (Saratoga, July 16, 1840).

Andrews, T. M., Counsel at Law, New York (Saratoga Springs, Sept. 6, 1840).

Andrews, H. P., aged 23 years, step-brother of P. B. P. Wiggins, 9 years (Saratoga, Sept. 3, 1844).

Andrews, John C., Prof. of Music, Troy (Saratoga, July 3, 1843).

Andrews, Rev. Emerson, Baptist (Phila., July 11, 1843).

Andrews, James N., Madison Co., Miss. (New Orleans, Feb. 13, 1844).

Angier, Mrs. Anne Louisa, Buffalo, daughter of Judge James Lanman, Ct. (Saratoga, Aug. 25, 1843).

Anthon, Rev. Henry, D.D., Rector of St. Mark's Episcopal Church (New York, Oct. 29, 1839).

Anthon, Geo. C. (New York, Dec. 18, 1844).

Anthon, Master H. (New York, Oct. 10, 1839).

Anthony, Darius, Church Elder, Methodist Episcopals Oneida Conference (New York, Aug. 3, 1841).

Appleton, Caroline Leroy (Boston, Jan. 11, 1842).

Appleton, Miss Caroline F., sister to Saml. (Boston, Dec. 20, 1841).

Appleton, Mrs. Mary Anne (Boston, Dec. 10, 1841).

Appleton, F. A., son of above (obt. June 30, 1843) (Boston, Dec. 10, 1841).

Appleton, Wm. (Boston, Dec. 10, 1841).

Appleton, Miss Hettie Sullivan (Boston, Dec. 10, 1841).

Appleton, Mrs. Saml., daughter to Danl. Webster (Boston, Jan. 11, 1842).

Appleton, Saml. (Boston, Jan. 11, 1842).

Appleton, Master, infant son, 7 weeks old (Boston, Jan. 11, 1842).

Appleton, Harriet Henrietta Cutler (Nov. 27, 1841).

Appleton, Saml. *See* Goodwin, M. (Boston, Jan. 25, 1842).

Appleton, Chas. Hook (Nov. 27, 1841).

Arkley, Mrs., 4, Saxe-Coburg Place (Jan. 27).

Arms, Dr. C. C., Waterbury, Vt. (Saratoga, July, 19, 1843).

Arms, Mrs. C. C., Waterbury, Vt. (Saratoga, July, 19, 1843).

Armstrong, J. A., Detroit, Mich. (Saratoga, Aug. 28, 1844).

Armstrong, Abaigail (Saratoga, Aug. 26, 1844).

Arnold, Anthony B., Providence (Boston, April 20, 1842).

Arnold, J. R., of Savannah, Georgia (Boston, June 17, 1842).

Arnold, Wm., Dentist, 5, Warren Street (New York, Oct. 11, 1839).

Arthur, Benjn. Haight, U.S. Army, 2nd Lieut., 1st Regt. Infantry (New York, Nov. 23, 1839).

Arthur, Mrs. Edwd. P., New York { Saratoga, Oct. 7, 1839. 2 sisters married 2 brothers.

Arthur, Mrs. John A., Burlington

Arthur, Mrs. Mary Antoinette, Shoreham, Vt. (Sept. 14, 1844).

Arrieta, Señor Pablo de, of Habana (Saratoga, Aug. 14, 1844).

Ashurst, Helen E. (Lewis, Feb. 7, 1843).

Ashurst, Richd., aged 5 years (Phila., Feb. 3, 1843).

Ashurst, John, aged 3½ years (Phila., Feb. 3, 1843).

Ashurst, Richd. (Lewis, Feb. 7, 1843).

Ashurst, Steven (Lewis, Feb. 7, 1843).

Ashmun, Geo., late Speaker of House of Representatives, Mass. (Boston, Feb. 20, 1842).

Ashton, Emily, Jamaica Plain (Boston, Feb. 10, 1841).

Atherton, Chas., Esq.

Atkinson, Annie (Louisville, May 18, 1844).

Atwood, Henrietta (Phila., Dec. 29, 1842).

Aubin, J., Amesbury, Mass. (Boston, June 4, 1842).

Austin, widow of Benjn., aged 84 years (Feb. 10, 1842).

Austin, Miss H. G., sister of Mrs. Coolidge (Feb. 23, 1842).

Austin, Thos. H. (Boston, Feb. 18, 1842).

Ashmutz, Mrs.

Austin, Mrs. Catharine, wife of J. T. Austin, Atty. Gen. of Mass., mother of (Boston, April 8, 1842).

Austin, Ivers T. (Boston, April 8, 1842).

Austin, Miss Maria A. R. (Boston, April 8, 1842).

Auchonuty, Mrs. (New York, Nov. 30, 1839).

Averell, Horatio (Troy, Oct. 2, 1841).

Averell, Mrs. *See* Webb (Troy, Oct. 2, 1841).

Averell, J. Watson (Troy, Oct. 2, 1841).

Ayerell, Miss Jane (Troy, Oct. 2, 1841).

Avery, Rev. John, Presbyterian Church, Cleveland, Ohio (July 25, 1840).

Ayerigg, John B., M.C., New Jersey (Washington Feb. 20, 1841).

Babcock, E. Westerly, R.S., now Rhode (New York, Nov. 13, 1839).

Babcock, Dr. B. W., Hamilton, New York (Washington, April 15, 1841).

Bace, Geo. W. (Phila., Oct. 4, 1843).

Bache, Richd., U.S.N. (Washington, March 16, 1841).

Bacon, John (Louisville, Kentucky, May 15, 1844).

Bacon, Henry W., of Boston (Saratoga, July 22, 1844).

Bacon, Thos. H. (Boston, Feb. 8, 1844).

Backus, Leir S., editor (Washington, April 26, 1841).

Badlong, James, of Pawtucket, Mass. (New York, July 25, 1840).

Badia, Fayme, Island of Cuba (New York, Feb. 17, 1840).

Bagure, Dr. Thos. (Washington, June 25, 1841).

Bailey, Hannah (Phila., March 3, 1843).

Baird, John, born 1766, aged 78 years, father of Mrs. Washington Putnam (Saratoga, Aug. 31, 1844).

Baker, R. L., U.S.A. (Saratoga, Sept. 7, 1843).

Baker, Wm. Edgar (New York, Nov. 8, 1839).

Baker, D. B., Wilmington (Phila., Sept. 29, 1842).

Baker, Miss C. (New York, April 18, 1840).

Baker, Joseph P. (New York, Aug. 5, 1839).

Balch, Mrs. Anna (New York, Oct. 15, 1840).

Balch, Joseph, Merchants' Insurance (Boston, June 15, 1842).

Baldwin, A. S., Lieut., U.S.N. (New York, April 6, 1845).

Baldwin, Dr. John (Washington, March 14, 1841).

Baldwin, Micah, of New York (Saratoga, Sept. 5, 1844).

Ball, Dr. Geo. C., M.D. (New York, Dec. 2, 1839).

Ball, Mrs. Geo. C., daughter of Henry Eagle (New York, Dec. 2, 1839).

Ball, Chas. Henry (2 ft. 10 in.), born Aug. 5, 1837 (New York, Dec. 2, 1839).

Ball, Geo. Wm.

Ballentine, Wm. (Natchez, April 26, 1844).

Bankville, Moses H., Manard.

Bancroft, H., of Brooklyn (5 ft. 8½ in.) (New York, July 17, 1844).

Baneger, Miss Marua (New York, Oct. 13, 1840).

Banks, Linn, M.C., Madison, Va. (Washington, June 28, 1841).

Barbour, John (Saratoga Springs, Aug. 1, 1840).

Barbour, Rosamond Kate (Saratoga Springs, Aug. 1, 1840).

Barbour, A. L. (Saratoga Springs, Aug. 1, 1840).

Barbour, Mrs. A. L. (Saratoga Springs, Aug. 1, 1840).

Barbour, Miss Florence (Saratoga Springs, Aug. 1, 1840).

Barclay, Geo., of New York (Saratoga, Aug. 25, 1840).

Barclay, Mrs. Geo., of New York (Saratoga, Aug. 25, 1840).

Barclay, Miss M. A. (Saratoga, Aug. 25, 1840).

Barclay, John A. (Phila., Oct. 9, 1843).

Barker, R. D., Macon, Miss. (Washington).

Barker, David, poet 1816–1874 (New York, Nov. 18, 1839).

Barker, Mrs. David (New York, Nov. 18, 1839).

Barlay, A. (New Orleans, April, 5, 1844).

Barlow, Timothy (New York, Dec. 7, 1839).

Barlow, Rev. Wm., Ornaburgh, St. Laurence Co. (New York, Nov. 30, 1839).

Barnard, R. F., Counsel at Law, Sheffield, Mass. (Saratoga, Aug. 22, 1844).

Barnard, D. D., M.C., New York (Albany, Feb. 5, 1841).

Barnard, Cora (Albany, Feb. 5, 1841).

Barnard, Sarah (Albany, Feb. 5, 1841).

Barnard, J. G., U.S. Engineer, chief engineer American army in the field, 1815–1882 (Saratoga Springs, Aug. 20, 1844).

Barnes, Albert, Pastor of first Presbyterian Church (Phila., Dec. 19, 1844).

Barnes, Miss Susan Pain (New York, July 25, 1843).

Barney, John (Baltimore, Dec. 11, 1840).

Barnum, F. K., 2nd Infantry (Saratoga, Aug. 25, 1844).

Barre, E. L., New York (Saratoga, Aug. 16, 1843).

Barre, Mons. L. (Saratoga, Aug. 16, 1843).

Bartol, James L. (Baltimore, Dec. 7, 1840).

Barrow, Alex.

Barrow, Robt. H. (New Orleans, Feb. 17, 1844).

Barrow, Robt. J. (Louisville, July 30, 1844).

Barrow, R. R., M.C., Louisiana (Saratoga, July 28, 1840).

Barrus, Rev. H. G., Methodist Episcopal Church (Boston, Feb. 27, 1842).

Barry, R. T., M.D., U.S.N. (Washington, Feb. 11, 1841).

Barry, Garrett, 2nd Infantry, U.S.A. (Saratoga Springs, Aug. 6, 1842).

Barry, Saml. F., New York (5 ft. 5½ in.) (Saratoga, Aug. 6, 1844).

O

Barry, Mrs. Saml. F. (Saratoga, Aug. 6, 1844).

Bartlet, Richd., of New York (Saratoga Springs, Aug. 7, 1840).

Bartlett, Washington A., Lieut., U.S.N. (New York, Jan. 2, 1845).

Bartlett, Edwin, New York (Saratoga, Sept. 8, 1843).

Bartlett, Thos., 74 years of age (Boston, Dec. 15, 1841).

Bartlett (1804–1855), Elisha, Prof. Theory Practice Med. (Boston, May 24, 1842).

Barton, Wm., designer of U.S. Arms.

Bastianilli, Titus, de Livourne, Italy (Saratoga Springs, Aug. 17, 1840).

Bates, Isaac C. (Boston, Dec. 24, 1841).

Bates, Robt. B., obt. 1842, Counsel at Law (New York, Aug. 27, 1839).

Bates, James M., of Bedford, Westchester Co. (New York, Jan. 20, 1840).

Bates, John Seymour (Aug. 15, 1839).

Battelle, C. (New York, Aug. 13, 1839).

Batty, W. B.

Bayard, Mrs. Richd. H., Wilmington, Delaware (Saratoga Springs, Aug. 15, 1840).

Bayley, Miss Annie M. (New York, Oct. 2, 1839).

Bayne, Miss Eliza J., miniature painter (Washington, May 3, 1841).

Bayne, Mrs. Arameta, mother of above (Washington, May 9, 1841).

Beach, Wm. A., Counsel at Law (Saratoga Springs, Aug. 30, 1841).

Beach, Mrs. M. L., Charlestown (Phila., Oct 13, 1843).

Beadle, Rev. E. R., missionary to Syria (New Orleans, Feb. 23, 1844).

Bear, Rev. John (Baltimore, Nov. 20, 1840).

Beatty, Wm. B. (New York, Nov. 14, 1848).

Beaujeau, Mme. Mary, married to G. W. Hawley, 1841 (New York).

Beck (1794–1851), John B., M.D., Prof. of Materia Medica and Medical Jurisprudence in College of Physicians and Surgeons (New York, Aug. 15, 1839).

Beck, Chas. F., M.D. (Phila., Jan. 23, 1844).

Beebe, Mrs. Jane, Secconde Noce, Mrs. Hutchins. See Hutchins (New York, Dec. 19, 1839).

Begoden, Achille (Bordeaux, Sept. 23, 1839).

Behn, Mrs. Amelie (New Orleans, March 23, 1844).

Behn, James R. (2 ports.) (New Orleans, March 22, 1844).

Belknap, Col. S. F., of Concord, Mass. (Saratoga, July 25, 1845).

Bell, Saml. F., Principal of Rhinebeck Academy, New York (Saratoga Springs, Aug. 15, 1840).

Bell, Wm., of Three Forks, Barren Co. (Louisville, May 10, 1844).

Bell, Abraham, Peel's Museum (New York, Oct. 6, 1839).

Belmont, August (2 ports.), agent for House of Rothschild (New York, Sept. 17, 1839).

Beman (1785–1871), Rev. Dr. Nathan S. S., Pastor of first Presbyterian Church (2 ports.) (Troy, Sept. 23, 1841).

Beman, Miss Louisa C. (Troy, Sept. 23, 1841).

Bencher, Abraham (Washington).

Benedict, Danl. L. (Saratoga Springs, Sept. 3, 1840).

Benedict, Mrs. L. (Saratoga Springs, Sept. 3, 1840).

Benedict, Rowell G., of Boston (Saratoga Springs, Dec. 31, 1841).

Benedict, A., 12, Wall Street, Counsel at Law (Saratoga, Aug. 20, 1842).

Benedict, Ezra C., Counsel at Law, New York (Saratoga, Aug. 20, 1842).

Benedict, Mrs. A., of New York (Saratoga, Aug. 20, 1842).

Benedict, W. P. (Louisville, May 14, 1844).

Benezet, Philip, Esq., aged 69 years.

Benham, Mrs. Mary Louisa, Alexandria, D.C. (New Orleans, May 15, 1844).

Benham, Ada Louisa, Alexandria, D.C. (New Orleans, April 15, 1844).

Benjamin, Chas., of Demerara, Br. Guiana (Boston, Jan. 10,' 1842).

Benjamin, Mrs. Chas. (Boston, Jan. 10, 1842).

Benjamin, Miss Theodora L. (Boston, Jan. 10, 1842).

Benne, Francis, Hamburgh (Washington, March, 1841).

Bennett, James M., jeweller (Phila., Jan. 23, 1843).

Bennett, Theo. B. (Charlestown, July 8, 1844).

Benson, Eliza (Baltimore).

Benson, Henry (Baltimore).

Benson, Mr. (New York, April 14, 1844).

Benson, Mrs. (New York, April 14, 1844).

Benson, J., sen., New York (5 ft. 9 in.) (Saratoga, Aug. 25, 1844).

Benson, John M. (4 ft. 8 in.) (Saratoga, Aug. 25, 1844).

Bents, Mrs. Joseph, 30, Courtland Street (Nov. 29, 1839).

Bent, Mr. Geo. C., South Boston (Saratoga, Sept. 5, 1843).

Bent, Mrs. Geo. C., South Boston (Saratoga, Sept. 5, 1843).

Berdun, Mrs. Francis C. (New York, March 16, 1841).

Bergh, Mrs. Edwin (New York, April 14, 1845).

Bergh, Mr. Edwin (New York, Jan. 9, 1840).

Berhard, L. Corn, doctor (Boston, June 24, 1842).

Berhard, Alex. (Boston, June 24, 1842).

Bernard, J. G.

Barratt, James G. (Washington, Jan. 28, 1841).

Berry, Morris M., of Utica (Saratoga Springs, July 20, 1840).

Berry, Capt. Chas. C., of Brooklyn, New York (Saratoga, July 21, 1843).

Berti, Signor Anselmo, of Mentone (New York, Oct. 20, 1839).

Berti, Signora Mary, from Baltimore. See Mrs. J. Dessac (New York, Oct. 20, 1839).

Berti, Candido (New York, Oct. 20, 1839).

Berti, Olimpia, born at New York, Oct. 20, 1835 (New York, Oct. 20, 1839).

Berti, Rosina, born June 14, 1839 (New York, Oct. 20, 1839).

Betts, Royston (Baltimore, Dec. 14, 1840).

Beylle, Augustus (Phila., Dec. 15, 1842).

Bibby, Gouvr. S. (New York, April 24, 1840).

Bibby, Mrs. Maria K. Gouvr., daughter of late Pres. Munro of Va. (New York, April 24, 1840).

Biddle, Henry J., civil engineer (Phila., Feb. 17, 1841).

Biddle, James S., U.S.N. (New York, Sept. 24, 1839).

Bidwell, Rev. W. W., Presbyterian (Phila., July 21, 1840).

Bidwell, Marshall S., Counsel at Law (2 ports.), Oct. 22, 1839 (Saratoga, Aug. 4, 1842).

Bigelow, Capt. Chas. Henry, engineer (Boston, March 14, 1842).

Bigelow, Geo. Tyler (Boston, Feb. 18, 1842).

Bigelow, John T., Sec. of Commonwealth, Mass. (Boston, April 9, 1842).

Bigelow, Alpheus, Esq., jun., M.A., Counsel at Law, Weston, Middlesex, Mass. See Estes (Saratoga, July 26, 1844).

Bigelow, Rev. Andrews, of Taunton, Mass., Pastor of first Congregational Church. See Lawrence (Boston, April 25, 1842).

Bigelow, Mrs. Andrews (Boston, April 25, 1842).

Billings, Joseph H., Roxbury, Mass. (Saratoga, July 25, 1844).

Billings, Amus, New York (6 ft.) (Saratoga, July 10, 1844).

Billings, N. B., New London, Ct. (Saratoga, July 27, 1843).

Billings, Mrs. H. B., New London, Ct. (Saratoga, July 27, 1843).

Bishop, E. H., Newhaven, Ct. (Saratoga, Aug. 10, 1843).

Bispham, W. W., 112, Arch Street (Phila., Nov. 15, 1842).

Bispham, Chas. (New Jersey, July 15, 1844).

Bittinger, Rev. Eden C., Pastor of first Presbyterian Church of Washington (5 ft. 10½ in.) (Saratoga, Aug. 12, 1844).

Blache, A. (New Orleans, Jan. 4, 1844).

Blackwell, A., of Belfast (Baltimore, Nov. 28, 1840).

Blagden, Thos. (Washington, April 21, 1841).

Blagden, Rev. G. W., Pastor of Old South Church, Boston (Saratoga, Aug. 5, 1842).

Blair, Frank P., journalist, editor (Washington, May 6, 1841).

Blake, Geo. S., Naval Officer (Phila., Jan. 15, 1841).

Blake, Edwd., of Boston (Saratoga Springs, Aug. 13, 1849).

Blake, Mrs. Edwd., of Boston (Saratoga Springs, Aug. 13, 1849).

Blake, J., 112, Sullivan Street (New York, Feb. 21, 1840).

Blake, J., jun. (New York, Feb. 21, 1840).

Blandchard, Wm. S., Student in Theology, Lane Seminary, Walnut Hill, Cincinnati, Ohio (Saratoga, Sept. 3, 1844).

Bliss, W. W. S., 1st Lieut., U.S.N. (New York, Aug. 20, 1839).

Bliss, Dr. Elam, 85, Beckman Street (New York, Aug. 2, 1839).

Bliss, Col. Geo., of Springfield, Mass., Pres. of Gt. Western Rail Road (Saratoga, July 23, 1842).

Blondel, Wm., Prof. of Music (New York).

Blossom, Col. Wm., of Canadaigua, New York, Delegate of Western Rail Road, Boston (Saratoga Springs, Dec. 31, 1841).

Blunt, G. W., of New York (Boston, May 27, 1842).

Blunt, A. Bowdile W., Counsel at Law, 32, Prince Street (New York, Sept. 28, 1839).

Blunt, Eliza S. (2 ft. 8 in.), born Feb. 11, 1837 (New York, Sept. 28, 1839).

Boardman, H. A., Walnut Street Church (Phila., July 22, 1843).

Boardman, Mrs. H. A. (Phila., Oct. 13, 1843).

Boardman, Andrew, English, Manchester (New York, Aug. 7, 1839).

Boardman, Wm. W., M.C. (Newhaven, Ct., Feb. 25, 1841).

Boardman, Mary Jones, born Jan., 1836 (Phila., Oct. 13, 1843).

Boardman, Chas. H., born May, 1838 (Phila., Oct. 13, 1843).

Boardman, John L., born Oct., 1840 (Phila., Oct. 13, 1843).

Boardman, Henry A., born Jan., 1843 (Phila., Oct. 13, 1843).

Bodley, H. T., Atty. at Law (Lexington, May 29, 1844).

Bogert, Dr. Cornelius R., M.D. (New York, Nov. 16, 1839).

Bogert, Wm. J., New York (Saratoga, Aug. 18, 1842).

Bogert, Dr. S. V. R., M.D., Geneva, Ontaria Co., Boston (New York, Dec. 31, 1841).

Boisaubin, A., Morristown, New Jersey (Saratoga Springs, Aug. 11, 1840).

Bolton, W. G., U.S.N. (Saratoga, Sept. 25, 1843).

Bolles, A., jun., elected Sec. State (Boston, April 1, 1842).

Bomford, G., Col. of Ord. (Washington, March 20, 1841).

Bomford, Geo. C. (Washington, March 19, 1841).

Bomford, Geo. E. (Washington, March 24, 1841).

Bomford, H. (Washington, March 15, 1841).

Bomford, Miss R. (Washington, March 18, 1841).

Bond, Widow Southey, Mt. Vernon, North Carolina (Saratoga, Aug. 12, 1844).

Bond, Rev. Alvan, Norwich, Ct. (Saratoga, Aug. 7, 1843).

Bonden, Andrew, New York (Saratoga, Sept. 11, 1844).

Bonfanti, Gins di Milano (Saratoga, Aug. 8, 1844).

Bonneville, L. de, Prof. of Harward University, Cambridge (Boston, Dec. 28, 1841).

Bonnin, Wm. Wingfield, Florence, Italy (New Orleans, April 6, 1844).

Booth, Washington (Baltimore, Dec. 3, 1840).

Boott, Kirk (Boston, Dec. 29, 1841).

Borden, Edwd. P. (Phila., May 9, 1843).

Bordley, J. Beale, painter (Baltimore, Nov. 26, 1840).

Borghese, Edouard (Saratoga, Aug. 8, 1844).

Bostwick, Eliz. M., wife of Horatio N. (Burlington, June 3, 1843).

Bostwick, W. M. L. (Boston, Dec. 28, 1841).

Bostwick, Chas. Bryon, 42, Hispinard (New York, Nov. 20, 1839).

Botts (1802–1869), John, M.C., minor, Va. (Washington, June 29, 1841).

Bowers, Geo. P. (New Orleans, 1844).

Bowman, N., Francisville, Louisiana (New Orleans, March 12, 1844).

Bowie, R. Ashurst, 263, Arch Street (Phila., Jan. 25, 1843).

Bowlis, Mathias, Maine (Saratoga Springs, Aug. 22, ·1840).

Boyce, Capt., U.S. Coast Surveyor (Washington, March 27, 1841).

Boyd, Wm., from Glasgow (New York, Sept. 14, 1839).

Boyd, Mrs. See Crerar (New York, Sept. 12, 1839).

Boyd, Geo. Wm., jun. (3 ft.), 3 years old (New York, Sept. 12, 1839).

Boyed, Lynn, M.C., Kentucky (Washington, June 29, 1841).

Brackett, Mrs. E. (Phila., May 3, 1843).

Bradbury, James (New Orleans, Feb., 1844).

Bradbury, Miss Josephine (New Orleans, Feb. 27, 1844).

Bradbury, Mary Anne (New Orleans, Jan. 30, 1844).

Bradbury, E. W. (New Orleans, Feb. 6, 1844).

Bradhurst, H. M. (New York, March 5, 1840).

Bradshaw, Laura Hale (Boston, Jan. 3, 1842).

Bradshaw, Andrew (Boston, Jan. 3, 1842).

Bradley, W. A. (Washington, April 17, 1841).

Bradley, J. N., publisher of Boston Daily Mail (Saratoga Springs, Dec. 9, 1841).

Bradley, Thos., of Dukes Co., Member of Senate of Mass. (Boston, Feb. 10, 1842).

Brady, H., Brig.-Gen., U.S.A. (plain clothes) (Washington, March 25, 1841).

Brady H., Brig.-Gen., U.S.A. (uniform) (Washington, March 25, 1841).

Bradford, G. S., Worcester Co., Mass. (Saratoga, Aug. 7, 1844).

Bradford, Olive D., Plainfield, Ct., obt. (Saratoga, July 27, 1844).

Brander, Heslop G. (New York, Nov. 8, 1839).

Brasier, E. F. (New Orleans, Sept. 6, 1844).

Brantz, Lewis, Pres. of Balt. port dePorte (Baltimore, Dec., 1840).

Brayant, Henry (Boston, May 28, 1842).

Breckenridge, Henry M. (Pittsburg, Feb. 4, 1841).

Breed, Mrs. Persis N. (Louisville, Kentucky, May 14, 1844).

Breed, James E. (Louisville, Kentucky, May 14, 1844).

Breed, Mary Kemp (Louisville, Kentucky, May 14, 1844).

Breese, Mrs. W. G. (Saratoga Springs, Aug. 19, 1840).

Breese, W. G., of Cincinnati (Saratoga Springs, Aug. 19, 1840).

Brent, Miss Kate, gd.-daughter of D. Carroll (Washington, March 8, 1841).

Brice, Wm. H. (Baltimore, Dec. 5, 1840).

Bridgeport, Nathaniel Hewit (2 ports.) (Phila., Sept. 22, 1842).

Briggs, Mrs. Louisa (Phila., Jan. 19, 1844).

Briggs, Eliza (Phila., Jan. 17, 1844).

Briggs, Adele (Phila., Jan. 9, 1844).

Brigham, L. H. of Boston (Saratoga, July 22, 1842).

Brigham, Wm., Atty. at Law (Boston, Jan. 23, 1842).

Brigham, J. C. See American Bible Society (New York, May 7, 1840).

Brill, Robt. (Phila., Sept. 27, 1842).

Brimley, Geo. (Boston, April 8, 1842).

Brockway, John H., M.C., Ellington, Ct. (Washington, Feb. 25, 1841).

Bronson, Dr. Tracy, M.D., Newton, Trumbull, Ohio (New York, June 22, 1840).

Brooks, Sidney, of Boston (Saratoga Springs, Aug. 13, 1842).

Brooks, Mrs. Saml. R., New York (Saratoga, Sept. 4, 1844).

Brooks, Mr. Saml. R., New York (Saratoga, Sept. 4, 1844).

Brooks, John, 79 years of age, of Boston (Saratoga, July 24, 1844).

Brooks, Chauncey (Saratoga, Aug. 18, 1844).

Brooks, Henry, of New York (Saratoga, Aug. 4, 1843).

Brooks, Mrs. Henry, of New York (Saratoga, Aug. 4, 1843).

Brookhouse, Mrs. Agnes M. (Boston, Feb. 26, 1842).

Brown, O. W. James (New Orleans, March 25, 1844).

Brown, Carolina E., Boston (Saratoga, Aug. 20, 1844).

Brown, Francis (New York, Nov. 27, 1839).

Brown, John Cater, Providence (Saratoga, Aug. 3, 1843).

Brown, Saml. G., Prof. of Beth. & C., Dartford Coll., Hanover, New Hampshire (5 ft. 9 in.) (Saratoga, Aug. 17, 1844).

Brown, Albert G., M.C., Miss. Gallatin (March 3, 1841).

Brown, Mr. Chas. H., Wharfinger (Saratoga, Aug. 31, 1843).

Brown, Mrs. Chas. H., Indian Wharf (Saratoga, Aug. 31, 1843).

Browne, Miss Sarah A. (New York, Aug. 5, 1839).

Browne, D. R. (New York, Aug. 5, 1839).

Browne, G. W. (New York, Aug. 5, 1839).

Browne, Rev. G. S. (Saratoga Springs, Aug. 26, 1841).

Browne, F. B. E., M.D., Huntsville, Alabama (New Orleans, Feb. 3, 1844).

Browne, Alex. (Phila., Jan. 13, 1843).

Browne, M. B. (Phila., March 4, 1843).

Browning, Mr., of England, aged 73 years, London (New York, Oct. 30, 1839).

Bruce, Robt. (New Orleans, March 1, 1844).

Bruce, Wm. Jerome (New Orleans, 1844).

Brune, Wm. Henry (Saratoga, Aug. 9, 1843).

Brundred, Miss Mary Ann, of English relations (New York, Jan. 3, 1840).

Brunel, Fredk. A., jun. (New York, Sept. 23, 1839).

Brunel, Mme. Marie Oliver, and dog Fideline, of Havana (New York, Sept. 23, 1839).

Brumeid, Thos., third Presbyterian Church (Phila., Aug. 8, 1842).

Bryan, Judge Jos. H., Alabama (Washington, March 30, 1841).

Bryant, John, jun. (Boston, May 18, 1842).

Bryant, Mrs. John, jun. (Boston, May 18, 1842).

Bruyes, F. (New Orleans, April 9, 1844).

Bruyes, Henri (New Orleans, April 9, 1844).

Buany, Signor Pablo, Santiggo de Cuba (6 ft. ½ in.) (New York, Oct. 8, 1841).

Bucklin, Mrs. Eunice, godmother to (Troy, Oct. 8, 1841).

Bucklin, Julia Andres. *See* Andres (Troy, Oct. 8, 1841).

Buckingham, Eliza C., Norwich, Ct. (3 ft. 8¼ in.), aged 5½ years (Saratoga, July 27, 1844).

Budd, Henry (Phila., July 21, 1843).

Buel, David, Counsel at Law (Troy, Sept. 24, 1841).

Buell, Phineas L., Granville, Mass. (Washington, May 3, 1841).

Bujac, M. J. (Phila., Jan. 3, 1844).

Bujac, Alfred (New Orleans, Jan. 3, 1844).

Bull, Wm. Henry, 106, Franklin Street (New York, Oct. 1, 1839).

Bull, Jireh, New York (5 ft. 8½ ins.) (Saratoga, July 18, 1844).

Bullard, Chas., of Boston (Saratoga, July 22, 1842).

Bullard, Henry B. (New Orleans, 1844).

Bun, Dr. Hudson S. (Phila., Aug. 14, 1843).

Bunch, Robt. (New York, Oct. 2, 1839).

Bunnel, Mr. E. F. (Boston, Nov. 8, 1841).

Bunnel, Mrs. E. F., sister of Hon. Levy Woodberry (Boston, Feb. 26, 1842).

Buntin, S. F., Newbury Port, Mass. (Saratoga Springs, Dec. 4, 1841).

Buracu, J. C. (Phila., March 9, 1844).

Burdge, Wm., Yeoman of Shropshire, England (Saratoga, July 22, 1844).

Burgwyn, J. Collinson, North Carolina (Saratoga Springs, Aug. 14, 1840).

Burgwyn, Wm. K., Roanoke, nr. Halifax (Boston, May 23, 1842).

Burke, Edmund, M.C., New Hampshire (Washington, Feb. 22, 1841).

Burke, G., ex-Legislator, Pres. of Canal Bank (New Orleans, April 2, 1844).

Burnap, Mrs. G. W. (Baltimore, Dec. 3, 1840).

Burnap, Rev. G. Wm. (Baltimore, Dec. 14, 1840).

Burnside, Saml. M., Worcester, Mass. (Saratoga Aug. 12, 1843).

Burr, David H., draughtsman, N.O. of Repres. (Washington, April 9, 1841).

Burr, Edwin, Counsel at Law, of New York (Saratoga, Aug. 22, 1842).

Burroughs, Rev. Dr. Chas., Rector of St. John's Church, Portsmouth (2 ports.) (Boston, Dec. 28, 1841).

Burroughs, Mrs. Mary, obt. March 28, 1833, wife of (Boston, Dec. 15, 1841).

Burroughs, G., 83 years of age (Boston, Dec. 15, 1841).

Burroughs, Eliza (Boston, Dec. 15, 1841).

Burroughs, Rev. Henry, jun., Rector of St. Paul's Church, Camden, New York (Boston, May 10, 1842).

Burroughs, Mrs. Henry (2 ports.) (Boston, May 10, 1842).

Burroughs, Master G. (2 ports.) (Boston, May 10, 1842).

Burroughs, Miss Rebecca (Boston, Dec. 15, 1841).

Burroughs, Miss Caroline (Boston, Dec. 15, 1841).

Burroughs, Henry (Boston, Dec. 15, 1841).

Burruss, John W. (New Orleans, Feb. 22, 1844).

Burt, N. H. (Phila., April 12, 1843).

Butt, Miss Antoinette C., New York (Saratoga, Aug. 5, 1844).

Butler, S. N., M.C., South Carolina (July 7, 1841).

Butler, Rev. Dr. David, St. Paul's Episcopal Church (Troy, Sept. 15, 1841).

Butler, Miss Harriet (Troy, Sept. 15, 1841).

Butler, James Lawrence (New York, Aug. 28, 1839).

Butler, James Lawrence (New York, Nov. 17, 1839).

Butler, W. O., M.C., Kentucky (Washington, June 26, 1841).

Butler, Mrs. Benjn., wife of late Atty. Gen. of U.S.A. (Saratoga Springs, Aug. 31, 1840).

Butler, Miss (child) (Saratoga Springs, Aug. 31, 1840).

Burton, Mrs. Eliza E. (Phila., July 7, 1843).

Burton, Mary A. (Phila., July 7, 1843).

Burton, John (Phila., July 7, 1843).

Burton, Gideon (Phila., Feb. 3, 1843).

Burton, Rebecca P. (Phila., July 7, 1843).

Bush, James P. (Boston, May 11, 1842).

Bush, Mary (Boston, Feb. 24, 1832).

Bush, Saml. L. (Boston, May 11, 1842).

Bush, Geo., Prof. New York University, New York (New York, Aug. 25, 1839).

Busby, Marteo, of Syracuse (Saratoga Springs, Aug. 14, 1840).

Bussey, Mrs. Judith, of Jamaica Plain (July 8, 1842).

Byrne, Theo. (New Orleans, March 14, 1844).

Byrne, J. B. (New Orleans, March 14, 1844).

Cabot, Saml. (Boston, Feb. 15, 1842).
Cabot, Mrs. Saml. (Boston, Feb. 15, 1842).
Cabot, Miss E. P. (Boston, Feb. 15, 1842).
Cabot, Miss Sarah (Boston, Feb. 15, 1842).
Cabot, Ed. C. (Boston, Feb. 7, 1842).
Cabot, Mrs. Ed. C., née Miss M. E. Robinson (Boston, Feb. 7, 1842).
Cabot, Louis (Boston, Feb. 7, 1842).
Cadwalader, Henry, Lieut., U.S.N. (Boston, May 30, 1842).
Cahoone, Wm., of New York (Saratoga, July 30, 1840).
Cahoone, Mrs. Wm., of New York (Saratoga, July 30, 1840).
Cahoone, Rev. Wm., jun. (Saratoga, July 30, 1840).
Caldwell, Chas., M.D. (Louisville, May 21, 1844).
Caldwell, Thos. L., M.D., chief surgeon (Louisville, May 21, 1840).
Caldwell, Rev. D., Rector of Lexington (Va., Feb. 12, 1844).
Calhoun (1782–1850), John C., sen., Sec. of State, Tyler's Cabinet (Washington, March 8, 1841).
Calhoun, James S., Georgia (Georgia, Feb. 2, 1841).
Callaghan, P., Counsel at Law, New York (Saratoga, Aug. 8, 1842).
Callender, Wm., clerk, police office (New York, Oct. 29, 1839).
Callender, Chas. J. (Boston, Nov. 17, 1841).
Calyo, Signor Nicolino, from Naples (New York, Aug. 8, 1839).
Camp, H. B., Deaf and Dumb Asylum, Harford (Saratoga Springs, Aug. 27, 1841).
Camp, Mrs. H. B. (Saratoga Springs, Aug. 27, 1841).
Campbell, Colin, South Carolina (Saratoga, July 19, 1842).
Campbell, Hugh (Phila., March 11, 1843).
Campbell, Mrs. Mary (Phila., March 11, 1843).
Carroll, Mrs. Nicholas (New York, March 13, 1839).
Carroll, Mr. Nicholas (New York, Dec. 21, 1839).
Carson, Mr. James (late of Belfast, Ireland), Kingston, Jamaica (Aug. 7, 1840).
Carson, Mrs. James (Aug. 7, 1840).
Carter, Mrs. James, mother of Mrs. J. W. Seved (Boston, May 14, 1842).
Carter, Mrs. Geo. D. (Troy, Sept. 20, 1841).
Carter, Addison B. (Va. June 14, 1841).
Carter, John (Georgetown, May 14, 1841).
Carvalho, S. N., painter, Charleston (Washington, March 20, 1841).
Cary, Mrs. Wm., daughter of Col. Perkins of New York (Boston, June 25, 1842).
Cary, Miss Anne (Boston, June 25, 1842).
Cary, Gertrude ƒ (Boston, June 26, 1842). Twins,
Cary, Grace ⎰ 2 years of age.
Cary, John L. (Baltimore, Dec. 1, 1840).
Cary, Thos. G. (Boston, Feb. 15, 1842).
Cary, Thos. G., jun. (Boston, Feb. 15, 1842).
Cary, Mrs. Thos. G., sen. (Boston, Feb. 15, 1842).
Cary, Richd. (Boston, Feb. 15, 1842).
Cary, Emma (Boston, Feb. 15, 1842).
Cary, Caroline (Boston, Feb. 16, 1842).
Cary, M. L. (Boston, Feb. 16, 1842).
Cary, Eliza C. (Boston, Feb. 16, 1842).
Cary, Sarah (Boston, Feb. 16, 1842).
Casey, Zadok, M.C., Illinois, Mt. Vernon, Jefferson (Feb. 3, 1841).
Cassing, Saml., New York (5 ft. 9¼ in.) (Saratoga, Aug. 29, 1844).

Campbell, Miss Jane Violetta. See Tredwell (New York, May 18, 1840).
Campbell, Mrs. W. (New York, Oct. 21).
Campbell, Mr. Brayton, Atty. at Law (New York, Oct. 13, 1840).
Campbell, James C., U.S.N. (Boston, Feb. 26, 1842).
Campbell, Mrs. H. M., mother of Mrs. D. Lynch (Saratoga, July 9, 1844).
Campbell, John, Parmasus (Washington, March 4, 1841).
Campbell, B. U. (Baltimore, Jan. 12, 1841).
Campbell, Andrew, inventor (Baltimore, Nov. 18, 1840).
Carlston, Geo. J. (Boston, May 18, 1842).
Carlisle, Geo., of Cincinatti (Saratoga, Sept. 2, 1841).
Carmicheal, Mr., Governor of Sing Sing (Saratoga Springs, Aug. 5, 1841).
Carmicheal, Mrs., Mt. Pleasant, Westchester (Saratoga Springs, Aug. 5, 1841).
Carmicheal, Rev. M., Hempstead, L.I. (Saratoga Springs, Aug. 10, 1841).
Carmicheal, Mrs. D., of Fred. Va. (Baltimore, Dec. 1, 1840).
Carol, Fidel, of Matanzas, Cuba (Boston, May 6, 1842).
Carpender, Jacob S. (New York, April 7, 1840).
Carpenter, widow of Benjn., Cambridge, Mass. (2 ports.) (Boston, May 12, 1842; June 4, 1842).
Carr, Edwd., of York, England (Phila., Dec. 9, 1842).
Carrière, Leopold, du Conservatoire de Paris et Theatre Royal de l'operat Comique (New Orleans, Jan. 7, 1844).
Carrington, Edwd., Providence, R.I. (Saratoga, Aug. 23, 1843).
Carrol, Danl., son of Wm. (Washington, March 8, 1841).
Carrol, Danl., of Dudington (Washington, March 8, 1841).
Carroll, Thos. B., editor of the Budget (Troy, Sept. 25, 1841).
Cassing, Mrs. Saml., New York (5 ft. 3¼ in.) (Saratoga, Aug. 29, 1844).
Castein, Victor (killed in duel) (New Orleans, April 6, 1844).
Catlin, Miss Helen D., niece of E. H. Derby. See Derby (Boston, Nov. 4, 1841).
Cespedes, Rosa de, Habana and Cuba (Dec. 26, 1842).
Cilliman, N. B. S., Atty. at Law (Troy, Sept. 24, 1841).
Chadwick, Chris. C. (Boston, March 11, 1842).
Chambers, James R., born Feb., 1829 (New Orleans, April 13, 1844).
Chambers, Mary (New Orleans, April 13, 1844).
Chambers, Wm. H. (New Orleans, April 13, 1844).
Chambers, Sidney (New Orleans, April 13, 1844).
Chambers, Josephine (New Orleans, April 13, 1844).
Champion, Miss A. S. (Troy, Sept. 16, 1841).
Champion, Aist (Troy, Sept. 16, 1841).
Chance, Wm., jun. See Timmins (New York, June 4, 1844).
Chancey, Henry, New York (Saratoga, Sept. 8, 1843).
Chandler, Wm., Lieut., U.S.N. (Jan. 30, 1841).
Chanemontet, Lucien (New Orleans, Feb. 5, 1844).
Chanlee, Rev. P. W., Charlestown, South Carolina (New York, March 7, 1840).
Chanlee, Mrs., daughter of B. Winthrop. See Winthrop (New York, March 7, 1840).

Chanlee, Miss Marguerite (New York, March 7, 1840).

Chaunay, Henry (5 ft. 7 in.) (Saratoga, July 16, 1844).

Channing, Henry Wm. (New York, Feb. 17, 1840).

Channing, Roscoe H., 8 years of age (New York, Feb. 17, 1840).

Channing, Mrs. R. G. (Boston, March 17, 1842).

Chapin, Loring D., Member of New York Legislature, etc. (Aug. 17, 1839).

Chaplin, Edwd. K. (Natchez, July 20, 1844).

Chapman, Henry P. (New York, Aug. 6, 1839).

Chapman, Mrs. Maria. *See* Weston (Feb. 12, 1842).

Chapman, Miss Helen M., Va. (Washington, May 1, 1841).

Chapman, T. A., Va. (Washington, April 30, 1841).

Chapman, John S. (Kentucky, March 14, 1841).

Chapman, Miss Emily (Washington, May 1, 1841).

Chapman, Miss Virginia (Washington, May 1, 1841).

Chapman, D. R. (Boston, June 22, 1842).

Chapman, Mrs. (Boston, June 22, 1842).

Chapman, Jane Eliza (Boston, June 22, 1842).

Chapman, Mr. Jonathan, Mayor of City of Boston (Boston, May 21, 1842).

Chapman, Mrs. (Boston, May 21, 1842).

Chapman, Jonathan ∫ (Boston, May 21, 1842).
Chapman, Eliza W. D. \ Children of above.

Chase, Nelson, New York (Saratoga, Sept. 2, 1843).

Chase, Theod. (Boston, Jan. 29, 1842).

Chase, Clarise A., *née* Miss Bigelow (Boston, Jan. 29, 1842).

Chase, Theod., jun. (Boston, Jan. 29, 1842).

Chase, Geo. Bigelow (Boston, Jan. 29, 1842).

Chase, Chas. Henry (Boston, Jan. 29, 1842).

Chaunay, Henry (5 ft. 7 in.).

Chauncey, C. W., U.S.N. (2 ports.) (Washington, Feb. 24, 1841).

Chauncey, J. L., Lieut., U.S.N. (Washington, March 5, 1841).

Chauncey, Rev. P. S. (June 19, 1841).

Chauncey, Mrs. Maria G. (Washington, March 5, 1841).

Chauncey, Miss Mary (little child) (Washington, March 5, 1841).

Chauncey, J. L., Lieut., U.S.N. (uniform) (Washington, March 5, 1841).

Chauncey, C. W., U.S.N. (Washington, Feb. 17, 1841).

Cheltama, Mr., of Amsterdam (Saratoga, Aug. 25, 1840).

Cheltama, Mrs. (Saratoga, Aug. 25, 1840).

Cherbonnier, Mons. Pierre (Baltimore, Nov. 21, 1840).

Cherbonnier, Mme. (Baltimore, Nov. 21, 1840).

Cherbonnier, Victor (Baltimore, Nov. 21, 1840).

Cherbonnier, Mlle. Corine (Baltimore, Nov. 21, 1840).

Cherbonnier, Alida (Baltimore, Nov. 21, 1840).

Chesborough, Mr. Isaac M., of Providence, R.I. (Nov. 27, 1839).

Chesborough, Mrs. (Nov. 27, 1839).

Chester, John, Detriot, Mich. (Troy, Sept. 20, 1841).

Chester, Mrs. John, daughter of Judge Geo. Morell (Troy, Sept. 20, 1841).

Chester, Rev. A. T., Presbyterian Church (Saratoga Springs, July 14, 1840).

Chester, Mrs. A. T. (Saratoga Springs, July 14, 1840).

Chester, Rev. C. H., of Schuylesville, New York (Saratoga, Sept. 9, 1844).

Chester, Joseph L., New York (Saratoga, Aug. 16, 1845).

Chester, Master (Troy, Sept. 23, 1841).

Chester, Master (Troy, Sept. 23, 1841).

Chester, Miss, Burlington, New Jersey (1842).

Chester, Miss E. H., Burlington, New Jersey (Nov. 6, 1842).

Chester, Miss M. W., Burlington, New Jersey (Nov. 6, 1842).

Chew, Benjn., aged 70 years, Chief Justice of Pennsylvania.

Chew, R. S., Deputy of State (Washington, March 30, 1841).

Child, Dr. Wm. (Boston, Dec. 2, 1841).

Childe, Mr., civil engineer, of Albany (Saratoga, July 25, 1842).

Childe, Mrs. Laura, *née* Dwight. *See* Dwight (Saratoga, July 25, 1842).

Childe, Lelior, aged 7, daughter of above (Saratoga, July 25, 1842).

Childs, Mrs. S. R.. of New York (Saratoga, Aug. 18, 1840).

Chillas, David (Phila., Oct. 10, 1842).

Chipman, Henry Midm., Acting Master in *John Adams* (Boston, March 3, 1842).

Chisolm, John (Oct. 20, 1842).

Chittenden, J. C., M.C., of Adams (New York, June 12, 1841).

Chisebro, M. G., Mayor of Canandaigua (Boston, Dec. 31, 1841).

Christ, E., New York (Saratoga, Aug. 6, 1844).

Christ, Geo., of New York (Boston, June 21, 1842).

Chooet, Dr. Abraham, aged 85 years, celebrated Physician and Anatomist.

Chouning, J. C. (New York, Jan. 5, 1844).

Chur, J., Prof. of Music (Natchez, April 15, 1844).

Church, Joseph M., Skaneatell, Onnondaga Co., New York (Feb. 5, 1840).

Church, H. T. L., of Troy ∫ (New Orleans, Sept. 25,
Church, Myron H. \ 1841). Twins.

Cilliman, N. B. S. (Troy, Sept. 24, 1841).

Claghorn, John [*sic*] (Phila., Dec. 31, 1842).

Clapp, Alex., Huntingdon, Yale (Boston, Dec. 25, 1841).

Clapp, Agnes (New Orleans, March 23, 1844).

Clapp, Theod. (New Orleans, Feb. 24, 1844).

Clapp, Rev. T., of Ravenswood, L.I.

Clapp, Revel, Albany, New York (6 ft.) (Saratoga, Aug. 29, 1844).

Clapp, Mrs. Revel, Albany, New York (Saratoga, Aug. 29, 1844).

Clark, F., of Troy (July 8, 1840).

Clark, Widow Mary Lee, New Jersey (Washington, March 3, 1841).

Clark, J. C., M.C., New York (Washington, April 19, 1841).

Clark, Mr., brother of J. Clark; S. of New York.

Clark, Gen. A. (5 ft. 9½ in.), Amsterdam Mount Co., New York (Saratoga, Aug. 25, 1844).

Clark, Mrs. Susan Maria, wife of J. C., Maine (Washington, April 19, 1841).

Clark, Miss Josephine Sophia, Maine (Washington, April 19, 1841).

Clarke, Lot (Lockport, July 24, 1843).

Clarke, Lester M., Fairfield (July 24, 1843).

Clarke, Master T. (Saratoga, Sept. 2, 1843).

Clarke, Dr. John, M.D. (Saratoga Springs, July 21, 1840).

Clarke, Mrs. John (Saratoga Springs, July 21, 1840).

Clark, C. M., of Ranock, North Carolina (Saratoga, Aug. 12, 1844).

Clark, Mrs. C. M. (Saratoga, Aug. 12, 1844).

Clarke, Augustus, of Boston (Saratoga, Aug. 18, 1842).

Clarke, Mrs. Augustus, of Boston (Saratoga, Aug. 18, 1842).

Clarke, J. Theo., of Boston (Saratoga, July 18, 1843).

Clarke, Miss Eliza.

Clarke, Rev. F. (New Orleans, March 2, 1844).

Clarkson, Col. C. S., Cincinnati, Ohio, served under Gen. Harrison "last war" (June 14, 1841).

Clason, A. W. (New York, Dec. 5, 1839).

Clevenger, Shaval Vail, of Cincinnati, Ohio, sculptor, died passage from Italy, 1844 (Oct. 9, 1840).

Clay, Wm. (Sept. 10, 1839).

Clay, Clement C. (Alabama, March 5, 1841).

Clay, Henry (March 10, 1841).

Clephane, James (Washington, March 17, 1841).

Clephane, Louis, son of above (Washington, June 24, 1841).

Cleveland, Aug., of New York (Saratoga, Aug. 12, 1840).

Clifford, Geo. Odriard (New Orleans, April 1, —).

Clifton, Miss Cecilia, of Boston (Mrs. J. Young) (Baltimore, Dec. 18, 1840).

Clifton, C. W. (Jackson, March 8, 1844).

Clintsman, James C. D. (Phila., Nov. 4, 1843).

Clinton, Chas. A., Counsel at Law (New York, Dec. 7, 1839).

Clinton, Mrs. (New York, Dec. 7, 1839).

Clinton, Catherine S. (New York, Dec. 7, 1839).

Clinton, Augusta, born Dec. 9, 1835 (New York, Dec. 7, 1839).

Clinton, Maria Franklin, born April 12, 1839 (New York, Dec. 7, 1839).

Clinton, Franklin, U.S.N. (New York, Dec. 7, 1839).

Clynch, Gen. D. L., St. Mary's, Georgia (April 4, 1841).

Coale, Saml. Chase (Saratoga, Aug. 9, 1843).

Coall, Geo. B. (Dec. 3, 1840).

Coburn, Jos., Lieut., 3rd Regt. (Phila., July 14, 1842).

Cochrane, Mrs. A., of Glasgow (New York, Sept. 29, 1843).

Coddington, J. J., jun., of New York (Saratoga, Sept. 2, 1844).

Cockroft, James, M.D., 24, Scythe Street (Feb. 7, 1840).

Coffin, Wm. S. (Boston, June 3, 1842).

Coffin, Geo., of Boston (2 ports.) (Saratoga Springs, July 27, 1840).

Coffin, James D., drowned (Boston, Dec. 11, 1841).

Coffin, N. W. (Boston, Nov. 19, 1841).

Coffin, Miss Mary Augusta, aged 21 years and 11 months (New York, Nov. 7, 1839).

Cohen, A. (New Orleans, Aug. 6, 1844).

Cohen, Joshua S., M.D. (Baltimore, Dec. 17, 1840).

Coit, Dr. Benjn. B., M.D., Corras Society, Sec. of Medical Society.

Colby, A. G. O., of New Bedford, Mass. (Boston, June 7, 1842).

Cole, Thos., painter (New York, Oct. 25, 1840).

Cole, Lyman (Phila., Feb. 15, 1843).

Colegate, James, Treas. Dept. (March 29, —).

Colen, John H., from Copenhagen, lithographer and drawer (Aug. 9, 1843).

Coles, L. G., New York (Saratoga, July 19, 1843).

Collmare, A. F., of Boston (Saratoga, Aug. 16, 1844).

Collins, Geo. B. (Dec. 2, 1839).

Collis, John H. (New York, Nov. 11, 1839).

Collis, Geo. Whitmor (New York, Nov. 11, 1839).

Coindrau, Mons. A. (Boston, Dec. 25, 1841).

Collyer, Robt. H., M.D., Isle of Jersey, England, now New Orleans (Nov. 19, 1839).

Collier, John A., Counsel at Law, Binghampton, Co. Broome (Saratoga Springs, July 16, 1840).

Collier, Mrs. John A. (Saratoga Springs, July 16, 1840).

Colman, Henry, Mass. (April 19, 1841).

Coit, Henry A., 55, Clinton Street (Nov. 18, 1839).

Coit, Adelaide Johnson (June 20, 1840).

Coit, Adelaide, jun. (June 20, 1840).

Coit, Dr. Benjn. B., M.D., Sec. of Medical Society, Corras Society (June 20, 1840).

Coit, Mrs. *See* Johnson (Feb. 24, 1840).

Colt, John Oliver, Baltimore (Saratoga, Aug. 27, 1844).

Comstock, Ann Rebecca (Phila., Jan. 14, 1843).

Condit, Rev. Joseph D., South Hadley, Mass. (Saratoga, Aug. 11, 1842).

Condit, Jonathan B., Pastor of second Church, Portland, Maine (Aug. 13, 1840).

Cone, Geo. D., Troy Conf. Acad. West Poultney, Vt. (5 ft. 7 ins.) (Saratoga, July 20, 1844).

Conrotte, Pierre de la (New Orleans, March 25, 1844).

Constantin, T. H., Bordeaux (Sept. 23, 1839).

Cook, Henry Wm. (Baltimore, Dec. 14, 1840).

Cook, Mrs. Wm. (Baltimore, Dec. 14, 1840).

Cook, Rev. Isaac P. (Baltimore, Dec. 14, 1840).

Cook, Saml. C. (Phila., Jan. 30, 1843).

Cook, Wm. A. (New York, March 6, 1840).

Cook, M. Nelson, portrait painter (Saratoga Springs, Sept. 9, 1840).

Cook, Mrs. (Saratoga Springs, Sept. 9, 1840).

Cookcroft, James, M.D., 24, Forsyth Street.

Cooke, Edwd. P., 368, Broadway (Dec. 18, 1839).

Cooke, Joseph (5 ft. 8 ins.) (Saratoga, Aug. 10, 1844).

Cooke, Ransom (Saratoga, June 28, 1843).

Cooke, A. S. (Aug. 12, 1839).

Cooke, Mrs. Edwd., London (London, Sept. 15, 1837).

Coolidge, Mrs. (Boston, March 4, 1842).

Coolidge, Miss H. T. A. (Boston, Feb. 10, 1842).

Coolidge, C. Austin (Boston, Dec. 20, 1841).

Cooper, Alfred (Phila., Oct. 24, 1842).

Cooper, B. C., husband of Almira H. (Phila., Aug. 5, 1844).

Cooper, Rev. Ezekiel of Meth. Epis. (Phila., Jan. 30, 1843).

Cooper, Almira H. (Phila., Aug. 5, 1844).

Cooper, James B., Capt., U.S.N. (taken from description) (Phila., Oct. 28, 1842).

Cooper, Mark A., M.C. (Feb. 2, 1841).

Cooper, Mrs. Rebecca, first wife of James B. (Phila., Oct. 14, 1843).

Cooper, Miss R. M., daughter of above (Phila., Oct. 14, 1843).

Cooper, Mrs. Eliz., second wife of J. C. (Phila., May 2, 1843).

Cooper, Miss Hannah, daughter of second wife (Phila., May 2, 1843).

Copcutt, Francis, from England (Sept. 24, 1839).

Copp, Saml., jun., St. Louis, Miss. (Nov. 23, 1839).

Corbin, Wadel, ed. of *Paul Pry*, of England (New York, Aug. 7, 1839).

Corey, John A., Atty. at Law and Counsel at Law (Saratoga, Aug. 2, 1840).

Cornell, Robt., late Alderman of fifth Ward (New York, Jan. 14, 1840).

Cornell, Mrs. A. (New York, Jan. 14, 1840).

Cornell, Geo. James (New York, Jan. 14, 1840).

Cornell, Chas. R., New York (Saratoga, Sept. 2, 1843).

Coryell, S. S. (Phila., Nov. 23, 1842).

Coster, Washington, Esq., engineer (2 ports.) (New York, Nov. 11, 1839).

Cotting, Amos, jun. (Boston, April 4, 1842).

Cotting, Chas. (Boston, April 4, 1842).

Cotting, Francis (Boston, April 4, 1842).

Cotting, David (Boston, April 4, 1842).

Cotting, Amos (Boston, April 7, 1842).

Cownig, Henry (New York, Nov. 26, 1839).

Cox, Wm. A., Trenton, New Jersey (Sept. 29, 1839).

Cox, Rev., Rector of St. John's Episcopal Church (Troy, Sept. 16, 1844).

Cox, Rev. Saml. Hamson, D.D., first Presbyterian Church, Brooklyn, Prof. Extraordinary of Biblical and Christian History, in the Union Theological Seminary, New York (Saratoga, Aug. 21, 1844).

Coyault, Ernestine (New Orleans, March 9, 1844).

Coyer, C. F., New York (Saratoga, Aug. 23, 1844).

Cozzens, Geo. H. (Saratoga, Aug. 31, 1844).

Coyne, Joseph, Cheshire, England (New Orleans, March 9, 1844).

Crackbon, Joseph (Boston, June 14, 1842).

Craig, Joseph, from Dublin (Dec. 14, 1839).

Craig, Mrs. Joseph, parents of Mrs. Anderson (Dec. 14, 1839).

Cranch, Wm. G., son of Judge C. (June 26, 1841).

Cranch, W. Chas., J.D.C. (Washington, April 14, 1841).

Crawford, A. McLeod (Phila., Oct. 11, 1842).

Crawford, M. W. (Phila., Oct. 13, 1842).

Crawford, J. Agnew (Phila., Oct. 8, 1842).

Crawford, Rev. S. Wm. (Phila., Oct. 11, 1842).

Crawford, Mrs. S. Wm. (Phila., April 4, 1842).

Crawford, Miss M. M. (Phila., Oct. 18, 1842).

Crawford, Annie (Phila., Nov. 14, 1842).

Crawford, Rev. Robt., Presbyterian Church (July 20, 1840).

Crawford, Miss Martha E. (Baltimore, Dec. 15, 1840).

Crawford, Wm., jun. (Baltimore, Dec. 15, 1840).

Crawford, Wm. C. (Baltimore, Dec. 15, 1840).

Crerar, Peter, son of Mrs. Wm. Boyd (Sept. 14, 1839).

Crerar, John, aged 12½ years, son of Mrs. Wm. Boyd (Sept. 12, 1839).

Creyon, A. J. (Phila., March 21, 1843).

Crist, Abraham, Counsel at Law (Aug. 27, 1839).

Crocker, Wm. A., Taunton, Mass. (Saratoga, Aug. 15, 1844).

Crocker, Mrs. Wm. A. (Saratoga, Aug. 15, 1844).

Croghan, G., jun., Louisville, Kentucky (Washington, May 3, 1841).

Crolius, Col. Clarkson, U.S.N. (New York, Feb. 15, 1840).

Croom, W. W., Florida (Saratoga, June 30, 1843).

Crosby, Sarah H., Bangor, Maine (Saratoga, Aug. 16, 1844).

Crosman, G. H., Capt., 6th Infantry, U.S.A. (March 31, 1842).

Croswell, Rev. Wm., of Auburn Co., New York (Boston, June 4, 1842).

Crowninshield, Mrs. G. R. (Boston, Nov. 5, 1841).

Cruft, Edwd., jun., formerly of Boston (lame) (Louisville, May 18, 1844).

Cullum, Geo. W., Capt., U.S. Engineers (Saratoga, Aug. 10, 1844).

Cummings, Rusus K. (Boston, Nov. 13, 1841).

Cummings, Mrs. John, sister of Mrs. J. Kennedy (New York, Aug. 13, 1839).

Cummings, Brig.-Gen. T. S., miniature painter (New York, Aug. 2, 1839).

Cummings, Dr. John G., M.D., son-in-law to Mrs. A. Cochrane, Glasgow (New York, Sept. 29, 1843).

Cummins, Dr. B. (Phila., July 25, 1843).

Cummins, Mrs. Geo. (Saratoga, July 26, 1843).

Cummins, Mary, wife of Dr. B. (Phila., July 26, 1843).

Cumpston, Rev. Edwd. H., Oct. 1841 (April 20, 1840).

Cumpston, Mrs. Edward H., née Miss Skinner, 1842 (April 20, 1840).

Cunningham, Miss Jane, of Belfast, Ireland (Oct. 18, 1839).

Curtis, Mrs. Chas. P. (Boston, April 15, 1842).

Curtis, C. P., jun. (Boston, April 8, 1842).

Curtis, H. P. (Boston, April 8, 1842).

Curtis, Thos. J. (Boston, April 8, 1842).

Curtis, Rodrick (Sept. 2, 1840).

Curtis, G. (Boston, April 27, 1842).

Curtis, C. P., sen., Counsel at Law. See Greenough (Boston, April 8, 1842).

Cushing, Robt. M., aged 6 years (Boston, Feb. 15, 1842).

Cushing, John Gardiner, aged 7½ years (Boston, Feb. 15, 1842).

Cushing, Eliza C., daughter of late Mrs. Watson. See Watson (June 10, 1842).

Cushing, Jos., jun. (Saratoga, Aug. 18, 1843).

Cushing, Thos. P., 4, Mount Vernon Street (Boston, Dec. 21, 1841).

Cushman, Rev. R. W., Pastor of Bowdoin Square Baptist Church (Boston, June 21, 1842).

Cushman, Edwd. F., banker, 14, Wall Street (New York, March 1, 1840).

Cushman, Mrs. Alex., New York (Saratoga, July 29, 1844).

Cuthbert, Wm. H., Charleston, South Carolina (Saratoga, Aug. 7, 1843).

Cutler, Rev. Curtis, Congregational Church, Peterborough, New Hampshire (Saratoga, Aug. 4, 1842).

Cutler, Rev. B. C., D.D., Rector of St. Ann's Church, Brooklyn (Saratoga, Aug. 14, 1844).

Cutter, Wm., editor of Coleman's Monthly Miscellany (New York, Aug. 17, 1839).

Cuyler, John M., asst.-surgeon, U.S.N. (April 24, 1841).

Dale, John B., Lieut., U.S.N. (Baltimore, Jan. 27, 1841).

Dallas, G. M., Counsel at Law, Vice-Pres. U.S.A. (Phila., Jan. 20, 1843).

Dallas, A. James, Eminent Counsel, obt. Jan., 1819, aged 57 years, Jefferson Politician, Sec. of War.

Dallas, A. J., jun., U.S.N. (Boston, March 2, 1840).

Dallas, Alex. J., Commodore, U.S.N. (Phila., Jan. 21, 1843).

Dalman, Susan Ann (New Orleans, Feb. 5, 1844).

Dalman, Josephine Lafayette (New Orleans, Feb. 5, 1844).

Dalman, Peter (New Orleans, Feb. 5, 1844).

Dalmany, Peter, 18 years of age, born in Kentucky, slave belonging Mrs. Dalman (New Orleans, Feb. 6, 1844).

Dane, Capt., 5th Infantry, U.S.A. (June 27, 1841).

Danforth, Rev. Joshua, Presbyterian Church, Alexandra (Jan. 28, 1841).

Daniel, T. H. (Va., 1844).

Daniel, Miss Anne, daughter of Judge Daniel (Saratoga, Aug. 16, 1843).

Daniel, Miss E. R., Richmond, Va., daughter of Judge Daniel (Saratoga, Aug. 16, 1843).

Davenport, Chas. F., post office, New York (Boston, May 24, 1842).

Davidge, W. D. (Baltimore, Dec. —, 1840).

Davidge, T. H. (Baltimore, Dec. 3, 1840).

Davidson, Lionel, of London Bank (Dec. 27, 1839).

Davis, John D. (Pittsburg, March 27, 1841).

Davis, John, Judge of Western District (Boston, May 31, 1842).

Davis, Rev. Saml. C., Rector of All Faith Parish (Washington, March 6, 1841).

Davis, Col. D., Concord, New Hampshire (Saratoga, Aug. 20, 1843).

Davis, David (Boston, Nov. 10, 1841).

Davis, Henry R. T. (Phila., Nov. 10, 1842).

Davis, J. B. (Phila., 1842).

Davis, John (New Orleans, Jan. 13, 1844).

Davis, Geo., deputy coll., Custom House, New York (3 ports.) (Aug. 12, 1839; Aug. 19, 1839; Sept., 1842).

Davis, M. L., Esq. *See* Greene (Oct. 29, 1839).

Davis, John, Judge, U.S. District Court; Mag. apt. Feb. 7, 1801, resigned July 16, 1841, aged 81 years (Boston, Nov. 29, 1841).

Davis, H. T., godson of above (Boston, Jan. 22, 1842).

Davis, Isaac P. (Boston, Jan. 22, 1842).

Davis, John R. (Baltimore, Dec. 5, 1840).

Davis, Mrs. Wendall Thornton. *See* Russell (Boston, Nov. 27, 1841).

Davis, A. B. (Dec. 3, 1840).

Davis, Widow Rebecca (Boston, Dec. 13, 1841).

Davis, Nathaniel M., Plymouth, Mass. (Boston, Dec. 16, 1841).

Davis, Wm., Plymouth, Mass. (Saratoga Springs, July 6, 1844).

Davis, Mrs. J. W., daughter-in-law of Judge John Davis (Boston, Dec. 9, 1842).

Davis, W. Watson (Boston, Dec. 9, 1841).

Davis, John Wm. (Boston, Dec. 9, 1842).

Davis, Robt. S. (Boston, Dec. 9, 1842).

Davis, Frank B. (Boston, Dec. 9, 1842).

Davis, Wm. R. (Boston, Dec. 9, 1842).

Davies, Thos. S. (Jan. 16, 1840).

Davison, G. M., stationer (Saratoga Springs, July 31, 1841).

Dawson, Wm., M.C., Greenborough, Georgia (Feb. 2, 1841).

Dax, Cath., Albaret Dept. Lands, France (Saratoga, Aug. 8, 1844).

Day, Geo. E., New Haven, Ct. (April 30, 1840).

Day, Mrs. Benjn., New York (Saratoga, Aug. 14, 1842).

Dayton, A. O., 4th Auditor of Treasury (Feb. 3, 1841).

Dayton, Elias B. (2 ports.), aged 78 years, entered and served in U.S.A. as a volunteer in 1776, terminated his active service as Brig.-Gen. in Militia of State of New Jersey, 1825, a Member of Society of Cin. (New York, April 28, 1840).

Dean, Eben. (Boston, Nov. 24, 1841).

Deane, Chas., Edinburgh Street (Boston, March 2, 1842).

Deas, Fitzallen, Lieut., U.S.N. (Washington, March 5, 1841).

De Buys, Mlle. Félice (New Orleans, April 2, 1844).

De Buys, Mlle. Adèle (New Orleans, April 2, 1844).

Decatur, Mrs. J. P. (Phila., Jan. 28, 1843).

Decatur, Anna (Phila., Jan. 28, 1843).

Decatur, Andrew (Phila., Jan. 28, 1843).

Decatur, Channa (Phila., Jan. 28, 1843).

Decatur, Lieut. Stevens (Phila., Jan. 28, 1843).

Decatur, Susan (Phila., Jan. 28, 1843).

De Baun, Mrs. Abraham, mother of Mrs. Zebedee King (New York, March 16, 1840).

Deeble, Edwd., book binder (Jan. 27, 1841).

Deemes, Rev. Chas. M. F., Methodist Church (2 ports.) (New York, Feb. 27, 1839).

Deforest, Lockwood, New York (Saratoga, July 24, 1843).

DeKay, James E., M.D. (New York, Oct. 18, 1839).

DeKay, Master Henry (New York, Oct. 18, 1839).

Delafield, Clarence (New York, March 4, 1840).

Delauney (1828–1891), Jules, French portrait painter (New Orleans, Jan. 4, 1844).

Delavan, Edwd. C., Temperance Lecturer (Saratoga, Aug. 3, 1842).

Delprat, John C. (New York, Nov. 28, 1839).

Delprat, Fanny (New York, Nov. 28, 1839).

Delprat, Margaret (New York, Nov. 28, 1839).

Delprat, Henrietta (New York, Nov. 28, 1839).

Delprat, John Chas. (New York, Nov. 28, 1839).

Delprat, James Stewart (New York, Nov. 28, 1839).

Dem, J. A. (New York, Dec. 18, 1844).

Deming, Henry E., of New York (Saratoga, July 21, 1843).

Deming, E. (Aug. 24, 1839).

Denike, Willitt (Jan. 8, 1840).

Denison, R. S., of New York (Saratoga, July 11, 1844).

Denison, Mrs. R. S., of New York (Saratoga, July 11, 1844).

Dennis, Edwd. P., nephew to Capt. Berry (Saratoga, July 21, 1843).

Dennis, E. C., Auburn, New York (Boston, Dec. 31, 1841).

Dennett, Wm. H. (Boston, Nov. 8, 1841).

Denny, John Tappen (New York, Oct. 30, 1839).

Denny, D., of Boston (Saratoga, July 15, 1844).

Denny, Geo., of Westboro', Mass. (Boston, May 24, 1842).

Denny, Mrs. D., of Boston (Saratoga, July 15, 1844).

Denny, Thos., 11, Clonton Place, New York (New York, Oct. 30, 1839).

Denny, Mrs. Thos., sister of T. W. Tappen (New York, Oct. 30, 1839).

Denny, Thos., jun. (New York, Oct. 30, 1839).

De Pass, J. M. (New Orleans, May 21, 1844).

De Pestre, Edwd., of Malanza, Cuba (Phila., Dec. 28, 1842).

Derby, E. H. *See* Catlin (Boston, Nov. 4, 1841).

Derby, Mrs. E. H. (Boston, Nov. 4, 1841).

Derby, Richd. C. (2 ports.) (Boston, March 15, 1841).

Derby, Mrs. Richd. C. (Washington, March 18, 1841).

Dermott, Miss A. K. (Washington, Feb. 9, 1844).

Dessac, Mrs. John, of Phila. (New York, Sept. 24, 1839).

Devereux, John C., jun., from Utica, New York (New York, Aug. 21, 1840).

Dewey, Capt. Saml. W., U.S.N., 77, South Street (New York, Nov. 30, 1839).

Dewel, Miss Jane Eliza (Saratoga Springs, July 26, 1841).

Dewitt, Wm. H., of Albany (Saratoga, July 8, 1840).

Dexter, James, Counsel at Law, Albany (Boston, April 23, 1842).

Dexter, Miss Catharine (Boston, Nov. 9, 1841).

Dexter, Thos. A., Counsel at Law (Boston, May 25, 1842).

Dexter, Mrs. Thos. A. (Boston, May 25, 1842).

Dexter, Mrs. Anne, mother of Thos. (Boston, April 12, 1842).

Dexter, Geo. M., Auburn, New York, Ct. (Boston, Feb. 28, 1842).

DeYoux, Mons., of Macon, Seine et Loire, France (standing without leg) (New Orleans, March 22, 1844).

DeYoux, Mons. (with leg—seated) (New Orleans, March 22, 1844).

DeYoux, Mme. (New Orleans, March 22, 1844).

Dickinson, Mrs. John D., mother of Mrs. Taylor (Troy, Sept. 6, 1841).

Dikenson, Miss Eliz., daughter of Mrs. James Vale. *See* Townsend (Troy, Sept. 13, 1841).

Didier, Mrs. Edmund (Baltimore, Nov. 27, 1840).

Didier, Master (Baltimore, Nov. 27, 1840).

Didier, Miss Mary (Baltimore, Nov. 27, 1840).

Didier, Edmund (Baltimore, Nov. 27, 1840).

Diedericks, Robt. (New York, Oct. 29, 1840).

Digges, Dr. Wm. D. *See* Brent (Washington, March 8, 1841).

Diller, Anna, Dowington (Chester Co., Pa., April 17, 1843).

Diller, Roland M., Westchester (Chester Co., Pa., March 28, 1843).

Diller, Jona., Esq. (done from description), probably father of above (Chester Co., Pa., March 20, 1843).

Diller, Isaac (Phila., March 21, 1843).

Dinsmoor, Anna Jarvis (Saratoga, Sept. 16, 1844).

Dixon, Geo., Washington (Phila., Sept. 19, 1842).

Doane, James C., Cohasset, Mass. (Boston, March 2, 1842).

Dobbyn, W. A., late of 5th Dragoon Guards (Phila., March 1, 1843).

Doly, Judge James, Wisconsin, Terry (April 3, 1841).

Doly, Mrs. James, Wisconsin, Terry (April 3, 1841).

Donaldson, James L., 1st Lieut., U.S.A. (Saratoga Springs, Aug. 15, 1841).

Domenech, Francisca Ponce, Puerto Rico (Saratoga, July 6, 1843).

Donellan, Rev. R. C., St. Matthew's Church (Washington, Feb. 5, 1841).

Dorman, Dr. Olbert (Washington, Jan. 25, 1841).

Dorr, Albert H. (2 ports.) (Boston, Jan. 18, 1842).

Dorr, Miss Susan E. (Boston, Jan. 19, 1842).

Dorr, J. F., of New York (Saratoga, July 18, 1844).

Dorsay, W. H. (Va., Dec. 21, 1843).

Downes, John, Commodore, U.S.N. (Saratoga Springs, July 22, 1842).

Downes, John, jun., U.S.N. (Saratoga Springs, July 22, 1842).

Downs, Miss Julia M. (2 ports.) (Saratoga Springs, July 28, 1842).

Downing, Saml. W., Capt., U.S.N. (Saratoga, Aug. 12, 1840).

Downing, Mrs. Saml. W. (Saratoga, Aug. 12, 1840).

Drake, James, Habana (Saratoga, Aug. 1, 1843).

Drake, John, of New York (Oct. 1, 1840).

Drake, Mrs. Magdelen, mother of Mrs. Townsend (Oct. 1, 1840).

Draper, John Haggerty (New York, Jan. 26, 1840).

Draper, Fanny (New York, Jan. 26, 1840).

Draper, W. B. (New York, Jan. 26, 1840).

Draper, Simeon, jun. (New York, Jan. 26, 1840).

Draper, Mrs. S. H., *née* Miss Haggerty (New York, Jan. 26, 1840).

Draper, Mary (New York, Jan. 26, 1840).

Dubois, Gen. Nathanl. (Washington, March 2, 1841).

Dubois, Miss Sarah, now Mrs. Wagstaff, June 1843 (2 ports.) (Saratoga, Aug. 11, 1842).

Dubois, Cornelius (Dec. 13, 1839).

Dubois, Geo., Washington (Dec. 30, 1839).

Dubois, Dr. Henry A. (June 22, 1840).

Dubois, Edmund F. (Baltimore, Dec. 14, 1840).

Du Colombier, Prosper Martin (Va., April 11, 1843).

Dudley, Col., Cincinnati, Ohio, served under Harrison "last war" (June 24, 1841).

Duffee, F. Harold, late editor of the *Jeffersville Courier* (Phila., May 2, 1843).

Duffin, Charlotte E. (New Orleans, Feb. 15, 1844).

Dufour, Mons. Louis, of Dunkerque, France, in America since 1800 (Aug. 18, 1840).

Dufour, Cyprian (New Orleans, March 20, 1844).

Dugan, Miss Ann (Jan. 28, 1843).

Dugan, Joseph (Jan. 28, 1843).

Dumaresq, Mrs. James (March 29, 1842).

Dummins, Georges W. (Smyrna, Jan. 26, 1843).

Dumont, Wm. (New York, Sept. 20, 1843).

Dunbar, A. W. (2 ports.) (New Orleans, Feb. 8, 1844).

Duncan, G. Currie (New Orleans, Jan. 20, 1844).

Duncan, Saml. P. (Saratoga, July 29, 1843).

Duncan, S. D. (Natchez, July 22, 1843).

Duncan, Stephen (Natchez, July 29, 1843).

Duncan, J. W. (Natchez, April 30, 1844).

Duncan, Mrs. Francis A. (New Orleans, March 22, 1844).

Dunham, Wm. S. (New York, Oct. 31, 1839).

Dunham, Mrs. Margaret (New York, Oct. 31, 1839).

Dunham, R. B. (New York, Oct. 31, 1839).

Dunham, W. F. (New York, Oct. 31, 1839).

Dunham, Harriet Louisa (New York, Oct. 31, 1839).

Dunitry, Alex. (Washington, June 26, 1841).

Dunlap, James, Concordia (New Orleans, Feb. 21, 1844).

Dunny, Signor Pablo, Santiggo de Cuba (Dec. 30, 1839).

Du Pan, F. (New Orleans, Feb. 5, 1844).

Dural, Chas. G. (Phila., Oct. 14, 1842).

Durel, Paulin (New Orleans, Jan. 15, 1844).

Durel, T. (New Orleans, Jan. 4, 1844).

Dwight, Widow James, of Springfield, Mass. *See* Childe (Saratoga, July 23, 1842).

Dwight, Francis, of Albany, New York. | Saratoga, July 23, 1842. Sons of above.

Dwight, Geo., Springfield, Mass. |

Dwight, Mrs. Geo. (Saratoga, July 23, 1842).

Eagle, Henry, 486, Broadway (New York, Dec. 3, 1839).

Eagle, Miss Matilda, 486, Broadway (New York Dec. 13, 1839).

Eagle, Mrs. Henry (New York, Dec. 2, 1839).

Eagle, Robt. Nelson (New York, Dec. 19, 1839).

Eammach, Mr. N. S., Inst. (New Orleans, Feb. 18, 1844).

Earhart, Wm. (Natchez, April 27, 1844).

Earhart, Saml., aged 2 years (Natchez, April 27, 1844).

Earhart, Mrs. Wm. (Natchez, April 27, 1844).

Eason, James N., Charleston, South Carolina (Saratoga, July 10, 1843).

Eastburn, Mrs. James, of England (New York, Feb. 3, 1840).

Eaton, J. H., 1st Lieut., 3rd Infantry, U.S.A. (Saratoga, Aug. 6, 1842).

Eaton, Lewis (Washington, June 12, 1841).

Ebaugh, Rev. John S., Minister D.A., Phila. (Saratoga, Aug. 21, 1843).

Eckford, Mrs. Henry, gd.-mother to Henry DeKay (New York, Oct. 18, 1839).

Eckley, Wm. H. E. (Nov. 24, 1841).

Eckley, David (Boston, April 16, 1842).

Eckley, Fanny A. (Boston, April 16, 1842).

Eckley, Master Arthur A. (Boston, April 16, 1842).

Eddy, Rev. E. C., Gen. Agent of the A. B. C., F. M. (Saratoga Springs, Aug. 17, 1840).

Edes, Peter (New York, Oct. 15, 1840).

Edmond, Wm., of Mobile (Troy, Sept. 11, 1841).

Edmond, Mrs. Wm., of Mobile (Troy, Sept. 11, 1841).

Edmond, Master (Troy, Sept. 11, 1841).

Edmondson, Dr., of Baltimore (Saratoga, Aug. 15, 1842).

Edmondston, P. M., Charleston, South Carolina (Boston, Dec. 28, 1841).

Edwards, T. B., son of James (Washington, April 21, 1841).

Edwards, James, New Orleans (Saratoga, Aug. 2, 1844).

Edwards, Mrs. Dr. S. (Washington, April 15, 1841).

Edwards, Harriette (Washington, April 13, 1841).

Edwards, S., M.D., U.S.N. (Washington, April 15, 1841).

Edwards, Lewis E. (Washington, April 15, 1841).

Edwards, Mrs. Mary E., wife of Lewis (Washington, April 15, 1841).

Edwards, James E., Comm. of Pensions (Washington, April 21, 1841).

Edwards, Lewis, son of James (white figure) (Washington, April 21, 1841).

Edwards, John, son of James (Washington, April 21, 1841).

Elam, T. U. (New Orleans, Feb. 19, 1844).

Elam, J. E. (New Orleans, Feb. 19, 1844).

Eldridge, Widow Mrs. P. A. (Boston, April 12, 1842).

Eldridge, G. F. (Boston, April 12, 1842).

Eigenbrodt, Rev. Wm. E., of Brainbridge (New York, May 2, 1840).

Eliot, Saml. A., Mayor of Boston 1837–1839 (Boston, June 15, 1842).

Eliot, Frank E., of Washington, D.C. See Lamb (Boston, Jan. 17, 1842).

Ellicott, B. W. (Baltimore, Aug. 18, 1841).

Elliot, Chas. A., of Boston (Baltimore, Nov. 21, 1840).

Ellis, Chiseldon, of Waterford (New York, July 16, 1840).

Ellis, G. A., Capt., Merchant, New Bedford, Mass. (Saratoga, Aug. 9, 1842).

Ellis, Rev. John M., Mich. (Jan. 30, 1840).

Ellison, Francis B., Lieut., U.S.N. (Boston, Aug. 23, 1841).

Ellsworth, Oliver, son of Gov. W. W. Ellsworth, Harford, Ct. (Boston, May 19, 1842).

Ely, Major Edwd. B.

Embury, Daniel.

Embury, Miss Anna Rissaud, gd.-daughter of Daniel J. R. Manley (Brooklyn, Oct. 25).

Emerson, Fredk., author, Boston (Saratoga, July 22, 1840).

Emerson, Miss Lucy B. (Boston, Nov. 20, 1842).

Emlen, Geo., Counsel at Law (2 ports.). 1st port. (Phila., Aug. 14, 1843); 2nd port. (Saratoga, April 24, 1843).

English, Theo. Dunn, poet (Phila., Dec. 1, 1842).

English, Adelaide (New Orleans, Jan. 10, 1844).

Erving, J., Major, 3rd Artillery, U.S.A. (Boston, April 22, 1842).

Erwin, H. C., gd.-son of Henry Clay (Lexington, June 1, 1844).

Erwin, Isaac (Natchez, Feb. 8, 1844).

Espino, Guillermo (Venezuela, July 13, 1843).

Estes, Mrs. E. C., of Brooklyn, New York, daughter of Alpheus Bigelow, jun. See Bigelow (Saratoga, July 26, 1844).

Etienne, D. G., Prof. of Music (Saratoga, Aug. 8, 1844).

Etting, Reuben (Phila., May 16, 1843).

Eustis, W., U.S.A. (Feb. 2, 1841).

Eustis, A. B. (Phila., Nov. 28, 1842).

Eustis, Mrs. A. B. (Phila., Oct. 31, 1843).

Eustis, Mrs. F. A. (Phila., Oct. 31, 1843).

Eustis, Mr. F. A. (Phila., Oct. 31, 1843).

Euvrard, Mons. F., Officer de la Marine, Fran-Havre de Grace (Saratoga, Aug. 2, 1841).

Evans, Watton W., engineer, New Brunswick, New Jersey (Jan. 16, 1840).

Evans, F. W. (Baltimore, Jan. 14, 1841).

Evans, Geo. (Maine, March 20, 1841).

Everdell, Wm. (New York, Nov. 10, 1839).

Everdell, Mrs. Wm. (New York, Nov. 10, 1839).

Ewbank, Thos. (New York, Nov. 10, 1839).

Ewing, Mrs. Cornelia, Lonsdale (Saratoga, Aug. 27, 1840).

Ewing, Hubert (Phila, Oct. 11, 1843).

Fahnestock, Levi (Baltimore, Dec. 3, 1840).

Faitonte, Wm. S., Newark (New Orleans, March 19, 1844).

Faile, Miss Ann D., Westchester, New York (Saratoga, Aug. 6, 1844).

Falconer, James H. (New York, Nov. 19, 1844).

Farley, Mrs. John (Washington, Feb. 5, 1841).

Farnswith, John C. (Saratoga, Nov. 9, 1841).

Farrar, Col. P. W. (New Orleans, Dec. 29, 1843).

Farrell, Dr. J. (March 20, 1844).

Faxon, Geo. N. (Boston, Dec. 2, 1841).

Fay, Major John J. (Buffalo, New York, March 15, 1841).

Fearnhead, Wm. (Betterville, Sept. 7, 1830).

Fell, Reese D., Guardian of the Poor (May 22, 1843).

Fellows, James, 32, Dy Street, Maiden Lane, New York (Saratoga, Aug. 7, 1839).

Fellows, Mrs. James, (Saratoga, Aug. 7, 1839).

Felton, Cornelius C., Cambridge, Mass., Pres. Harvard (Aug. 12, 1841).

Felton, S. M., of Charleston, Mass. (Saratoga, July 26, 1845).

Felton, Mrs. Luther (Saratoga, Sept. 4, 1843).

Fenderick, Chas., artist (Washington, June 23, 1841).

Fenner, John H. (Saratoga Springs, July 24, 1841).

Ferrell, Miss Frances E., of Natchez (Saratoga Springs, Aug. 25, 1840).

Ferrers, Signor Chas., of Turin, Italy (Saratoga, Aug. 10, 1844).

Ferrers, Signora Jane, from Belfast, Ireland (Saratoga, Aug. 10, 1844).

Ferrers, Signora Emile (Saratoga, Aug. 10, 1844).

Field, Rev. Thos. P., Pastor of second Congregational Church, Danvers Mass. (Saratoga, Aug. 4, 1842).

Field, A. L., Lynn's Hotel, aged 20 years (Boston, June 13, 1842).

Field, Osgood, of New York (New Orleans, April 13, 1844).

Field, Dr. Frost (New Orleans, April 13, 1844).

Figure, female, no name on back.

Feist, Michael Chas., of Frankfort, Germany (New York, Nov. 14, 1839).

Fillebrown, T., jun. (Washington, Feb. 27, 1841).

Fillebrown, J. S., U.S.N. (Boston, Dec. 25, 1841).

Fillmore, Millard, M.C., Pres. of U.S.A. (New York, June 14, 1841).

Finlay, Robt., Santa Cruz (March 29, 1840).

Fish, Wm. K. (Holmesbury, Pa., Oct. 17, 1842).

Fisher, C. H. (Phila., Jan. 17, 1843).

Fisher, Rev. Geo. H., Reformed D. E. Church, New York (Saratoga, Aug. 5, 1843).

Fisher, Fredk. Geo., aged 78 years, father of Clara F., of Drury Lane, London (New York, Nov. 9, 1839).

Fisk, T. W. (Natchez, April 30, 1844).

Fister, D., clockmaker (Washington, May 1, 1841).

Fitch, Rev. Chester, New Marlboro', Mass. (Aug. 20, 1841).

Fitch, Wm., New York (Saratoga, Aug. 23, 1843).

Fitch, Rev. Prof., Detroit Branch of University of Mich. (Aug. 13, 1840).

Fitzwilliam, Miss Maria (Feb. 25, 1840).

Fitz, Virginia W. (New Orleans, Sept. 6, 1844).

Flandin, Mons. Pierre, of Lyon, France (Oct. 25, 1839).

Fletcher, Rev. Joshua, of Baptist Church (Saratoga, Aug. 12, 1840).

Fletcher, Mrs. Joshua (Saratoga, Aug. 12, 1840).

Flint, Mrs. Anne (Saratoga Springs, Aug. 5, 1841).

Flower, Geo. (Washington, Feb. 3, 1841).

Flower, Rees Wall (Phila., June 12, 1843).

Floyd, Miss Rosamond M., of New York (Saratoga, Aug. 5, 1842).

Fluker, D. J. (Louisiana).

Flutton, John, of Phila., aged 107 years, native of New York, silversmith.

Follin, Noel (New York, Oct. 31, 1839).

Follin, Miss Maria (New York, Oct. 31, 1839).

Folsom, Chas. W., Cambridge College, Mass. (Boston, Nov. 20, 1841).

Folsom, Geo. Mackean (Boston, Nov. 9, 1841).

Folsom, Chas. (Boston, Nov. 9, 1841).

Folsom, Rev. Nathanl. S., first Parish Congregational Church, Haverhill, Mass. (Boston, Dec. 31, 1841).

Folsom, Geo., Counsel at Law (New York, Jan. 21, 1840).

Fondey, Townsend, of Troy (Boston, May 31, 1842).

Fondey, Mrs. Townsend, late Miss Hollister (Boston, May 31, 1842).

Fontaine, Veuve Gilbert, *née* Lenoir (New York, Oct. 6, 1840).

Foote, Euphemia (New York, Oct. 31, 1839).

Foote, John (New York, Oct. 31, 1839).

Foote, Saml. (New York, Oct. 31, 1839).

Foote, Thos. M. (Buffalo, May 8, 1841).

Forbes, R. B. (Boston, Dec. 31, 1841).

Forbes, Mrs. Margaret, sister of Col. Thos. Perkins (Boston, Feb. 23, 1842).

Forbes, Bennett (2 ports.) (Boston, Dec. 31, 1841).

Forbes, J. M., of Milton Hill (Boston, Jan. 28, 1842).

Forbes, Mrs. J. M. (Boston, Jan. 28, 1842).

Forbes, Alice, aged 3½ years ⎱ (Boston, Jan. 28,
Forbes, Elen, aged 3½ years ⎰ 1842). Twins.

Forbes, Miss Emma P., sister to J. M. (Boston, Jan. 28, 1842).

Forbes, Master Bennett (Boston, Dec. 31, 1841).

Forbes, Miss Alice (Boston, Dec. 31, 1841).

Forest, John, Lt.-Col., 51st Regt. (New Orleans, Feb. 10, 1844).

Forman, Widow Anna Maria, wife of Geo. (New York, June 18, 1840).

Forman, Lawrence T. ⎱ (New York, June 18, 1840).
Forman, Lewis   ⎰ Three sons of above.
Forman, Wilson

Forsyth, Miss Virginia (Phila., Oct. 18, 1842).

Forsyth, John, Sec. of State.

Foster, Joseph (Boston, April 5, 1842).

Foster, Mrs. Joseph (Boston, April 5, 1842).

Foster, A. Laurence, M.C. (New York, June 12, 1841).

Foster, Jacob, Boston (Saratoga, July 20, 1844).

Foster, Geo. (April 10, 1844).

Foster, Saml., aged 44 years (Natchez, 1844).

Foster, Adams (Phila., Oct. 22, 1842).

Foster, Mrs. Lafayette (New York, Dec. 18, 1844).

Foster, Mary (Phila., Oct. 22, 1842).

Foster, James (Phila., Aug. 9, 1843).

Foster, Lieut., Fogette S. (Norwich).

Fowle, Edwd. (New York, July 29, 1839).

Fowler, L. N., practical phrenologist (New York, Nov. 28, 1839).

Fowler, Theodocius A., 176, Baker Street (Nov. 12, 1840).

Fox, Dr. Geo. W., M.D. (Natchez, April 24, 1844).

Fox, Henry F., from Dublin (Aug. 5, 1839).

Francis, D. G.

Franklin, Benjn., aged 84 years.

Freeman, Dr. Saml., M.D. (Saratoga Springs, July 29, 1841).

Frelinghuysen, Fredk., son-in-law to Geo. Griswold (Saratoga, July 8, 1843).

Frelinghuysen, Mrs. Matilda E. (Saratoga, July 6, 1843).

French, A., Albany, New York (Saratoga, Aug. 5, 1844).

Frost, John, Prof. de Belles lettres (Phila., Jan. 28, 1843).

Frost, Dr. Geo. Wm., M.D., Staten Island (Aug. 9, 1839).

Frothingham, Wm., of Boston (New York, Sept. 6, 1839).

Frothinghand, Mrs. A. R. (Brooklyn, Aug. 5, 1844).

Fuentes, Rafael de (New Orleans, Dec. 29, 1843).

Fuller, Mrs. Gym., Green Street (New York, March 17, 1840).

Fulton, W. S., sen. (Arkansas, June 12, 1841).

Fuyel, Daniel A. (Lexington, March 25, 1844).

Funes, Juan, Gregorio de Madrid (Saratoga, Aug. 10, 1843).

Furniss, Wm. (New York, Aug, 31, 1840).

Gadsby, Wm. (Washington, April, 17, 1841).

Gaines, Maj.-Gen., U.S.A. (Washington, March 20, 1841).

Gaines, Mrs. (Washington, March 20, 1841).

Galbraith, James D., W.S.W. (Lychburg, Feb. 23, 1844).

Gale, E. Thompson (Troy, New York, March 8, 1841).

Gamble, Roger L., M.C. (Georgia, July 2, 1841).

Garbeille, Peter G., sculptor (New Orleans, Jan. 26, 1844).

Garcia, Signor J., New York (Saratoga, Aug. 9, 1844).

Gardette, E. B., M.D., dentist (Phila., April 14, 1843).

Gardiner, Col. D. S., of East Florida (Washington, June 9, 1841).

Gardiner, John, W. T., Lieut., Dragoons (Washington, March 1, 1841).

Gardiner, Edwd. (Boston, Feb. 15, 1842).

Gardiner, Mr., Spring Island, Counsel at Law (New York, Oct. 13, 1840).

Gardiner, W. H. (Boston, Feb. 15, 1842).

Gardiner, Mrs. W. H. (Boston, Feb. 15, 1842).

Gardiner, Caroline L. (Boston, Feb. 15, 1842).

Gardiner, John T. (Boston, Feb. 15, 1842).

Gardiner, Chas. (Boston, Feb. 15, 1842).

Gardiner, L. R. Barrut, Capt., U. S. Infantry.

Gardner, Hordell (Saratoga, July 21, 1840).

Gardner, Henry S. (Boston, May 26, 1842).

Garidelli, Achille, Italian, Nice (Sept. 7, 1839).

Garland, Hugh A. (Feb. 16, 1841).

Garland, John, Lieut.-Col., U.S.A. (March 26, 1841).

Garland, A., Lieut., U. S. Marines (Phila., 1843).

Garnis, John P., Cincinnati, Ohio (Saratoga, July 18, 1844).

Garr, Geo. (New Orleans, April 1, 1844).

Garretson, Rev. John (2 ports.), Bellville, New Jersey (Saratoga, July, 31, 1840).

Garrettson, F., of Rimbeck Duchess Co. (Saratoga, Sept. 14, 1844).

Garrettson, Mrs. F., New York (Saratoga, Sept. 14, 1844).

Gassaway, Mrs. Kitty E. A. (Washington, March 24, 1841).

Gates, Seth M., M.C., New York (June 25, 1841).

Gautier, Dr. J., New Jersey.

Gayot, Leonard, 102, Leonard Street (Sept. 20, 1839).

Gazzon, A. H., Alabama (Washington, March 12, 1841).

Geddes, Geo., of Geddes, New York (Saratoga, July 10, 1844).

Gedney, Geo. W. (Oct. 5, 1839).

Gedney, Thos. R., Lieut., U.S.N. (2 ports.) (Washington, March 16, 1844).

Geib, Wm. (Phila., May 5, 1843).

George, Robt., Baltimore (Saratoga, Aug. 27, 1844).

Germain, Rev. R. G., St. Mary's Hall (Burlington, June 9, 1843).

Geusau, Baron, Vienna (Dec. 6, 1839).

Gibbene, Daniel L. (Boston, May 31, 1842).

Gibert, James T., M.D. (Oct. 16, 1839).

Gibbons, Wm., Savannah, now New Jersey (July 22, 1843).

Gibbons, Julia (New York, Jan. 5, 1840).

Gibbons, Sarah H. (New York, Jan. 5, 1840).

Gibbs, Alex. (Saratoga, Aug. 10, 1843).

Gibbs, Miss Anna R. (Saratoga, Aug. 10, 1843).

Gibbs, Miss Nancy, New Bedford, Mass. (Saratoga, Aug. 10, 1843).

Gibson, Wm., Prof. of Surgery at University at Perth (March 7, 1843).

Gibson, Isaac, New York, (Saratoga, Aug. 8, 1844).

Gibson, Chas. Hammond, gd.-son of Mrs. Saml. Hammond.

Gibson, John Gardiner. *See* Hammond.

Gibson, G. F., Baltimore (Saratoga, July 12, 1844).

Gibson, John, editor of *True American* (Washington, March 24, 1841).

Gifford, Chas., of Hudson (2 ports.), with dog (New York, Oct. 17, 1839).

Gilbert, John G., stage-manager of Tremont Theatre (Boston, Nov. 9, 1843).

Giles, Miss Eliz. G., of Worcester (Boston, March 2, 1842).

Gill, Owen A. (Baltimore, Jan. 9, 1841).

Gillespie, Archibald H., Lieut., U.S. Marines (Phila., Nov. 14, 1842).

Gillett, L. Warrington (Baltimore, Jan. 26, 1841).

Gillis, John P., Lieut., U.S.N. (Boston, May 4, 1842).

Gilman, W. S., of Alton, Illinois (New York, Aug. 6, 1839).

Gilmor, Robt. (Baltimore, Aug. 11, 1840).

Gilmor, Wm. (Baltimore, Nov. 27, 1840).

Gilmor, Chas. S. (Baltimore, Dec. 8, 1840).

Gillmore, A. R., Syracuse, New York (Boston, Dec. 31, 1841).

Gilpin, John F., Guardian of the Poor (May 22, 1843).

Gilpin, H. D. (Washington, Feb. 20, 1841).

Glynn, James, Lieut., U.S.N. (Boston, March 26, 1842).

Gobert, Charlotte, widow of Chas. G., mother of Mrs. Parker (New York, April 12, 1840).

Goddard, Wm. B. (son) (Phila., April 12, 1843).

Goddard, J. M. (son) (Phila., March 8, 1843).

Goddard, Janet (daughter) (Phila., April 1, 1843).

Goddard, Susan N. (daughter) (Phila., Oct. 20, 1843).

Goddard, Mrs. Kingston (daughter-in-law) (Brooklyn, Sept. 20, 1843).

Goddard, Rev. Kingston (son) (Brooklyn, Sept. 20, 1843).

Goddard, M. (father) (Phila.).

Goddard, John Bonsall (gd.-son) (Phila., Oct. 4, 1842).

Goddard, Harvey Beck (gd.-son) (Phila., Oct. 4, 1841).

Goddard, Paul Fredk. (gd.-son) (Phila., Oct. 4, 1841).

Goddard, Louisa, wife of Dr. Paul B. G. (April 1, 1842).

Goddard, Eliz., of Brookline (Saratoga, July 17, 1844).

Godon, Sylvanus Wm., Lieut., U.S.N. (Saratoga, Aug. 2, 1842).

Godone, Signor Gaspare, of Acarine, Capital of Pierremont (Broadway, Aug. 10, 1839).

Godone, Signora Gaspare (Broadway, Aug. 10, 1839).

Godone, Miss Fanny (Broadway, Aug. 10, 1839).

Godone, John (Broadway, Aug. 10, 1839).

Godone, Napoleon (Broadway, Aug. 10, 1839).

Godone, Gaspare, jun. (Broadway, Aug. 10, 1839).

Godone, Ferdinand (Broadway, Aug. 10, 1839).

Godwin, Parke, editor (New York, July 29, 1839).

Gold, Thos. A., of Pittsfield, Counsel at Law (Aug. 24, 1841).

Goldsborough, John R., Lieut., U.S.N. (Jan. 27, 1841).

Goldtrap, Thos., Ware (Phila., July 9, 1844).

Goodinch, Rev. Chas. (Rector of St. Paul's Church (New Orleans, Feb. 12, 1844).

Goodrich, Wm. H. (Saratoga, Aug. 27, 1841).

Goodrich, C. B. (Boston, Nov. 18, 1841).

Goodrich, S. G., author of *Peter Parley's Tales*, etc. (New York, Oct. 26, 1839).

Goodridge, S. G., Boston (Saratoga, Aug. 25, 1840).

Goodwin, Maria. *See* Appleton (Boston, Jan. 27, 1842).

Gordon, H. (6 ft. 3½ in.), Va. (Saratoga, July 25, 1844).

Gould, Alex. (Baltimore, Dec. 3, 1840).

Gourgas, Francis R., Member of House of Representatives (Boston, Jan. 21, 1842).

Gourlie, John H., broker (New York, Dec. 12, 1839).

Grace, Eliz. (Habana, Cuba, Dec., 1842).

Graf, Fredk. B. (Baltimore, Dec. 10, 1840).

Grafton, C., jun. (Boston, April 25, 1842).

Graham, David, jun., 770, Broadway, New York (Saratoga, Aug. 22, 1840).

Graham, Mrs. (Saratoga, Aug. 22, 1840).

Graham, Robt. H., sen. (Saratoga, Aug. 22, 1840).

Graham, Nathan. B., New York, 84, Eight Street (New York, Nov. 23, —).

Graham, R. M. C. (New York, Nov. 23).

Graham, James Lorimer (New York, Nov. 23).

Grandval, Mons. de Gengoa de la Rochelle (Nov. 19 1839).

Granger, Francis (Washington, June 12, 1841).

Grant, G. P., Hartford Co. (Saratoga, Sept. 2, 1844).

Grant, Reuben H., Gen. (Macon, Miss.).

Grant, Miss Eliz. W., and her sister-in-law (Boston, Nov. 6, 1841).

Grant, Mrs. Patrick, obt. 1843 (Boston, Nov. 6, 1841).

Granth, Mrs. W. H. (Washington, April 28, 1841).

Grass, Fredk. (Phila., April 12, 1843).

Grasse, Rev. Isiah G., Rector of St. Matthew's, New York (Feb. 15, 1840).

Gratz, Benjn. (Lexington, Kentucky, May 20, 1844).

Gratz, James (Phila., Aug. 18, 1843).

Graves, T. B., of N. Ross, Co. Wexford, Ireland (Saratoga, Aug. 23, 1844).

Gray, Miss Anne Augusta (Brooklyn, Mass., Dec. 27, 1841).

Gray, Henry G. (Boston, Feb. 1, 1842).

Gray, Edwd., of Baltimore (Saratoga Springs, July 8, 1840).

Gray, Watson (Dec. 24, 1840).

Gray, Miss Eliza (Dec. 21, 1840).

Gray, Mrs. Horace (Boston, Nov. 22, 1841).

Gray, Master (Boston, Nov. 22, 1841).

Gray, John (Boston, March 24, 1842).

Gray, John H. (Boston, Nov. 30, 1841).

Gray, Mrs. John H. (Boston, Nov. 30, 1841).

Grayson, J. C., U.S. Marines (Boston, May 11, 1842).

Greene, Walter C. (Nov. 18, —).

Greene, Saml. N., of Boston. *See* Hassard and Livingstone (New York, Nov. 13, 1839).

Greene, W. P., of Norwich (Boston, March 14, 1842).

Greene, Miss Rose (Washington, May 8, 1841).

Greene, Hugh W. (Boston, March 2, 1842).

Greene, Mrs. D. J. (Brooklyn, Nov. 2, 1839).

Greene, Wm. J. (Brooklyn, Dec. 31, 1839).

Greene, Wm. Davis, stepson of M. L. Davis (Nov. 30, 1839).

Greene, Anna Lloyd (Boston, Dec. 23, 1841).

Greene, Miss L. E. E. (Boston, Feb. 15, 1842).

Greene, Miss Sarah (Boston, April 9, 1842).

Greene, Eliz. Clarke, widow of (Boston, April 9, 1842).

Greenleaf, Wm. C. (Washington, April 15, 1841).

Greenleaf, Miss Caroline (Cambridge, Dec. 9, 1841).

Greenough, David D., Counsel at Law, of Jamaica Plain (Boston, May 20, 1842).

Greenough, James (Boston, May 20, 1842).

Greenough, Mr. W. W. (Boston, April 9, 1842).

Greenough, Mrs. W. W., daughter of Mrs. Chas. P. Curtiss (Boston, April 9, 1842).

Greenough, Wm., sen. (Boston, April 29, 1842).

Greenwood, John, Boston (Saratoga, July 9, 1844).

Greenwood, Chas. R. (Boston, Nov., 1841).

Greenwood, Rev. Francis W. P., Minister of King's Chapel, Boston, obt. 1843 (Boston, Nov. 9, 1841).

Greenwood, Mrs. W. F. (Boston, Nov. 9, 1841).

Greenwood, Augustus (Boston, Nov. 9, 1842).

Greenwood, Alice Lloyd (Boston, Nov. 9, 1841).

Greenwood, Francis W., jun. (Boston, Nov. 9, 1841).

Greenwood, Mary L. (Boston, Nov. 9, 1841).

Gregory, H. M., Binghampton (New York, July 20, 1840).

Gregory, D., ex-Mayor of Jersey City (Saratoga, Aug. 23, 1843).

Gregory, Mrs. D. (Saratoga, Aug. 23, 1843).

Gregory, Mary Louisa (Saratoga, Aug. 23, 1843).

Gregory, Miss Clara B. (Saratoga, Aug. 23, 1843).

Greig, John, Cananadaigua (New York, June 14, 1841).

Griffin, E. T. (Baltimore, Dec. 2, 1840).

Griffith, John M., New York (Troy, Sept. 10, 1841).

Griffith, Mrs. Catharine (Troy, Sept. 10, 1841).

Griffith, Miss M. E. S. (Troy, Sept. 10, 1841).

Griffith, R. R. (Baltimore, Aug. 16, 1844).

Griffiths, Miss Jane (Baltimore, Dec. 24, 1840).

Griffiths, James P. (Phila., Feb. 4, 1843).

Griffiths, Mary F. (Phila., Feb. 7, 1843).

Griffiths, Anna Clifford (Phila., Oct. 10, 1842).

Griffiths, Robt., Englesfield (Phila., Oct. 10, 1842).

Grimes, J. Stanley, Lecturer Phrenology and Chemistry (Saratoga, Aug. 10, 1840).

Griswold, Rufus Wm., editor of *New World* (New York, Sept. 4, 1839).

Griswold, Wm., of New York (July 10, 1840).

Griswold, Geo., 57, Chamber Street, New York (2 ports.) (Saratoga, July 8, 1843).

Griswold, Mrs. Geo., 57, Chamber Street, New York (2 ports.) (Saratoga, July 8, 1843).

Groning, K., of London (New Orleans, March 23, 1844).

Grosette, Augustus, first tenor in Theatre Royal d'Anvers (New Orleans, Feb. 14, 1844).

Grosvenor, S., of New York (Saratoga Springs, Aug. 23, 1844).

Grosvenor, Miss Eliza, of New York (Saratoga Springs, Aug. 23, 1844).

Grout, S., Vt. (Troy, Sept. 24, 1841).

Guild, E. G. (Boston, Nov. 11, 1841).

Gumbell, Rev. Joseph M., of Buffalo (Washington, March 2, 1841).

Gwin, Mrs. Wm. M., wife of Marshal of Southern District, Viskburg of Miss. (Saratoga Springs, Aug. 25, 1840).
Gwynn, Wm., Counsel at Law (Baltimore, Dec. 25, 1840).

Habersham, John Rae, of Georgia (Boston, March 2, 1842).
Habersham, Richd. W., M.C., Clarksville (Haversham, Jan. 30, 1841).
Haggerty, John Lewis, 55, Chamber Street (New York, Jan. 26, 1841).
Haggerty, Mrs. John Lewis, 55, Chamber Street (New York, Jan. 26, 1841).
Haggerty, Miss Maria (New York, Jan. 26, 1841).
Haggerty, Ogden (2 ports.) (New York, Jan. 26, 1840).
Haggerty, John A. (New York, Jan. 26, 1840).
Haggerty, Miss Eliz., now Mrs. B. Draper (New York, Jan. 26, 1840).
Haggerty, Wm. C. (New York, Jan. 26, 1840).
Haggerty, Mrs. Ogden, wife of Ogden (New York, Jan. 22, 1840).
Haggerty, Anne, daughter of above (New York, Jan. 22, 1840).
Haggerty, Ogden, jun., son of O. H., obt. Nov., 1844 (New York, Jan. 22, 1840).
Hagner, Thos., Florida (Saratoga, July 20, 1842).
Hagner, T. R., (Washington, March 3, 1841).
Hagner, Lieut. P. V., Ord. Corps, U.S.A. (Feb. 15, 1841).
Hagner, Lieut. C. N., topographical engineer (Feb. 15, 1841).
Haight, Mrs., daughter-in-law of D. L. Haight (Saratoga, July 26, 1843).
Haight, Miss Lydia (Saratoga, July 26, 1843).
Haight, Saml., Consul of U.S.A. at Anvers (New York, Dec. 20, 1844).
Haight, D. L., Anvers (New York, July 21, 1843).
Haines, Miss E. R. (New York, Nov. 23, 1844).
Hak, P., of New York (Saratoga, July 9, 1844).
Halberstadt, J. (2 ports.) (Phila., March 9, 1839; Jan. 2, 1840).
Hall, Francis C. H., relation of Mrs. Hamilton Smith (Louisville, May 15, 1844).
Hall, F. C., Lieut., U.S. Marines (Phila., Oct. 5, 1842).
Hall, Rev. Richd. Dayson, Rector of St. Mary's (W. Phila., Aug. 16, 1842).
Hall, Edwd. A. (New Orleans, Jan. 6, 1844).
Hall, E., Norfolk, Va. (Saratoga, Sept. 8, 1843).
Hall, D. A. (Washington, March 11, 1841).
Hall, Joseph (Boston, Jan. 6, 1842).
Hall, Saml. (Baltimore, Jan. 6, 1841).
Hall, Dudley (Boston, April 9, 1842).
Hall, J. McClean (New Orleans, Jan. 25, 1844).
Hall, Rev. Robt. B. (2 ports.), Plymouth, Mass. (Saratoga, July 6, 1843).
Hall, Mrs. Robt. B. (Saratoga, July 6, 1843).
Hall, Isaac M., Rochester, New York (Oct. 16, 1840).
Hall, Mrs. Caroline (Oct. 16, 1840).
Hall, Miss (little child) (Oct. 16, 1840).
Hall, Miss Lucy Ann Thompson (baby) (Oct. 16, 1840).
Hall, Miss Anne (Saratoga, Aug. 31, 1840).
Halleck, J. Wager (Washington, Feb. 19, 1841).
Hamblin, Thos. T., manager of Bowery Theatre (New York, Aug. 26, 1839).

Hamilton, A. W., Kentucky (Saratoga, Aug. 12, 1843).
Hamilton, David, Albany, New York (Saratoga, July 19, 1844).
Hamilton, Alex. (Bridgeport, April 9, 1841).
Hamilton, B. S. (New Orleans, April 6, 1844).
Hamilton, C. G. (Halifax, Nova Scotia).
Hammond, widow, Mrs. Saml., jun., formerly Miss Greene, obt. March 22, 1844 (2 ports.) (Boston, Nov. 16, 1841; May 1, 1842).
Hammond, Gardiner Greene, with dog Turk (2 ports.) (Boston, May 1, 1842).
Hammond, Saml. (2 ports.) (Boston, May 1, 1842).
Hammond, John L., son of Mrs. Saml. H. (Boston, Nov. 4, 1841).
Hammond, Mrs. Saml. (Boston, Nov. 4, 1841).
Hammond, John Carver Palfrey, gd.-son of Mrs. Saml. (Boston, Nov. 4, 1841).
Hammond, Chas., son of Mrs. Saml. (Boston, Nov. 5, 1841).
Hammond, Chas., gd.-son of S. H. See Gibson (Boston, Dec. 26, 1841).
Hancock, Mary L., daughter of late Gov. of Mass. (Boston, June 8, 1842).
Hand, Geo. E., Detroit (Aug. 12, 1840).
Hansell, W. L., Guardian of the Poor (May 22, 1843).
Hardisty, H., jun. (Dec. 2, 1840).
Hare, Robt., Counsel at Law (Phila., Dec. 28, 1842).
Harlan, Richd., M.D. (Phila., Sept. 21, 1842).
Harris, Henry, Deputy Marshal (Boston, Nov. 3, 1841).
Harris, Rev. Thaddeus Mason, aged 74 years, Episcopal Church, obt. April 3, 1842 (Boston, Jan. 14, 1842).
Harris, J. Morrison (Baltimore, Dec. 9, 1840).
Harrison, C. Woodland, of Phila. (Aug. 12, 1840).
Harrison, Mrs. Raindrop, of Va. (Phila., Aug. 12, 1840).
Harrison, Saml. T. (2 ports.) (Baltimore, Dec. 10, 1840).
Harrison, Miss Marguerite (Baltimore, Dec. 10, 1840).
Harrison, Geo. L., Baltimore (Saratoga, July 31 1844).
Harrison, Wm. N. (Baltimore, Dec. 9, 1840).
Harrison, M., Lieut., U.S. Engineers (Boston, Dec. 28, 1841).
Harrison, Thos., 74 years of age, New York (Saratoga, Aug. 10, 1844).
Harrison, W. H., 9th Pres. of U.S. (Washington, Feb. 20, 1841).
Harris, Alex. (Jan. 21, 1844).
Harrod, Chas. and family (New Orleans, March 22, 1844).
Harrod, Mrs. M. (New Orleans, March 22, 1844).
Harrod, Miss G. P. (New Orleans, March 22, 1844).
Harrod, Eliz. (New Orleans, March 22, 1844).
Harrod, Master B. M. (New Orleans, March 22, 1844).
Harsen, Dr. Jacob, M.D. (New York, Feb. 17, 1840).
Hartt, Chas. P. (Troy, Sept. 15, 1841).
Hart, Robt. M. (Baltimore, Nov. 22, 1840).
Hart, Miss Cordilia (Saratoga Springs, Sept. 4, 1840).
Hart, S., Miss. (Saratoga, July 15, 1843).
Hartt, Mrs., Missouri (New Orleans, March 23, 1844).
Hartt, Hiram (New Orleans, March 22, 1844).
Harvey, Jacob, Esq. (New York, Oct. 20, 1840).
Harvey, Mrs. Jacob (New York, Oct. 20, 1840).
Harvey, Miss Mary (New York, Oct. 20, 1840).

Harvey, Miss Rebecca (New York, Oct. 20, 1840).
Hassard, Mrs. Thos., Bloomingdale, Boston (New York, Nov. 13, 1839).
Hassard, Saml. Nicholson, Bloomingdale, Boston (New York, Nov. 13, 1839).
Hassard, John Rose Greene (New York, Nov. 13, 1839).
Hassler, C. A., asst.-surgeon, U.S.N. (Washington).
Hassler, Mrs. Mariane, Bristol, Pa. (Boston. June 7, 1841).
Hassler, J. R. Chas., surveyor, obt. Nov. 19, 1843 (Phila.).
Hassler, Mrs. Anna (Washington, March 29, 1841).
Hassler, May Carry (baby) (Washington, March 29, 1841).
Hassler, Edwd. (Washington, March 29, 1841).
Hassler, Caroline (Washington, March 29, 1841).
Hassler, J. T. S., asst., U.S. Coast Survey (Washington, March 26, 1841).
Hassler, Mrs. J. T. S. (Washington, March 26, 1841).
Hassler, Ferdinand Rudolph (little boy) (Washington, March 26, 1841).
Hassler, Edwd., U.S.N. (Washington, March 29, 1841).
Hastings, John, M.C. (Ohio, June 17, 1841).
Hastings, Miss F. (Phila., Aug. 7, 1844).
Hastings, Geo. (Brooklyn, Aug. 7, 1844).
Hastings, Mrs. Geo. (Brooklyn, Aug. 6, 1844).
Hatchkiss, Gideon (New York, Jan. 16, 1843).
d'Hauterive, Baron (Phila., Dec. 5, 1842).
d'Hauterive, Auguste (Phila., Dec. 12, 1842).
d'Hauterive, Maurice (Phila., Dec. 12, 1842).
d'Hauterive, Baronne (Phila., Dec. 12, 1842).
d'Hauterive, Marie (Phila., Dec. 12, 1842).
Haven, Luther, of Leicester, Mass. (Boston, May 24, 1842).
Havens, R. N., Pittsburgh, Pa. (July 30, 1839).
Hawley, Emily Jane. See Hawley and Beaujeau (Nov. 30, 1844).
Hawley, T. B. W. (July 27, 1839).
Hay, Col. Wm. (Leamington, 1837).
Haydon, Wm. (New Orleans, Jan. 17, 1844).
Hays, Jacob, aged 67 years, chief constable (New York, Oct. 25, 1839).
Hays, Mrs. Jacob (New York, Oct. 30, 1839).
Hays, Benjn. J., jun., constable (New York, Oct. 28, 1839).
Hays, Gilbert J. (New York, Nov. 1, 1839).
Hays, Mrs. Wm. Henry, daughter of Mrs. Monk (New York, Oct. 27, 1839).
Hays, Wm. Henry (New York, Oct. 27, 1839).
Hays, Miss Mary C. (New York, Oct. 27, 1839).
Hayward, W. H. (New Orleans, Feb. 12, 1844).
Hayward, Selham W. (Boston, Feb. 23, 1842).
Hazard, Isaac Peace, of Peace Lake, R.I. (Boston, Dec. 30, 1841).
Head, Saml. (Phila., Jan. 3, 1840).
Healy, Geo. H. (Aug. 20, 1839).
Heath, Miss Abby L. H. (Brookline, April 4, 1842).
Heaton, A., New Haven (Saratoga, July 24, 1843).
Hebert (1816–1880), P. O., Gen., Corps of Engineers (April 20, 1841).
Hechavarria, Prudencio de, Habana, Chamberlain to Isabella, Queen of Spain (Saratoga, July 19, 1843).
Heckster, Edwd., New York (Saratoga Springs, 1840).
Heintzelman (1807–1862), S. P., Asst. Quartermaster-General, U.S.A. (Phila., April 4, 1843).

Heiskell, H. L., surgeon, U.S.A. (April 17, 1841).
Hellis, Horace de A., Marquis de Santangelo (Washington, March 14, 1841).
Hellyer, John B., of London (Boston, Jan. 13, 1842).
Henderson, Robt. S., 8, City Hall Place (Aug. 20, 1839).
Hepburn, Mrs. B. H., New York (Saratoga, July 24, 1840).
Henderson, John, sen., Miss. (Feb. 11, 1841).
Henderson, Rev. M. H., Epis., Newark, New Jersey (Aug. 22, 1840).
Hendrickson, Chas. (Phila., Feb. 23, 1843).
Henry, Joshua, of New York (Saratoga, July 10, 1840).
Henry, Miss Jane Agnes (New Orleans, Feb. 29, 1844).
Henry, Miss Helen (Phila., Aug. 4, 1840).
Heran, D. Melville, of New York (Saratoga, July 26, 1844).
Heran, Mrs. D. Melville, of New York (Saratoga, July 26, 1844).
Heran, Miss Mary, of New York (Saratoga, July 26, 1844).
Herbst, Miss M., of Amsterdam, Holland.
Hernandez, Joseph, Brig.-Gen. (Washington, April 13, 1841).
Heron, I. E., Major, U.S.A. (Saratoga, July 14, 1844).
Herriman, Widow A., sister of Mrs. J. Clark, New York (Saratoga Springs, Aug. 12, 1840).
Herriman, Miss Eliza W. (Saratoga Springs, Aug. 17, 1840).
Herron, A. R. (Memphis, March 12, 1844).
Hertell, John P., New York Custom House (Aug. 19, 1839).
Hetzell, A. K., Capt., U.S.A., 2nd Infantry (April 17, 1841).
Hetzell, Saml. Selden, son of A. K. (Washington, April 19, 1841).
Heyl, Mary Louisa Henrietta (New Orleans, Jan. 28, 1844).
Hicks, Eliz., 32, Warren Street (Oct. 31, 1839).
Hicks, Effie, 32, Warren Street (Oct. 31, 1839).
Hield, Mr. Wm., Park Theatre, died June, 1843 (New York, Aug. 9, 1839).
Hield, Mrs. (New York, Aug. 9, 1839).
Higginson, J. (Boston, April 25, 1842).
Hill, Wm. Dudley, Mass. (Saratoga, Sept. 6, 1844).
Hill, Miss Rebecca J. (Washington, May 1, 1841).
Hinckman, Chas., of England, 60, Cherry Street (Nov. 7, 1839).
Hindman, Thos. C., Col., U.S.A. (Alabama, June 25, 1841).
Hinds, Rev. N. P. (Phila., April 28, 1843).
Hinds, Emily (Phila., April 28, 1843).
Hinds, Ann (Phila., May 1, 1843).
Hinkle, Louis Chas. (Dec. 16, 1839).
Hinsdale, Bissoll, Rochester (Saratoga, Aug. 4, 1843).
Hinslow, Rev. Horace, Pastor of second Presbyterian Church, Lansingbergh (Saratoga, July 16, 1840).
Hixon, J. Vila, of New York, gd.-son of Rev. Dr. Saml. (Boston, Jan. 5, 1842).
Hoar, E. Rockwood, of Concord, Mass., Atty. Gen. (Saratoga, July 26, 1845).
Hoban, James, Counsel at Law (Washington, June 23, 1841).
Hobbeer, Selah R. (Washington, March 23, 1841).

Hobbie, Drake (done from description), died Feb. 28, 1841 (Washington).

Hoffman, Colder Cade, brother to Martin Hoffman (Aug. 24, 1839).

Hoffman, Lindsay Murray, judge and writer.

Hoffman, Emily.

Hoffman, Martin (Aug. 19, 1832).

Hoffman, Miss Mary Catharine (Boston, Feb. 16, 1842).

Hoffman, P. V., of New York (Saratoga Springs, July 25, 1842).

Hoffman, Mrs. P. V., of New York (Saratoga Springs, July 25, 1842).

Hoffman, David, Counsel at Law, lawyer and writer (Baltimore, Dec. 9, 1840).

Hogan, widow, 15, Waverly Place, New York, obt. 1841 (New York, Oct. 23, 1840).

Hogan, Hogan (Alton, March 20, 1841).

Holcomb, A. A., U.S.N. (Washington, March 16, 1841).

Holland, T. (Phila., July 25, 1843).

Hollands, Henry (March 19, 1844).

Hollenbach, G. M. (Saratoga, July 24, 1844).

Hollister, A. P. (Sept. 14, —).

Hollister, Miss Julia W., New Berne, North Carolina (Saratoga, Sept. 13, 1844).

Holman, T. (Phila., July 25, 1843).

Holmer, Eleazer, of Boston (Saratoga, July 20, 1844).

Holmer, Mrs. Eleazer, of Boston (Saratoga, July 20, 1844).

Holmer, W. F., of Boston (Saratoga, July 20, 1844).

Holmer, Mrs. W. F., of Boston (Saratoga, July 20, 1844).

Holt, Hines, M.C. (Georgia, Feb. 2, 1841).

Hone, Isaac S., of New York, deputy collector of Custom House (Saratoga, Aug. 12, 1843).

Hooper, R. C. (Boston, Jan. 15, 1842).

Hooper, Mrs. E., of Marblehead (Boston, Jan. 10, 1842).

Hooper, Nathanl., of Marblehead (Boston, Jan. 10, 1842).

Hooper, Saml. (Boston, Jan. 10, 1842).

Hooper, Mrs., daughter of Mrs. Wm. Sturgis (Boston, Jan. 10, 1842).

Hooper, Wm., son of Saml. (Boston, Jan. 15, 1842).

Hooper, Ellen, daughter of R. W. Hooper (Boston, Jan. 10, 1842).

Hooper, Edwd. Wm., son of R. W. Hooper (Boston, Jan. 10, 1842).

Hooper, Alice B. (Boston, Jan. 10, 1842).

Hooper, Anna Maria (Boston, Jan. 10, 1842).

Hooper, Wm. H., of Marblehead (June 17, 1842).

Hooper, John G., jun., of Marblehead (May 6, 1842).

Hooper, John, jun., of Marblehead (Boston, April 12, 1842).

Hooper, Mrs. John, of Marblehead (Boston, April 12, 1842).

Hooper, Robt., jun., Pres. Boston Bank (Boston, March 30, 1842).

Hooper, R. (Boston, March 30, 1842).

Hooper, John (Boston, March 30, 1842).

Hooper, Henry (Boston, March 30, 1842).

Hoover, Rev. Chas., Newark, New Jersey (Jan. 10, 1840).

Hopkins, Erastus, former Pastor of second Presbyterian Church, Troy, New York (Saratoga, July 6, 1843).

Hopkins, G. W. (New York, March 3, 1840).

P

Hopkins, G. W., M.C. (Washington, July 8, 1841).

Hopkins, Mark, Pres. of William College (April 20, 1840).

Hopkinson, James (Phila., April 25, 1840).

Horn, James, New York (Saratoga, Aug. 30, 1843).

Horner, Fortescue (Cheltenham, June 17, 1839).

Horton, Rev. Wm., of St. Thomas's Church, Dover, New Hampshire (Boston, June 7, 1842).

Hosken, Lieut. J., British R.N., Commander of Great Western Steamboat (Saratoga, July 20, 1844).

Housten, James Alex., surgeon in America since Nov., late editor of *Belfast Christian Patriot* (New York, April 1, 1840).

Howard, John, Pres. of Springfield Bank (Saratoga, July 21, 1842).

Howard, Miss M. O. (Saratoga, July 21, 1842).

Howard, Miss H. W. (Saratoga, July 21, 1842).

Howard, A. W. (Boston, Nov. 9, 1841).

Howard, Daniel D., New York (Saratoga, July 22, 1843).

Howe, Wm. A. (Boston, April 7, 1842).

Howe, Mrs. Eliz., Brookline (Brookline, April 4, 1841).

Howland, Edgar, New York (Saratoga, July 25, 1844).

Howland, Mrs. G. S., sister of Mrs. R. Williams (New York, June 8, 1840).

Howland, Julia L. (her daughter) (New York, June 8, 1840).

Howland, S. S., 12, Washington Square, New York (Saratoga, Aug. 10, 1840).

Howland, G. G., 12, Washington Square, New York (Saratoga, Aug. 10, 1840).

Howland, Miss Rebecca, New York (Saratoga, Aug. 26, 1843).

Howland, Miss Joanna, New York (Saratoga, Aug. 26, 1843).

Hoyt, G., of New York (Saratoga, Sept. 5, 1844).

Hubard, Edmund W., M.C., Buckingham (July 8, 1841).

Hubbard, Wm. H., of New York (Saratoga, July 3, 1843).

Hubbard, Reuben, Rector of St. John's, Stillwater, New York (Saratoga, June 29, 1843).

Hubbard, Henry (Charlestown, Feb. 22, 1841).

Hubbard, A. H., Norwich, Ct. (Boston, May 7, 1842).

Hubbard, Thos. A., son of above (Boston, May 27, 1842).

Hubbard, Saml. R., New York (Saratoga, Aug. 7, 1844).

Hudson, Chas., M.C., Worcester, Mass. (Aug. 7, 1843).

Huertas, Florencia, Cuba (Phila., Jan. 27, 1842).

Huger, Benjn., Capt., Ord. Corps (Washington, Feb. 2, 1841).

Huger (1764–1855), Francis, Lieut. (Jan. 27, 1841).

Huggins, H. F. (Washington, April 13, 1841).

Hughes (1825–1868), Ball, sculptor from London, doing bust of Edouart (Boston, Nov. 2, 1842).

Hughes, Mrs. Ball (Boston, Nov. 2, 1842).

Hughes, Miss Augusta (Boston, Nov. 2, 1842).

Hughes, Georgina (Boston, Nov. 2, 1842).

Hughes, Hon. Dr. John, Bishop of Basileopolis in Asia Minor, Coajutor and Admins. of the Bishops of New York (Oct. 22, 1840).

Hughes, Wm. D., Inspector of Custom (New York, July 10, 1839).

Hulin, R. D., clerk of Union Hall (Saratoga, Sept. 4, 1844).

Hull, Laurence, M.D., sen., of Angelica, from Senate District (New York, Oct. 25, 1839).

Hull, Geo., Lieut.-Gov. of Mass. (Boston, May 27, 1842).

Hull, Isaac, Commodore, U.S.N. (Saratoga, July 27, 1842).

Hull, Parker L., Counsel at Law (Saratoga, July 27, 1842).

Humbert, Francis (Aug. 22, 1839).

Humphrey, Miss Frances (New Orleans, March 1, 1844).

Humphrey, Miss Mary (New Orleans, March 1, 1844).

Humphrey, Henry B., of Boston (Saratoga, July 20, 1844).

Humphries, Ella, of New Orleans (1844).

Hunt, H. T., 2nd Lieut., U.S.A. (Saratoga, July 29, 1843).

Hunt, Wm., Counsel at Law, of Lockport, New York (Boston, June 25, 1842).

Hunt, Wm., English, arrived Aug. 17, 1835 (Jan. 31, 1840).

Hunt, Mrs. John (Saratoga, Aug. 18, 1843).

Hunt, Miss Jane M. (Saratoga, July 21, 1842).

Hunt, John (Saratoga, July 21, 1842).

Hunt, Wm. M. (Saratoga, April 20, 1842).

Hunt, Henry L. (Saratoga, April 15, 1843).

Hunt, R. M. (Saratoga, Aug. 15, 1843).

Hunt, John, of Mobile (Saratoga Springs, Aug. 17, 1840).

Hunter, S. Hillen (Saratoga, Aug. 16, 1844).

Hunter, Gen. Alex. (2 ports.) (Washington, April 27, 1841).

Hunter, Mrs. Daniel.

Hunter, Mrs. Sarah Ann (Washington, April 27, 1841).

Hunter, Mrs. Louisa (Phila., Oct. 20, 1841).

Hunter, Miss Jane (Washington, April 30, 1841).

Hunter, Mary (Washington, April 30, 1841).

Hunter, Dr. Lewis B., surgeon, U.S.N. (Phila., Jan. 3, 1842).

Huntingdon, Wolcott, Norwich, Ct. (Saratoga, July 16, 1843).

Huntingdon, Mrs. Wolcott, Norwich, Ct. (Saratoga, July 16, 1843).

Huntingdon, J. W., sen., Norwich, Ct. (Feb. 25, 1841).

Huntingdon, Wm., of New York (Saratoga, Aug. 6, 1841).

Hurlbut, E. P., Counsel at Law, 73, Adam Street (Sept. 9, 1839).

Huskins, Rev. Saml. N., Epis. Williamsburgh L.I. (Saratoga, Aug. 26, 1840).

Hussey, Geo. (New York, March 15, 1840).

Hutchings, Eusibus (Louisville, Kentucky, May 12, 1844).

Hutchins, F., 120, Chatham Street (New York, Dec. 19, 1839).

Hutchins, Mrs. F. (already described as Mrs. Jane Beebe. See Beebe, not 2 figures) (New York, Dec. 19, 1839).

Hutchins, Augustus (New York, Dec. 19, 1839).

Hutchins, Alex. (New York, Dec. 19, 1839).

Hutchinson, Thos. H., Charlestown, South Carolina (Sept. 20, 1839).

Hutton, J. Francis, 20, Wall Street (Aug. 5).

Hyde, Edwd. G. (New Orleans, Feb. 1, 1844).

Ingersoll, Edwd. (Phila., Oct. 24, 1842).

Ingersoll, Mrs. Edwd. (Phila., Oct. 24, 1842).

Ingersoll, Adèle (Phila., Oct. 24, 1842).

Ingersoll, Fanny (Phila., Oct. 24, 1842).

Ingle, Susan C. (Washington, March 15, 1841).

Ingle, Joseph (Washington, March 16, 1841).

Ingraham, Prof. J. W. (Natchez, June 17, 1841).

Ingraham, Edwd., Counsel at Law (Phila., Sept. 29, 1842).

Ingraham, Judge D. P. (New York, Aug. 12, 1841).

Inman, H., 17, White Street, portrait painter (New York, Oct. 1, 1840).

Inman, Miss Mary L. (New York, Oct. 1, 1840).

Innes, Mrs. Anne, of New York (Saratoga, Aug. 12, 1842).

Ireland, Geo. (New York, Oct. 15, 1840).

Irons, J. F., 1st Lieut., U.S.A. (Boston, Feb. 5, 1842).

Irvin, Richd., of New York (Saratoga, Sept. 5, 1843).

Irvin, Mrs. Richd., of New York (Saratoga, Sept. 5, 1843).

Irvin, Wm., of New York (Saratoga, Sept. 5, 1843).

Irvin, Miss Mary, of New York (Saratoga, Sept. 5, 1843).

Irvin, Miss Susan Williams, of New York (Saratoga, Sept. 5, 1843).

Irving, Sanders (New York City, June 12, 1842).

Irwin, W. W., Rep. Penna (March 2, 1841).

Irwin, Mrs. W. W. (March 2, 1841).

Isnard, Master (Boston, April 22, 1842).

Isnard, Mons. Max, French Consul (Boston, April 22, 1842).

Iverson, Mrs., wife of Judge T. (Washington, March 31, 1841).

Ives, Geo. K., of Boston (Saratoga, June 28, 1843).

Ives, Mrs. H. B., of Providence (Saratoga, June 28, 1843).

Ives, R. H. (Boston, Dec. 22, 1841).

Ives, Mrs. Anne A., Providence, R.I. (Saratoga, July 10, 1843).

Jack, Col. C. J., Counsel at Law (Phila., Sept. 21, 1842).

Jackson, Rev. Henry, Pastor of first Baptist Church (Saratoga Springs, July 27, 1840).

Jackson, Mrs. Henry, New Bedford (Saratoga Springs, July 27, 1840).

Jackson, Capt. Isaac, of Boston (New Orleans, Feb. 8, 1844).

Jackson, Rev. W. G., Eastville, Va. (Saratoga Springs, Aug. 17, 1841).

Jackson, Miss Emily, New York.

Jacob, Isaac (New Orleans, March 20, 1844).

Jacobs, Ralph (New Orleans, March 20, 1844).

Jacobs, Elisha (Boston, Dec. 10, 1841).

Jacobs, Mrs., née Coffin (Boston, Dec. 10, 1841).

Jacobs, Sarah Ann (Boston, Dec. 10, 1841).

Jacobs, Benjn. (Boston, Dec. 10, 1841).

Jacobus, Rev. Melanathon, first Presbyterian Church, Brooklyn (New York, Oct. 2, 1840).

James, J. W., of Boston (Saratoga, Aug. 23, 1843).

Jameson, Robt. (Alexandria, March 12, 1841).

Jannerett, James N., Charleston, South Carolina (Saratoga, Aug. 23, 1841).

Janson, Eugene (Phila., Oct. 25, 1842).

Jarvis, Leonard (Saratoga, Sept. 9, 1843).

Jarvis, Mrs. Leonard (Saratoga, Sept. 9, 1843).

Jay, Miss Anne, of New York (Oct. 13, 1842).

Jay, Peter Augustus (New York, Aug. 11, 1840).

Jay, John (New York, March 10, 1840).
Jay, Mrs. John (New York, March 10, 1840).
Jay, Miss Eliza (New York, March 10, 1840).
Jay, Miss Sarah Louisa, of New York (Saratoga, Aug. 11, 1840).
Jay, Wm., Counsel at Law, of New York (Saratoga, Aug. 11, 1840).
Jeffries, Dr. John, M.D. (description) (Boston, Dec. 20, 1841).
Jeffries, Mrs. John (Boston, Dec. 20, 1841).
Jeffries, John, jun. (Boston, June 15, 1842).
Jenifer, Daniel (Feb. 2, 1841).
Jenkins, Miss Agnes B., Pittsfield, Mass. (Saratoga, July 15, 1844).
Jenkins, Adam Hubley (Nov. 23, 1839).
Jenkins, J. Robt. (Baltimore, July 27, 1844).
Jenkins, Thornton A., Lieut., U.S.N. (Baltimore, Dec. 10, 1840).
Jenkins, Mrs. Thornton A. (Baltimore, Dec. 10, 1840).
Jewitt, Isaac F. (New York, Feb. 26, 1840).
Jocelyn, Benjn. (New York, Nov. 8, 1839).
Jocelyn, Titus (New York, Nov. 8, 1839).
Johnson, C., M.C. (Tennessee, June 21, 1841).
Johnson, Wm. Fell (Baltimore, Dec. 20, 1840).
Johnson, H. A., Boston (Saratoga, July 21, 1844).
Johnson, Chas. T., obt. Feb., 1843 (Sept. 21, 1839).
Johnson, Mrs. Chas. T. (Sept. 21, 1839).
Johnson, Theo. T. (New York, Feb. 24, 1840).
Johnson, Miss Louisa, sister of Mrs. Colt (New York, Feb. 24, 1840).
Johnson, Rev. Saml. R., brother of Dr. J., Lafayette, Indiana (New York, May, 1, 1840).
Johnson, Chas., Norwich, Ct. (Saratoga, July 25, 1843).
Johnson, Chas. Coit, Norwich, Ct. (Saratoga, July 25, 1843).
Johnson, Oliver, asst.-editor *New York Tribune* (Phila., Dec. 11, 1844).
Johnson, E., Mass. (Saratoga, July 24, 1844).
Johnson, Frank, leader of Brass Band, Phila., of 128th Regt. (Saratoga, Aug. 13, 1840).
Johnson, Mrs. Helen, obt. 1843 (Saratoga, Aug. 13, 1842).
Johnston, Buckingham (Phila., Oct. 24, 1842).
Johnston, A. R., 1st Dragoon Guards (Boston, Nov. 3, 1841).
Jones, Thos., Ap. Commodore, U.S.N. (April 19, 1841).
Jones, M. P., son of above (April 19, 1841).
Jones, S. G., U.S.A. (West Point, Aug. 24, 1839).
Jones, Wm. Page, U.S. Lieut., Artillery (April 10, 1841).
Jones, Roger, Brig., U.S.A. (Washington, March 20, 1841).
Jones, Adelaide (New York, Nov. 1, 1843).
Jones, Mrs. Mary (Charleston, Oct. 13, 1843).
Jones, Beach, Pastor of Presbyterian Church (Bridgetown, Oct. 13, 1843).
Jones, Major H. (Annapolis, Oct. 24, 1842).
Jones, Miss M. A., sister of Mrs. Dunham.
Jones, H. B., Congress Hall (Saratoga, July 16, 1842).
Jones, Paul T. (Phila., Oct. 12, 1842).
Jones, Miss T. Floyd, L.I. (April 15, 1840).
Jones, Nathanl., M.C., New York (Warwick, March 5, 1841).
Jordan, W. H. S. (Boston, Nov. 16, 1841).

Josephs, A. K., Counsel at Law (New Orleans, March 20, 1844).
Joy, John B. (Boston, Nov. 30, 1841).
Joy, Mrs. John B. *See* Webster (Boston, Nov. 30, 1841).
Joy, Joseph (Boston, Nov. 30, 1841).
Joyce, Saml. (New York, July 25, 1843).
Judah, S. W. (New York, July 25, 1843).
Judah, Mrs. J. W. M., daughter of Hayman Levi, of New York (Saratoga, Aug. 3, 1844).

Kain, Wm. (Dec. 4).
Karney, Robt. W., Atty. and Counsel at Law, Notary Public, Nassau Street (Aug. 17, 1839).
Kassam, Miss Francis (Saratoga, July 16, 1841).
Kay, Mrs. Mary, of Lafayette (New Albany, Jan. 27, 1844).
Kean, Miss Cristine (New York, April 21, 1840).
Kearney, P., Lieut., jun., 1st Dragoons, U.S.A. (May 18, 1841).
Kearney, P., jun., Aide to Gen.-in-Chief (Saratoga, Sept. 9, 1843).
Keel, R. S., New York (Saratoga, Aug. 9, 1844).
Keese, Hon. Oliver, Judge, of Keesse Villa, Essex City, New York (Saratoga, Aug. 3, 1842).
Kellogg, Francis L. (Troy, Sept. 28, 1841).
Kellogg, Julia A. (Troy, Sept. 28, 1841).
Kellogg, Chas. Augustus, New York (Troy, Oct. 2, 1841).
Kellogg, Mrs. Warren, New York (Troy, Sept. 28, 1841).
Kellogg, Henry L., New York (Troy, Sept. 13, 1841).
Kellogg, James Pain, New York (Troy, Oct. 2, 1841).
Kemeys, Wm. (Nov. 27, 1839).
Kempshall, Thos., M.C., New York, Rochester (Washington, March 8, 1841).
Kempton, Geo., Robertsville, South Carolina (Nov. 4, 1839).
Kandall, W. W. (New Orleans, March 11, 1844).
Kendell, John Irwin (New Orleans, March 11, 1844).
Kennedy, Isaac, Tioga Co., Spencer (Saratoga, July 20, 1844).
Kennedy, John, of Mobile, Alabama (Aug. 3, 1839).
Kennedy, Mrs. John. *See* Cummings (Aug. 3, 1839).
Kent, James, Chancellor, New York, with Judge Story, Supreme Court (New York, Oct. 20, 1840).
Kernson, Chas., Charleston, South Carolina (Saratoga, July 22, 1844).
Kerr, Geo. W., Newborough (New York, Aug. 10, 1839).
Keyser, P., Guardian of Almshouses (Phila., May 22, 1843).
Kidder, Frederic I., surgeon, Claremont, New Hampshire (Boston, Feb. 2, 1842).
Kidder, J. G., of Boston (Saratoga, Aug. 15, 1842).
Kielchen, P. A., Russian Consul (Boston, April 22, 1842).
Kilty, A. H., Lieut., U.S.N. (Boston, Feb. 13, 1842).
Kimball, Moses, Boston Museum (Boston, June 25, 1842).
Kimball, Mrs. Elijah, New York (Saratoga, Aug. 15, 1843).
Kimball, Abraham, Salem, Mass. (Saratoga, July 26, 1843).
Kindall, H., Providence, O.S. (Saratoga, Aug. 7, 1843).
King, Henry G., St. Louis, Mass.
King, John Gableson (Boston, Jan. 24, 1842).
King, Miss Caroline H. (Boston, Jan. 24, 1842).

King, Thos. Butler, M.C., Waynesville, Georgia (Washington, Feb. 2, 1841).
King, Mrs. Sarah (2 ports.) (Phila., Nov. 11, 1842).
King, Francis, of Phila. (Saratoga Springs, Aug. 10, 1843).
King, D. Rooney (2 ports.) (Germanstown, July 5, 1844).
Kingsbury, C. V., Lieut. (Troy, Sept. 24, 1841).
Kinsman, Col. John D., Portland, Maine (Washington, March 20, 1841).
Kitchum, Abbey (New Orleans, Jan. 10, 1844).
Kitchum, Louisa (New Orleans, Jan. 10, 1844).
Kneass, Napoleon Bonaparte, New Orleans (New Orleans, Oct. 7, 1839).
Kneeland, Mrs. Eve C., of New York (Saratoga, Sept. 9, 1843).
Kneeland, Saml., jun. (Boston, May 30, 1842).
Kneeland, H., sculptor (New York, Nov. 11, 1843).
Knight, Nehemiah R. (Providence, Feb. 24, 1841).
Knight, Geo. (Phila., Nov. 1, 1842).
Knight, John Francis (Phila., Nov. 1, 1842).
Knox, Hugh, of New York (Troy, Sept. 14, 1841).
Knox, Dr. E. R., Carlisle, Pa. (Aug. 24, 1840).
Konig, Mr., Hanover (Baltimore, Jan. 9, 1841).
Konig, Mrs., Hanover (Baltimore, Jan. 9, 1841).
Krebs, John N. (Baltimore, Dec. 3, 1841).
Krebs, James Wesley (Baltimore, Oct. 16, 1839).
Kruttschnitt, J., Germany (New Orleans, March 21, 1844).
Kuhn, Geo. H. (Boston, June 15, 1842).
Kursheeot, Edwd. Israel (New Orleans, March 2, 1844).
Kyle, Mrs. John A. (Oct. 9, 1839).
Kyle, Margaret (Phila., March 10, 1843).
Kyle, Alex., sen., Prof. of Flute (April 24, 1839).
Kyle, John A., jun., Paymaster Officer, U.S.A. (Sept. 10, 1839).
Kyle, John A., sen., Prof. of Flute (Oct. 9, 1839).

Laburee, Rev. Benjn. (New York, May 8, 1840).
Lacombe, Mr. Emile Henry (New York, Jan. 20, 1840).
Lacombe, Mrs. Emile Henry (New York, Jan. 20, 1840).
La Costa, Henry (New York, Aug. 22, 1839).
Laidey, T. T. S., Ordn., U.S.A. (Saratoga, Sept. 17, 1843).
Lamb, Widow Rosanna, aged 81 years (Boston, Jan. 8, 1842).
Lamb, Thos. (Boston, Jan. 17, 1842).
Lamb, Mrs. Thos., sister of Frank E. Eliot. *See* Eliot (Boston, Jan. 17, 1842).
Lamb, Emily G. (Boston, Jan. 17, 1842).
Lamb, Margy. Eliot (Boston, Jan. 17, 1842).
Lamb, Wm. Eliot (Boston, Jan. 17, 1842).
Lamb, Chas. Duncan (Boston, Jan. 17, 1842).
Lamb, Anthony, late Magistrate of New York, Jay Street (Saratoga, Aug. 7, 1840).
Lamb, Miss Sarah (Saratoga, Aug. 7, 1840).
Lamb, Mrs. Anthony (Saratoga, Aug. 7, 1840).
Lambers, Mons. Leger, Riviere de Loup Dist. Des Trois Rivieres (Saratoga, Aug. 19, 1843).
Lambert, Rev. Thos. R., chaplain (2 ports.) (Saratoga, Aug. 7, 1841; Boston, June 7, 1842).
Lambers, Mme., Riviere de Loup Dist. Des Trois Rivieres (Saratoga, Aug. 19, 1843).
Lambert, W. G., jun. (New York, July, 1843).
Lamport, John T., City Atty. J. (Troy, Sept. 23, 1841).

Lanckenan, Richd. (New York, May 14, 1840).
Langdon, B. F., of Castletown, Va. (Saratoga Springs, Aug. 17, 1841).
Langtree, S. D. (Washington, Feb. 3, 1841).
Langworthy, Rev. Isaac P., Pastor of Congregational Church (Saratoga, Aug. 19, 1842).
Langworthy, Mrs. Isaac P., Chelsea, Mass. (Saratoga, Aug. 19, 1842).
Larcombe, Hivinar or Twinaz, Religious Instructor of East Penitentiary (Phila., March 6, 1843).
La Roche, Anna Mercier (Phila., Dec. 12, 1843).
La Roche, Percy Chas. (Phila., Dec. 12, 1843).
La Roche, Susan (Phila., Dec. 12, 1843).
La Roche, R., M.D., father of above (Phila., Dec. 12, 1843).
La Roche, Adele (Phila., Dec. 12, 1843).
Larrabee, Wm. F., and dog (2 ports.) (New York, March 11, 1840).
Latham, W. G. (New Orleans, Jan. 23, 1844).
Lathrop, J. H., Yonawanda (March 15, 1841).
Lathrop, J. Hallowell, Maine (March 19, 1841).
Latimer, Miss Juliet (Washington, April 28, 1841).
Latrobe, Benjn. H., civil engineer, Baltimore (Baltimore, Dec. 14, 1840).
Latting, J. Jordan, of New York (Saratoga, July 23, 1844).
Latting, Joseph, of New York, Saltingdown, L.I. (Saratoga, July 23, 1844).
Laurence, Robt. (Washington, April 26, 1841).
Laurenson, F. B., Litterlouna (Baltimore, Nov. 25, 1840).
Laurie, Mrs., wife of Rev. James L. (Washington, March 26, 1841).
Lavelier, Octavia.
Law, Edwd. (Phila., Dec. 6, 1842).
Lawler, Levi M., Alabama (June 26, 1841).
Lawrence, Abbot, M.C. (Boston, March 11, 1842).
Lawrence, Mrs. (Boston, Feb. 18, 1842).
Lawrence, James (Boston, Feb. 18, 1842).
Lawrence, Miss Annie B. (Boston, Feb. 18, 1842).
Lawrence, Abbott, jun. (Boston, Feb. 18, 1842).
Lawrence, Kitty B. (Boston, Feb. 18, 1842).
Lawrence, T. B. (Boston, Feb. 18, 1842).
Lawrence, Wm., Boston (Saratoga, July 19, 1844).
Lawrence, Amos, philanthropist (Boston, March 22, 1842).
Lawrence, R. M., son of above (Boston, March 21, 1842).
Lawrence, C. Wm. (Sept. 28, 1839).
Lawrence, Richd. M., 351, Broadway (Dec. 21, 1839).
Lawrence, Miss Adrian (Dec. 21, 1839).
Lawrence, Joseph, M.C., Pa. (June 26, 1841).
Lawson, Thos., Surg.-Gen., U.S.A. (June 22, 1841).
Lawton, Joseph G. (Pottsville, Jan. 30, 1843).
Lazarus, Mrs. Mary, late Miss Moss (Louisville, Kentucky, May 13, 1844).
Lazarus, Henry (2 ports.) (Louisville, Kentucky, May 13, 1844).
Leavitt, Joshua, 146, Nassau Street (Jan. 24, 1840).
Lee, Cassius F., clerk of U.S. Court, Alexandria, D.C. (Saratoga, Aug. 22, 1843).
Lee, John R., Buffalo (Saratoga, Aug. 23, 1843).
Lear, Louisa L. (Washington, March 15, 1841).
Lecombe, A. (Saratoga, July 26, 1844).
Le Conte, Dr. John, of Georgia (Saratoga Springs, Aug. 6, 1841).
Le Conte, Mrs. John, of Georgia (Saratoga Springs, Aug. 6, 1841).
Lee, John, M.C. (New Orleans, March 2, 1841).

Lee, Rev. Alfred, Rockdall, Pa. (Saratoga Springs, Aug. 6, 1840).
Lee, Mrs. Alfred, Rockdall, Pa. (Saratoga Springs, Aug. 6, 1840).
Lee, Ann, slave, born at Alexandria, Va.
Lee, Dr. Chas. A., M.D. (New York, Dec. 20, 1839).
Lee, Capt. James, jun., aide-de-camp, of 6th Brigade, New York States Artillery (2 ports.) (Nov. 20, 1840).
Leet, Isaac, M.C., Pa. (Washington, Feb. 22, 1841).
Lefevre, Rev. C. F. (New York, March 3, 1840).
Lefevre, Mrs. (New York, March 3, 1840).
Lefevre, Miss Ellen (New York, March 3, 1840).
Lefevre, Williams (New York, March 3, 1840).
Lefevre, G. (New York, March 3, 1840).
Leftwich, Col. Aug. (Lynchburg, March 7, 1844).
Leiper, Geo. G. (Baltimore, Jan. 26, 1841).
Lekain, Mrs. J., aged 85 years, mother of Saml. Appleton, died 1843 (Boston, Jan. 25, 1842).
Lequer, N., of Brooklyn, L.I. (Saratoga, July 23, 1842).
Leroy, Miss Jane (Nov. 23, 1839).
Lester, Gerard C. (Aug. 2, 1839).
Levering, Fredk. A. (Baltimore, Dec. 9, 1840).
Levy, Hayman, Mayor of Camden, South Carolina. See Judah (Aug. 3, 1844).
Levy, Capt. Uriah S., U.S.N. (Saratoga Springs, Aug. 20, 1842).
Lewis, Mr. Chas. H. (Louisville, Kentucky, May 14, 1844).
Lewis, Mrs. Chas. H. (Louisville, Kentucky, May 14, 1844).
Lewis, Benjn. Francklin (baby) Louisville, Kentucky, May 14, 1844).
Lewis, S. S., of Boston, agent for steamers (Saratoga, July 26, 1845).
Lewis, Chas. D., Life Guards, New York Militia Vol. (New York, Oct. 20, 1840).
Lewis, —, M.D. (March 14, 1843).
Lewis, Mr. Chas. A., New London, Ct. (Saratoga, Aug. 10, 1844).
Lewis, Dixon H., M.C. (Alabama, March 5, 1841).
Lewis, Mrs. Chas. A., New London, Ct. (Saratoga, Aug. 10, 1844).
Lex, C. (Phila., Oct. 19, 1843).
Lincoln, Albert L. (Boston, June 18, 1842).
Linder, G., from London (Oct. 20, 1839).
Lindsay, Oliver B. (Phila., Jan. 16, 1843).
Lindsay, G. F., Capt., Asst.-Quartermaster, U.S.N. of Marines (Boston, Feb. 11, 1842).
Lindsay, Mrs. Mary, wife of G. F. (Phila., Dec. 16, 1842).
Lindsley, C. H., Troy Whig Office (Sept. 16, 1841).
Litchtenhein, S. A., jun., New York (Saratoga, July 20, 1844).
Little, W. C., of Albany (Saratoga Springs, Aug. 8, 1840).
Little, J., of New York (Saratoga, July 19, 1844).
Little, Mark, Albany (Aug. 18, 1841).
Livingston, Mrs. Mortimer (Saratoga, Aug. 20, 1841).
Livingston, Miss Angelica (Saratoga, Aug. 20, 1841).
Livingston, Miss Jerrulline (Saratoga, Aug. 20, 1841).
Livingston, Miss Sylvia (Saratoga, Aug. 20, 1841).
Livermore, Mrs. and Mr. (New York, Aug. 11, 1842).
Livingston, Mr. A. H., Boston (New York, April 27, 1840).

Livingston, Mrs. A. H., formerly Miss Greene (New York, April 27, 1840).
Livingstone, Mrs. Mortimer (New York, July 28, 1840).
Loan, A. (New Orleans, Feb. 2, 1844).
Lockwood, Roe, 411, Broadway (Edouart's landlord) (New York, Feb. 20, 1840).
Lockwood, John A., M.D., U.S.N. (Phila., Oct. 4, 1842).
Logan, Archibald, settled in Lexington in 1785, born Aug. 5, 1769 (May 24, 1844).
Logan, A. D., of New York, Counsel at Law (New York, Oct. 26, 1840).
Long, E. B. (Baltimore, Dec. 9, 1840).
Longer, Mlle. Nanette (New Orleans, March 23, 1844).
Longer, Angèle (New Orleans, March 23, 1844).
Longfellow (1807–1882), H. F. W., of Cambridge, poet (Boston, Dec. 7, 1841).
Lord, Willis, seventh Presbyterian Church (Phila., Sept. 2, 1842).
Lord, Ivory, of Maine (Boston, Nov. 9, 1841).
Loring, Mr., of Boston (Saratoga, Aug. 15, 1840).
Loring, Mrs. (Saratoga Springs, Aug. 15, 1840).
Lorillard, Peter (2 ports.). See Reynolds and Wolfe (Saratoga, Aug. 25, 1840; July 17, 1844).
Loring, Anna (Boston, Jan. 24, 1842).
Loring, Mrs. Relief (Boston, Jan. 21, 1842).
Loring, Ellis Gray, Counsel at Law, Washington, son of Mrs. R. L. (Boston, Jan. 24, 1842).
Loring, Geo. B. (Boston, Dec. 1, 1841).
Lothrop, Eliza L. (Boston, Nov. 20, 1842).
Lourret, Andrew, Prof. at Conservatoire (Phila., March 21, 1843).
Lovett, Capt. Fredk. M., of Packet Ship (Boston, June 13, 1842).
Love, Mrs. W. E. (Boston, March 9, 1842).
Love, Wm. E., jun. (Boston, April, 1842).
Love, Wm. E., sen., polyphonist (New York, Aug. 9, 1839).
Lovering, Joseph S. (Phila., Oct. 5, 1842).
Lovett, Fredk. W., Boston (New Orleans, Feb. 8, 1840).
Low, Capt. Moses A. (July 18, 1840).
Lowell, Mrs. F. C. (Boston, Nov. 24, 1841).
Lowell, Miss Georgia (Boston, Nov. 24, 1841).
Lowell, Miss Mary (Boston, Nov. 24, 1841).
Lowell (1819–1891), J. R. (Boston, Nov. 30, 1842).
Lowrey, Chas. J. (Troy, Oct. 5, 1841).
Lowry, Robt. H. (Dec. 2, 1840).
Luard, Peter Francis (Leamington, Jan. 2, 1838).
Lucas, Chas. Z. (Baltimore, Dec. 25, 1840).
Ludlow, Mrs. Livingstone (Phila., July 30, 1844).
Ludlow, J. Livingstone (Phila., July 30, 1844).
Ludlow, Mrs. E. G., bust only (New York, Aug. 10, 1839).
Ludlow, Mary Constance (Aug. 10, 1839).
Ludlow, Miss Susan (Aug. 10, 1839).
Ludlow, Wm. H. (Aug. 10, 1839).
Luke, T. N., Liute Falls, Herk Co., New York (Saratoga, Aug. 20, 1841).
Lurty, Maria (Saratoga, July 12, 1841).
Lyman, Mr. Lewis (Troy, Oct. 1, 1841).
Lyman, Mrs. Lewis. See Willard (Troy, Oct. 1 1841).
Lyman, Miss M. B., governess to Mrs. T. G. Cary (Boston, Feb. 18, 1842).

Lyman, John C., of Boston (Saratoga, July 25, 1843).
Lyman, Mrs. Gen. John.
Lyman, Miss Julia.
Lyman, C. (Phila., Feb. 9, 1843).
Lynch, D., Lieut., U.S.N. (Saratoga Springs, July 9, 1844).
Lynch, Mrs. D. *See* Mrs. H. M. Campbell (Saratoga Springs, July 9, 1844).
Lyons, Col. N. A. (Feb. 19, 1844).

Mabbe, Widow Ann, of Tony Town, aged 60 years, Westchester (New York, Feb. 22, 1840).
Mabee, Thos. B. (New York, Feb. 22, 1840).
Mabee, Mrs. Thos. B. (New York, Feb. 22, 1840).
Mackay, Capt. J. (Saratoga, Aug. 26, 1844).
Mackenzie, Thos. G. (Saratoga, Aug. 14, 1843).
Mackie, John S. (March 9, 1840).
McKay (or McKie), Alex. L., son of Thos. McKie, agent of the Snake Indian Fur Co., fought Vancouver, New York (New York, Oct. 6, 1839).
Macomb, Mrs., wife of Maj.-Gen. (Sept. 5, 1840).
Macomb, Miss Sarah (Phila., March 24, 1843).
Macomb (1820–1872), W. H., U.S.N., son of Maj.-Gen. (Washington, March 10, 1841).
Macomb, Mrs. J. N., daughter of Maj.-Gen. (Phila., March 24, 1843).
Macomb, J. N., Lieut., U.S.A. (Phila., March 23, 1843).
Macomb, Maj.-Gen. Alex., Comm.-in-Chief, U.S.A. *See* Miller.
Macrae, Capt. N. C., 3rd Infantry (April 24, 1841).
Macrae, Capt., same as above (in uniform).
Macrae, Mrs. N. C. (Washington).
Macrae, Miss E., sister of Capt. M. (Washington, April 30, 1841).
Macrae, A. (Va., March 13, 1841).
Maeder, J. G., Prof of Music, Boston (Saratoga, Aug. 16, 1844).
Magher, John H., Counsel at Law (Sept. 10, 1839).
Magruder, Geo. A., Lieut., U.S.N. (Phila., Oct. 27, 1842).
Magruder, Mrs. M. M. (Phila., Oct. 27, 1842).
Magruder, J. Bankhead, 1st Lieut., U.S.A. (Boston, Feb. 5, 1843).
Mallory, Frs., M.C. (Va., July 8, 1841).
Man, Saml. F., Cumberland, R.I. (2 ports.), one standing, one sitting (Saratoga, Aug. 16, 1843).
Mandeville, Rev. Henry, Pastor of Utica (Saratoga Springs, Aug. 6, 1840).
Mangum, Willies P., Sen. Red, Mount Orange (North Carolina, Feb. 4, 1841).
Manice, D. F., of New York (Saratoga, Aug. 17, 1843).
Mankin, Henry (Baltimore, Nov. 24, 1840).
Manley, Dr. James R., M.D. (Aug. 20, 1839).
Manley, Dr. James, jun. (Nov. 5, 1839).
Manley, Miss Petronella P. (Brooklyn, Oct. 25, 1839).
Manning, Mr. W. L., Fort Carrington, Franklin Co. (Saratoga, Sept. 9, 1844).
Manning, Mrs. W. L. (Saratoga, Sept. 9, 1844).
Manwaring, Prof. Giles, jun., Principal of Schenectady Lyceum (Saratoga, Aug. 3, 1841).
Mapes, Miss Sophia Gurthride (New York, Aug. 20, 1839).
Mapes, Miss Louisa (New York, Aug. 20, 1839).
Mapes, Master Chas. (New York, Aug. 20, 1839).

Mapes, Col. James (2 ports.) (New York, July 29, 1839; Aug. 20, 1839).
Mapes, Mrs. James (New York, Aug. 20, 1839).
Mapes, Miss Mary Eliz. (New York, Aug. 20, 1839).
Mapes, Chas., Major (New York, Aug. 18, 1839).
Marbury, John, Georgetown, D.C. (May 8, 1841).
Marbury, Francis F., Atty. and Counsel at Law, 32, Warren Street (Oct. 3, 1839).
Marcy (1786–1857), W. L., ex-Gov. of State of New York (2 ports.), second Saratoga, Sec. of War and Sec. of State (Sept. 28, 1839).
Marras, Signor Constantino (Troy, Sept. 15, 1841).
Marras, Signora Constantino (Troy, Sept. 15, 1841).
Marriates, N. K., (2 ports.) (Washington, April 1, 1841).
Marsh, Rev. J., Vice-Pres. of Temperance, of Brooklyn, New York (Saratoga, Aug. 3, 1842).
Marshall, A. Ashton. *See* Alexander (Dec. 18, —).
Massias, A. A., Major, Staff, U.S.A. (New Orleans, Feb. 4, 1841).
Marston, Mrs. Eliz. (Phila., May 3, 1843).
Marston, John (Phila., May 3, 1843).
Marther, Chas. A., of Troy (Saratoga, Aug. 29, 1840).
Martinez, H. T. (Washington, March 8, 1841).
Martin, Edwd., New Brighton, Staten Island (Aug. 28, 1839).
Martin, John L. (Jan. 23, 1841).
Martin, Geo. W. (New Orleans, March 11, 1844).
Martins, Señor Marcos, A. R., Brazil Para. (Troy, Sept. 2, 1841).
Marston, Mathew Randall (Phila., May 3, 1843).
Marston, John, Commander (Phila., May 3, 1843).
Mason, John (Boston, Nov. 6, 1841).
Mason, Mrs. Isabella (Boston, Nov. 6, 1841).
Mason, Arthur (Boston, Nov. 6, 1841).
Mason, Miss Isabella (Boston, Nov. 6, 1841).
Mason, Alice, and cat (Boston, Nov. 6, 1841).
Mason, Henry (March 11, 1840).
Mason, L., Prof. of Music (Boston, Jan. 14, 1842).
Mason, Robt. M. (New York, Nov. 22, 1839).
Massett, J. Schwartz, of London, England (Boston, Nov. 5, 1841).
Massol, Florian (Louisville, Kentucky, May 7, 1844).
Mauran, Joshia, Providence (Saratoga, Aug. 10, 1843).
Mauran, O. (New York, Feb. 6, 1840).
Mavrateno, N.
Maxey, Mr. T., late Minister to Belgium, Maryland (Saratoga, Sept. 7, 1843).
Maxey, Mrs. T. (Saratoga, Sept. 7, 1843).
Maxwell, Grace Catharine (Brooklyn, Sept. 20, 1843).
Maxwell, Georgianna M. (Brooklyn, Sept. 20, 1843).
Maxwell, Margaret (Brooklyn, Sept. 20, 1843).
Maxwell, Matilda (Brooklyn, Sept. 20, 1843).
Maxwell, W. H., Counsel at Law (Aug. 21, 1840).
Maxwell, J. B. B. (Feb. 20, 1841).
May, Saml. (Saratoga, July 16, 1844).
May, Mrs. Mary (Saratoga, July 16, 1844).
May, Miss Abby W. (Saratoga, July 16, 1844).
May, Miss Mary G. (Saratoga, July 16, 1844).
May, Jullian, of Washington (New Orleans, March 23, 1844).
Mayer, Christian, aged 77 years (Baltimore, Jan. 9, 1841).
Mayer, Mrs. Christian (Catharine) (Baltimore, Jan. 9, 1841).

Mayer, Beata (Baltimore, Nov. 25, 1841).
Mayer, Mr. Brantz. *See* Brantz (Baltimore, Nov. 25, 1841).
Mayer, Mary, Mrs. Brantz (Baltimore, Nov. 25, 1841).
Mayer, Catharine (Baltimore, Nov. 25, 1841).
Mayer, Chas. Fredk. (Baltimore, Nov. 25, 1841).
Mayer, Mr. Chas. F. (Baltimore, Nov. 30, 1841).
Mayer, Mrs. Chas. F. (Baltimore, Nov. 30, 1841).
Mayer, Henry Chas. (Baltimore, Nov. 30, 1840).
Mayer, Chas. F., jun. (Baltimore, Nov. 30, 1840).
Mayer, Frank (Baltimore, Nov. 30, 1840).
Mayer, Alfred (Baltimore, Nov. 30, 1840).
Mayer, Lewis (Baltimore, Nov. 30, 1840).
Mayers, W. H., Fort Smith, Arkansas (Saratoga, July 8, 1844).
Maynard, Moses Banckville, New York (April 14, 1841).
Maynard, Edwd. M.D., surgeon-dentist (Washington, March 11, 1841).
McBrid, Miss Mary, of New Orleans.
McCaleb, May, daughter of Judge McC. (New Orleans, March 14, 1843).
McCaleb, Corinna, daughter of Judge McC. (New Orleans, March 14, 1843).
McCall, Robt. (Phila., Aug. 14, 1843).
McCall, Henry, Louisiana (Saratoga, Aug. 12, 1843).
McCammon, Wm. J. (Phila., Dec. 3, 1840).
McClellan, Geo., M.D. (Phila., March 25, 1843).
McCloskey, Rev. P., St. John's Church, Chenectady (Saratoga, Aug. 16, 1843).
McCollum, T. Vandalia, midshipman on board *John Adams*, U.S.N. (Boston, March 2, 1842).
McCormick, Rev. Andrew, Episcopal Church (Washington, April 10, 1841).
McCoskey, Robt., New York (Saratoga, July 22, 1843).
McCready, Fredk., sen. (New York, Sept. 9, 1839).
McCready, Mrs. Fredk. (New York, Sept. 9, 1839).
McCready, Miss Mary (New York, Sept. 9, 1839).
McCready, Fredk., jun. (New York, Sept. 9, 1839).
McCready, Ann (New York, Sept. 9, 1839).
McCready, Master Mapes (New York, Sept. 9, 1839).
McCurdy, R. N., of 59, Clinton Place, New York (Saratoga, Aug. 16, 1844).
McCurdy, Mrs. Gertrude M. (Saratoga, Aug. 16, 1844).
McCurdy, T. F. (Saratoga, Aug. 16, 1844).
McCurdy, Miss G. M. (Saratoga, Aug. 16, 1844).
McCurdy, Sarah (Saratoga, Aug. 16, 1844).
McDonald, Wm. (New York, Nov. 22, 1844).
McDougall, J. Alex. (New York, Aug. 31, 1842)
McDougall, Mrs. Eliza (New York, Aug. 31, 1842).
McEvers, Miss Jane Emmest (Saratoga Springs, Aug. 23, 1844).
McEvers, Miss Mary Bache (New York, Dec. 19, 1839).
McGebee, M. (Woodville, Feb. 24, 1844).
McGebee, C. G. (Woodville, Feb. 24, 1844).
McIntyre, Rev. James, Presbyterian, Elkton, Maryland (Saratoga, Aug. 26, 1841).
McIntyre, Peter, New York (Saratoga, July 19, 1843).
McIntyre, A. (Saratoga, June 26, 1843).
McKay, Alex. L. (New York, Oct. 6, 1837).
McKay, Gordon, Pittsfield, Mass. (Saratoga, July 15, 1844).
McKean, Wm. W., Lieut., U.S.N. (Washington, March 9, 1841).

McKee, Wm. (Phila., July 20, 1843).
McKeon, John, late M.C., 512, Broom Street.
McLeod, D. C., M.D., U.S.N. (New Orleans, March 20, 1844).
McMichael, B., of Ireland (Saratoga, Aug. 16, 1844).
McMurray, John (New Orleans, Feb. 11, 1844).
McNair, Dr. Walter (Phila., Oct. 1, 1843).
McNeil, Chas. (New Orleans, April 5, 1844).
McThuson, Saml., Washington (New York, Feb. 18, 1840).
Mead, Mr. Saml. O., of Boston (Saratoga, July 20, 1844).
Mead, Mrs. Saml. O., of Boston (Saratoga, July 20, 1844).
Mead, Miss Maria L. W., Waterston (Saratoga, July 20, 1844).
Mead, Jane Maria (May 4, 1843).
Mead, Maria (May 4, 1843).
Meade, Mr. Geo. (Washington, Feb. 13, 1841).
Meade, Mrs. Geo. (Washington, Feb. 13, 1841).
Medcalf, Mr. Chas. M. (Baltimore, Dec. 30, 1840).
Mees, E. (New Orleans, Jan. 20, 1849).
Meigs, Dr. C. D. (Phila., Oct. 16, 1842).
Meigs, Emily (Phila., Oct. 16, 1842).
Meigs, H. O. (Phila., Oct. 16, 1842).
Meigs, M. C., U.S. Corps Engineers. *See* Rogers (Washington, Feb. 26, 1841).
Mercer, Anna Eliz. (New Orleans, Feb. 10, 1844).
Mercer, W. Newton (Feb. 20, 1844); also standing (Feb. 20, 1844).
Merck, Theo. (Nov. 25, 1839).
Meriwether, John, M.C., Eatonton (June 18, 1841).
Merrill, Rev. Abraham D., Methodist Episcopal Church (Boston, March 21, 1842).
Merrill, H. W., Lieut., U.S.A. (Saratoga, July 25, 1843).
Merritt, Widow Michael (Feb. 25, 1840).
Merry, Capt. Thos. H., sen. (New York, Aug. 25, 1839).
Merry, Mrs. Thos. H. (New York, Dec. 3, 1839).
Merry, Anna Tallos, daughter of Capt. Thos. Merry (New York, Dec. 3, 1839).
Merry, Charlotte, daughter of Capt. Thos. Merry (New York, Dec. 5, 1839).
Merry, Mary, daughter of Capt. Thos. Merry (New York, Dec. 5, 1839).
Merry, Thos. B., grandson of Capt. Thos. Merry (New York, Dec. 3, 1839).
Merryman, John (Dec. 19, —).
Mesier, Edwd. S., 9, Murray Street, New York (New York, March 15, 1840).
Mesier, Alice, aged 5 years and 4 months (New York, March 15, 1840).
Mesier, Josephine, aged 2 years and 5 months (New York, March 15, 1840).
Meyers, — (Louisville, May 11, 1844).
Michelina, Juan José, from Carucas, Venezuela (Oct. 20, 1839).
Mickle, R., Union Bank (Baltimore, Jan. 9, 1841).
Micon, W. C., Counsel at Law (New Orleans, Feb. 27, 1844).
Middleton, Thos. D., New York (Saratoga, July 24, 1844).
Miles, Chough R., Counsel at Law, Millbury, Mass. (Saratoga, Aug. 14, 1844).
Miles, Mrs. Chough R. (Saratoga, Aug. 14, 1844).
Miller, A. S., Capt., 1st Regt. Infantry (Saratoga, Aug. 21, 1841).

Miller, Major Morris L., aide-de-camp, U.S.A. (Washington, Feb. 19, 1841).

Miller, Mrs. Morris, daughter of Gen. Alfred Macomb (Washington, Feb. 19, 1841).

Miller, Edwd., civil engineer (Phila., Jan. 12, 1843).

Miller, John (Washington, March 3, 1841).

Miller, Benjn. F., P. Pal. Supt. (Potomac, Georgetown, Feb. 1, 1841).

Miller, Daniel H. (Aug. 29, 1839).

Miller, Chas. D. (Phila., Jan. 18, 1843).

Miller, Mrs. Chas., widow of Chas. (Boston, March 10, 1842).

Millikin, Miss Mary (Natchez, April 26, 1844).

Mills, Madison, surgeon, U.S.A. (Washington, Feb. 27, —).

Mills, Robt. (Washington, June 20, 1841).

Mills, Wm., of Glasgow (New Orleans, Jan. 28, 1844).

Mills, Wm. H. (Boston, Nov. 9, 1841).

Mills, James R., Boston (Saratoga, Aug. 16, 1844).

Milnor, Jos. K., American Ass. Co. (Aug. 19, 1839).

Miner, Mrs. (Columbus, Ohio, Dec. 7, 1841).

Miner, Wm. (Columbus, Ohio, Feb. 22, 1841).

Minerbi, Señor S., of Trieste (Saratoga, July 15, 1840).

Misson, Lewis M., surgeon, U.S.N. (April 15, 1841).

Missroon, John S., Lieut., U.S.N. (Saratoga, Aug. 2, 1842).

Mitchell, John K., Lieut., U.S.N. (Washington, March 1, 1841).

Moale, John C. (Baltimore, Nov. 23, 1840).

Moeller, J. B., Capt., U.S.N. (Saratoga, Aug. 10, 1844).

Moffat, Dr. W. B., of New York (Saratoga, Aug. 6, 1841).

Moffat, Mrs. W. B., of New York (Saratoga, Aug. 6, 1841).

Moffat, Mr. M., of New York (Saratoga Springs, 1841).

Moffat, Dr. John, of New York (Saratoga Springs, Aug., 1841).

Moffat, Miss Sophia Y., of New York (Saratoga Springs, Aug., 1841).

Moffat, Miss Maria, of New York (Saratoga Springs, Aug., 1841).

Moffat, Miss Caroline (New York, Aug. 20, 1841).

Monell, Claudius L. (Oct. 15, 1839).

Monroe, James, jun., 1st Lieut., 6th Regt. (Boston, April 22, 1842).

Montanya, James de la (Haverstraw, Rockland, Feb. 16, —).

Montendon, Mons. Julian (Washington, March 19, 1841).

Montgomery, Wm. H., U.S.N. (Phila., Oct. 29, 1842).

Montgomery, Miss Julia M. (April 15, 1841).

Moore, Wm. Henry (Oct. 30, 1839).

Moore, Rev. Josiah, of Duxbury, Mass. (Boston, May 26, 1842).

Moore, A. B., portrait painter (Troy, Oct. 8, 1841).

Moore, Henry E. (New Orleans, March 20, 1843).

Moore, Mrs. Cornelia S., of New Brunswick, New Jersey (New York, Oct. 30, 1839).

Moorhead, J., Commander, U.S.N. (Saratoga, Sept. 4, 1842).

Morell, Geo. W., jun. (Troy, Sept. 26, 1841).

Morell, Mrs. Geo. W., wife of Judge G. Morell, of Detroit, Mich. (Troy, Sept. 25, 1841).

Moreton, John L., 31, Broadway, Sec. of Acad. of Designs (Jan. 20, 1840).

Morgan, Mrs. Jane (New Orleans, March 23, 1844).

Morgan, Saml. (New Orleans, Jan. 21, 1844).

Morgan, H. Y., Aurora, New York (Boston, June 7, 1842).

Morgan, John C., Jersey City (Aug. 16, 1839).

Morgan, Joseph Wm., Jersey City, brother of above (Aug. 23, 1839).

Morgan, Evan J. (Dec. 8, 1840).

Morgan, Mrs. Benjn.

Morgan, Christopher, M.C., New York (New York, Feb. 20, —).

Morison, Hector (New York, April 14, 1839).

Morris, Calvery, of Ohio (Jan. 22, 1841).

Morris, Mrs. Richd. Valentine, widow of Commodore V. Morris, of New York (Sept. 1, 1840).

Morris, Robt. H., Recorder of City of New York (New York, March 11, 1840).

Morris, Mrs. Robt. H. (New York, March 11, 1840).

Morris, Mrs. Geo., 51, Greenwich Street (Nov. 18, 1839).

Morris, Emma (Nov. 18, 1839).

Morris, Robt., aged 50 years, chief financier in the Revolution, signed the Declaration of Independence.

Morris, Miss (Saratoga, Aug. 1, 1843).

Morison, Hector (2 ports.) (New York, March 3, 1843).

Moss, S. (New Orleans, Jan. 13; 1844).

Moss, Baby (New Orleans, Jan. 17, 1844).

Moss, Mrs. and her son (New Orleans, Jan. 17, 1844).

Moss, Ernest (New Orleans, Jan. 17, 1844).

Moss, Saml., jun. (New Orleans, Jan. 10, 1844).

Moss, Saml., jun. (New Orleans, Feb. 10, 1843).

Moss, James, jun. (New Orleans, March 19, 1844).

Mott, James (Baltimore, Dec. 8, 1840).

Mott, Master James (Baltimore, Dec. 8, 1840).

Mott, R. W., Manchasset, L. F. (Sept. 27, 1839).

Mulligan, John W., jun., New York (Saratoga, Aug. 25, 1843).

Mummy, A. J. (New Orleans, April 2, 1844).

Munger, Widow Nancy (Saratoga, April 15, 1840).

Munger, Nancy (Saratoga Springs, Aug., 1840).

Munger, H. F. (Saratoga, Aug., 1840).

Munger, Richd. (Aug., 1840).

Murphy, Miss Ellen, of Dublin, Ireland, married Saml. Joyce, Dec., 1841. See Beaujeau (July 20, 1839).

Murphy, Eliz. E. (Phila., Oct. 5, 1843).

Murphy, Thos. (Baltimore, Dec. 10, 1840).

Murray, John R. (March 17, 1844).

Murray, John B. (March 30, 1840).

Murray, James (Baltimore, Dec. 30, 1840).

Mauray, O. (New York, Feb. 6, 1840).

Murrell, John D. (Lynchburg, March 2, 1844).

Myerle, David (Lexington, Kentucky, Feb. 16, 1841).

Myers, P. D. (Phila., Jan. 6, 1843).

Myers, Mary Ann (Phila., April 5, 1843).

Myers, E. Geo. (Phila., April 5, 1843).

Myers, James (Phila., April 5, 1843).

Myers, Lititia (Phila., April 5, 1843).

Myers, Newton D. (Phila., April 5, 1843).

Myers, Rebecca Swain (Phila., April 5, 1843).

Myers, Wilbur F. (Phila., April 5, 1843).

Mylne, W. C., of Glasgow (New Orleans, Feb. 23, 1844).

Nack, James, poet (deaf and dumb) (Oct. 3, 1839).

Nagel, Giovanni, pupil of Paganini (Saratoga, Aug. 28, 1842).

Nagel, Mrs. Chas., sister of Mrs. Peyser (Saratoga, Aug. 12, 1843).

Nash, Mr. I. A., Pittsfield, Mass. (Oct. 21, 1840).

Neilson, Dr. John (New York, Sept. 26, 1839).

Neilson, John, jun. (March 25, 1839).

Nesbit, Eugenius A., M.C. (Georgia, Feb. 2, 1841).

Nevins, James (Phila., Aug. 14, 1844).

Newbold, Chas. (Phila., Dec. 22, 1842).

Newbold, Chas., jun. (Phila., Dec. '24, 1842).

Newell, Miss Ellen A. (Boston, June 4, 1842).

Newell, Martha (Phila., Oct. 23, 1843).

Newell, Maria (Phila., Oct. 23, 1843).

Newell, Mary (Phila., Oct. 23, 1843).

Newton, A. G. (Washington, March 24, 1841).

Newton, Rev. Richd., Rector of St. Paul's (Phila., Feb. 1, 1843).

Nicholl, Mary L. (Saratoga Springs, Aug. 4, 1842).

Nichols, Miss Rebecca Dole (New York, Sept. 17, 1839).

Nichols, Anne Clark (New York, Sept. 17, 1839).

Nicholson, A. O. P. (Tennessee, June 28, 1841).

Nicholson, Josh. H., Legislateur (Maryland, Feb. 17, 1841).

Nicholson, John Carallorn (New Orleans, Aug., 1843).

Nicolson, John B., Commodore (Washington, Feb. 5, 1841).

Niles, John M. (Ct., March 3, 1841).

Niles, Rev. Ma., first Church, Marblehead (Mass., June 7, 1841).

Nims, J., portrait painter (New York, May 16, 1840).

Niven, Chas. (Washington, Jan. 28, 1841).

Nixon, James Oscar (Aug. 8, 1839).

Noah, Miss J. P. (New York, Nov. 2, 1840).

Noe, Louvisae, Lafayette (New Orleans, Jan. 27, 1844).

Norman (?), Dr., D.D., Presiding Elder of New Orleans.

Norris, Geo. (Baltimore, Jan. 11, 1841).

Norris, G., Somerville (Dec. 11, 1840).

North, Harvey, New Orleans (Saratoga, Aug. 15, 1843).

North, Athalic, New Orleans (Saratoga, Aug. 15, 1844).

North, J. Bartram, Capitol Hill (Washington, Feb. 18, 1841).

Norton, Herman, Corres. Sec. of American Ptost. Society, New York (Saratoga, July 20, 1844).

Nourse, Mrs. Michael (Washington, March 24, 1841).

Nourse, Mr. Michael, chief clerk, Register Office (Washington, March 24, 1841).

Noyes, Wm. T. (Troy, Sept. 14, 1841).

Nugent, Miss Augusta (New York, Sept. 20, 1839).

Oakley, Chas. S., gd.-son of John D. Roome (Nov. 23, 1839).

Oakley, Mrs. Maria Louisa (Nov. 23, 1839).

Oakley, Anne Caroline (Nov. 23, 1839).

Oakley, Margaret Roome (Nov. 23, 1839).

Oakley, Chas. S. (New York, Aug. 25, 1839).

Oakley, James B. (New York, Aug. 24, 1839).

Oakley, Wm. F. (3 ports.) (New York, June 3, 1840).

Oakley, Miss E. (Saratoga Springs, Aug. 13, 1841).

Oakley, Judge J. (New York, Nov. 15, —).

Oakley, Cornelius, jun. (Dec. 13, 1839).

O'Brien, John, Atty. at Law, Durham, Green Co. (Nov. 23, 1839).

O'Brien, John G. (Phila., Nov. 28, 1842).

O'Connor, Daniel, builder, New York (Saratoga, Aug. 17, 1843).

O'Donnell, J. H. (Baltimore, Aug. 15, 1842).

O'Donnell, Rev. James, O.S.A., St. Paul's Church (Brooklyn, Oct. 2, 1840).

O'Donoghue, Rev. Francis, R.C., of Killarney, Co. Kerry, Ireland, now New York (Sept. 16, 1840).

Ogden, T. Murray (New York, March 9, 1840).

Ogden, Isaac G., jun. (Sept. 2, 1839).

Ogden, Mrs. G., jun. (Sept. 2, 1839).

Ogden, Miss, sister of Isaac.

Ogden, Miss Euphemia (New York, April 25, 1840).

Ogden, Isaac, sen. (April 17, 1840).

Ogden, Sarah, gd.-daughter of Isaac (New York, April 17, 1840).

Ogden, Wm. S., Lieut., U.S.N. (Boston, May 30, 1842).

Ogden, Nicholas G., cashier of Phœnix Bank, New York (New York, April 18, —).

Ogden, Caroline (New York, April 18, —).

Ogden, G. (New York, April 18, —).

Ogden, Mrs. N. G. (New York, April 18, —).

Ogden, Miss Laura (New York, Jan. 20, 1840).

Ogden, D. A. (New Orleans, Jan. 22, 1844).

O'Hallaran, Capt., 39th Regt., Brit. Army of St. John's (Saratoga Springs, Sept. 4, 1840).

Onderdonk, Henry M. (Sept. 13, 1839).

Onderdonk, Wm. H. (Sept. 11, 1839).

Onderdonk, Miss Eliz.

Onderdonk, John C., obt. Oct. 15, 1840 (taken from death) (New York, Oct. 16, 1840).

Ormsby, Stevens, Col., Louisville Legion (Louisville, May 13, 1844).

Orne, Mr. Wm. W., of Springfield (Saratoga, July 25, 1842).

Orne, Mrs. Wm. W., daughter of Mrs. Dwight (Saratoga, July 25, 1842).

Osborn, Saml. (Nov. 28, 1839).

Osgood, Josiah, Boston (Saratoga, July 15, 1840).

Osgood, Isaac P., Counsel at Law (Boston, Nov. 5, 1841).

Osgood, Mrs. P. (Boston, Nov. 5, 1841).

Osgood, John H. (Boston, June 30, 1842).

Osgood, Miss (Boston, June 30, 1842).

O'Sullivan, H. (Washington, Feb. 15, 1841).

O'Sullivan, Thos. S. (Washington, June 4, 1841).

O'Sullivan, J. L. (Oct. 5, 1840).

O'Sullivan, T. L., of *Democratic Review* (New York, Oct. 5, 1840).

Owner, James, jun., Post Office Dept. (March 3, 1841).

Oxley, Mrs. Chas. (New Orleans, March 1, 1844).

Oxley, Chas. (New Orleans, March 5, 1844).

Packwood, Saml. (New York, March 1, 1840).

Pado, A. O. (New Orleans, June 16, 1844).

Paez, Signor Ramon, son of Gen. P., Pres. of Venezuela, W. Indies (Caracas, Sept. 27, 1839).

Page, Benjn., Capt., U.S.N. (Saratoga Springs, Aug. 14, 1840).

Paige, Mr. T. W. (Boston, Nov. 30, 1841).

Paige, Mrs. T.W. (Boston, Nov. 30, 1841).

Paige, Harriet White (Boston, Nov. 30, 1841).

Paige, James Wm. (Boston, Nov. 30, 1841).

Pain, Mr. John, New York (Saratoga, Aug. 15, 1844).

Pain, Mrs. John, New York (Saratoga, Aug. 15, 1844).

Palfrey, Miss Maria (New Orleans, Feb. 14, 1844).

Palmer, Mr. Geo. W. (Saratoga, July 10, 1843).

Palmer, Mrs. Geo. W. (Saratoga, July 10, 1843).

Palmer, James S., Lieut., U.S.N. (Saratoga Springs, Aug. 3, 1840).

Papineau, Louis Joseph Amedee dit Montigny (Saratoga Springs, July 15, 1840).

Pardow, Geo., Warwickshire, England (New York, Jan. 18, 1840).

Pardow, Mrs. (New York, Jan. 18, 1840).

Parejo, A. de Andalusia (Saratoga, Aug. 10, 1843).

Parker, James C. (New York, April 12, 1840).

Parker, Mrs. *See* Mrs. Gobert (New York).

Parker, S. O., son of above.

Parker, James Contandt, son of Mrs. P.

Parker, Miss Gertrude, aunt of James C. (New York, April 17, 1840).

Parker, Mr. John, of Boston, obt. Oct., 1844 (Saratoga, July 23, 1844).

Parker, Mrs. John (Saratoga, July 23, 1844).

Parker, Daniel C. (Boston, Jan. 19, 1842).

Parker, Mrs. Daniel C. (Boston, Jan. 19, 1842).

Parker, Henry (Boston, Jan. 19, 1842).

Parker, Miss Emily Taylor (Boston, Jan. 19, 1842).

Parker, Gen. D., late Adjt. and Inspector-Gen., U.S.A. (March 26, 1841).

Parker, Richd. G. (Boston, June 6, 1842).

Parker, Geo. Phillips, Temperance (Boston, June 2, 1842).

Parker, C. C., son of Gen. (Phila., Oct. 25, 1842).

Parker, Wm. B., of Amsterdam, Holland (Boston, Dec. 24, 1841).

Parker, J. W. (Iowa, July 7, 1841).

Parmly, Saml. (2 ports.) (Feb. 13, 1840).

Parmly, Saml., dentist, 9, Park Street N. (New York, Dec. 10, 1839).

Parmly, Mrs. Saml.

Parmly, Ehrick, 9, Park Street N. (New York, Dec. 10, 1839).

Parmly, Mary, 9, Park Street N. (New York, Dec. 10, 1839).

Parmly, Anna, 9, Park Street N. (New York, Dec. 10, 1839).

Parmly, Julia, 9, Park Street N. (New York, Dec. 10, 1839).

Parmly, Eliz. Montague, 9, Park Street N. (New York, Dec. 10, 1839).

Parmly, J., brother of Saml. (New York, Dec. 8, 1839).

Parmly, David R., cousin of Saml. (Feb. 6, 1840).

Parsons, Wm., Pres. of Mass. Bank (Boston, Feb. 24, 1842).

Parsons, Mrs. (Boston, Feb. 24, 1842).

Parsons, Miss Eliz. (Boston, Feb. 24, 1842).

Parsons, Miss Martha (baby) (Boston, Feb. 24, 1842).

Parsons, Theophilus, jurist (Boston, Feb. 24, 1842).

Paterson, Wm., Prof. of Flute, of Augustus, Georgia (Sept. 13, 1839).

Pattison, Elias (Troy, Sept. 17, 1841).

Pattison, Richd. (Troy, Sept. 17, 1841).

Pattison, Edwd. (Troy, Sept. 17, 1841).

Patten, H. Joseph (New York, July 29, 1840).

Patterson, John H., M.D. (Dec. 18, 1840).

Patterson, Wm. Lindsay, Lochmailen (New Orleans, Feb. 21, 1844).

Patterson, J. Harman, U.S.N. (Washington, Feb. 17, 1841).

Patterson, Mr. Abraham B. (Baltimore, Dec. 8, 1840).

Patton, Charlotte Harper (Phila., Nov. 13, 1832).

Paulding, James K., Sec. Navy (Jan. 21, 1841).

Paulding, P. Kemble, son of above (Washington, Feb. 2, 1841).

Payne, John Howard (Washington, April 22, 1841).

Payot, Mons. (Saratoga, Aug. 2, 1841).

Payot, Mme. Marchande de Modes, Paris (Saratoga, Aug. 2, 1841).

Payot (child), not named (Saratoga, Aug. 2, 1841).

Payson, Miss Mary P. (Boston, June 13, 1842).

Peabody, Geo. F. (Phila., June 30, 1843).

Peabody, Rev. Ephraim, minister of Unitarian Church, New Bedford, Mass. (Boston, June 21, 1842).

Peacock, Miss Julia (St. Louis, Feb. 23, 1844).

Peagram, Capt., U.S.A. (Saratoga Springs, Aug. 20, 1840).

Pearson, James A. (Birmingham, June 8, 1838).

Pearson, E. (New York).

Peaslee, Chas. (Phila., June 30, 1843).

Peasley, Miss Emely A. (Saratoga, Sept. 8, 1843).

Peck, Bela (Saratoga, Aug. 18, 1841).

Peck, widow of Prof. Peck, Prof. of Natural History, Harvard College (Boston, June 18, 1842).

Peck, Emma, of Indiana (Phila., Oct. 23, 1843).

Peck, John (Jan. 10, 1840).

Pecquet, Paul (New Orleans, Dec. 29, 1843).

Peet, Capt. Francis, Ship Pemulyn (New Orleans, Dec. 27, 1843).

Peet, Munson, son of above (March 1, 1843).

Peik, Chas. A. (Saratoga, July 30, 1844).

Pell, Duncan C., auctioneer, 114, Franklin Street (Nov. 13, 1839).

Penfold, Edwd., New York (Saratoga, July 22, 1843).

Peniston, Chas., M.D. (New Orleans, Jan. 17, 1844).

Penniman, Jesse A., M.D. (New Braintree, June 3, 1843).

Penrose, John R. (Phila., July 7, 1843).

Perkins, Col. Thos. (3 ports.) (Boston, Feb. 16, 1842).

Perkins, Mrs. Thos. (Boston, Feb. 16, 1842).

Perkins, Miss S. E. (Boston, Feb. 16, 1842).

Perkins, Geo. C. (Boston, Feb. 16, 1842).

Perkins, Thos. H., jun. (4 ports.) (Boston, March 15, 1842).

Perkins, Mrs. Thos. H., jun. (Boston, Feb. 15, 1842).

Perkins, P. D. (Boston, Feb. 15, 1842).

Perkins, F. C., shot by accident, July, 1843 (Boston, Feb. 15, 1842).

Perkins, A. T. (Boston, Feb. 15, 1842).

Perkins, Miss Louisa (Boston, Feb. 15, 1842).

Perkins, Rev. Justin, Missionary to Persia (Saratoga, Aug. 27, 1842).

Perrin, Mrs. H. C., Worcester, Mass. (Saratoga, July 16, 1842).

Perrine, G., M.D., Mobile, Alabama (Washington, March 20, 1841).

Peter, Wm. (Phila., Nov. 12, 1842).

Peters, Mr. Abraham (Baltimore, Jan. 20, 1841).

Pettingell, John H. Dennis, Barnstable Co.; Mass. (Saratoga, Aug. 9, 1843).

Peyroux, C. (New Orleans, Jan. 3, 1844).

Peyser, Dr. D. M., of Poland (Saratoga, Aug. 1, 1841).

Peyser, Mrs. D. M. *See* Nagel (Saratoga, Aug. 1, 1841).

Peyton, Miss Susan S., of Richmond (Saratoga Springs, Aug. 25, 1844).

Phelps, Miss Caroline (Boston, Jan. 8, 1842).

Phelps, Miss Maria E., New York (Saratoga, Aug. 14, 1840).

Phelps, Mrs. Thos. Wm. (New York, Aug. 5, 1839).

Phelps, Miss Eliz. (New York, Aug. 5, 1839).

Phelps, A., Greenfield, Mass. (Saratoga, Aug. 1, 1844).

Phelps, Abel, of Boston (Saratoga, July 22, 1844).

Phelps, Miss Maria (Saratoga, July 22, 1844).

Phillips, Mr. John, son of late Gov. of Mass. (Boston, March 17, 1842).

Phillips, Mrs. John (Boston, March 17, 1842).

Philips, Alex. (New Orleans, June 3, 1844).

Philips, Rosina (New Orleans, June 3, 1844).

Philips, Thos. F. (Phila., Oct. 1, 1843).

Philips, Thos. Wm. (New Orleans, March 1, 1844).

Phœnix, T. Phillips, M.C. (City of New York, Aug. 23, 1841).

Pickens, Francis Wm. (Edgefield, March 4, 1841).

Pickering, Timothy.

Pickering, Arthur, of Boston (Saratoga, July 23, 1842).

Pickering, Joseph Thos. (Saratoga, July 30, 1839).

Picket, James H. (Lexington, June 1, 1844).

Pickett, Richd., lost in the *Lexington* steamer, burnt at sea on Jan. 13, 1840, of Boston (New York, Sept. 5, 1839).

Pickett, E. S., Newbury Port, Mass. (New York, June 6, 1840).

Pickman, C. Gayton (Cambridge, March 1, 1842).

Picton, J. M. W., M.D. (New Orleans, April 4, 1844).

Pierce, Joshua H., lithographer (Jan. 19, 1840).

Pierce, Franklin, sen. (New Hampshire).

Pierpont, Mary Lord (Boston, June 13, 1842).

Pierpont, Rev. J., poet reformer (Boston, June 13, 1842).

Pierpont, Mrs. Lord (Boston, June 13, 1842).

Pierrepont, Henry Evelyn (Brooklyn, L.I., Aug. 14, 1840).

Pierson, E., New York (Saratoga, July 21, 1843).

Piper, James (Phila., Dec. 24, 1842).

Piper, Ferdinand, Lieut., U.S.N. (Boston, June 17, 1842).

Pitard, A. D. (New Orleans, Feb. 5, 1844).

Pitchlynn, P. P., Speaker of the General Council of the Choctaw Nation (W. Arkansas, March 12, 1841).

Pitman, John T., clerk, U.S. District Court, Providence (Saratoga, Aug. 10, 1842).

Plaguemaine, Eliz. Reames (New Orleans, Dec. 7, 1828).

Platen, Wm., M.D. (Georgetown, D.C., May 4, 1841).

Platt, Mr. Z. (Detroit, Mich., Aug. 10, 1843).

Platt, Mrs. Z. (Saratoga, Aug. 10, 1843).

Pleasant, Mary, wife of Saml. (Phila.).

Pleasanton, A. J. (Phila., Jan. 28, 1843).

Pleasanton, Mrs. Caroline (Phila., Jan. 28, 1843).

Pleasanton, Ann Josephine (Phila., Jan. 28, 1843).

Pleasanton, Clementine (Phila., Jan. 28, 1843).

Pleasanton, Augustus (Phila., Jan. 28, 1843).

Pleasanton, Adelaide (Phila., Jan. 28, 1843).

Pleasanton, Mary Virginia (Phila., Jan. 28, 1843).

Plumb, B. W. (Nov. 17, —).

Plumb, B. W. (Dec. 8, 1844).

Plumbe, John, jun (Boston, Nov. 2, 1841).

Plumer, W., jun., M.C., New Hampshire (Boston, Jan. 28, 1842).

Plummer, S. M., U.S.A. (Nov. 17, 1841).

Plunkett, Alfred (New York, July 30, 1839).

Plunkett, Mrs. Alfred (taken from description), obt. (New York, July 30, 1839).

Plunkett, Ernest (New York, July 29, 1839).

Plunkett, Eliza (New York, July 29, 1839).

Plunkett, Eugene (Washington, March 11, 1841).

Poinsett, Joel R., Sec. of War (Jan. 21, 1841).

Poinsett, M. (Feb. 10, 1841).

Poizart, Cecilia (Phila., July 24, 1843).

Poizart, J. R. (Phila., July 24, 1843).

Pollard, Miss Margaret (Washington, April 30, 1841).

Polk, Wm. (Saratoga, Aug. 5, 1841).

Pomeroy, Robt., of Pittsfield, Mass. (Saratoga, July 18, 1844).

Pomeroy, Mrs. Robt., of Pittsfield, Mass. (Saratoga, July 18, 1844).

Pomeroy, Miss Mary Agnes (Saratoga, July 18, 1844).

Pomeroy, Mrs. Phebe B. (Troy, Sept. 31, 1841).

Pomery, Dr. Thaddius, aged 78 years, of Stockbridge, Mass. (Saratoga, Aug. 20, 1842).

Poole, Franklin (Nov. 28, 1839).

Poor, John A., Counsel at Law, Bangor, Maine (Saratoga, Aug. 15, 1844).

Poor, Rev. David, Methodist Episcopal Minister (Greenfield, Aug. 26, 1841).

Popham, Major W., aged 88 years (New York, Nov. 5, 1839).

Porter, Capt. Benjn., Danvers (Saratoga, July 26, 1843).

Porter, John A., of Newbury Port (Saratoga, Aug. 4, 1843).

Porter, Dr. Joshua, surgeon on board the *Constitution* in the Revolution, brother to Gen. P., died Oct., 1831, aged 72 years (Saratoga, Aug. 26, 1844).

Porter, Minerva (Saratoga, Aug. 26, 1844).

Porter, David D., Lieut., U.S.N. (Washington, March 19, 1841).

Porter, Miss Roberto V. (Washington, April 23, 1841).

Porter, John A., of Newbury Port (Saratoga Sept. 2, 1844).

Porter, James (New Orleans, Feb. 10, 1844).

Post, W. B., Esq., Waldron (New York, Sept. 25, 1840).

Post, Mrs. (New York, Sept. 25, 1840).

Post, W. B., jun. (New York, Sept. 25, 1840).

Post, A. Kintzing (New York, Sept. 25, 1840).

Post, Mrs. A. Kintzing (New York, Sept. 25, 1840

Post, Miss S. M. (New York, Sept. 25, 1840).

Post, Miss Y. E. (New York, Sept. 25, 1840).

Post, Miss Helene Louisa (New York, Sept. 25, 1840).

Post, Mrs. A., mother of Mrs. W. W. Livermore of New York (Saratoga Springs, Aug. 11, 1842).

Potter, James Brown Mason, Usqueyany, R. T. (Boston, Dec. 30, 1841).

Potter, Chas., Providence, R.I. (Saratoga, Aug. 2, 1841).

Potter, Woodburne (Phila., April 20, 1841).

Pottey, Rev. E. J., Methodist Episcopal Church, of Springfield, Mass.

Povey, John, of Park Theatre (New York, Feb. 3, 1843).
Powell, Rev. Wm., Epis. Union Hill, Westchester Co., New York (West Farms, Aug. 20, 1841).
Powell, Wm. A. (New York, 1840).
Power, Rev. Dr. John, R.C., Vicar-Gen. of New York, Rector of St. Peter's Church, Barclay S. (Oct. 23, 1840).
Powers, E. E., Columbus, Georgia (Saratoga, Sept. 12, 1844).
Pratt, Mrs. (Washington, April 5, 1841).
Pratt, Mrs. S. B., Boston (Saratoga, July 27, 1844).
Pratt, Horace L. Edgar, A.B. of New York University (Saratoga, Aug. 12, 1844).
Pratt, Francis McKay (little child) (Louisville, May 17, 1844).
Prelm, Wm. Kostock, Germany (New Orleans, March 23, 1844).
Prentice, Mrs. Harriet? (Louisville, May 20, 1844).
Prentice, Courtland, editor of *Louisville Journal* (Louisville, May 14, 1844).
Prentice, Geo. D.
Prentiss, John H., M.C., Cooperstown (New York, Jan. 27, 18—).
Prescott, Wm. H., author of *History of Ferdinand and Isabella*, obt. 1844, at sea on his voyage to Fayet. (Boston, Nov. 26, 1841).
Prescott, Rev. Edwd. G., Episcopal Church, Salem, Mass. (Boston, May 31, 1842).
Preston, Wm. C., sen., South Carolina (Columbia, Feb. 17, 1841).
Prewett, Mr. N. (Natchez, Feb. 24, 1844).
Price, Miss Harriet M., New York (Saratoga, Aug. 16, 1843).
Pride, Mrs. Geo. L. (New York, Sept. 17, 1839).
Pride, Geo. L. (New York, Sept. 17, 1839).
Pride, Hamilton Jackson (New York, Oct. 10, 1839).
Pride, Mary Jannette (New York, Nov. 6, 1828).
Priest, John F. (Boston, May 26, 1842).
Primrose, Robt., New Berne, North Carolina (Saratoga, Sept. 30, 1844).
Primrose, Miss Mary A. (Saratoga, Sept. 30, 1844).
Prince, James (Boston, March 31, 1842).
Prince, Wm. E., U.S.A., 1st Infantry (Boston, Feb. 5, 1842).
Prout, Robt. M. (Baltimore, Dec. 12, 1840).
Prue, Mary Augusta, New York (Saratoga, Aug. 26, 1844).
Pudington, Henry T. (New York, March 1, 1844).
Purdy, John F. (New York, Sept. 16, 1839).
Purdy, L. Lovell (New York, Sept. 17, 1839).
Putnum, Rev. Israel W., Pastor of first Church, Middleborough, Mass. (Saratoga, July 20, 1842).
Putman, Capt. Nathaniel, jun., Zenobia (Saratoga, Aug. 12, 1843).
Putnam, Rev. Allen Edwd., of New England, farmer (Boston, June 15, 1842).
Putnam, Rev. Geo., Minister of Presbyterian Church, Roxbury (Boston, June 15, 1842).
Putnam, Miss Catharine (Boston, June 8, 1842).

Quick, James B., of New York (Saratoga, Aug. 18, 1842).
Quincey, Josiah, Pres. of Senate, Mass. (Boston, Jan. 8, 1842).
Quincey, Mrs. (Boston, Jan. 8, 1842).
Quincey, Tertius and dog (Boston, Jan. 8, 1842).
Quincey, Mary A. (Boston, Jan. 8, 1842).

Quincey, Miss May Sophie (Boston, Jan. 9, 1842).
Quincey, Mrs. Josiah (Boston, Jan. 9, 1842).
Quincey, Josiah, Pres. of Harvard Coll., Cambridge (Boston, Jan. 8, 1842).
Quincey, John, New York (Saratoga, Aug. 26, 1843).
Quincey, Mr. Edmd. (Boston, Feb. 15, 1842).
Quincey, Mrs. Edmd., daughter of Daniel C. Parker (Boston, Feb. 15, 1842).

Radford (Cheltenham, Nov. 23, 1829).
Rahe, Adrian, Martinique (Sept. 24, 1839).
Ramsey, Geo. D., Capt., Ord. (Washington, April 6, 1841).
Ramsey, Capt. Wm., U.S.N. (Saratoga, Sept. 14, 1844).
Ramsey, Rev. Wm., Missionary to India (Phila., Jan. 20, 1843).
Ramsey, J. M. (March 29, 1840).
Randall, Benjn., M.C. (Maine, June 18, 1841).
Randall, A., Counsel at Law (Annapolis, March 8, 1841).
Randolph, Wm. B. (Jan. 26, 1841).
Rankin, Edwd. E. (Saratoga, July 8, 1844).
Ranson, Lena Ann (New York, Oct. 31, 1839).
Rapelye, Geo., of New York (Saratoga Springs, Aug. 6, 1841).
Rariden, James, M.C., Indiana (Centerville, Wayne, Feb. 26, 1841).
Rathbone, J. B., of New York (Saratoga, Aug. 5, 1840).
Rawson, Rev. James, Episcopal Methodist of Albany (Saratoga, Aug. 19, 1842).
Rawson, Mrs. Charlotte Ann (Saratoga, Aug. 19, 1842).
Ray, Rev. John W., Glen's Falls (Saratoga, Aug. 26, 1844).
Raymond, Susan (Smyrna, July 6, 1843).
Read, Wm. (Boston, June 3, 1842).
Reed, B. J. (Boston, Jan. 10, 1842).
Reed, Mrs. B. J., daughter of Mrs. Hooper. *See* Hooper (Boston, Jan. 10, 1842).
Reed, John H., gd.-son of Mrs. E. Hooper (Boston, Jan. 10, 1842).
Reed, Rev. Fitch, Methodist Episcopal Church (April 20, 1840).
Recard, Jean Baptiste, de Tule, Loraine, France (Saratoga Springs, July 13, 1840).
Redman, John, M.D.
Redmond, Wm., New York (Saratoga, Sept. 3, 1844).
Reed, Mrs. Eliz. W. (Phila., Jan. 2, 1843).
Reed, Washington (Phila., Jan. 2, 1843).
Reed, James (Chambersburg, Jan. 2, 1843).
Reed, John, M.C. (Barnstable, Mass., Feb. 20, 1841).
Reese, Dr. D. M., M.D., late Prof. in Albany Medical Coll. (Saratoga, Aug. 11, 1841).
Reese, Miss N. Frances (Saratoga, Aug. 11, 1841).
Reid, Capt. Saml., U.S.N. (New York, Nov. 23, 1844).
Reim, Geo. M., M.C. Berks, Pa. (Pa., June 25, 1841).
Reinboth, Jos. D. (Phila., Oct. 25, 1843).
Relf, Richd. (New Orleans, April 13, 1844).
Remington, Edwd. (New Orleans, Nov. 9, 1842).
Remsen, S. H., of New York (Boston, May 20, 1842).
Renalds, G. L., gd.-son of P. Lorillard (Saratoga, July 17, 1844).

Rencher, Abraham, M.C. (June 18, 1841).

Revel, D. Nathan.

Reynand, P., Vice-Consul for Brazil (New Orleans, Jan. 20, 1844).

Reynolds, Edwd., aged 81 years (Boston, Jan. 20, 1842).

Reynolds, Mrs. Edwd. (Boston, Jan. 20, 1842).

Reynolds, Chas. G. (Boston, Jan. 26, 1842).

Reynolds, Mrs. Chas. G. (Boston, Jan. 26, 1842).

Reynolds, John, M.C., Illinois (Belleville, St. Clair, Feb. 3, 1841).

Reynolds, Jos. P., Portsmouth, Va. (Washington, June 9, 1841).

Reynolds, Miss Mary, of Albany (Boston, Jan. 25, 1842).

Rhoads, Julius, Albany, New York (Saratoga, Aug. 13, 1844).

Ribas, Antonia Lorence, Madrid (Oct. 9, 1839).

Rice, Geo. (Boston, Jan. 23, 1841).

Rice, Henry, jun. (Boston, Jan. 23, 1841).

Rice, Louisa (Boston, Dec. 15, 1841).

Rice, Anna Maria (Boston, Dec. 15, 1841).

Rice, Susan G., Cambridge, Mass. (Saratoga, Aug. 20, 1844).

Rich, Jabez C., Lieut., U.S. Marines (Phila., Oct. 3, 1842).

Richard, Mons. Auguste (Baltimore, Nov. 20, 1840).

Richards, Nath., of New York, father of late Mrs. Jonathan B. Steele (Saratoga, Sept. 12, 1842).

Richards, Mrs. (Saratoga Springs, Sept. 12, 1842).

Richards, Mrs. Austin (New Orleans, Jan. 20, 1844).

Richards, Newton (March 23, 1844).

Richardson, Tobias Gibson (Louisville, May 17, 1844).

Richardson, Sally Allen (Louisville, May 14, 1844).

Richardson, Lucy (Louisville, May 14, 1844).

Richardson, widow of Nathan., of Salem, Mass., aged 91 years, March 2, 1842 (Boston, June 30, 1842).

Richardson, J. (Oswego, July 22, 1843).

Riddle, Miss Ellen M. (Boston, Nov. 10, 1841).

Ridgway, Mrs. (Phila., Oct. 27, —).

Riggs, E., New York (Saratoga, Aug. 3, 1843).

Ring, Zebedee. See DeBaun (New York, March 16, 1840).

Ring, Mrs. Zebedee (New York, March 16, 1840).

Ring, John I. (New York, March 14, 1840).

Ring, James T. (New York, March 21, 1840).

Ring, Geo. (Mrs. R. missing) (New York, March 21, 1840).

Ring, Zebedee, jun. (New York, March 21, 1840).

Ripley, Saml.

Ritchie, H. A. (Louisville, Kentucky, May 15, 1844).

Rivers, Dr., surgeon, U.S. Marine Hospital, Providence, R.I. (Saratoga, July 9, 1844).

Roades, Rev. B. H., of Boston (New York, Oct. 5, 1839).

Roades, Mrs. B. H., from Providence (New York, Oct. 5, 1839).

Robb, Mrs. E. M., Fredericton, New Brunswick (Saratoga, Aug. 24, 1843).

Roberts, T. L. (Natchez, April 27, 1844).

Roberts, A. F. (Washington, April 19, 1841).

Roberts, Rev. D. F., Licentiate Presbyterian Church, New York (Saratoga, Aug. 8, 1843).

Robertson, Wm. B., Member of Consulation (Louisiana, March 22, 1844).

Robins, Dr. Amatus, M.D. (Troy, Sept. 17, 1841).

Robinson, John M. (Illinois, Jan. 30, 1841).

Robinson, J. M. (Baltimore, Dec. 3, 1840).

Robinson, Benjn., M.D., Fayetteville, North Carolina (Saratoga, June 26, 1843).

Rochelle, J. Jacques Gaudin de la (New Orleans, Jan. 27, 1844).

Rockwell, Wm., Brooklyn (Dec. 31, 1839).

Rockwood, Chas. G. (New York, Nov. 27,—).

Rodman, Lewis, M.D. (Phila., June 16, 1843).

Rodman, Thos. P., Yarmouth Port, Mass. (Boston, May 20, 1842).

Rodney, Rev. John, Rector of St. Luke's Church (Germantown, Feb. 2, 1843).

Rogers, Geo. M. (Baltimore, Dec. 8, 1840).

Rogers, Rev. E. P., Pastor Congregational Church, Springfield, Mass. (fifth Church) (Saratoga Springs, Aug. 11, 1841).

Rogers, Miss Octavia Ann (Mrs. Meigs) (Washington, June 29, 1841).

Rogers, Willis T., of Troy (Sept. 14).

Rogers, James, M.C., South Carolina (March 8, 1841).

Rogers, Mrs. E. (Phila., Aug. 17, 1843).

Rogers, Evans (Phila., Aug. 16, 1843).

Rogers, Rev. Wm. M., Central Church (Boston, Jan. 26, 1842).

Rogers, Lloyd N., of Baltimore, Maryland (Saratoga Springs, Aug. 28, 1840).

Rogers, Miss Eleanor A., of Baltimore, Maryland (Saratoga Springs, Aug. 28, 1840).

Rogers, Edmd. Law (Saratoga Springs, Aug. 28, 1840).

Rolton, Dr. Otto, from Somerset, England (Jan. 3, 1840).

Rolton, Mrs. Anne, from Somerset, England (Jan. 3, 1840).

Roman, E. (St. John's, March 27, 1844).

Roome, Miss Sarah, daughter of J. P. (New York, Sept. 12, 1839).

Roome, Wm. Corner, 8th Avenue, 421 Street (Oct. 12, 1839).

Roonce, John P., Crier of the Courts of Oyer Terminer Supreme Customs (New York, Sept. 12, 1839).

Root, Mrs. Gen. (Delhi, New York, March 23, 1841).

Rosekrans, E. H. (Saratoga, July 12, 1844).

Ross, Jane (New Orleans, Jan. 22, —).

Ross, Leopold N. (Middlestown, Feb. 24, 1843).

Rossiter, Mrs. C. D. (Troy, Oct. 8, 1841).

Rotch, Miss Maria, Jamaica Plain. (Boston, Dec. 19, 1841).

Rotch, Mrs. V. (Phila., Oct. 27, 1842).

Roussel, Eugene (Phila., Nov. 2, 1843).

Roussel, Dr. Chas. S. (New York, Nov. 22, 1844).

Rubathan, Miss Matilda Jane, Wales, Great Britain (New York, Oct. 23, 1840).

Rudman, Wm. C. (Phila., Aug. 29, 1844).

Rue, Col. J., Washington, South Carolina (Sept. 11, 1839).

Rue, L. E. (New York, Nov. 13, 1839).

Ruffat, G. (New Orleans, Feb. 5, 1844).

Ruggles, Saml. B. (Saratoga, Aug. 21, 1840).

Ruggles, John (Maine, Feb., 1841).

Ruiz, Candid, Signor F., Havana (Saratoga Springs, Aug. 20, 1841).

Ruiz, Garcia, Havana (Saratoga Springs, Aug. 20, 1841).

Ruiz, Garcia, Havana (Saratoga Springs, Aug. 20, 1841).

Ruschenberger, W. S. W., surgeon, U.S.N. (Phila., Oct. 5, 1842).

Ruschenberger, Mrs. W. S. W. (Phila., Oct. 5, 1842).

Russell, G. Hammond (Boston, Nov. 6, 1841).

Russell, N. P., jun. (Boston, Nov. 8, 1841).

Russell, Miss M. A. P., sister of Mrs. Wendall Thornton (Nov. 27, 1841).

Russell, J. H. (Dec. 11, 1841).

Russell, G. R. (Boston, Feb. 26, 1842).

Russell, Mr. N. P. (Boston, Nov. 27, 1841).

Russell, Mrs. N. P. (Boston, Nov. 27, 1841).

Russell, Saml., Middleton, Ct. (Saratoga. July 16, 1843).

Russell, Wm. H. (Washington, March 17, 1841).

Russell, Hon. James, Counsel at Law, late Minister of Leg., Mass. (Saratoga, July 23, 1844).

Russell, Mr. Moses B. (Boston, May 20, 1842).

Russell, Mrs., miniature painter, of 21, School Street (Boston, May 20, 1842).

Ryder, Rev. Jns. (D.C.).

Ryder, Miss Sally, of Plymouth (Boston, Dec. 28, 1841).

Sackett, Alex., Cleveland, Ohio (Saratoga, Aug. 30, 1844).

Salisbury, John (New York, April 7, 1840).

Salisbury, Widow Mary (New York, April 7, 1840).

Salisbury, John L., child of Widow Mary (New York, April 7, 1840).

Salisbury, Mary B., child of Widow Mary (New York, April 7, 1840).

Salter, Fredk., actor, of England (New York, Nov. 7, 1839).

Sandford, Thos., aged 2 years and 9 months (New York, Jan. 20, 1840).

Samson, C. B. (Nov. 17).

Sanborn, Mrs. Prof. E. D., Havana, New Hampshire.

Sanderson, Henry S., Major (Baltimore, Dec. 22, 1841).

Sanderson, Master Henry P. (Phila., Sept. 27, 1842).

Sands, Joshua R., Commander of U.S.N. (Washington, May 4, 1843).

Santangelo, Mrs. Mary de Attelles (Washington, March 26, 1841).

Sargent, Epres, editor of *New York Mirror* (Sept. 7, 1839).

Sargent, S. J. W. (Saratoga, July 6, 1843).

Saunders, E. R., Bardstown, Illinois (Saratoga, Aug. 31, 1843).

Saunders, Mr. C. C. (Louisville, May 18, 1844).

Saunders, Mrs. C. C. (Louisville, May 18, 1844).

Savage, Coms. (New York, Jan. 20, 1840).

Sawyer, Nathan S., M.C., Gardiner (Saratoga, July 3, 1843).

Sayers, Wm. D., Port Gibson, Mass. (Saratoga, Aug. 24, 1843).

Sayers, Edwd. S. (Phila., March 1, 1843).

Sayers, Mrs. Jane (Phila., March 1, 1843).

Sayre, F., Atty. (Aug. 19, 1839).

Sayres, Emma Stalker (New Orleans).

Scammon, E. P., 2nd Lieut. (Washington, March 16, 1841).

Schiffelin, P. (New York, Nov. 23, 1844).

Schlesinger, M. E. D. (Phila., July 24, 1843).

Scholefield, J., of Birmingham (New Orleans, Feb. 22, 1844).

Schriver, Albert (Phila., Jan. 5, 1843).

Schugler, Conn., Sheriff of Rebsealain City (Troy, Sept. 16).

Scott, Wm. B., of New York (Saratoga, Aug. 22, 1842).

Scott, John S. (New Orleans, Feb. 28, 1844).

Scott, John G., Cooper Co., Mo. (Louisville, Kentucky, May 20, 1844).

Scott, James, Richmond, Va. (Saratoga, Sept. 6, 1843).

Scott, Ellen, Richmond, Va. (Saratoga, Sept. 6, 1843).

Scott, John M., New York (Saratoga, July 21, 1843).

Scott, Maj.-Gen. Winfield, U.S.A. (Saratoga, July 20, 1840).

Scott, H. L., son of Comm.-in-Chief (Saratoga, Sept. 7, 1843).

Scott, G. H., Lieut., U.S.N. (Boston, June 16, 1842).

Searle, Rev. Addison, chaplain, U.S.N. (Boston, May 5, 1842).

Seaton, W. W. (Washington, April 17, 1841).

Seaton, Mr. Gales (Washington, March 20, 1841).

Seaton, Miss Caroline (Washington, Jan. 30, 1841).

Sedgewick, Miss E., of New York (Saratoga, Dec. 19, 1844).

Sedgewick, Miss Susan R. (Saratoga, Dec. 19, 1844).

Sedgewick, Miss Catharine M. (Saratoga, Aug. 18, 1842).

Sedgwick, Catharine M., authoress, of Stockbridge, Mass. (Saratoga, Aug. 18, 1842).

Seguin, Anne (Phila., Jan. 17, 1843).

Seguin, Edwd. (Phila., Dec. 26, 1842).

Selden, J. M. (Washington, June 21, 1841).

Selden, W., Treas., Treasury Dept. (Washington, May 28, 1841).

Selden, Saml., of Rochester (Saratoga Springs, Aug. 27, 1840).

Selden, Mrs. Saml., of Rochester (Saratoga Springs, Aug. 27, 1840).

Selden, Mrs. E., wife of Wm. (May 29, 1841).

Selleck, Miss Charlotte G., New York (New Jersey, Aug. 28, —).

Sever, Mr. James W. (Boston, May 14, 1842).

Sever, Mrs. James W. (Boston, May 14, 1842).

Seward, Wm. H., Governor of State of New York (New York, Oct. 2, 1839).

Seward, Benjn. J., brother of above, Westfield, obt. (New York, Oct. 2, 1839).

Seward, Miss Sarah J., of Rochester (Saratoga Springs, Aug. 29, 1840).

Sewall, Dr. Thos. (Washington, Feb. 20, 1841).

Sewall, Mr. S. E., Counsel at Law, Boston (Saratoga, July 9, 1844).

Sewall, Mrs. S. E. (Saratoga, July 9, 1844).

Seymour, Rev. Eben., of Bloomfield, New York, Pastor of Presbyterian Church (Saratoga, July 27, 1840).

Shanks, M., of Washington (June 22, 1841).

Sharper, Mrs. Henry (New York, Oct. 27, 1842).

Shaw, Francis G. (Boston, Feb. 10, 1842).

Shaw, C. Howland, Berion Street (Boston, Feb. 26, 1842).

Shaw, J. O., son of Chief Justice Shaw (Boston, June 16, 1842).

Shaw, Mr. Joel, dagguerotype (Saratoga, Aug. 24, 1842).

Shaw, Mrs. Joel (Saratoga, Aug. 24, 1842).

Shaw, Lemuel, Chief Justice Supreme Judical Court, Mass. (Boston, June 16, 1842).

Shea, James, of New York, died Sept., 1843 (Aug. 14, 1840).
Sheafe, Major Henry (Boston, Dec. 4, 1841).
Sheffield, P. K. (New Orleans, Jan. 24, 1844).
Shields, E. J., M.C. (Memphis, Tenn., Aug. 18, 1841).
Shepard, Isaac F., author of *Pebble from Costalia Village*, penielingo dr. (Boston, Nov. 27, 1841).
Shepard, Rev. Geo. C., D.D., Rector of St. John's Epis. (Saratoga, July 26, 1844).
Shepard, Mrs. Geo. Chas., Jamaica Plain, Mass. (Saratoga, July 26, 1844).
Sheppard, A. H., M.C. (June 18, 1841).
Sheppard, R. D. (New Orleans, Feb. 23, 1844).
Shermahorn, Abraham, of 36, Bond Street, New York (New York, Feb. 5, 1840).
Sherman, Thaddeus, jun. (New York, July 24, 1843).
Sherman, J., New Haven, Ct. (Saratoga, Aug. 30, 1844).
Sherman, Edwd. S., New York (Saratoga, July 17, 1844).
Sherman, Rev. Chas., Presiding Elder of Albany District in the Methodist Episcopal Church (Saratoga, Aug. 2, 1841).
Sherwood, Col. T. M., Auburn, New York, Vice-Pres. of Western R. R. (Boston, Dec. 31, 1841).
Shieffelin, Mrs. Richd. L. (New York, March 10, 1840).
Shieffelin, Richd. L. (New York, March 10, 1840).
Shieffelin, Julia (March 1, 1840).
Shieffelin, Bradhurst (March 10, 1840).
Shieffelin, H. M. (March 4, 1840).
Shieffelin, Sydney A. (March 4, 1840).
Shieffelin, Mrs. H. M., daughter of Mrs. Wagstaff (New York, March 5, 1840).
Shimmin, Chas. T. (Boston, Dec. 22, 1841).
Shimmin, Thos. D. (Boston, Dec. 25, 1841).
Shipman, Rev. Thos. L., Norwich County (Saratoga, Aug. 9, 1842).
Shippey, Josia W., Paterson, New Jersey (Sept. 5).
Shortes, M. (Brooklyn, Sept. 30, 1843).
Shrival, R. G. (Phila., Dec. 27, 1842).
Shurmday, Dr. Saml., M.D., Essex, New York (Aug. 20, 1840).
Sickles, Miss Mary H., of New York (April 7, 1842).
Sigourney, D. A., cashier of Washington Bank (Boston, Nov. 19, 1841).
Silliman, Augustus A., 30, Wall Street (Dec. 13, 1839).
Silsby, J. H., of Congress Hall (Saratoga Springs, Aug. 14, 1841).
Simons, Allen (New Orleans, Dec. 29, 1843).
Simons, —, of Circular Rail Road (Saratoga, Aug. 30, 1842).
Sizen, Nelson, Blandford, Mass. (Washington, May 3, 1841).
Skilton, Edwd., Charlestown (July 20, 1840).
Skinner, Rev. Pastor Thos. H., New Mercer Street Church (Feb. 11, 1840).
Skinner, Mr. E. L., of Auburn, New York (Saratoga Springs, Aug. 19, 1842).
Skinner, Mrs. E. L., of Auburn, New York (Saratoga Springs, Aug. 19, 1840).
Slack, Chas. A. (Grosse Tete, Louisiana, Jan. 24, 1844).
Slade, Wm., M.C. (Vt., July 3, 1841).
Slater, H. N., Providence, R.I. (Saratoga, July 27, 1844).

Slave, belonging Mrs. Oxley (New Orleans, March 1, 1844).
Sloat, J. D., Commodore, U.S.N. (Saratoga, Aug. 13, 1844).
Sloo, Thos. (New Orleans, Jan. 26, 1844).
Smeets, Wm. A., of New York, brother of Mrs. Cheltama. *See* C. (New York, Sept. 28, 1840).
Smith, Mrs. Hamilton (Louisville, May 15, 1844).
Smith, Hamilton, jun. (Louisville, May 15, 1844).
Smith, Mary (Louisville, May 15, 1844).
Smith, Master (baby) (Louisville, May 15, 1844).
Smith, M. E., sister of Hamilton S., sen. (Louisville, May 15, 1844).
Smith, Wm. Ballard, brother of Miss M. E. (Louisville, May 15, 1844).
Smith, Miss Eliz., daughter of Bishop B. B. Smith (Louisville, May 15, 1844).
Smith, Miss Virginia, daughter of Bishop B. B. Smith (Louisville, May 15, 1844).
Smith, Louisa H. (Louisville, May 15, 1844).
Smith, Wm. Asa, Brooklyn (New York, Jan. 20, 1840).
Smith, Richd. Somers, 2nd Lieut., U.S. Infantry (Saratoga Springs, Aug. 6, 1842).
Smith, Fisher C. (Phila., Feb. 10, 1843).
Smith, Col. Kenderton (Phila., May 3, 1843).
Smith, G. W., of Lafayette, Indiana (Oct. 2, —).
Smith, Daniel S., 347, Greenwich Street (Oct. 4, —).
Smith, Mrs. S. L., of W. H. Tremont Theatre (Boston, May 6, 1842).
Smith, Robt., from Clithers, Lancashire, England, Providence, R.I. (Sept. 17, 1839).
Smith, Miss Caroline E. (Troy, Sept. 16, 1841).
Smith, Wm. A. (New York, Jan. 16, 1840).
Smith, Thos. P., Saratoga (Charlestown).
Smith, T., Registrar (Washington, Jan. 27, 1841).
Smith, Mrs. W. G. (Boston, March 10, 1842).
Smith, Rev. E. G., late editor of *Quarterly Christian Spec.* (New York, Sept. 6, 1839).
Smith, T. R. (Saratoga, Aug. 18, 1844).
Smith, Gen. P. S., of Florida (Washington, June 7, 1841).
Smith, John Cotton, jun., Ct. (Saratoga, July 26, 1844).
Smith, Mrs. Mary H., Sparon, Ct. (Saratoga, July 30, 1844).
Smith, Rev. Eli, Missionary to Syria (Saratoga Springs, Aug. 15, 1840).
Smith, Rev. P., Mass. (Aug. 1, 1840).
Smith, Rev. Daniel, Bridgeport (Saratoga Springs, Aug. 15, 1840).
Smith, Geo. B., Street Commissioner from 1820–1835 (New York, March 25, 1840).
Smith, James O., 134, Prince Street (New York, Feb. 26, 1840).
Smith, Oliver H., sen. (Indiana, Feb. 26, 1841).
Smith, Truman, M.C. (Litchfield, Feb. 25, —).
Smith, C. H., Major-Paymaster, U.S.A. (Feb. 3, 1841).
Smith, Chas., of Warren R. Tor. (Saratoga, July 12, 1844).
Smith, Mrs. Chas., of Warren R. Tor. (Saratoga, July 12, 1844).
Snell, Prof. E. S., Amhurst Coll., Mass. (Boston, Dec. 20, 1841).
Snelling, Mrs. Caroline (Phila., Aug. 13, 1844).
Snelling, Saml. R. (Phila., Aug. 13, 1844).
Snowdon, Edgar, Mayor of Alexandria, D.C. (Washington, May 14, 1841).

Strong, A. M., Albany (Saratoga, Aug. 1, 1843).

Strong, Rev. Edwd., Pastor of Street Church, New Haven, Ct. (Saratoga, Aug. 20, 1844).

Stuart, Dr. James C., M.D., of Syracuse (Saratoga Springs, July 10, 1841).

Stuart, Robt. L., of New York (Saratoga, Aug. 18, 1841).

Stuart, James, European Agent (Saratoga, Aug. 15, 1843).

Stuart, Wm., Baltimore (Washington, March 25, 1841).

Sturgis, Capt. Josiah, Revenue Service (Boston, Nov. 27, 1841).

Sturgis, Mrs. Wm., daughter of Judge John Davis (Boston, Jan. 10, 1842).

Sturgis, Widow Eliz., sister of Col. Thos. Perkins; 86 years of age (Boston, Jan. 24, 1843).

Sturgis, Saml. P. (Boston, Jan. 23, 1842).

Sturgis, H. P. (Boston, Dec. 2, 1841).

Sullivan, Susan (Brooklyn, Sept. 20, 1843).

Sullivant, Mr. Michael L., Columbus, Ohio (Saratoga, Aug. 26, 1841).

Sullivant, Mrs. Michael L., Columbus, Ohio (Saratoga, Aug. 26, 1841).

Sumner, Mr. Increase, Great Barrington, Mass. (Saratoga, July 13, 1843).

Sumner, Mrs. Increase, Great Barrington, Mass. (Saratoga, July 13, 1843).

Sumner, Miss Francis (Saratoga, Aug. 9, 1843).

Sumter, T. D., M.C. (June 26, 1841).

Sung, Chin, from China (Washington, Feb. 10, 1841).

Sung, Chin, from China (Washington, Feb. 10, 1841).

Surget, F., Louisiana (Saratoga, Aug. 10, 1843).

Sutherland, Mary Florence (Brooklyn, March 11, 1843).

Sutherland, Lieut. D. J. (Phila., March 8, 1843).

Suydam, Alderman Lambert (Boston, Aug. 6, 1841).

Suydam, James, New York (New York, Feb. 28 1840).

Swain, Wm. W. (Boston, Feb. 1, 1843).

Swain, Mrs. Eliza (Phila., July 28, 1842).

Swain, Wm. (Phila., Sept. 14, 1842).

Swan, Thos., Esq. (Baltimore, Dec. 11, 1840).

Swan, Thos., jun. (Baltimore, Dec. 11, 1840).

Swan, Louisa T. (Baltimore, Dec. 11, 1840).

Swan, Mrs. Thos. (Baltimore, Dec. 11, 1840).

Swan, Wilson C. (Baltimore, Dec. 11, 1840).

Sweet, Nathanl. (Boston, Dec. 2, 1841).

Sweney, G., M.C. (Ohio, June 17, 1841).

Swift, Col. John, late Mayor (Phila., April 29, 1843).

Swift, W. H., Capt., U.S.A. (Saratoga Springs, July 14, 1842).

Swift, Henry A. (Dec. 13, 1839).

Swift, Dr. Wm., M.D., U.S.N. (Saratoga, July 18, 1844).

Sxerd, Joseph (Phila., Oct. 10, 1842).

Taggart, James B. (Washington, May 1, 1841).

Taliaferro, John (Fredrickburgh, Feb. 18, 1841).

Tallarie, C. A. (Antille, New Orleans, Feb. 7, 1844).

Tallmadge, N. P., Gen. (New York, March 25, 1841).

Tallmadge, Daniel B., Judge of Superior Court (Oct. 1, 1839).

Tallmadge, F. A., Counsel at Law and Senator, State of New York (Aug. 28, 1839).

Tallmadge, Miss T. T. (Aug. 29, 1839).

Tallmadge, Wm. A. (Sept. 2, 1839).

Q

Tallmadge, Fredk. (April 20, 1840).

Tanney, F. C., of New York (Saratoga, July 22, 1844).

Tanner, Mrs. F. C. (Saratoga, July 22, 1844).

Tappan, Henry P., Prof., New York University (Sept. 6, 1839).

Tappan, C. P. (Sept. 25, 1839).

Tappan, Wm. B. (Boston, April 4, 1842).

Tarbell, L. P., Deputy Sheriff (Boston, July 1, 1842).

Tarlton, Llewellyn Pitt, M.D. (Lexington, Kentucky, May 28, 1844).

Tayloe, Mr. Benjn., Ogle (Washington, Feb. 16, 1841).

Tayloe, Mrs. Benjn., Ogle (Washington, Feb. 16, 1841).

Tayloe, E. Thornton (Washington, Sept. 13, 1841).

Tayloe, Eugenie (Washington, Feb. 20, 1841).

Tayloe, Julia (Washington, Feb. 20, 1841).

Tayloe, Hester. *See* Dickinson (Washington, Feb. 20, 1841).

Taylor, Jonathan, M.C. (auto.) (Newark, Ohio, March 3, 1841).

Taylor, Mrs. Fanny, of New York (5 ft. 4 in.) (Saratoga, July 9, 1844).

Taylor, Wm., of Richmond, Va. (March 7, 1840).

Taylor, James, cashier of Commercial Bank, Albany (Saratoga, July 25, 1842).

Taylor, James A. (New York, Aug. 7, 1839).

Taylor, Mrs. Carolina Matilda (auto.) (Saratoga, Aug. 25, 1843).

Taylor, Master James, Belosts, Albany (Saratoga, Aug. 25, 1843).

Taylor, Miss Sarah Anne (Saratoga, Aug. 25, 1843).

Taylor, James (March 6, 1840).

Taylor, Rev. E. J., Unitarian (Boston, June 18, 1843).

Taylor, Mrs. T. V. (Richmond).

Taylor, Jacquelin P. (Richmond).

Taylor, Nathanl., New Haven (Saratoga, Aug. 27, 1841).

Texter, A. W., jun., Vice (Russian) Consul (Boston, June 16, 1842).

Teakle, Mr. E. W., of Butica (New York, Aug. 21, 1844).

Teakle, Mrs. E. W., of Butica (New York, Aug. 21, 1844).

Tennent, Dr. Henry, Pine Ridge, Miss. (Natchez, April 29, 1844).

Teneyck, Mrs. Andrew, widow, New Jersey (Dec. 12 1839).

Tenney, A. G., editor of Boston *Daily Evening Telegraph* (Boston, April 10, 1842).

Terret, B. A., 1st Lieut., 1st Regt. U.S. Dragoons (Washington, May 11, 1841).

Terret, Mrs. Marianne, wife of above (Washington, May 11, 1841).

Tevis, Robt., Shelbyville, Kentucky (Louisville, May 20, 1844).

Tevis, Mr. Henry L., Louisville, Kentucky (Saratoga, Aug. 7, 1843).

Tevis, Mrs. Henry L., Louisville, Kentucky (Saratoga, Aug. 7, 1843).

Thacher, Dr. Chas., M.D. (Boston, Dec. 2, 1841).

Thatcher, Rev. Washington, Oendago Co., New York (Saratoga, Aug. 14, 1841).

Thatcher, Mrs. Saml., of Cambridge, Mass., obt. Nov., 1846 (Boston, June 19, 1842).

Thayer, John Eliot, of Boston (Troy, Jan. 18, 1842).

Theall, Mrs. Benjn., 178, Walker Street (Nov. 29, —).

Thibault, Chas. (Oct. 4, 1839).

Thibault, Angelina (Oct. 4, 1839).

Thom, Geo., U.S.A. (Washington, Feb. 19, 1841).

Thomae, Geo. F. (Brooklyn, Aug. 6, 1844).

Thomae, Mrs. Geo. F. (Brooklyn, Aug. 6, 1844).

Thomas, Wm., Plymouth, Mass. (Saratoga, July 6, 1844).

Thomas, J. B., Plymouth, Mass. (Saratoga, July 6, 1844).

Thomas, Henry (New Orleans, Feb. 1, 1844).

Thomas, J. Hanson, M.D. (Baltimore, Dec. 22, 1840).

Thomas, Sterling (Dec. 14, 1840).

Thompson, Chas., Seneca Falls (Saratoga, Aug. 2, 1843).

Thompson, Mrs., mother of Thos. Thompson (Boston, Nov. 1, 1841).

Thompson, Rev. James, sen., Independent Church, Barre, Mass. (Saratoga, Aug. 4, 1842).

Thompson, Rev. James. H., jun., Independent Church, Salem, Mass. (Saratoga, Aug. 4, 1842.)

Thompson, Hugh B., Prof. of Language (Lexington, Kentucky, June 6, 1844).

Thompson, Thos. (Boston, Nov. 1, 1841).

Thompson (1819–1886), Mr. Jerome, portrait and historical painter (New York, Oct. 15, 1839).

Thompson, Mrs. Jerome (New York, Oct. 15, 1839).

Thompson, James M., proprietor of Thompson's Express (Saratoga, July 6, 1843).

Thompson, Mrs. James M. (Saratoga, July 6, 1843).

Thompson, Edwd. R., Lieut. (Phila., Oct. 31, 1843).

Thompson, G. L. (Washington, March 19, 1841).

Thompson, Mrs. M. A., wife of G. L. (Washington, March 19, 1841).

Thompson, Saml. J. (Baltimore, Dec. 11, 1840).

Thomsen, Laurence (Dec. 15, 1840).

Thomson, M. M. (New Orleans, Jan. 28, 1844).

Thomson, Henry L., New York (Saratoga, July 17, 1844).

Thomson, James, jun. (Saratoga, July 17, 1844).

Thorn, Rev. John, Carlisle, Pa. (Saratoga, Sept. 17, 1844).

Thornton, J. Wingate, Counsel at Law (Boston, Dec. 2, 1841).

Thornton, Miss Eliz. G. (Baltimore, Dec. 31, 1840).

Thornton, Miss Magt. D. (Baltimore, Dec. 15, 1840).

Thornton, Miss F. Antonia (Baltimore, Dec. 14, 1840).

Thornton, Mrs. F. A. (Baltimore, Dec. 14, 1840).

Thorp, Nathan (Washington, May 13, 1841).

Thorp, Rahway, New Jersey (Saratoga, July 23, 1844).

Thorp, Mrs. C. E. (Saratoga, July 23, 1844).

Tibault, E. V. (New Orleans, Jan. 30, 1844).

Tickner, M. L. (New York, Oct. 10, 1839).

Tiremann, Daniel F., alderman, 16th Ward (New York, Nov. 22, 1839).

Tilden, Miss C. B., Jamaica Plain (Boston, Dec. 10, 1841).

Tilden, Mrs. Bryant P., died March 26, 1842 (Boston, Dec. 10, 1841).

Timberlake, Miss M., Va. (Washington, April 29, 1841).

Timmins, John S. (New York, Jan. 10, 1840).

Timmins, Mrs. John, daughter of Pardow. See Pardow (New York, Jan. 10, 1840).

Timmins, John P., nephew of above (New York, Jan. 10, 1840).

Timmins, Wm. Chance, nephew of J. S. Timmins (New York, Jan. 10, 1840).

Timmins, Miss Mary (New York, Jan. 9, 1840).

Timmins, Henry, son-in-law of Mrs. G. Greene (Boston, April 12, 1842).

Tisdale, Wm., jun. (Boston, Feb. 21, 1842).

Tisdale, Saml. T., 212, Water Street (Aug. 20, 1839).

Tisdall, Fitzgerald, Cork, Ireland (New York, Feb. 28, 1840).

Tittermary, Miss Margaretta (Louisville, Kentucky, May 10, 1844).

Tobias, Chas. (New Orleans, Aug. 26, 1844).

Todd, Major Wm. (2 ports.), Somerset City, New York; aged 86 years, was at the Revolutionary War (New York, June 4, 1840).

Todd, Rev. (Phila., Aug. 4, 1840).

Tooley, James (Natchez, April 24, 1844).

Tooley, James, miniature painter (Phila., Dec. 10, 1843).

Tomlinson, T. A., M.C. (New York, June 12, 1841).

Tomkins, Mr. Daniel H. See Staples (New York, Jan. 25, 1840).

Tomkins, Mrs. Daniel H. (New York, Jan. 25, 1840).

Tomkins, Miss Laura (New York, Jan. 25, 1840).

Tomkins, Wm. (New York, Jan. 25, 1840).

Thomson, Waddy, M.C. (Greenville, Feb. 23, 1841).

Torrey, Mrs. Eliz. B. (Boston, Feb. 15, 1842).

Totten, Sarah. See Myers, sister of (New York).

Totten, James, U.S.A. (Saratoga, Aug. 10, 1844).

Totten, Mrs. Julia K. (Saratoga, Aug. 10, 1844).

Townsend, Miss Mandeline (New York, Oct. 1, 1840).

Townsend, John R. (New York, Oct. 1, 1840).

Townsend, Mrs. R., née Drake (New York, Oct. 1, 1840).

Townsend, Marguerite (baby), aged 5 months (New York, Oct. 1, 1840).

Townsend, Mrs. Marguerite, aged 78 years (New York, Oct. 1, 1840).

Townsend, Mrs. Harrick N. (Troy, Sept. 13, 1841).

Tracey, Chas., Counsel at Law, Utica, New York (Saratoga, July 10, 1844).

Traston, Rev. M., Methodist Episcopal Church of Westbrook, M.C. (Boston, May 10, 1842).

Travers, John Taylor (Saratoga, July 25, 1843).

Travers, Mary Taylor (Phila., Jan. 20, 1843).

Travers, Joseph (Phila., Jan. 20, 1843).

Travers, Georgina (Phila., Jan. 20, 1843).

Travers, Eliz. (Phila., Jan. 20, 1843).

Travers, Franklin, (Phila., Jan. 20, 1843).

Travers, Octavius (Phila., Jan. 20, 1843).

Treat, S. (Saratoga, July 20, —).

Tredwell, widow, Mrs. Mary Eliz., sister of Miss J. V. Campbell (New York, May 18, 1840).

Tree, Lambert, chief clerk of Post Office (June 23, 1841).

Tripp, Stephen, of Providence, New Jersey (Saratoga, Aug. 25, 1841).

Trist, N. P. (Havana, Jan. 21, 1841).

Trowbridge, C. C., Detroit, Mich. (Saratoga, Aug. 28, 1844).

Trumbull, Joseph, M.C. (Harford City, Feb. 25, 1841).

Tseroyeasthaw, aged 30 years, or the man who keeps you awake, Chief of the five Nations.

Tucker, Nathan (Boston, Jan. 6, 1844).

Tucker, John (Phila., March 16, 1843).

Tucker, Louise (Mrs. John) (Phila., March 16, 1843).

Tucker, John, jun. (Phila., March 16, 1843).

Tucker, Louisa (Phila., March 16, 1843).

Tucker, Louisa A. (Boston, April 23, 1842).

Tucker, Richd. D., Jan. 6, 1842, father of Mrs. J. H. Gray (Boston, Dec. 15, 1841).

Tuckerman, J. Francis, M.D., assist.-surgeon, U.S.N. (Boston, Feb. 26, 1842).

Tuckerman, Miss Sophia M. (Boston, April 16, 1842).

Tuckerman, H. F. (Boston, Nov. 17, 1842).

Tumel, Mme. Eliza, New York (Saratoga, Sept. 2, 1843).

Turell, Chas. J. (New York, Aug. 1, 1844).

Turner, Rev. Ed., Congregational Church, Jamaica (Boston).

Turner, Richd. J. (Dec. 12, 1840).

Turner, Chas. G. (Feb. 10, 1841).

Turpin, Dr. Wm., M.D. (New York, Aug. 8, 1839).

Tuttle, A. C., of New York (Sept. 2, 1840).

Tyler, John, Pres., U.S.A. (Washington, April 20, 1841).

Tyler, Geo. C., Custom House (Aug. 10, 1839).

Tyler, Geo., Custom House, New York (Aug 10, 1839).

Tyler, Geo. Fredk., New York (Saratoga, July 26, 1840).

Tyler, John, 10th Pres., U.S.A. (Presented to the American Nation, June, 1911, by Mrs. F. Nevill Jackson; this portrait now hangs in the White House, where it was originally taken.) (Washington, 1841).

Tyson, J. Washington, U.S.A. (Phila., Dec. 30, 1842).

Tyson, Job R., Counsel at Law (Phila., Aug. 19, 1841).

Twinamè, Wm., Liverpool, England (Saratoga, Aug. 25, 1844).

Ufikoff, Geo. H. (Feb. 22, 1843).

Ullman, Daniel, Counsel at Law (Nov. 16, 1839).

Upham, Henry (Boston, 1841).

Upham, Mrs. S. M., of Boston (Saratoga, Aug. 13, 1840).

Usher, Miss Marcella, obt. March 8, 1841 (Aug. 5, 1839).

Vail, Mrs. James, London (Troy, Sept. 13, 1841).

Valentine, David J., assist. clerk, Common Council (New York, Nov. 7,—).

Van Antwerp, Miss Anne Sickles (May 13, 1840).

Van Antwerp, Margt.

Van Buren (1782–1862), Martin Pres. (Washington, Jan. 21, 1841).

Van Buren, A. (Washington, Jan. 21, 1841).

Van Buren, Martin, jun. (Washington, Jan. 21, 1841).

Vance, Wm. L., Memphis (March 5, 1844).

Vandenhoff, —, tragedian (New York, Nov. 20, 1839).

Vandenhoff, Miss Caroline, niece of above (New York, Nov. 20, 1839).

Van Derlyn, John, jun., Pancrama (Saratoga, July 8, 1840).

Vanderwort, Joseph B. (Jan. 2, 1840).

Vanderwoort, P. (Sept. 24, 1839).

Van Doren, J. L., New York (Saratoga, July 19, 1844).

Van Horsugh, Rev. J. R. C., St. Peter's Church (Washington, March 9, 1841).

Vanleer, Miss R., Jamaica Plain (Dec. 10, 1841).

Van Kleeck, Rev. Robt. B., Rector of St. Paul's Church (2 ports.) (Troy, Sept. 16, 1841).

Van Kleeck, Mrs. Robt. B. (Troy, Sept. 16, 1841).

Van Murbecke, H. C. (Oct. 12, 1839).

Van Renselaer, H. (St. Lawrence, June 14, 1841).

Van Renselaer, Rev. Cortland (Washington, Feb. 16, 1841).

Van Renselaer, Cortland, son of above (Phila., Oct. 28, 1842).

Van Renselaer, Philip L. (Phila., Oct. 28, 1842).

Van Renselaer, Mrs. C. (Washington, May 4, 1841).

Van Rensselaer, Richd., Counsel at Law, Albany (Saratoga, Aug. 29, 1840).

Van Rensselaer, Mrs. Richd. (Saratoga, Aug. 29, 1840).

Van Rensselaer, Miss Maria Eliza (Saratoga, Aug. 29, 1840).

Vasquez, Dr. Domingo, M.D. (New Orleans, Dec. 24, 1843).

Vasser, Mr., Poughkeepsie (Saratoga, July 18, 1843).

Vaughn, Edwd. M., Atty. at Law (Lexington, Kentucky, June 1, 1844).

Van Wart, Irving (New York, June 2, 1840).

Van Wart, Mrs. Irving (New York, June 2, 1840).

Van Wart, Henry, brother-in-law of Washington Irving (Birmingham, England, April 13, 1838).

Van Wart, Henry, jun. (Birmingham, England).

Van Wart, Henry (Boston, Nov. 18, 1841).

Van Wart, Mrs. Henry (Boston, Dec. 10, 1841).

Veilae, John Jay, Maj.-Gen., Lansingburgh, New York (Saratoga, Aug. 12, 1843).

Venman, Chas., officer of ship Œmulyn (Dec. 24, 1842).

Vermilge, J. B., Newark, New Jersey (Saratoga, Sept. 5, 1844).

Verplank, Saml., 36, Franklin Street (Jan. 17).

Villani, Signor J., Duche de Mèdene, Italy (Sept. 23, 1839).

Vogel, Wm. (New Orleans, March 21, 1844).

Vogel, Mrs. Wm. (New Orleans, March 21, 1844).

Vogel, Maax (New York, Sept. 6, 1844).

Von Bretton, James (Phila., Nov. 2, 1842).

Von der Smith, D. B., of Lancaster (Saratoga, July 26, 1844).

Vreleler, J. V. E., Geneva, New York (Troy, Dec. 31, 1841).

Vultee, Miss Caroline A. (New York, Oct. 7, 1839).

Wade, James Taylor.

Wade, Christine, slave to above.

Wade, James J. (Port Gibson, New Orleans, Feb. 28, 1844).

Wadsworth, Rev. Chas., Pastor second Presbyterian Church (Saratoga Springs, Aug. 31, 1844).

Wager, Philip S. (Phila., Sept. 20, 1842).

Wagner, Peter J. (New York, Feb. 8, 1841).

Wagner, Tobias (Phila., Feb. 16, 1843).

Wagstaff, Miss S. A. (March 5, 1840).

Wagstaff, Mrs. David (March 5, 1840).

Wainwright, R. A., Lieut., U.S.A. (Troy, Sept. 24, 1841).

Wainwright, Miss E. M., daughter of Dr. W., of New York (Boston, April 4, 1842).

Wainwright, Wm. Lambert (Roybruy, May 16, 1842).

Wainwright, Peter (a) and dog Ponto (b) (Roybruy, May 16, 1842).

Wainwright, Mr. Peter, Treasurer of Saving Bank (Boston, March 31, 1842).

Wainwright, Mrs. Peter (Boston, March 31, 1842).

Wainwright, Susanna Hartwell (Boston, March 31, 1842).

Wainwright, Eliz. Mayhew (Boston, March 31, 1842).

Wait, B., Charlestown, Mass. (April 4, 1844).

Waldo, Francis, New York (Saratoga Springs, July 24, 1840).

Waldron, Victor (New York, Aug. 18, 1839).

Walker, Robt. J., sen., Miss. Sec. Treasury under Polk (Madisonville, March 25, 1841).

Walker, Wm. H. (Louisville, May 11, 1844).

Walker, Amasa (Boston, March 22, 1842).

Walker, Rev. W. F., Rector of Bethseda Church (Saratoga Springs, Aug. 17, 1841).

Walker, Wm. (New York, Sept. 5, 1839).

Walker, Prof. James, Cambridge, Mass.; afterwards Pres. of Harvard (Saratoga, July 15, 1843).

Walker, Henry C. (New Orleans, March 14, 1844).

Walker, Mr. S., and dog Hannibal (b) (New Orleans, Jan. 26, 1844).

Walker, S. P. (Washington, May 10, 1841).

Walker, Alex. (Nov. 29, 1840).

Wall, Carret D. (New Jersey, Feb. 4, 1841).

Wall, James W. (New Jersey, Jan. 9, 1843).

Wallace, G. Weed, 1st Infantry Regt. (Aug. 24, 1839).

Wallack, Robt. (Washington, April 30, 1841).

Wallack, James H., lessee of National Theatre, obt. April 23, 1844 (New York, Nov. 7, 1839).

Walworth, Mr. Hyde R., chancellor, State of New York (Saratoga Springs, Aug. 29, 1840).

Walworth, Mrs. Hyde R. (Saratoga Springs, Aug. 29, 1840).

Ward, S. G. (Boston, Jan. 5, 1842).

Ward, Mr. Henry H., of New York (Saratoga Springs, Aug. 31, 1840).

Ward, Mrs. Eliza H., New York (Saratoga Springs, Aug. 31, 1840).

Ward, Wm. J. (Baltimore, Aug. 18, 1843).

Ward, Emma Rosalie (Baltimore, Aug. 18, 1843).

Ward, Arietta J. (Baltimore, Aug. 18, 1843).

Ward, J. T. (Washington, April 20, 1841).

Ward, K. A., of Rochester, New York (Saratoga Springs, Aug. 24, 1840).

Ward, Mrs. K. A., of Rochester, New York (Saratoga Springs, Aug. 25, 1840).

Ward, Wm. G. (New York, Oct. 8, 1840).

Ward, Miss Anna Eliza (New York, Oct. 8, 1840).

Ward, Miss Louisa (New York, Oct. 8, 1840).

Ward, John (New York, Oct. 8, 1840).

Ward, Wm. G., jun. (New York, Oct. 8, 1840).

Ward, Chas. Henry (New York, Oct. 8, 1840).

Ward, Mrs. W. G. (New York, Oct. 8, 1840).

Ward, Mr. Saml. (New York, Oct. 30, 1840).

Ward, Mrs. Lucy (New York, Oct. 30, 1840).

Ward, Master Gideon Lee (New York, Oct. 30, 1840).

Ward, Miss Lucy Geneive (New York, Oct. 30, 1840).

Ward, Robt. Drederichs (New York, Oct. 30, 1840).

Warden, Mrs. Emily, wife of David W. (Phila., Nov. 6, 1843).

Warner, Mr. Geo. E. (New York, Aug. 27, 1839).

Warner, Mrs. Geo. E. (New York, Aug. 27, 1839).

Warner, Col. Andrew, Deputy Co. Clerk (New York, Sept. 26, 1839).

Warner, Mrs. Andrew (New York, Jan. 6, 1840).

Warner, Miss Catharine Anne (New York, Jan. 7, 1840).

Warner, L. T. (New York, Nov. 25, 1844).

Warre, John, Dr. (Saratoga, Nov. 5, 1841).

Warren, Miss Emily (Boston, Nov. 5, 1841).

Warren, Mrs. Wm., Lafayette (Saratoga, July 8, 1840).

Warren, Susan (Saratoga, July 8, 1840).

Warren, Eliza (Saratoga, July 8, 1840).

Warren, Lott, M.C. (Georgia).

Warren, Wm., Lafayette, Atty. at Law (Saratoga, July 8, 1840).

Washburn, Emery, Senator of State, Mass., Worcester (Boston, March 1, 1842).

Washburn, Mrs. Emery. See Giles (Boston, March 1, 1842).

Washington, A. G.

Washington, B., M.D., U.S.N. (April 16, 1841).

Washington, Dr. James A. (Saratoga, Aug. 18, 1841).

Waterman, Richd., R.I (Saratoga, Aug. 14, 1844).

Waterman, J., New Orleans, obt. Sept. 1, 1841 (Saratoga, Aug. 25, 1841).

Waterman, Rufus, Providence (Saratoga, Aug. 18, 1843).

Waterman, Edwd. (Phila., April 1, 1843)

Waterston, Robt., sen. (2 ports.) (Boston, March 10, 1842).

Waterston, Rev. R. C., Pitt's Street Chapel (Boston, Dec. 22, 1841).

Waterston, Mrs. R. C. (Boston, Dec. 22, 1841).

Waterston, Helen Ruthven, daughter of Pres. Josiah (Boston, Dec. 22, 1841).

Watkins, Mr. F. (April 1, 1841).

Watkins, Wm. Hamilton, of Pres. M. E. Church (New Orleans, Jan. 10, 1844).

Watson, James R., Lieut., U.S.N. (Boston, May 22, 1842).

Watson, Saml. Edmiston, Lt.-Col., U.S. Marines (Boston, March 18, 1842).

Watson, Rev. John L., Trinity Church (Boston, Nov. 19, 1841).

Watson, Mrs. John L. See Cushing (Boston, Nov. 19, 1841).

Watson, Eliz. (Boston, June 10, 1842).

Watson, Benjn. N. (Boston, June 17, 1842).

Watson, Rev. John L., Episcopal Church (Boston, May 2, 1842)

Watson, Hugh L. (Brooklyn, Sept. 25, 1843).

Watson, Winslow M., editor of Daily Whig (Troy, Sept. 14, 1841).

Watterson, H. M., M.C. (Tenn., June 27, 1841).

Watts, H. M. (Phila., Jan. 21, 1843).

Watts, Talbot (Boston, Nov. 9, 1841).

Watts, Alex., New York (Saratoga, Aug. 21, 1844).

Waugh, S. B., portrait painter (Phila., Sept. 30, 1842).

Waugh, James Hoffman (Feb. 13, 1841).

Wayland, Daniel (New York, April 25, 1840).

Wayland, Rev. John (New York, April 10, 1840).

Wayland, Rev. Francis, sen. (Saratoga Springs, July 1, 1840).

Wayland, Miss Sarah (Saratoga Springs, July 1, 1840).

Wayland, Miss Anne (Saratoga Springs, July 1, 1840).

Wayland, Prof. F., Pres. of Brown's University, Providence, R.I. (New York, April 25, 1840).

Way, Edwd., of England, Montreal (Saratoga).

Webb, Mr. W. W., brother of Mrs. Averell (Troy, Sept. 15, 1841).

Webb, Mrs. W. W. (Troy, Sept. 15, 1841).

Webb, R. S., nephew of Mrs. Horatio Averell. *See* Averell (Troy, Oct. 2, 1841).

Webster, Daniel, Boston, Mass., orator, statesman, Sec. of State (Saratoga, Aug. 20, 1840).

Webster, Dr. John Lee (Phila., Jan. 11, 1843).

Webster, Mrs. J. W. (Boston, Nov. 18, 1841).

Webster, Sarah Hickling (Boston, Nov. 18, 1841).

Webster, Catharine Prescoot (Boston, Nov. 18, 1841).

Webster, Harriet W. (Boston, Nov. 18, 1841).

Webster, Mrs. Caroline S., sister of Mrs. John B. Joy (Washington, May 3, 1841).

Wedge, Simon (Dec. 21, 1840).

Weeks, James H., brother-in-law to Mrs. E. M. Weekes (Boston, Nov. 18, 1841).

Weeks, Mrs. E. M., sister of N. Faxon (Boston, Nov. 18, 1841).

Weil, R. (New Orleans, Jan. 27, 1844).

Weir, Robt. W., painter, West Point (Aug. 8, 1839).

Weld, Moses Wm. (Boston, May 25, 1842).

Wells, J. (Boston, May 26, 1842).

Welles, Benjn., of Boston (Saratoga, Aug. 17, 1843).

Welles, Mrs. B. (Saratoga, Aug. 17, 1843).

Welles, Eliza S., daughter of above (Saratoga, Aug. 17, 1843).

Welles, Susan C., daughter of above (Saratoga, Aug. 17, 1843).

Welles, Miss G., daughter of above (Saratoga, Aug. 17, 1843).

Wells, W., of Cambridge (Boston, Dec. 29, 1841).

Welles, Benjn. S. (Boston, Nov. 12, 1841).

Wells, Rev. Ranford, Newark, New Jersey (Aug. 2, 1840).

Wells, F. Fairchild (Troy, Oct. 5, 1841).

Wendall, Dr. Herman, M.D., Albany (Aug. 15, 1840).

Wendel, Mr. John, of New York (Saratoga, Sept. 11, 1844).

Wendell, Mrs. John, of New York (Saratoga, Sept. 11, 1844).

Wentworth, Miss A. E. (Boston, Jan. 5, 1842).

West, M. J. (Arkansas, Feb. 20, 1844).

West, Chas. E., Principal of Rutgers Female Institution (New York, Oct. 24, 1839).

West, Mrs. Catharine, of London, daughter-in-law of Benjn. West, painter and Pres. of R.A. (Oct. 18, 1839).

West, Fredk., Sunday Morn. Atlas (New York, July 31, 1839).

Westcott, Mr. James R. (Saratoga Springs, Aug. 28, 1841).

Wescott, Mrs. (Saratoga Springs, Aug. 28, 1841).

Wescott, Miss Mary E. (Saratoga Springs, Aug. 28, 1841).

Wescot, Mrs. Joseph (Saratoga, July 7, 1843).

Westcot, Mr. Joseph (Saratoga, July 7, 1843).

Westcot, Miss Louisa P. (Saratoga, July 7, 1843).

Westcot, J. H., jun. (Saratoga, July 7, 1843).

Westcott, Mr. Alanson (Saratoga Springs, Sept. 9, 1840).

Westcott, Mrs. Alanson (Saratoga Springs, Sept. 9, 1840).

Weston, G. B., Duxbury, Mass. (Boston, June 9, 1842).

Weston, H. E., brother of Mrs. Chapman (Boston, Feb. 14, 1842).

Weston, T. L., jun. (New York, Aug. 21, 1839).

Weston, Valentine W., sen. (New York, Aug. 21, 1839).

Wethered, P., jun., Kent Co., Maryland (Saratoga, Aug. 28, 1844).

Westmore, Wm. S., of New York (Saratoga, July 31, 1842).

Wett, C. B. S. (Charleston, Nov. 20, 1842).

Wharton, W. C. (Phila., March 19, 1842).

Wharton, Chas. Henry, J.P. (Washington, Jan. 26).

Wharton, Edwd. (New Orleans, March 9, 1844).

Wharton, Franklin (Feb. 11, 1844).

Wharton, C.

Wheaton, Rev. N. S., Rector of Christ Church, South Carolina (New Orleans, April 2, 1843).

Wheelock, Mrs., of Medfield, Mass., 81 years of age (Boston, April 20, 1842).

Whelen, Edwd. T. (Phila., Aug. 12, 1844).

Whipple, Mrs. Geo., Oberlin, Ohio (Saratoga, Sept. 11, 1844).

Whipple, Master Geo. Hall (Saratoga, Sept. 11, 1844).

White, John R. *See* Tallmadge (Phila., Oct. 5, 1839).

White, Mrs. Eliz., of Washington (June 27, 1841).

White, James C., of Washington (June 27, 1841).

White, Miss Mary Hannah (June 27, 1841).

White, Grenville B., of Boston (Saratoga, Aug. 25, 1843).

White, Saml. J. (New Orleans, April 5, 1844).

White, Geo., author of *Memoir of State, History of Manufactures* (Washington, April 13, 1841).

White, Mr. Stephen, nr. Buffalo (New York, April 16, 1841).

White, Mrs. Mary, nr. Buffalo (New York, April 16, 1841).

White, Miss Mary (Saratoga, July 21, 1844).

White, Miss Louisa (Saratoga).

White, Wm. B. (Saratoga, Aug. 13, 1842).

White, Ferdinand E. (Boston, April 21, 1842).

White, Mrs. Ferdinand E. (Boston, April 21, 1842).

Whiteman, Miss Sophia Hannah (Aug. 2, —).

Whiteman, Miss Emely Adams (Aug. 2, —).

Whiteman, Miss Francis Eliz. (Aug. 2, —).

Whitman, Geo. (New Orleans, Washington).

Whitman, David, sen., father of J. B.

Whiteman, Mrs. David, obt. April 25, 1835.

Whitman, John B. (Oct. 2, 1840).

Whitman, T. B., jun., 41, John Street, New York (New York, July 31, 1839).

Whitmore, Stephen, M.C., Gardiner (Saratoga, July 3, 1843).

Whitmore, Nathanl. M., M.C., Gardiner (Saratoga, July 3, 1843).

Whitney, Mrs. M., wife of Gen. Moses W., Milton Hill, Mass. (Saratoga, Aug. 13, 1842).

Whitney, Rev. Peter, formerly Pastor of N. Boro', Mass., aged 79 years, obt. Jan., 1821 (Boston).

Whitney, Mrs., obt. Feb., 1816 (taken from description) (Boston).

Whitesides, Rev. Henry F. M. (Phila., April 29, 1843).

Whitaker, Thos. S. (New York, Sept. 23, 1840).

Whittaker, Horace, Norwich, Ct. (Saratoga, July 26, 1843).

Whitwell, Rev. R., St. Amand West, Epis. Prov., Canada (Saratoga, July 26, 184–).

Wickes, A. W., of Troy Citizen Corps (Sept. 27, 1841).

Wiersbiki, Lord F. O., of Poland (Boston, Nov. 26, 1841).

Wiggins, Mrs. Mary S., *née* Porter (Saratoga, Aug. 26, 1844).

Wiggins, Peter B. Porter (Sept. 2, 1844).

Wight, Amhurst, Counsel (Aug. 13, —).

Wight, Mrs. A. W. (Aug. 14, —).

Wight, Amhurst (Aug. 15, —).

Wight, Miss Jane Eliz. (Aug. 14, —).

Wilbor, J. B. (Dec. 8, 1844).

Wilbor, W. H. (Nov. 30, 1839).

Wilbor, J. B., jun. (Aug. 18, 1839).

Wild, Dr. Chas., M.D., of Brookline, Mass. (Boston, March 29, 1842).

Wilde (1789–1847), Richd. Henry, M.C., Georgia, (Boston, Nov. 4, 1841).

Wilde, Benjn. (Oct. 18, —).

Wilder, Sampson V. S., 1, Washington Place (New York, April 1, 1840).

Wilder, Mrs. Sampson V. S. (New York, April 21, 1840).

Wilder, Miss Josephine Christina (New York, April 21, 1840).

Wilder, Miss Francina, now Mrs. T. H. Rhed (Dec. 2, 1840).

Wilder, Vrylina (New York, April 21, 1840).

Wilder, Dr. A. H., M.D., Groton, Mass. (Saratoga, March 4, 1843).

Wildes, Moses, New England, Cofy [*sic*] House (Boston, April 22, 1842).

Wilkes, Dr. Geo., M.D., New York (New York, May 30, 1840).

Wilkes, Hamilton (June 4, 1840).

Wilkeson, Judge (Washington, April 14, 1841).

Wilkeson, Mrs. Judge (Washington, April 15, 1841).

Wilken, Sarah G., Coshen, Orange Co., New York (Saratoga, Aug. 10, 1844).

Wilkin, S. J., M.C. (Orange City, Aug. 8, 1844).

Wilkins, Mrs. Sophia, of Quebec (Saratoga, Aug. 24, 1844).

Wilkinson, Theo. J. (New Orleans, Jan. 6, 1844).

Willard, Mrs. W. Y. (Troy, Sept. 27, 1841).

Willard, Mr. W. Y. (Troy, Sept. 27, 1841).

Willard, Aaron, of Boston (Saratoga, July 22, 1844).

Willard, Miss Caroline (Saratoga, July 22, 1844).

Willard, F. A., M.D., of Boston (Saratoga, July 22, 1844).

Willard, Joshua, of Boston (Saratoga, Sept. 8, 1843).

Willcox, Caroline E., daughter of Mrs. Marston (Phila., May 3, 1843).

Willcox, Ellen S., daughter of Mrs. Marston (Phila., May 3, 1843).

Williams, Mr. R. S., of Natchez (New York, June 5, 1840).

Williams, Mrs. R. S., of Natchez (New York, June 5, 1840).

Williams, Saml. S. (New York, June 5, 1840).

Williams, Mrs. Saml. S. (New York, June 5, 1840).

Williams, Miss A. G., of New York (Saratoga Springs, Aug. 23, 1844).

Williams, Thos., aide-de-camp to Gen.-in-Chief (Saratoga, Aug. 26, 1841).

Williams, Thos. H. (Boston, Dec. 3, 1840).

Williams, Miss Harriet A. (Saratoga Springs, Aug. 29, 1840).

Williams, Thos. W., M.C., Ct. (New London, Feb. 24, 1841).

Williams, Mrs. Thos. W. (New London, Feb. 24, 1841).

Williams, Mrs. F. A. (Washington, April 17, 1840).

Williams, Gen. Wm., Norwich, Ct. (Saratoga, Aug. 12, 1841).

Williams, Mrs. Wm., Norwich, Ct. (Saratoga, Aug. 12, 1841).

Williams, Rev. J. N., Prof. Episcopal Church (Boston, March 5, 1842).

Williamson, Nichls. (New York, Jan. 16, 1840).

Willies, Miss (Phila., Jan. 18, 1843).

Willis, Wm. (Aug. 12, 1839).

Williston, John, Portsmouth, Va. (Boston, Nov. 20, 1841).

Wilson, Capt. J. Dayton, Service, 34, Cortland Street (Oct. 4, —).

Wilson, Thos. (New York, Aug. 10, 1839).

Wilson, James W. (New York, Aug. 13, 1839).

Wilson, W. H., of Boston (Saratoga, Aug. 4, 1844).

Wilson, Mrs. W. H., of Boston (Saratoga, Aug. 4, 1844).

Wilson, Robt. T., Baltimore, Maryland (Saratoga, Aug. 25, 1844).

Wilson, D. M., police officer of Capitol (March 10, 1841).

Wilson, Mr. Ebenezer, Atty. at Law, obt. 1843 (Troy, Sept. 23, 1841).

Wilson, Mrs. Ebenezer (Troy, Sept. 23, 1841).

Wilson, James H. (Phila., April 21, 1843).

Wilson, Mrs. James P., Hartsville (Phila., Feb. 13, 1843).

Wilson, Hiram A., of Louisville Acad., Clifton Park (Saratoga Springs, July 20, 1844).

Wilson, Miss Emily, New York (Saratoga, Aug. 12, 1844).

Wilson, Joseph, purser, U.S.N. (Jan. 20, 1842).

Wilson, Mrs. Joseph.

Wilson, Mr. Joseph G. (Boston, March 1, 1842).

Wilson, Miss L. E.

Wilson, Leonard J.

Wilson, Miss Harriet R.

Wilson, John.

Winchester, W., Manager of Water Co. (Baltimore, Dec. 14, 1840).

Winchester, Alex. (Baltimore, Dec. 3, 1840).

Winchester, James (Baltimore, Dec. 22, 1840).

Winder, W. S., nr. Govanstown (Phila., Sept. 25, 1842).

Winship, Capt. Jona., of Brighton (Boston, Nov. 24, 1841).

Winslow, Col. R. S., New York (Saratoga, Aug. 7, 1844).

Winter, Wm. D. (New Orleans, Feb. 15, 1843).

Winthrop, B., aged 77 years, obt. 1845 (New York, March 7, 1840).

Winthrop, Hon. Robt., M.C., Speaker, House of Representatives (Boston, May 20, 1842).

Wirgman, Chas. (Dec. 8, 1840).

Wirgman, O. P. P. (Baltimore, Dec. 2, 1849).

Wirt, Henry G., M.D. (Washington, May 18, 1841).

Wise, Henry A., politician (Va., Feb. 12, 1841).

Wister, Wm. (Phila., Dec. 9, 1842).

Wister, Mary (Phila., Oct. 4, 1842).

Witmore, Mrs. Sarah E. (Troy, Sept. 28, 1841).

Wizzs, Chas. P. (New Orleans, Jan. 21, 1844).

Wilcott, Saml., Counsel at Law, Hopkinton, Mass (Boston, Nov. 15, 1841).

Wolcott, T. H. (March 15, 1842).

Wolf, Louis Leo, of New York (Saratoga, July 28, 1842).

Wolf, A. H., of New York (Aug. 12, 1841).

Wolfe, Mr. John, 86, Chamber Street, New York (Saratoga Springs, Aug. 25, 1840)

Wolfe, Mrs. John, daughter of Peter Lorillard (Saratoga Springs, Aug. 25, 1840).

Wolfe, Miss Mary Lorillard (Saratoga Springs, Aug. 25, 1840).

Woolsey, G. M. (New York, Aug. 12, 1840).

Wood, Miss Sarah, New Bedford, Mass. (Saratoga, Aug. 30, 1844).

Wood, Fredk., 410, Broadway (Aug. 12, 1839).

Wood, B. B., watchmaker (Boston, March 12, 1842).

Wood, James C., Auburn, New York (Boston, Dec. 31, 1841).

Wood, J. Ben. (New York, Dec. 14, 1844).

Wood, Mary C. (New York, Dec. 17, 1844).

Wood, F. (Natchez, April 25, 1844).

Wood, Dr. Wm. Maxwell, U.S.N. (Phila., March 6, 1843).

Wood, Eliz. Moore, daughter of above (Phila., March 6, 1843).

Woodbridge, Rev. Geo. Richmond, Va. (Saratoga, Aug. 14, 1840).

Woodbury, Levi, statesman. *See* Treasury (New Hampshire, Jan. 22, 1841).

Woodruff, H., Bank, State of New York (Jan. 8, 1840).

Woodward, Wm. (Baltimore, Jan. 2, 1841).

Woodward, J. A. (June 19, 1841).

Woodwards, Rev. A., Rector of St. Luke's Parish (New Orleans, April 2, 1844).

Wool, John E., Brig.-Gen. (Troy, Oct. 3, 1841).

Worcester (1784–1835), Mr. J. E., of Cambridge (Dec. 7, 1841).

Worcester, Mrs. J. E., of Cambridge (Dec. 7, 1841).

Worth, Wm. T., Col., 8th Infantry (Saratoga, May 20, 1840).

Wray, P. A., of Alabama (Saratoga, Aug. 3, 1844).

Wright, H. Allen (New York, Nov. 30, 1839).

Wright, Silas (New York, March 5, 1841).

Wright, Dr. Thos., M.D. (New York, Nov. 25, —).

Wright, Edwd. H., Newark (New York, Aug. 12, 1841).

Wucherer, John R. (Phila., March 9, 1843).

Wurts, Wm. A., Lieut., U.S.N. (Phila., Oct. 5, 1842).

Wurts, Master, son of above (Phila., Oct. 5, 1842).

Wyse, Nno. M., War Dept. (Washington, March 4, 1841).

Wyse, E. W., of Baltimore (New Orleans, March 20, 1844).

Yandell, Dr., Prof. in Chemistry.

Yard, Edwd. M., Lieut., U.S.N. (March 1, 1842).

Yates, Giles F., of Schnectady, New York (Saratoga Springs, July 25, 1840).

Yeatman, Miss Emma (Washington, April 1, 1841).

Yellot, Wm., 89, Wall Street (New York, Aug. 3, 1839).

Yohannan, Mar, Bishop of Ooroomiah, Persia (2 · ports.) (Saratoga Springs, Aug. 27, 1840).

Yorger, Orville, Memphis (Tenn., Feb. 26, 1844).

Young, Dr. B. Favert (Natchez, Jan. 21, 1844).

Young, Mrs. M. J., and slave (Natchez, Jan. 21, 1844).

Henrietta, slave (Natchez, Jan. 21, 1844).

Young, Wm. Cosser (Natchez, Jan. 21, 1844).

Young, Robt. Temple (Natchez, Jan. 17, 1844).

Wm., slave to (Natchez, Jan. 17, 1844).

Young, Marguerite Allison (Natchez, Jan. 17, 1844)

Young, Robt. Wade (Natchez, Jan. 17, 1844).

Young, Jane (New Orleans, Jan. 22, 1844).

Young, Chas. Saml. (New Orleans, Jan. 22, 1844).

Young, McClintock (Jan. 22, 1841).

Young, Augustus, M.C. (Vt., July 3, 1841).

Young, Richd., sen., of Quincey (Feb. 2, 1841).

Young, Rev. Thos. J., St. John's Church (Saratoga, Sept. 5, 1844).

Young, Saml., Phœnix Bank, New York (Saratoga, July 10, 1840).

Young, Rev. Dr. Alex. (Saratoga Springs, July 17 1843).

Zacharis, J. W. (New Orleans, Jan. 28, 1844).

Zacharis, John A. (New Orleans, March 8, 1844).

Zender, T. D. L., mesmerist (New Orleans, Sept. 25, 1842).

Index

Auguste Edouart's Silhouettes of Eminent Americans, 1839–1844
was composed by Heritage Printers, Inc., Charlotte, North Carolina, printed
by The Meriden Gravure Company, Meriden, Connecticut, and bound by Complete Books Company, Philadelphia, Pennsylvania. The type is Baskerville, and
the paper is Mohawk Superfine. Design is by Edward G. Foss.